HIGH CORRIDORS

HIGH CORRIDORS

QANTAS 1954-1970

John Gunn

University of Queensland Press
ST LUCIA • LONDON • NEW YORK

First published 1988 by University of Queensland Press
Box 42, St Lucia, Queensland, Australia

Typeset by Midland Typesetters
Printed in Australia by Globe Press Pty Ltd, Melbourne

Distributed in the UK and Europe by University of Queensland Press
Dunhams Lane, Letchworth, Herts. SG6 1LF England

Distributed in the USA and Canada by University of Queensland Press
250 Commercial Street, Manchester, NH 03101 USA

Cataloguing in Publication Data

National Library of Australia

Gunn, John, 1925- .
 High corridors : Qantas 1954-1970.
 Bibliography.
 Includes index.

 1. Qantas Airways — History. 2. Airlines —
Australia — History. I. Title.

387.7'065'94

British Library (data available)

Library of Congress

Gunn, John. 1925- .
 High corridors : Qantas. 1954-1970 / John Gunn.
  p.   cm.
 Bibliography: p.
 Includes index.
 1. Qantas Airways. 2. Air lines — Australia — History. I. Title.
HE9889.Q33G864 1988   87-30165
387.7'065'94—dc19

ISBN 0 7022 2128 7

To Capt. G.U. (Scottie) Allan, Capt. Edgar Johnston,
and Capt. R.J. (Bert) Ritchie

Contents

Illustrations

Preface

Qantas lost almost all its aircraft fleet in World War II and its
international route to England in partnership with BOAC was
severed. The airline's near physical demise was followed by
departmental disinterest in its survival as an airline organisation. Only the extraordinary will of its chairman, Fergus
McMaster, and the tenacity of its managing director, Hudson
Fysh, supported by a body of brave pilots and a loyal and overworked staff, kept Qantas in existence. The Qantas initiative
in opening an alternative air link from Perth to Ceylon in 1943
across the Indian Ocean was central to its emergence, when
the war ended, as Australia's chosen instrument for the nation's international airline operations.

In the confused postwar years, as air links were once again
established with England using uneconomic and unsuitable
modified wartime landplanes, Qantas consolidated not only its
professionalism as an airline operator but also its support from
the Australian government. In the face of intense pressure
from England to buy what it considered outmoded and uncompetitive British aircraft, Qantas won the backing of the
Australian prime minister, Ben Chifley, to re-equip with the
fast, pressurised American Constellations. By 1954 it was
ready to take over the long eastbound air route across the
Pacific and, serving North America as well as England, enter
what was now a new world of international airline operations.

High Corridors covers the history of Qantas as Australia's
national airline from this new beginning until its fiftieth anniversary in 1970 when, with the arrival of the huge jumbo
jets, international airlines embarked on what was to become an

era of mass travel. The marketing of "products" and the central importance of the computer, with its world links to the desks of travel agents, were to become as necessary as the aircraft fleet and its operation.

The first volume of the history of Qantas, *The Defeat of Distance*, was about individuals and pioneering. The second volume, *Challenging Horizons*, was about survival and improvisation in the war and postwar years. This third volume is the history of an established and expanding corporation, under the brilliant leadership of Cedric Oban Turner. It is a more complex story, far removed in scale from the prewar romance of aviation pioneering and the uncertainties and dangers of wartime operations. The Qantas environment from 1954 as Australia's national airline was, as its corporate structure was shaped under Turner and its engineering and technical expertise grew impressively, bounded by pressures and competition from more and more countries and by its often stormy relationships with its political masters and their departments and with its partner, BOAC. This volume, too, follows the final years of Hudson Fysh's long career in Qantas and the bitter, often tempestuous and tragic relationship between Turner and Fysh.

In this volume, as in previous ones, I have been greatly helped by people in England and the United States who were closely involved with Qantas, as well as by many of those in Qantas who shaped the events that made this history. As before, however, while their comments and perspectives have been invaluable, I have always relied on the written word of the day and the many primary sources of documentation for the substance of the book.

Again, I must thank for their help the Department of Prime Minister and Cabinet, the Department of Aviation, the Australian Archives, the Mitchell Library (Sydney), the Royal Air Force Museum, London (who maintain the archives of British Airways), the Boeing Aircraft Company, Lockheed Aircraft Corporation, United Technologies, and Rolls-Royce. I would also like to thank once again Brian Reed for his great help in the selection of photographs. The many people who served or still serve Qantas and who gave their time and advice are too numerous to list here but, without them, my task would have been impossible.

Political and Strategic Roles
1954–1955

In March 1954, Hudson Fysh knelt before Queen Elizabeth II to receive the accolade, in a ceremony at Government House, Sydney. Thirty-four years before, he and Paul McGinness had met the Queensland grazier, Fergus McMaster, in a hotel in Brisbane and persuaded him to back their youthful plans for an aerial service in Queensland. Now both McGinness, the initiator, and McMaster, the source of strength and wisdom during the early years, were dead. The airline they had brought into being flew to the United Kingdom, Hong Kong, Japan and South Africa as well as to New Guinea, New Caledonia and the New Hebrides. It was poised, as Australia's chosen instrument in international aviation, to begin on 15 May a great extension of its routes across the Pacific to San Francisco and Vancouver and, with that service, introduce to its fleet the new Super Constellation airliner. Sir Hudson Fysh, chairman and managing director of Qantas Empire Airways, headed an organisation earning over £13 million and carrying more than 118,000 passengers each year, and employing some five thousand people. It had great depth of expertise in the technical evaluation of aircraft and airline operations, and in the complexities of high finance and international aviation politics. It commanded the attention of prime ministers and it reflected, in its relationships with other countries, the Australian national interest. Fysh's knighthood recognised decades of loyal, diligent and tenacious service in the founding and building of an institution that had all but abolished Australia's long isolation from the United Kingdom and Europe. It should have marked for him, as he

1

1

On 15 May 1954, VH-EAG, the Super Constellation operating the first Qantas trans-Pacific service, has the external power supply disconnected prior to moving away from its parking position. By a remarkable coincidence, the prototype Boeing 707 had made its first public appearance only hours before on the other side of the Pacific. At Boeing's Renton factory in Seattle, Washington, the date was still 14 May 1954. Two days later, VH-EAG would fly close to Seattle en route from San Francisco to Vancouver but more than five years would elapse before the Qantas Super Constellations had to relinquish their status as flagships of the fleet to the jetliners.

approached sixty, a happy climax to a remarkable career and a new period in his life of ease in his professional role and serenity in personal relationships. He had earned both. Instead, he was about to embark on a decade of bitter conflict, increasing loneliness, self-doubt, and considerable unhappiness.

There were six members of the Qantas board, four of them (at the end of 1954) knights. Fysh felt deeply that they were all, either constantly or at times, against him. Sir Daniel McVey he regarded as a constant critic. Fysh described him in a diary entry as jealous, subtle, and cunning and a partner in intrigue with Sir Keith Smith.[1] Both G. P. N. Watt and the Qantas vice-chairman, W. C. Taylor, had also, he wrote, intrigued against him when the Labor government had taken control of the airline.[2] A new board member appointed in July 1954, Dr Roland Wilson (soon to be knighted), was to regard him, as the years passed, with increasing contempt and hostility. There seemed, to Fysh, to be always tension or antagonism of some sort.[3] He was, he wrote, at times "picked on in the board room".[4] An underlying challenge to his authority was to grow, "perhaps", he wrote, "engendered by my own personal deficiencies".[5] Above all he faced increasing pressure from his able and ambitious general manager, C. O. Turner, who, he wrote, "felt it most effective to refer as little as possible to his board, and keep affairs in his own hands, [affairs] which he had not properly discussed with me as chairman of the board, at our daily meetings".[6]

His board members were men of high intelligence and long experience. He had no admirers among them. It may have been excessive to describe their particular conflicts with Fysh as "intrigue", but that is certainly how he perceived it. G. P. N. Watt perhaps came closest to identifying the problem, from the viewpoint of board members. "Hudson Fysh", he said many years later, "was an able man but not a modern man." Frustration was the basis of their discord in what Fysh himself described as "the period of complexity" in the airline's affairs.

> Looking at the names of my fellow board members . . . and the high degree of intelligence and business ability which they expressed, it can be realised that they never applied the rubber stamp [Fysh recorded]. Long and arduous discussions took place at our monthly board meetings and, under the stress of the times, difficulties arose which involved personalities. During the last ten years of my service . . . on occasion I became involved in some personal strife and unhappiness which, I feel, was brought about basically by the sharp difference in outlook on a number of matters which was apparent between the Chief Executive and myself. The effects of this were carried through to some board members, there being a lack of that full support and understanding which is so essential from a Chief Executive to his Chairman . . . The fact also was, of course, in my long pioneering service, that I was receiving far too much personal publicity and public applause for the triumphant new happenings taking place, whereas it was the board collectively – and the management – which, in the nature of things, had done most of the work. I tried hard to minimise this but jealousies arose . . .[7]

Fysh's chief executive visited London in April to discuss partnership questions with BOAC in what Sir Miles Thomas, in welcoming him, described as a new era of flying equipment, with new activities for QEA on the Pacific. He hoped these new activities would go from strength to strength and form an essential part of "the BOAC-cum-Qantas route round the world". Turner, outlining Qantas plans for the immediate future, said QEA intended to put Consellation 1049s into service on the Pacific in mid-May as a mixed-class aeroplane. They would keep the Constellation 749s on the Kangaroo Route for the time being. In total, Qantas would have a fleet of eight Constellation 1049s and were going to take over the BCPA option on three Comet 2s, though they were concerned about the delay in delivery dates. BOAC, in their turn, said they planned to put Comets onto first-class services on the Kangaroo Route in December. (Qantas had no possibility of starting Comet services for a further nine to twelve months.) Sir Miles suggested the

3

possibility of BOAC taking over the three BCPA Comets as Qantas might have difficulty in operating a small fleet of only three. Turner, though he politely replied that he would explore the possibility, said it was QEA policy to take and operate the Comets. He did not, he said, think the Australian government would agree to Qantas withdrawing from all first-class services. Turner indicated that QEA had given the Bristol Aeroplane Company a letter of intent to purchase six Mark 250 Britannias for delivery in 1958 "or thereabouts".[8]

A few days later, at a meeting of BOAC's sales director Keith Granville, Basil Smallpiece, the financial comptroller, and Sir Victor Tait, operations director, Granville told Turner of BOAC's difficulties in the immediate future arising from a loss of twenty to twenty-five per cent of total fleet capacity following the withdrawal of the certificate of airworthiness of all Comets. He asked if QEA could help in any way. Turner proposed the possibility of providing immediate relief without creating political difficulties on the Pacific service by the purchase of two DC6 aircraft, formerly operated by Philippine Air Lines, for use by Qantas on the Pacific. This could, he thought, free Constellation 1049s for Qantas on the Kangaroo Route and, in turn, enable the Kangaroo Route partnership to release Constellation 749s for use on other BOAC routes. He pointed out that it would be politically and economically difficult for QEA to operate the DC6s beyond October 1954.[9]

McVey, visiting England in July, spent a night at Bristol and wrote to Fysh: "The Bristol people are well on their toes. The Britannia, I am convinced, will be a first-class aircraft. The Proteus engine is now evidently giving satisfaction since certain

The prototype Boeing 707 flew for the first time on 15 July 1954.

4

necessary modifications have been made to it . . . All in all, Hudson, I find it difficult to share your views about the Britannia. I think we will need some and I am reasonably certain we shall be satisfied with them."

Fysh replied on 22 July:

> There has been a QEA board development . . . I was informed by our new Minister over the phone that it had been decided by the Government to put Dr Wilson on our board . . . I expressed disappointment that for the first time I had not been brought into the picture in a matter of this sort [and] given the opportunity of at least expressing an opinion that it is quite wrong in principle to have Government Departmental officers on the board of QEA. The Minister's reaction was that he, as incoming Minister, had received a direction on the matter and that was that . . . No doubt this mooted appointment is an attempt to do away with the great difficulties which have existed during the past year with the Treasury in regard to QEA financial affairs, but it seems to me that the appointment only throws us back to the position we were in when the Labor Government first took over QEA[10]

To Dr Roland Wilson Fysh wrote, on the same day: "I wish to extend my personal congratulations and good wishes for the outcome of this new association for the benefit of the Company which we serve". (The new minister for civil aviation was Athol Townley who succeeded H. L. Anthony on 9 July; the new board member, Roland Wilson, was secretary to the Department of Treasury. He was later to succeed Hudson Fysh as chairman of Qantas.)

The Qantas board and the management, under C. O. Turner, had much to occupy them beyond the tensions recorded by the chairman. On 15 May, QEA's *Southern Constellation* inaugurated

As de Havillands and the UK government began unprecedented research into the cause of the Comet 1 disasters, the Comet 3 flew for the first time on 19 July 1954. Eighteen feet (5.5 metres) longer than the Comet 1, the Mark 3 was also fitted with pinion fuel tank on the wings, clearly visible in this photograph. Only one Comet 3 was built; it was used to develop the Comet 4 which carried the first fare-paying passengers on a Comet since 1954 when BOAC began trans-Atlantic Comet services on 4 October 1958.

5

the Qantas service across the Pacific and brought within reach the possibility for Qantas to achieve in its own right around-the-world services as Australia's sole overseas operator. The take-over by Qantas of British Commonwealth Pacific Airlines (BCPA) that had made this possible left problems in the absorption of BCPA staff and in a major reorganisation of capital. Aircraft fleet policy had to be assessed, particularly as it was affected by the BCPA commitment to purchase the Comet 2 aircraft. The Boeing Company had, on 15 July 1954, flown for the first time the prototype of its Boeing 707 airliner. Although no orders had been received for it from commercial operators, Qantas was well aware that the new airliner was based on Boeing experience in the design and construction of more than one thousand B47 jet bombers, which gave it background experience on large jet aircraft far exceeding that of any other manufacturer. Commercially, Qantas was coming to grips with the new tourist class services, begun on 1 April between Sydney and London, where fares at twenty per cent below normal first class were being offered for travel with less leg room and more modest catering facilities. Tourist fares were also introduced on the main Pacific trunk services, causing a review of the operation of Sandringham flying boat services between Sydney and Suva and Sydney and the New Hebrides. (Passengers were now able to fly Sydney-Fiji at a lower fare in a pressurised and faster land plane.) There were looming problems with the salary structure for senior executives and there was growing concern about the air cargo position on the Kangaroo Route. Development of the old Wentworth Hotel was under way and it was, by year's end, to have the distinction of becoming the first hotel in Australia to have bathrooms and full conveniences for every room. Work was begun on the construction of a new head office building at the corner of Hunter and Elizabeth streets on a site that had been purchased for the purpose in 1949.

On 21 May 1954, at a meeting of shareholders, British Commonwealth Pacific Airlines Limited was put into liquidation. For QEA the final terms of settlement for the cash and assets taken over from BCPA was a net gain of approximately £2 million to Qantas; in effect a capital subscription by the Commonwealth government to which the company agreed to issue two million new shares of £1 each. The reorganisation of the Pacific services involved not only Qantas, the Commonwealth government, and BCPA but also Tasman Empire Airways Limited (TEAL) and the governments of New Zealand and the United Kingdom. The arrangements were complex.

The Commonwealth government bought the United Kingdom and New Zealand shareholdings in BCPA for £A1 million. It then transferred its shareholding in BCPA to Qantas in consideration of the transfer to the Commonwealth of the Qantas shares in TEAL and the issue of the new Qantas shares. Qantas obtained from BCPA a loan of £A1 million. It bought the United Kingdom shareholding in TEAL and transferred these shares together with the existing thirty per cent shareholding in TEAL to the Commonwealth. Qantas subscribed half of the new capital called up by TEAL (approximately £A1 million) to cover the purchase of DC6 aircraft and spares from BCPA and transferred forthwith the TEAL shares thus obtained to the Commonwealth. At the end of the day, BCPA ceased to exist as an airline and TEAL became jointly owned by the Australian and New Zealand governments.[11]

By June, C. O. Turner was able to inform Qantas and former BCPA staff that integration of the two had proceeded smoothly and was almost completed. Of 294 BCPA staff at 14 May, 262 had joined Qantas. Qantas, he wrote, accepted responsibility for Pacific operations as from 1 April, though the services were operated by BCPA with their DC6s for six weeks until 15 May, when the first Qantas Super Constellation service departed. He quoted a leader from the *Sydney Morning Herald* of 19 March that paid generous tribute to both companies and read:

> Qantas, whose expansion from small beginnings in Queensland in 1920 is one of the romances of aviation, will now rise in rank from ninth to fifth among the world's airlines. In addition to the Kangaroo Route to Britain, it operates trunk lines to Hong Kong and Japan. One of its most impressive achievements was the inauguration in 1952 of a fortnightly service between Sydney and Johannesburg, across the vast spaces of the Indian Ocean. Qantas's flying record, regarded with admiration and envy among international air operators, is a guarantee that the BCPA service is passing into excellent hands.[12]

Hudson Fysh, in a memorandum on 7 June, drew attention to the challenge ahead. "From the outset . . . we will be up against competition on the Pacific such as we have never experienced before".

BCPA had not actually signed any agreement to purchase Comet 2 aircraft but, as Turner pointed out in a board memorandum on 27 May, "it is undoubted that they were committed to take the aircraft if de Havillands could have met the contract conditions for [its] operation on the Pacific and could have delivered the aircraft on dates acceptable to BCPA". At the Christchurch Conference in October 1953, Australia had undertaken that on the merging of BCPA with Qantas, Qantas would take over BCPA's order for Comet 2s "subject to the usual technical considerations". It was understood that Qantas would use the aircraft on the Kangaroo Route and not on the Pacific. Turner now pointed out to the board that the position had changed entirely as a result of the recent grounding of the Comet 1. "The accidents to the Comet 1", he wrote, "and subsequent grounding have thrown doubt on the aircraft structure. The production of these aircraft has been stopped until the cause of the accidents has been found." Delays that had already occurred would, he said, prevent delivery of Comet 2s to Qantas until the end of 1956. If the cause of the Comet accidents was discovered, it could force considerable modification of the aircraft's design so that a completely new assessment of it would be necessary. The minister should, said Turner, be advised that the purchase of Comet 2 aircraft should now be treated as an entirely new project; Australia's position should be made clear to the United Kingdom. (BCPA had carried out negotiations with de Havilland for three Comet 2 aircraft and with Rolls-Royce for nineteen spare Avon engines. The specification and contract purchase had been negotiated to finality and a letter of intent to purchase dated 23 January 1953 existed. No monies had been paid and the contract document itself had not been signed by BCPA.)[13] Fysh wrote to the minister, H. L. Anthony, on 11 June setting out the company's revised views on the Comet and concluded: "It is not possible to fit the Comet 2 into our basic route planning and we therefore consider that we should not be held to any obligation which may be implied from the Christchurch discussions whereby we would purchase what has become an aeroplane of unknown specifications for delivery on an unknown date."[14] The new minister, Athol Townley, agreed in his reply: "I find it difficult to imagine that . . . what must be a modified aircraft will not involve a completely new assessment by every operator who has at any time indicated his interest in the purchase of this type".

By October it was evident that the Comet 1 series had been abandoned. There was no doubt, however, that the jet engine would, in the years ahead, power a new generation of civil airliners either as pure jets or, geared to propellers, as turboprops. These emerging types had all to be carefully watched and evaluated and judgments made about their economics and passenger appeal in comparison with improving piston-engined aircraft. Capt. Scottie Allan, now assistant general manager,

prepared a report on world aircraft developments for C. O. Turner. All the Comet 1s belonging to BOAC and South African Airways were, he said, being used as test pieces into the current investigation of the Comet accidents. It had been recommended that all future highly pressurised fuselages be tested in a pressurised water tank over sufficient periods to allow a 3,000-hour fatigue life. "A test of this nature will take about six months to complete provided no failures occur, so that the manufacture of Comet aircraft could not be recommenced for some considerable time", Allan wrote. It would be late in 1956 before Comets could be available, and "in the meantime, most operators who had Comet 2s on order have bought other types". Britain's lead in pioneering civil jet airliners had been lost and with it had gone the last real chance to break into the United States-dominated world market for long-range civil aircraft.

Despite the flight of the prototype Boeing 707, it was by no means clear that it would be a suitable jet airliner. Boeing did not expect to have a production 707 flying before 1956 and a two-year tanker and freighter flying programme of tests was anticipated before the aircraft could carry paying passengers. "Boeing", wrote Allan, "have released a brochure on the 707 but unfortunately it contains no basic performance information upon which we could make a comparison with other aircraft. Broadly, Boeing claims that its cost per ton-mile is about equal to the DC-6."

The Douglas Company had a design for a commercial jet but were firm in asserting that a military contract was necessary before risking the expense of building a prototype. "Their model [wrote Allan] has four jets in pods on a thirty-degree swept back wing and will have a gross weight of over 200,000 pounds. Its design cruise speed is about 520 miles per hour. It will not be

On 1 September 1954, the Super Constellation, powered by turboprop engines, made its first flight from Burbank. A total of four aircraft, fitted with the 5,500-horsepower Pratt and Whitney YT34 engines, were built and flown. Lockheed proposed two airline versions powered by T34s, the L1249A freighter and the L1249B passenger aircraft, but a lack of firm orders forced them to abandon the project.

9

built unless backed by a military order and would cost about four or five million dollars – and take three or four years to produce." Allan summarised the Douglas piston-engined types. The DC7 was overpowered, noisy, and of reduced range but was popular in the United States because of its high speed.

> The DC7C is a later and notable change which has followed as a result of the high overall noise level and low capacity of the DC7A. Five feet more wing is to be placed between each inboard engine and the hull, and the fuselage lengthened eighty inches . . . Compared with the [Lockheed] 1049C it should be about twenty-five miles per hour faster and have greater range, though with slightly less payload. The DC7C will lend itself admirably to the installation of a turboprop engine and Douglas are negotiating with engine manufacturers including Rolls-Royce . . . Engine availability [for the turboprop version] fixes its probable production to about 1959.

Lockheed, who had provided the current Qantas fleet, had a jet airliner design that was markedly different from the Comet (with engines buried in the wing roots) and the Boeing 707 (with engines hung from the wings on pods). The four engines, reported Allan, were installed in pairs aft of the passenger compartment in the fuselage "with the object of reducing noise and facilitating maintenance". Lockheed, also, did not expect to build any commercial jet type without first having a military contract to offset design and prototype costs. (This Lockheed design was never built.)

> Though Lockheeds have two large turboprop aircraft flying [Allan wrote], the C130 [a four-engined freighter ordered in quantity by the military] and the 1049E [a Constellation with four Pratt & Whitney T34 turboprop engines] they have plans also for a four-turboprop passenger, 450 miles per hour machine. This latter also awaits the production of the new series of turboprop engines which will not be available until 1959 so that, at least in the United States, the aircraft situation is likely to remain substantially unchanged until about 1959 . . . At least five years of good work will be had from present piston types before operators of the present large aircraft need expect serious competition.

He pointed out that turboprop aircraft had to operate at a height of some 35,000 feet and required a much greater pressurisation differential than existing fuselages.

Britain's turboprop Bristol Britannia had been flown for one day in September at the Farnborough Air Show. Two prototypes were flying in the test programme. Allan commented:

> There is an urgent necessity to build up hours on the aeroplane and to remove doubts on such items as the controllability of the

aeroplane at full load with two engines out on one side in turbulence, and the reliability of the electronic engine control systems etc. . . . Bristol expects that the fuselage will be required to undergo the water-tank pressurisation test for fatigue similar to that applied to the Comet. Besides the delay of about six months to complete this test, hull manufacture will be inactive while awaiting results. The production of completed aeroplanes is, however, more dependent on the production of engines than on production of airframes.

The later versions of the existing Proteus engine would, he said, provide such a marked difference in operating costs that "if Qantas took delivery of Proteus Britannias we would have to change to the later engine type [available 1959–60] which would be a very costly proceeding indeed".

Captain Allan summarised the Qantas perspective on future commercial jet and turboprop aircraft. To obtain economic results comparable with present piston aircraft, jet transports would have gross weights upwards of 230,000 pounds. They would cost $4 million to $5 million each. "The speeds claimed for these commercial jet projects is becoming more conservative than a year ago and now mostly vary between 500 and 550 miles per hour, instead of the 600 to 650 quoted a year ago." In the United Kingdom, jet bomber prototypes were tentatively proposed for future British commercial jets. "These include the Vickers Valiant, Avro Vulcan and Handley Page Victor which are all large aeroplanes in the 250,000-pound class. Each manufacturer makes claims as to the cheapness of operation of such jets . . . Our studies are less optimistic . . . figures on jet aeroplanes do not show appreciable reductions in costs per unit load." Comet 2s and 3s would not be available before 1957, Boeings before 1959, and Douglas and Lockheed jets before 1962. Availability of the British Valiant type was not known. There were no airline orders for any of these aircraft.

All the United States manufacturers had plans for building medium-size turboprop airliners of some 130,000 to 150,000 pounds but these plans depended on the production of economic engines in 1959. In Britain, only the Britannia was contemplated. (The highly successful Vickers Viscount, powered by Rolls-Royce Dart turboprop engines, was a small, short-range airliner of no interest to Qantas.) According to Captain Allan, "in 1959 a hypothetical turboprop aeroplane of 150,000 pounds gross would cruise at about 420 miles per hour appreciably more economically than present day piston types and, according to most authorities, 30 per cent cheaper than a contemporary jet".[15]

11

SUPER CONSTELLATION TO AUSTRALIA..the South Seas

QANTAS—Australia's Overseas Airline

Qantas's San Francisco office premises at 212 Stockton Street overlooking Union Square in late 1954.

BOAC, under British government direction to favour British aircraft, did not have the five years of relative unconcern that Scottie Allan had predicted for Qantas, secure in its Constellation fleet. Sir Miles Thomas wrote a memorandum to the board on 21 September expressing great concern about "the fluid state of production of the aircraft we have on order from de Havillands and Bristols". He drew attention to three new factors affecting the situation. The minister of supply and de Havillands, he wrote, had adopted an attitude on the Comet that seemed too optimistic and BOAC could not realistically participate in a programme of getting Comets of any kind back into service "before a long series of modifications, tests and re-tests" after the findings of the Farnborough tests and the sifting of evidence by the Court of Enquiry. On Bristols, he wrote: "Despite the protestations of the manufacturers to the contrary, it is also evident that the Britannia programme is going to be very late indeed and we must never forget that in this aeroplane, in our support of British manufacturing interests, we are taking on not only a new airframe but a new engine that has no military backing and no production experience . . .".

12

Sir Miles next raised the plans of Lockheed, Douglas, and Rolls-Royce. Douglas, he said, were actively engaged in discussions with Rolls-Royce with the idea of fitting the new turbo-prop RB109 engine to their DC7C airframe. Juan Trippe had told him that Pan American was intensely interested in this project. They wanted, Trippe had said, "the best airframe manufacturer in the world with the best engine manufacturer in the world". BOAC, he reminded board members, had started negotiations with Douglas and had the right to acquire the first ten and then a further five of these aircraft. Lockheed also, wrote Sir Miles, were redesigning the wing of the 1049 and proposing to fit an improved Wright piston engine, an American turbo-prop now under development, or the Rolls-Royce RB109. Any of these combinations could outfly in range and speed the Princess flying boat. So could the Douglas-Rolls-Royce combination. Sir Miles lamented that "we continue to suffer under the handicap of slow production by British aeroplane manufacturers". He said that BOAC had loyally demonstrated its desire to promote British aircraft "by putting in a very substantial bid for the Princess – to say the least of it, 'encouraged' by the previous minister of transport and civil aviation . . . It has met with but scant response and quite unashamedly I submit that we should now withdraw the bid." BOAC has also, he said, held out not only a welcoming hand but also substantial financial concessions to the independent operators; "if all that such action merits is a continuation of carping public criticism, then obviously the equation is unbalanced." He thought that withdrawal of the as yet unaccepted offer for the Princess flying boats "should help to clear the way for the purchase of British-engined American aircraft of proven airframe design".[16]

At Qantas, the BCPA takeover marked the beginning of a new scale of operations and ever-increasing complexity in functions and organisation. C. O. Turner, as general manager, was in his element and took on more and more responsibility.[17] Hudson Fysh, gradually distanced from detail, served on the executive committee of the International Air Transport Association and attended its annual general meetings, continued on the board of TEAL (becoming vice-chairman), was chairman of the Wentworth Hotel board and deputy chairman of the Australian National Travel Association. The pressures of combining the roles of managing director and chairman grew. The Qantas board also felt that Turner, as general manager, Allan, as assistant general manager, and some of the more senior executive officers should be paid more, in recognition of their demanding and complex duties. Fysh told Athol Townley on 30 August that the board had resolved

> as a matter of urgency, the Minister's attention be again invited to the inadequacy of the salaries of certain executive officers and the need for early remedial action. It was emphasised that, since the Board's recommendation for salary increases was made last year, the Company's sphere of operations had increased very considerably . . . In the judgement of the Board, the salaries now paid to these officers do not reflect the work values of the positions they occupy and the duties they are required to discharge. Mention was also made of the probable further changes likely to be made in the authorities and responsibilities of senior executives of the Company if the Minister approves of the Chairman relinquishing the title of Managing Director . . .[18]

The board recommended an increase for the general manager of £500 to £3,500 and for the assistant general manager of £500 to £3,000. The operations manager and chief engineer were to receive rises of £300 to £2,500. The minister agreed to the suggested increases on 2 September. He accepted the board's submission that it was "in the best position to judge the work of the Company's officers and to nominate salaries" but added that "this does not necessarily mean that no other factors are involved".[19] The minister, he made it clear, had to bear in mind the relative salaries of other senior persons whose salary levels were the responsibility of the government. The board, in fact, was concerned with pay rates throughout the entire organisation. Fysh told the newest board member, Roland Wilson: "A serious position has arisen in regard not only to our failure to recruit urgently required new staff but in holding employees. This is due to a general labour shortage and the fact that we are not paying rates competitive with industry."[20]

The new staff so urgently required were needed for the happiest of reasons: continuing traffic growth. Fysh described it to his minister as "the yearly increase in loadings offering which has never yet failed to come along since Civil Aviation first started up". With it also came the need for more aircraft. "The major matter which we have on our plate at the moment", he told Townley, "is the proposed order of additional aircraft to enable us to adequately cater for our commitments for the future . . . Your agreement to the purchase of the Skymaster has been a great help, and we hope to hear that the two additional Super Constellations have also been agreed, which will consolidate our position in the 1956 period and onward." The minister was about to leave, at year's end, on an extended overseas trip. In a briefing paper, Fysh advised him on the parallel partnership agreement between Qantas and BOAC.

"Revenue", wrote Fysh, "is pooled by operators and shared at present on a 50-50 basis. The total estimated revenue per annum in pool is as follows: passengers and baggage, £5,600,000; mails £6,800,000; cargo £1,400,000. QEA profit margin from the Kangaroo Route is about a gross of £600,000 per annum, so that it will be seen that if we lost cargo revenue we would immediately eliminate our profit." The agreement made between the United Kingdom and Australian governments to operate the route had, he said, been made in 1947 and there had been no subsequent official talks to vary the arrangement. He continued: "The basic principles which have been recognised for twenty years are that the UK and Australian airlines should not compete against each other but should combine to compete against other strong foreign operators such as Pan American, KLM, SAS and so on. The partnership has been an outstanding success." He reminded the minister that with the approval of the Commonwealth government, Qantas had recently ordered ten Super Consellation aircraft for $30 million. "The experts of the International Bank investigated our organisation and we are supplying details of our operating revenue and expenditure to the Bank every few months. Unless we continue not only to operate efficiently but also to show a profit from our services we will prejudice this credit arrangement."[21]

Sir Daniel McVey referred to threats to this BOAC-QEA partnership in a letter on 17 December to Viscount Swinton, secretary of state at the Commonwealth Relations Office in London. "The system now runs the risk of being seriously prejudiced", he said, "by the intrusion of 'independent' operators in a field (freighter operation) which is at present enjoyed exclusively by the parallel partners. Two 'independent' operators, Britavia (wholly owned, I understand, by the P & O shipping line) and Acquilla, have applied . . . to operate air services between London and Perth . . . If the application is granted, the loss of freight . . . by the partners will seriously affect the operating results of BOAC and Qantas." The parallel partnership, hc wrote, had been most successful as an instrument of closer Empire co-operation. "BOAC, as an operator, cannot very well intervene or protest on a matter which must be regarded as high Government policy; nor can Qantas in Australia. But parallel partnership operation is your baby and mine — yours far more than mine — and I think you would be glad to be informed of any move likely to jeopardise the continued success of the operation."[22] His effort was without success. Swinton responded:

> All-freight services . . . have become an important new factor to be considered in formulating air transport policies of the present and future. All our experience in the United Kingdom tends to support the view that if we are to take advantage of the new opportunities we must allow, and even encourage, participation by the independent companies in the air freight field. This has particular force when, as in the case of Britavia, the company can command the co-operation of the well-established shipping agencies . . . the peculiar requirements of all-freight in traffic handling and operating techniques and sales methods provided strong grounds for entrusting the responsibility for all-freight services to a separate operator not concerned primarily with the expanding market for passenger and mail traffic.[23]

Though this was the UK government's official attitude it drew criticism from Sir Miles Thomas, who was shown copies of the correspondence. He told Phillip Hood, in Sydney: "[It] is, as you correctly assume, a typical departmental letter. It is also not quite right factually . . . I think it would be useful if Sir Daniel McVey could follow up this matter."[24]

In its twenty-first annual report for the 1954 year, Qantas recorded that its aircraft flew 11 million miles (up ten per cent on the previous year) and increased its capacity by almost twenty per cent to 67,000,000 ton miles. It operated, like BOAC, three services weekly on the London route and carried 23,785 passengers (over 4,000 more than in 1953). Super Constellations had replaced the older Constellation 749As in August. Special Skymaster Cargo Carriers flew to Singapore to meet BOAC cargo services from London. On the new Pacific route, one frequency each week terminated at San Francisco, the second extending to Vancouver. In seven and a half months of operation, 7,899 passengers were carried. Japan services were flown twice weekly, carrying both civilian and military traffic. (In support of Australian forces in Japan and Korea, Qantas carried 6,033 service personnel plus mail and cargo.) Skymasters operated the Hong Kong and Tokyo routes to mid-1954, when pressurised DC6s were chartered from TEAL for the Tokyo flights until November, when the older Lockheed 749As released from other routes superseded them. Revenue on the Indian Ocean service to South Africa did not cover full costs. Qantas continued to accept responsibility for operating air services to New Caledonia and the New Hebrides and experienced a substantial increase in traffic on the services to New Guinea and Papua. During

1954 Qantas operated thirteen aircraft internally in New Guinea, mostly from Lae. All Qantas operations were accident free and without injury to passengers or crew members.[25]

The continuing expansion was taking its toll on Fysh. "I found I was getting jumpy under the pressure of it all", he wrote. "On 7 December 1954 I wrote to my minister, Athol Townley, suggesting that I should relinquish my duties as Chief Executive on 30 June, 1955, when I would be sixty, and continue as whole-time Chairman of the Board." Townley approved and informed Fysh that his salary would be the same as currently recommended (£5,000 per year), less the pension equivalent of his retirement allowance on ceasing to be an employee of Qantas as its chief executive. (His pension equivalent was £1,461, which brought his salary in the role of full-time chairman down to £3,539.) Townley wrote that as chairman he would be the channel of communication with the minister and the director-general on all policy matters. He was also advised that, as in Trans-Australia Airlines, the general manager (Turner) would then become chief executive but would not be a member of the Qantas board. Fysh had been manager or managing director of the old Q.A.N.T.A.S. and of QEA for thirty-two years.[26]

VH-EAT, one of three Beaver aircraft delivered in early December 1954, at Mascot prior to its departure for service on the New Guinea internal network. The new Engine Test House can be seen under construction in the left upper corner of the photograph.

1955

There was an important letter from the minister to Fysh on 1 January 1955 in which the government clearly indicated that

17

Qantas, in its relationships with the airlines of other countries, was more than a carrier of passengers and cargo by air. Townley referred to fare proposals filed by QEA at the recent IATA Traffic Conference in Venice.

> I think your Board will agree [he wrote] that changes on fares and freight rates by a Government-owned airline can have important political, as well as financial, implications and consequently as responsible minister I wish to be fully consulted about such changes. Admittedly the filing of schedules with IATA and even their acceptance by an IATA Conference still leaves the rates subject to approval on behalf of the Australian Government but you will appreciate that it could become very embarrassing for me if, at that stage, proposals emanating from a wholly Government-owned airline have to be vetoed.
>
> I would like to take this opportunity of also referring to a somewhat related subject – the "mail-pooling" rate under the Kangaroo partnership. The relevant clause in the inter-governmental agreement – which is now nearing finality – will provide that this rate shall be "agreed from time to time between the designated airlines with the approval of the contracting parties". We, for our part, would have preferred to have this rate a matter for agreement between the two Governments but this presented certain difficulties and consequently the formula I have mentioned is being adopted.
>
> As you are aware, the mail-pooling rate is important financially to the Commonwealth as well as to the company and it is most undesirable that your company – which is wholly owned by the Government – should agree even tentatively any mail-pooling rate that will not receive my approval on behalf of the Australian Government. To avoid such a happening, it is my desire that when any negotiations with BOAC on this subject are contemplated, your company should first consult my Department and secure my approval to the attitude which QEA will adopt in the negotiations on this subject.
>
> To formalise the position on these two matters, I have directed that paragraph 11 of the Financial Directive to your company be amended to read as follows: "11. Any arrangements involving the pooling of revenue as between the company and another operator, including any agreement as to the rates for mails, shall be subject to the prior approval of the Minister. Any agreement or any filing with IATA relating to rates for the carriage of passengers, mails or goods shall also be subject to the prior approval of the Minister."[27]

The political dimension of Qantas activities even in the most fundamental of commercial matters was now formally recognised and spelt out.

A more basic political and strategic element in the Qantas national role was made clear in the first official document from the government aimed at securing for the airline a second route to England, across the continent of the United States, and so providing Australia with a round-the-world air service. On 25 January the Australian embassy in Washington was instructed by the Department of External Affairs to present to the US authorities a note referring to the air transport agreement that had been signed between the two countries on 3 December 1946 and under which the two countries' airlines had since operated. The note said:

> The Australian Authorities have noted that since 1950 the traffic between Australia and Europe (particularly the United States) has shown a marked and increasing tendency to travel through North America, instead of along the traditional route between Australia and the United Kingdom through the Middle East. This reflects the growing political, commercial and other associations between Australia and the North American continent.
>
> Traffic between Australia and Europe (particularly the United Kingdom) is vital to Australia and is the very foundation of services between Australia and Europe now operated by the Australian airline through the Middle East. Apart from the considerations mentioned above, recent disturbing developments in South East Asia reflect upon the security of those services to Europe. These services are the principal support of the moderate fleet of large transport aircraft possessed by Qantas, which comprise a significant element of the reserve defence air fleet of Australia.
>
> For these reasons the Australian Government wishes to obtain authority for direct air connections of its own across North America and through to Europe, and accordingly desires to propose an amendment of the Annex to the Australia-United States Air Transport Agreement so as to permit the Australian-designated airline to operate its services also across the United States and beyond to Europe, serving on the West Coast, on any particular flight at the option of the operator, either San Francisco or Los Angeles and in the east, Chicago and/or New York. [28]

The embassy was informed that a formal note had also been presented to Canada in Ottawa requesting traffic rights on the route through Fiji, Canton Island, Honolulu, San Francisco, Montreal, Gander and on to Europe. It was, of course, an initiative of the profoundest consequence for Qantas. The United States, however, was quick to indicate, in talks that followed in Washington, that there were difficulties and the ambassador (Sir Percy Spender) was instructed from Canberra to restate the Australian problem. In a note to the US government he again stressed the unsettled conditions in Asian areas and pointed out that though alternative routes might be available across the Indian Ocean, they could not be considered as more than an unsatisfactory short-term means of maintaining essential Australian services for traffic to Europe and the United

Kingdom. The immediate effect of these unsettled conditions, said the note, was the diversion of traffic to the more secure routes through the United States. Careful study by Australia had emphasised the importance of New York on any through route. The note concluded: "Sir Percy Spender emphasises the importance which the Australian Authorities attach to this problem . . . [for] a satisfactory solution which is of marked defence and commercial significance to this country".[29]

On 2 March, the embassy told the Department of External Affairs that in an unexpected statement, the US had informed them that the Australian request could not be granted. Australia, said the US, already had adequate opportunity of providing for Australia-Europe traffic: it had three-quarters of the route mileage eastbound and westbound; the route now requested would place Australia in a competitively advantageous position; the balance of rights under the existing agreement favoured Australia and the route requested would give extensive fifth freedom rights to the Australian airline and mean a serious loss of traffic to the US. Further, the granting of the request would create a precedent. The final US argument was, however, the critical one: rights of a comparable nature were not available from Australia. The embassy note concluded: "It seems clear . . . that whatever the merits of our arguments, the United States attitude is primarily determined by the view that we have no adequate quid pro quo."[30] As with all such international air traffic arguments, the heart of the matter was the equitable horse-trade. C.O. Turner was in New York during these exchanges and discussed the impasse with the embassy. It was decided that no further action would be taken pending a visit by the minister to the United States. "We have tentatively agreed for the time being that we should press as a minimum for a route through San Francisco and New York, perhaps associating Los Angeles with San Francisco as a co-terminal . . .".[31]

While these important matters for Qantas were being advanced with the full weight of government support, there were irritations arising from the government connection in lesser affairs. Hudson Fysh received a letter from the acting minister (Harold Holt) querying the increases in salary for the general manager (Turner) and the assistant general manager (Allan) that had been approved by Townley in August. They seemed, he wrote "a little out of proportion to the increases recently generally approved for salaries of Permanent Heads". He was, he said, taking up the matter with the chairman of the Public Service Board.[32]

The assistant general manager, Capt. Scottie Allan, had left for Burbank on 8 January to discuss specifications (and with authority to sign a contract with Lockheed) for two new Super Constellations (model 1049G), modified up to the Qantas standard in the last six of the ten Qantas aircraft to include bunks and improved galley and toilet arrangements. In addition, these aircraft were to have a strengthened hull allowing the front freight compartment to carry 9,000 pounds instead of the original 5,000. The forward part of the cabin floor was, in addition, strengthened to allow a loading of 100 pounds per square foot so that heavy freight could be carried if necessary. (The basic price of the aircraft was just under $US2 million.)[33] Some weeks earlier a separate contract had been signed for the purchase of a DC4 aircraft (second hand, from Resort Airlines) for modification in the workshops of Flying Tiger to Qantas standards and for conversion as a freighter. Freight was rapidly increasing in significance. A press release by Hudson Fysh predicted an increase in air cargo capacity of 50 per cent on the Kangaroo Route, giving the Qantas-BOAC partnership a combined capacity of 120 tons per month in each direction.[34]

BOAC's perceptive regional representative in Sydney, Phillip Hood, had told his deputy chief executive in a memorandum on 20 January of QEA's definite government approval to buy two more 1049 Constellations for delivery in June 1956 and referred to Qantas efforts to obtain traffic rights through Canada. "Unless QEA has other expansions in mind," he wrote, "for what other purpose could these aircraft be required . . .? The purpose of the latter part of my letter is to suggest that the race to be first in the round-the-world stakes might be won by Qantas."[35] BOAC at home, however, had far more immediate and complex issues to resolve. Deputy chairman Whitney Straight wrote to Sir Miles Thomas on 1 February about the airline's future aircraft programme: "We are faced with a number of critical decisions about future aircraft procurement. We are being subject to political and other pressures . . .". He wanted the whole programme carefully considered in the light of what was right for BOAC. "We now have the reputation of being the experimental department of the British Aircraft Industry . . . what we need and now lack is a reputation for reliability." It was, Straight said, abundantly clear that the Comet 2, if it ever appeared in operation, would be obsolete in terms of economy, range, and capacity. The Comet 2 had, in his view, "become a 'political' aeroplane which we are buying not because we, as commercial airline operators, now need or want it, but solely because its purchase is considered to be a matter of political expediency". There was, however, general agreement that the Comet 3 was the right aeroplane. Straight suggested that

> the airlines that have ordered, or might order, Comets of any type should be called to a meeting in London . . . A proposal should then be put forward on the basis of a "new look" Comet 3 with BOAC to lead by stating that it has sufficient confidence to place an order for not less than twenty units . . . I am convinced that a bold step of this kind is essential and could, even at this late stage, recover for the British Aircraft Industry and de Havillands the prestige which has been lost, despite the fundamentally sound and imaginative conception of the Comet aeroplane.

Whitney Straight was gloomy about the Bristol Britannia. "The Bristol Company", he wrote, "has not yet demonstrated its ability to manufacture a successful commercial aircraft in this [Britannia] category. The Britannia's history to date does not provide a basis for much confidence and there are still some technical doubts about the aircraft . . . We know that the Proteus, which is an obsolete conception, cannot be made into a really effective engine . . . The BE.25 is the only engine with sufficient power to take advantage of the stretch inherent in the Britannia airframe . . . It would be both practical and politically expedient to indicate in a positive way our support for the BE.25." BOAC must, he said, "if we are to survive as an airline, obtain a reasonable quantity of reliable, modern equipment. I feel it would be wrong, therefore, to accept any smaller fleet of Douglas aircraft than that for which we have asked." On future types, he commented on BOAC's interest in a new British jet, which he said "must be, almost inevitably, the Vickers 1000."[36] Clearly QEA's reservations about British aircraft were shared by their BOAC partners.

The pace and complexity of the QEA expansion brought with it tensions at home, with the minister and his department, and misunderstandings abroad, with BOAC. Athol Townley wrote with some irritation to Hudson Fysh on 2 May about correspondence between C. O. Turner and the director-general of civil aviation which, he said, should properly have come, as matters of far-reaching policy, from Fysh to himself. Fysh had in fact, quite properly and in accordance with the QEA financial directive, informed his minister of the airline's programme of air services and objectives for 1955. They included an increase from two to three services a week to San Francisco (with one per week instead of three per fortnight continuing on to Vancouver); the operation of the Hong Kong service from April by Super Constellation; the replacement of flying boat operations to New Guinea and other Pacific islands with DC4 services from April as landplane facilities became available; and an increase from once fortnightly to once weekly from April in the South Africa service, with alteration in the route to include Djakarta. What had aroused the minister, however, were proposals from Turner to the director-general which in no way referred to those submitted by Fysh, but which included a weekly service from the Kangaroo Route between Sydney and Singapore via Perth and Djakarta; routing of the Australia-South Africa service between Cocos Island and Sydney through Singapore and Darwin, omitting Perth; and discontinuation of the Skymaster service through Cocos to Singapore. The minister concluded his admonishment: "I am told that all these proposals have the approval of your Board, but I am unable to determine what the Board's programme really is, and I would be glad if you would clarify the position."[37]

QEA was also, through Turner, on the verge of a serious mis-understanding with BOAC. Phillip Hood had, from Sydney, advised his deputy chief executive, Basil Smallpiece, of his assessment that Qantas had plans for operating across the United States and on to Europe. Smallpiece, however, had spoken directly with Turner himself and had received quite a different impression. He wrote to Hood:

> You may be quite right about the way in which things will turn out in regard to an Australian operation across America or Canada. But I taxed Turner on this point directly, and he gave me his assurance that QEA have *no* intention of operating beyond the Pacific seaboard. It would not augur well for the future of partner-ship arrangements if we could not take a statement of this sort at its face value. I think, therefore, you should take the attitude, in all your discussions with QEA, and contacts with other people, that BOAC understand and believe that QEA have no intention of doing more than they say. We should certainly give them no grounds for thinking that we may not be trusting their word; in fact, by our attitude, we should be building up a position in which it would be very difficult for them to break it.[38]

Hood, however, remained dissatisfied. "We did make an agreement in Christchurch", he wrote, "and it is my firm feeling that Australia is using the rather loose wording on the future of the through route via the Pacific to get in quicker than any-body else." Capt. Edgar Johnston, he said, had informed the UK air attaché in Australia that QEA had no present intention to extend their service across Canada to the United Kingdom but that if and when they did, they would immediately consult the UK.[39]

Hood also sent Smallpiece a press clipping from a New Zealand newspaper that lashed out at Qantas. It said: "When BCPA was disbanded and Tasman Empire Airways and Qantas cut up the spoils between them, many persons thought TEAL's problems were over for quite some time. In fact, the problems just began; the worst one mainly springing from our giving Australia a 50 per cent holding in TEAL . . . A crisis will no doubt come. When Qantas gets all the aircraft it has on order, Australia is expected to make things uncomfortable. No one here trusts Australians when it comes to civil aviation matters, for they have proved themselves ruthless in the past."[40] TEAL, Hood told Smallpiece, "is frankly fearful of being swallowed up by QEA and if the company displayed any signs of weakening, QEA would be standing by to engulf them . . . The New Zealand Government must face the issue without delay – either to go in for long distance air services or remain a regional operator with the attendant prospect of witnessing Pan American and CPA eating into the present monopoly traffic."[41]

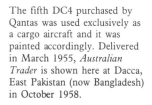

The fifth DC4 purchased by Qantas was used exclusively as a cargo aircraft and it was painted accordingly. Delivered in March 1955, *Australian Trader* is shown here at Dacca, East Pakistan (now Bangladesh) in October 1958.

The mystery of QEA's US ambitions was cleared up for BOAC on 4 March when Australia's acting minister for civil aviation, Harold Holt, issued a statement. The Department of External Affairs cabled Townley in Washington on 4 March 1955 that because of reports emanating from America on the

North American negotiations, taken up by Australian media,
it had been necessary to issue an official statement.

> Exploratory discussions [said the statement] have been going on
> for some months with the Canadian and United States authorities
> to secure the necessary rights to enable Qantas Empire Airways
> to extend its Pacific service across North America to Europe so
> as to fully participate in Australia-Europe traffic . . . There has
> been an increasing tendency for passengers to fly to Europe via
> North America instead of the traditional Kangaroo route through
> the Middle East . . . For this reason and also because of the
> strategic value of an alternate route to Europe the Government
> is anxious to secure the rights to enable the Pacific service to be
> extended to Europe . . .[43]

Basil Smallpiece was not amused. With great restraint he wrote
to Turner on 17 March, reminding him of their conversation
in London and referring to Holt's press release. "I do not know
whether your Government's policy has jumped ahead of you
during your absence, but I feel certain that had you been aware
that consideration was being given for fixing a date for the
commencement of this [trans-America] service, you would have
mentioned the matter to me while you were over here . . . I
am sure that it is wholly in accord with your feelings on the
matter that we should be absolutely frank on a matter such as
this. I therefore await with great interest your reply . . .".[43]

C. O. Turner replied at length, but did not address directly
the implied accusation in Smallpiece's letter. Qantas, he said,
had had nothing to do with the acting minister's statement,
which had been issued following uninformed comment in US
aviation journals.

> The reference [in the statement] to fixing a date for the
> commencement of such a service was possibly included with the
> idea of impressing both the US and Canada that we really meant
> business . . . Although the discussions were as between Govern-
> ments and were obviously of a highly confidential nature because
> of the defence aspects, I did go to a good deal of trouble to explain
> as frankly as I could the reasons which I thought were behind the
> applications. I did this on my own initiative with the idea of
> avoiding any possible misunderstanding between BOAC and QEA
> when it became known such talks were proceeding . . .

Turner set out some of the details of Canada's extra service into
Australia "which virtually flouted the terms of the bilateral
agreement", and problems with the US on the US-Australia
Pacific agreement. He concluded less than apologetically: "As
you know we had hoped that by this time BOAC would have
been operating a service through San Francisco to connect with

ours and we are disappointed that you will apparently not be able to consider this until well into 1957. It looks as if we need to get a better control of the through traffic because it appears that we are seriously losing to Pan Am and CPA, apparently because of the difficulties in obtaining accommodation on BOAC services across the Atlantic."[44]

The Qantas move, in Phillip Hood's eyes, had grave implications for BOAC financially. On 6 April, commenting on policy matters, he wrote: "It has always been my great hope to see the Union Jack on the Pacific. When I learnt that the winding up of BCPA entailed a junction at San Francisco with QEA I was most disappointed." For Qantas to cross the United States, he said, concessions would have to be granted at the Australian end. "The granting of rights to Pan American from Australia to South East Asia would be disastrous . . . Pan Am would then be in on the Kangaroo route, with obvious results to the partnership finances . . . Political necessity however, often overrides commercial considerations these days . . . Altogether I am sure BOAC must operate UK-Australia via the Pacific sooner or later . . .".[45] He told his chairman on 29 April: "QEA aspirations are being strongly backed by the Government . . . the more ambitious our partners become, the more need to watch our interests in this part of the world . . . New Zealand, with its strong British ties and almost embarrassing loyalty must get involved in Pacific developments as the plans of BOAC and QEA unfold."[46]

Sir Percy Spender, the Australian ambassador in Washington, reported to Townley on 3 May on Australia's efforts to secure rights for Qantas: "I saw Hoover this morning and handed him our latest note on transit rights for Qantas across the United States, I explained that I was approaching him because the Commonwealth considered the matter had important political aspects . . .". Hoover's administration, he said, "would give every possible consideration to our request. We should not, however, base any expectation upon this statement as there were many factors involved. All over the world the United States airlines were prevented from operating internal services, hence internal services in the United States were reserved for domestic airlines . . .".[47]

This Australian initiative to cross the United States and create a continuous airline route eastbound to England was, in fact, paralleled by a BOAC plan to operate westbound across the American continent to Australia. Sir Daniel McVey referred to conversations he had held in 1952 on behalf of Qantas in a letter from London to Hudson Fysh on 19 May 1955.

> At that time it was clearly understood by us all that BOAC would, at as early a date as possible, meet QEA at San Francisco and thereby provide a joint QEA-BOAC service to London via San Francisco. It was also understood that at a later date, when necessary Government negotiations had been satisfactorily concluded and when traffic and economic considerations justified it, BOAC would operate right through to Sydney via San Francisco and QEA would operate right through to London via San Francisco . . . This forward planning and ultimate objective are still uppermost in the minds of all over here. The extension of the BOAC service . . . is therefore only the first step.

McVey referred to Fysh's disappointment "over the drift in the relationships between BOAC and QEA", which, he wrote, seemed to be a regularly recurring trouble that caused agonisings on both sides. "This parallel partnership [McVey wrote] . . . needs hard work on both sides to make it successful . . . all of us recognise [it] as being the most powerful combination of interests in the international airline operating field . . . and in addition it can exercise a tremendous influence for good in British and Commonwealth relationships." He said he had chided Miles Thomas about the inordinate delay of BOAC in extending its service across America and was told that BOAC would have a Stratocruiser service operating by 1 October 1955. "Miles Thomas is in great heart and is very much on top of his job. Furthermore he is an enthusiastic believer in the parallel partnership method of operation." Cedric Turner, McVey added, "is held in the very highest regard over here and none of us need have any fears of his success as Chief Executive of QEA when the time comes for him to take over full executive authority and responsibility from you."[48]

Though QEA and BOAC, despite their differences, still saw their partnership as a powerful combination, Qantas now faced competition on its new Pacific route that it had never met on the long-established Kangaroo Route. A board paper reported on 27 May that though QEA had held its own with Pan American, Canadian Pacific had improved its competitive position. Revenue from cargo carrying had been increased overall, but at the expense of the Kangaroo Route. More seriously, average weekly loadings of mail received since the Australian Post Office had decided to reallocate a considerable proportion of mail to Pan American showed that QEA was losing between £130,000 and £150,000 a year in revenue. The paper summarised the American refusal of Australia's further application for rights from San Francisco to New York and beyond and said it had become "an urgent necessity for further preliminary talks with BOAC to clarify the future of the partnership services to the UK and Europe via the US and Canada". Closer to home, Qantas revenue from flying boat services continued to decline. Losses on the Noumea-Fiji extension grew. Only the Lae-Honiara service was profitable. A board paper in late May stated:

> The position is that we have informed the Department of Civil Aviation that we will cease flying boats on 4 June and action is now being taken to close down the base and dispose of the remaining three Sandringham flying boats . . . The boats are due for overhaul which would cost about £20,000 per aircraft and we could not expect to sell them for a price sufficient to cover this expense. As there are no buyers for time-expired aircraft it is proposed to break up the three flying boats . . . [and] it is assessed that we will recover parts useful to the Company to the value of over £5,000.[49]

Daniel McVey returned to the theme of the BOAC partnership in a letter to Fysh on 6 June, in which the once dominant issue of Australia as a unit of Empire was shown to be still alive and strong, through him, on the Qantas board.

> I do seriously think that both parties have a very deep obligation to make the partnership work [he wrote], and for reasons that lie outside and beyond the mutual advantages to be derived on the operation of their respective airlines. For one thing, there are

Qantas flying boat services from Rose Bay on Sydney Harbour came to an end with the departure for Noumea of the Short Sandringham *Pacific Warrior* on 1 June 1955. One of the four QEA Sandringhams was sold to Ansett Airways while the others were dismantled for spares; their Pratt and Whitney engines were interchangeable with the engines of the DC3s operating in New Guinea.

political aspects to be taken into account. QEA and BOAC must, at top level, refrain wherever possible from any action which might lead to embarrassment between the two Governments and, indeed, should try at all times to operate in such a fashion that the Governments are not tempted to intervene . . . The parallel partnership operation of BOAC and QEA is something more than an airline operating arrangement. It is an essay into the field of Empire building or, if you like, the maintenance and the strengthening of the partnership of the British Commonwealth of Nations as a united, if not a unified, political force.

These were sentiments that would have been powerfully supported by Fergus McMaster, founding chairman of Qantas. They were clearly in line with Hudson Fysh's own attitudes and with those of the Australian prime minister, R. G. Menzies. In February of 1955 the SEATO treaty had come into force, followed soon by the despatch of Australian troops to join the Commonwealth Strategic Reserve force in Malaya to counter terrorist forces (after eight years of British operations there). In May of the previous year, the French had been defeated in Vietnam. McVey did not see Australia as playing a role independent of Britain in such times.

It is all very well [wrote McVey] for some people to talk about the sovereign rights of Australia to do this or do that, and to advocate the exercise of independent judgment on what is good for Australia. So many people do that sort of thing. If every sovereign nation in the British Commonwealth were to adopt that attitude as a matter of national policy, it would be the beginning of the end of the British Commonwealth and the result would be that no one member country would amount to anything worthwhile as a force in world politics or affairs. The best test of whether a British country is fit to exercise sovereign rights is whether it is willing, when the need arises, to give up or pool some of those rights for the common good of the whole British Commonwealth . . . Coming down to purely materialistic considerations, Hudson, I have no doubt at all that Australia in general and QEA in particular will derive more long term financial benefits from the QEA-BOAC partnership than under any other system of operation. The history of QEA proves this; and now that QEA has become a strong partner—whereas formerly it was, we must all admit, a weak partner—it should not cause us to become impatient of the temporary weakness of BOAC. Make no error about it, Hudson, BOAC is a virile organisation, hampered at the moment only by a lack of aircraft and restrictions upon types of equipment they may buy, but that phase will pass. [50]

Ironically, within days of the receipt of this letter, Hudson Fysh wrote to the minister for civil aviation to suggest that the word "Empire" in the Australian airline's name, was no longer appropriate. "We have long been aware that the word 'Empire' in Qantas Empire Airways is nowadays meaningless", said Fysh. Americans, particularly, could not understand it. "We are considering changing this at some appropriate time and introducing the word 'Australian' in some way. Meanwhile, we are stressing on our aircraft and in publicity material 'Australia's overseas airline' and similar wording." Fysh did not, however, want a complete change of name. "In regard to the word 'Qantas' this is a name, as you know, which goes back to the beginnings of Australian commercial aviation and around which has not only centred our publicity and our records, but is a rallying point for the staff and their feelings. To give up the name by which we are known would eliminate the points mentioned . . . and would mean starting again. In fact, in the eyes of the world and the public, and in official circles, no longer would your international airline be the second oldest operating in the world and the oldest in Australia."[51] (Fysh was in error in this final phrase; the first airline to begin scheduled operations in Australia was Norman Brearley's West Australian Airlines.)

C. O. Turner left for London on 25 June for more partnership talks with BOAC. To prepare BOAC's deputy chief executive for his visit, Phillip Hood wrote discussing current issues.

> Sir Hudson delivered a long homily to me yesterday of which the main burden of his song was (i) QEA had always been anxious to operate an all-freight service and BOAC shows no enthusiasm—his tone generally indicated that we had held QEA back (ii) The UK and BOAC did not fully appreciate the entry of the shipping companies into the air sphere! (iii) acceptance of Britavia would unquestionably undermine the partnership . . . The fault is not altogether on our side but Qantas do incline to blame BOAC when obstructions are put in their way to develop. However, I am sure you will let Turner know, and minute accordingly, that history does not record BOAC as being the only culprit . . .

On the future of the Pacific, Hood commented:

> With the threat of a Pan American route from London to Sydney via the polar regions, Honolulu etc, the doubtful prospect of QEA obtaining rights across the US or Canada and the position today where Pan American is getting 53 per cent of the total Pacific business, QEA does not see the future at all clearly. CPAL gets 10 per cent of the business, leaving QEA 37 per cent. I am informed that QEA is losing more money on the Pacific than did BCPA . . . Somehow Pan American is away ahead of the field . . . QEA then, in my opinion, is looking for help and will jump at the chance of a partnership extension with BOAC, but of course Turner would never admit it . . . Hudson Fysh is personally most anxious for the continuation and extension of the partnership—I

have seldom known him so emphatic – but I do believe his thoughts
are not unconnected with the present losses on the Pacific . . . At
the moment they do feel slightly lonely battling against the might
of Pan Am.[52]

Critical to Qantas in its competition with Pan American was
the acquisition of the North American extension and the right
choice of aircraft to fly across the increasingly competitive Pacific
route. Pan American Airways had purchased a large number
of Douglas DC7Cs and delivery schedules showed that they
would put them into service on the Pacific towards the end of
1957. Qantas's Technical Development Department had
assessed the DC7C as some thirty miles an hour faster than
their Lockheed 1049Gs and now provided the board with an
assessment of the forward position for aircraft policy that raised
the question of whether Qantas could remain competitive in
the 1958–59 period. That assessment was more promising than
previous ones for the Britannia. Lockheeds had put forward
an attractive proposition for the exchange of three Constellation
1049Gs for their new 1649s for delivery at the end of 1957.
Both Lockheed and Douglas had announced plans for the
primary stage of their turboprop and jet era but the Lockheed
turboprop 310 lacked range for Qantas routes while Douglas
had what Qantas considered a very large and costly jet aircraft
with a gross weight of 257,000 pounds and delivery in 1959.
No orders for this jet had been received and from the little data
available, it appeared to Qantas to be a trans-USA or trans-
Atlantic aeroplane. The board was given figures showing that
the Britannia 300LR was very much better than either the
Lockheed 1649A or the Douglas DC7C and that delivery had
been offered towards the end of 1957.

A memorandum from the Technical Development
Department commented:

> The Board will remember our difficulty in recommending the
> Britannia was the possibility of the engine being doubtful, being
> insufficiently tested for commercial use by the time we would want
> to operate it and also because the new and greatly improved BE.25
> engine was likely to be available shortly thereafter. In withdrawing
> our letter of intent from Bristols for six Britannias we at the same
> time asked for a new proposition covering development of the air-
> craft with the BE.25 engine . . . Although we have pressed Bristols
> they have not yet come forward with a proposal which was
> promised last February . . . If the Bristol Company are able to
> make us a reasonable proposition and the Britannia were chosen
> to operate on some of our routes in 1957, it does not now appear
> that it would meet any really serious competition from American
> aircraft for some years.[53]

Bristol did, however, make an offer on 10 June for the Britannia Mark 300LR for £1,035,000 and for the Mark 250LR for an extra £25,000, though the offer was one of price only.[54]

At the board's meeting on 24 June 1955, a decision was taken that in every way matched in importance the issues of route extension and aircraft choice. It was resolved that "Mr C. O. Turner be appointed General Manager and Chief Executive of the Company, with effect from 1 July 1955". The board approved continuing allowances for Hudson Fysh as chairman including provision of a company car and driver, an entertainment allowance of £500 per year and personal accident insurance cover. "It was considered desirable", the board recorded, "to clarify the relationship between the positions of Chairman and General Manager and Chief Executive under the new organisation, and it was agreed that the Vice Chairman and Mr Watt would submit draft terms of reference for the Board's consideration."[55]

The need to clarify the relationship between Turner and Fysh under the new arrangement became immediately evident. A press release was issued on 24 June by C. O. Turner (through what was called the Editorial Group, headed by John Ulm). The full page release gave two brief sentences to Hudson Fysh and the rest to Turner. "Sir Hudson Fysh will continue as Chairman of the Board . . . Sir Hudson has been managing director of Qantas for 32 years."

Turner, said the carefully worded release, would assume all the chief executive's functions previously carried out by Sir Hudson. "Mr Turner, 48, has been a senior executive of the company for 20 years. He was appointed general manager in 1951. He had been assistant general manager since 1946." Background notes said that Turner was educated in Sydney and qualified as a chartered accountant, and that he lived in Sydney with his wife and four children at Turramurra, a Sydney north shore suburb, and was a keen golfer. "Mr Turner became general manager in 1951. The airline's rapid development since then has included re-equipping the mainline fleet with 14 Super Constellations (10 delivered, four on order) and expansion of its network with the opening of the Australia-South Africa service and the take-over of the Pacific service to the US and Canada."[8]

Hudson Fysh responded with a letter to Turner.

I regret that the statement for the Press covering top changes in QEA, which was got out by our Press Section, has caused the widespread impression that I am retiring from QEA except as

Chairman. The ordinary Board Chairman, as you know, does not play a very full part in Company affairs and does not give his full time to the job. Because of this it has been necessary for me to get out an amplifying statement, a copy of which I attach. It is unfortunate that the draft release which I handed you on 23 June was altered to eliminate the words "full time", and if these words had been left in a different impression would have been created.

I was also not shown a draft of the release as I should have been, nor was I shown a draft of the release for Staff News where also an unfortunate impression will be created. This is not what one appreciates seeing happen at the time of an important change over as is taking place, and I ask you to watch this sort of thing more closely in future, specially in matters where it is right and proper for me to be consulted.

As you must realise I have gone out of my way to always mention you and your part wherever appropriate, and I also expect you to watch my interests in the interests of the Company and proper procedure . . . With best wishes for your important talks in London. [57]

Fysh released his "statement amplifying the changes which are to take place at the top of Qantas Empire Airways" on 28 June.

It has been assumed by many [he said] that I am retiring from my past full time work for Qantas Empire Airways, but such is not the case. The position is that since the retirement of Sir Fergus McMaster from the Chairmanship eight years ago, I have held the dual positions of Chairman and Managing Director. As Managing Director I was the Company's Chief Executive, but the rapid growth of the Company and its now complex affairs made it apparent that for good organisation, and in order to handle the work, a split of these duties was necessary. Consequently the Minister for Civil Aviation has agreed that the position of Managing Director be dispensed with, and that I carry on as full time Chairman of the Board with appropriate responsibility for Policy matters . . . The Board of QEA have appointed Mr C. O. Turner, the present General Manager, as the Company's new Chief Executive Officer, responsible to the Board. His title will be General Manager and Chief Executive . . . [58]

Turner left immediately for the United Kingdom to discuss with BOAC what he described as two of the most important policy matters likely to affect the company's future. They were the operation of a route between Australia and the United Kingdom via the United States and "the question of operation of through cargo services within the Partnership and the application being made by the UK for independent operators to be granted rights to a service to Australia". As with all matters in the rapidly expanding Qantas, the issues were complex. Turner met Smallpiece in Singapore and heard the BOAC dilemma in some detail as it concerned Britavia's application for an all-freight service to Perth. The previous Conservative government in Britain had publicly committed itself to a policy of providing opportunities for independent operators. To provide capital necessary for this policy they had persuaded shipping companies to invest money in aviation. Alan Lennox-Boyd, the previous aviation minister, had stated in the House of Commons that he regarded all-freight services as primarily the domain of the independent operator. Therefore, to give effect to this policy, the Government had asked BOAC not to put in applications for freight services on the Atlantic; BOAC on their own initiative had subcontracted for the time being the operation of their all-freight service to Singapore to Skyways. The Conservative government had been returned after a general election with an increased majority and were under considerable pressure. Smallpiece told Turner that Britavia-P & O had made little or no progress in finding an opening for themselves and it was known that P & O, which owned seventy per cent of Britavia, were very set on getting in to the Far East routes, either through a freight service to Australia or other means. "Faced with this situation," said Smallpiece, "BOAC would much prefer to see Britavia allowed to have their all-freight service between London and Perth, rather than expose themselves to much more serious inroads on their position." BOAC, Turner was told, felt it wise to withdraw the partnership's opposition to the Britavia operation.

Turner responded to these arguments by again stressing that another operator would undermine the partnership. He also described to Smallpiece the precarious political position of Qantas in Australia. QEA's application to operate a Kangaroo service through Perth, Turner told him, had been approved by the minister without referring to Cabinet and had provoked a minor row. If there were renewed pressure in the immediate future in the UK for Australia to accept a British independent, it might well be that the Australian government would insist on nominating an Australian independent as a reciprocal operator instead of QEA. The introduction of an independent cargo service would undoubtedly lead to the development of independent services demanding the carriage of passengers and mails, which would mean the eventual disintegration of the partnership. He told Smallpiece that the matter was before Cabinet and that "we were fighting it on the basis that it was a direct attack on the existing partnership agreement between the UK and Australia".[59] Smallpiece told Turner he would not therefore press for an immediate decision on the Britavia issue.[60]

Turner later reported to the board: "It would appear that there is a serious divergence between Australia and the UK on this matter . . . Our concern is that the full story from the Company's standpoint should be placed before Cabinet. In view of the importance of 'closing the gap' through Perth, we have arranged to introduce our service through that point on 10 August, which is a month earlier than previously arranged." It was in his view an issue which, if resolved in favour of Britavia, could "mean the eventual disintegration of the [QEA-BOAC] partnership". Further, the UK government would continue to refuse BOAC permission to operate a through cargo service to Australia while the deadlock with Britavia continued. "He also indicated", wrote Turner, "that . . . they would continue to oppose the QEA application to run a through cargo service to the UK unless Britavia were granted the right to run a separate cargo service to Perth!" (In fact, the submission to Cabinet was withdrawn from Cabinet's agenda later in the year because of forthcoming general elections. It was not dealt with until after the elections.)

In discussions with BOAC Turner learned that they had radically changed their plans for the introduction of a transiting service from New York across the United States and now intended to bring its introduction forward from April 1957 to the coming November. Operations beyond San Francisco to Australia had to be renegotiated by BOAC as the rights to these under the Bermuda Agreement had rested with BCPA. Importantly, the BOAC connections from November would be replaced by QEA charter services from 1 January 1956. Turner cabled Fysh on 7 July: "This is the first step in agreement to operate services from Australia to UK via the US in partnership making best competitive use of joint equipment and rights." For political reasons it was agreed with BOAC that the cargo services remain on a sectional basis for the present "but they will be included in partnership pool from 1 July 1955 which greatly strengthens the position".

Turner found some conflict with BOAC about the operation of a UK service across the Pacific in competition with the Australian-supported service after 1958. However, he reported to the board that it was suggested that "after we have worked out our plans as operators we should approach our governments with recommendations for the future and that these recommendations will probably form the basis for inter-governmental talks . . . The last full scale inter-Commonwealth conference in connection with the partnership services was held in May 1949, so that there have been no official talks on partnership matters . . . for six years."

BOAC's Phillip Hood, at the same time, wrote to BOAC in London that San Francisco would develop into the same old problem as Singapore, "with strong prospects of friction between the partners". Under the United Kingdom's bilateral agreement with the United States, he foresaw that BOAC, because of the tremendous developments in California, would want to operate direct services there without change of aircraft, though maybe not for years to come. "If we are not careful we shall be back to the Kangaroo argument with QEA—the hardy annual we all know of too well—of too much non-pool frequency to the detriment of the pool partnership."

Turner's report on his visit to the United Kingdom had concluded:

> The Board will appreciate that there is now a serious difference in policy between BOAC and ourselves, because BOAC have not been permitted to purchase special aircraft to operate separate freighter services along the Kangaroo route, whereas we ourselves have two special Super Constellation freight carriers on order for delivery towards the end of next year . . . Investigation of the present state of air cargo services between the UK-Europe and Australia shows that we are very seriously handicapped by the "break of gauge" at Singapore and the comparatively slow service which is being operated by Skyways on behalf of BOAC between London and Singapore.[61]

While cargo revenue continued to grow in importance, revenue from mail remained essential to Qantas profitability and changes to the basis on which it was carried were of central importance. The accounting treatment of mail revenue on the Kangaroo Route differed materially from that on all other Qantas services; on the London-Australia route it was the responsibility of BOAC, while on all other Qantas routes mail carried was invoiced by Qantas. Also, mails of Australian and British origin were paid for at agreed rates based on distances established when the Empire Mail Scheme was first introduced in 1938 but foreign mails were paid for at the agreed Universal Postal Union gold franc rates. The Universal Postal Union at its Congress of Postal Administrations in Madrid in 1920 adopted a "gold franc" as the monetary unit of the union for settlements between postal administrations. The unit was intended to be a value-preserving instrument independent of any national currency.

Qantas noted in 1955 that the gold franc "is not money in the legal sense of the word but something which at any time may be converted into money at gold parity. Although the price of gold itself is subject to fluctuation, this is so slight that this metal has the reputation of being an article of merchandise with the most stable value."

At a meeting between Qantas and the Department of Civil Aviation on 25 March 1955 it had been agreed that Qantas would in future accept commercial mail rates for all its services. The rates agreed varied from 3.99 gold francs per tonne kilometre for first class mail to about one-quarter of this rate for newspapers. Australian domestic mails carried on international services were costed at 0.05 pence per pound irrespective of class. Converting gold francs to Australian currency was an intricate intellectual dance. "The gold franc", Qantas recorded, "is not a coin, not even a piece of gold, but simply a unit of weight of gold. It is a unit of weight, not of reckoning." It was possible to summarise these intricacies, however, by regarding a gold franc as worth 0.29032258 of a gram of gold at the fixed price of gold in local currency. The net effect of the Qantas agreement with the department was to reduce the Qantas mail revenue rate on the Australia-UK route to that applicable to all other QEA international services. [62]

C. O. Turner sent assistant general manager Scottie Allan to the United Kingdom at the end of July to further examine the Comet IV and the Bristol Britannia projects. Deliveries of the Britannias had been offered for June, July, and August of 1957 and were considered, if they lived up to specification, as an adequate reply to the DC7C aircraft. They were, however, regarded only as interim turboprops because the forward Britannia programme included a more advanced engine and a possible new wing design, both necessary in the Qantas view, to enable it to meet competition from American types in the 1959-60 period. Captain Allan was charged with evaluating whether the Proteus engine was sufficiently reliable to carry the Britannia through until improved engines were available in the 1960s and, equally important, to assess whether Bristols could produce aircraft on schedule and at the same time build up an organisation adequate to service the aircraft after they were produced.

Turner advised the board on 28 July that while the Lockheed 1649 and the Britannias were being investigated, new problems would be created in 1959 by the introduction of straight jet aircraft. BOAC, with the backing of the United Kingdom government, had ordered twenty Comet IVs; Douglas had announced the production of the DC8 and Boeing had received authority to produce a civilian version of the Boeing 707. Both these American aircraft, reported Turner, were likely to be available early in 1959. Nevertheless, he said, management was reluctant to recommend a programme that would mean a severance of the long connection with Lockheed, because it believed it to be the best-equipped organisation to meet the complex technical problems immediately ahead of the industry. "We believe that BOAC are planning to introduce the Comet IVs on the eastern routes, including the routes to Australia, so that whether we like it or not we must face the fact that these aircraft will be operating on our routes at speeds far in excess of those we can achieve with our present equipment or with any equipment likely to be available in 1957."[63]

De Havillands were now again exhibiting some of the optimism and push of the early Comet 1 days. The Comet IV, said the company's *Gazette* of August 1955, "is designed to dominate every route having stages up to three thousand miles. With this aircraft nowhere on earth will involve a journey of more than thirty-six hours." The Comet IV's first flight was scheduled for late 1957, by which time quantity production would be, it was promised, well advanced. By the date of entry into service, some 4,000 hours of development flying would have been completed. "Already, by virtue of 30,000 hours of airline flying [the *Gazette* continued], the searching inquiry of 1954 and the extensive programme of structural test and development work now reaching its culmination, the new Comet can claim to be the most thoroughly tried and tested airliner in existence."

The Qantas attitude to the Comet was not enthusiastic, but they had by no means dismissed it. The range of civil aircraft available to Qantas in 1955, or soon to become available, was extensive and the process of selection was critical to the airline's commercial future. The need to review replacement aircraft had been accelerated by the threat on the Pacific route by Pan American from the planned use of DC7C airliners. Scottie Allan had now returned from his mission overseas and was preparing a detailed written report for the board. Though that was only weeks away, C. O. Turner felt it advisable to warn the board on 25 August that neither the Lockheed 1649 nor the Britannia would be available in time to meet competition that was likely on Qantas routes from early 1957. "We could not", he said, "recommend the ordering of either of these two types at this stage." From America, the announcement by Lockheed of a new propjet aircraft called the Lockheed Electra, for delivery in 1959, and of the large straight jets of Boeing and Douglas complicated the competitive position.

> In regard to the Britannia LR300, it seems clear that we could not get them into route operations until 1958. Since they would be outmatched in 1959 by the Lockheed Electra turboprop ["propjet" and "turboprop" were interchangeable terms for aircraft powered by jet engines geared to propellers] and there is the possibility of three new types of straight jet aircraft coming forward at the same time, it would be difficult to recommend the purchase of the Britannia . . . The American straight jet aircraft DC-8 and the Boeing 707s appear to be too big for us to consider for application to our routes at this stage. However, there is still the question of the Comet IV . . . and we are forced to consider this aircraft because of our partnership with BOAC . . . Summarising the position, it appears we can do very little to assure that we will be fully competitive on the routes in 1957 so that it may be better to try and hold the position with our Super "G" Constellations through 1958-1959 (which are building up a very good reputation for reliability and service) until we can make a clear recommendation for an alternative type to commence operation in 1959 or 1960.[64]

Captain Allan's more detailed report, submitted to Turner on 12 September, did not change these Qantas views. The DC8 and Boeing 707 would, he said, be very large aeroplanes of between 260,000 and 300,000 pounds gross weight and would be more applicable to very high density routes. "At this stage," he reported, "we could not consider them." He thought the Comet IV, at 152,000 pounds, though less economic, more applicable to Qantas routes. "Its range is somewhat restricted and it could only cover Honolulu-Samoa at reduced payload. The full payload will be 190,000 pounds."[65]

A less dramatic aspect of the airline's operations, but central to the provision of competitive cabin service, came before the board in October. The tenancy of the buildings at St Mary's (west of Sydney) in which the Qantas frozen food factory was located was to end in March 1956 (as the federal government required the buildings as part of a new munitions factory). Urgent action was now necessary to relocate the frozen food factory, as it was estimated that all existing supplies would be consumed by mid-1956. A new frozen food factory on an area of land owned by the Department of Civil Aviation, on the northern side of the railway line that passed the QEA Mascot hangar area, was now proposed. The existing In-Flight Kitchen at Rose Bay and the Cabin Services Section, temporarily housed in a hangar at the airport, were to be included in the new building. The Catering Department at Rose Bay still operated in the wartime canteen acquired on lease ten years earlier from the Department of Civil Aviation. Originally modified to include administrative offices, a training school, an in-flight kitchen, a central catering store, and cabin service facilities, it had well outgrown its use and the Cabin Services Section and training school had been transferred to temporary accommodation at Mascot. The result of the division of functions was increased cost, staff problems, and extreme difficulty in maintaining high standards of food preparation because of the necessity to transfer food from Rose Bay to Mascot.

QEA had now been using precooked frozen food on its aircraft for six years with unqualified success. In the past twelve months the St Mary's factory had produced some 212,000 pounds for use in QEA and BOAC aircraft. Apart from the ability to provide food of consistently high standard and uniform quality, the use of frozen food had eliminated the danger of food contamination from fresh foods bought locally at other ports and had proved far more convenient to handle in modern aircraft on long haul flights. An early start on the new building was urged, in a board submission by Turner, to meet the removal date from St Mary's of March-April 1956 and allow for cold storage in Sydney of accumulated supplies before recommencing production in the new factory in July-August.

C. O. Turner now brought into the QEA organisation as an adviser on international affairs Capt. Edgar Johnston, a man

The Engine Test House at Mascot in late 1955. Hangar 85 can be seen in the left background. Note the embankment that partly obscures the parked aircraft. This was the Sydenham to Botany railway which was a single-line operation used only for freight. Until it was diverted in the early 1960s, the railway line forced QEA to move aircraft engines along the busy public roads between the engine workshop, the Test House and the hangars.

who had from 1919 (as a senior officer in the then aviation branch of the Defence Department and later as deputy director of civil aviation) an intimate knowledge of the development of Qantas. Edgar Johnston had played a considerable part in the complex and sometimes heated negotiations that had led to the partnership agreement between Qantas and Imperial Airways in 1934. He had seen the introduction and demise of the flying boat era as well as the Imperial Airways initiative for the revolutionary Empire Air Mail Scheme (which had never come to fruition). He had watched what had seemed at times during World War II the near annihilation of Qantas and was aware of the stormy and intricate postwar years when an uncertain and uneconomic service between Australia and England had been resumed. In a memorandum of 27 October, Turner advised the board that Edgar Johnston had agreed to a fixed minimum remuneration of £2,300 and a maximum of £3,500 per year. It was obvious that he was needed.

> Captain Johnston is departing immediately to represent us in Japan on bilateral negotiations between the Australian and Japanese Governments [wrote Turner]. I should mention that I have cleared Capt. Johnston's representation of the Company with the newly appointed Director-General of Civil Aviation who welcomes the fact that Capt. Johnston will be available for these talks. [The new director-general, succeeding Air Marshall Sir Richard Williams, was D. G. Anderson.] Immediately following these talks, Capt. Johnston's next urgent task will be to represent the Company in the organisation of the proposed "front" to stabilise the current international mail carriage rate at a minimum of four gold francs and, for this purpose, we consider it necessary that he should discuss the proposals with other international airlines, particularly BOAC . . . It will be appreciated, too, that we are still in the middle of negotiations with Canada and the US in connection with rights for a routing to the UK via North America, on which Capt. Johnston's services will be required . . . It will be realised that Capt. Johnston will be very fully engaged over the next few months.[66]

The bilateral negotiations with Japan that Turner referred to began on 11 November and were carried out in a friendly atmosphere, with capacity provisions agreed according to the usual Bermuda pattern. Concurrently, there was impending conflict with France, who now wished to substitute Sydney for Brisbane on services to Noumea. Qantas argued that its ability to continue to operate its regional services in the Pacific, which it saw as of considerable value to the French communities concerned, would be seriously affected by any additional operations between the points served by QEA. To the north, the Philippines government had directed that Philippines Air Lines should re-enter the international sphere and it was expected that bilateral discussions with Australia would start in the new year.

While all these matters affecting the international reach and presence of the Australian airline continued, the partnership between BOAC and Qantas remained central to its commercial operations. With the impending BOAC extensions across America and the Qantas negotiations for a service through New York to Europe, management had now to consider whether it was justifiable to seek revision of the understanding reached with BOAC at Christchurch, New Zealand with a view to the eventual operation by both BOAC and QEA of end-to-end services between London and Sydney via the United States in partnership. Shortage of equipment had prevented BOAC from extending its services between New York and San Francisco to meet Qantas at San Francisco, as envisaged in the Christchurch arrangements, and the partnership had been obliged to rely on US domestic operators to service the American sector for through passengers between England and Australia. Selling customers a passage involving connecting services and changes of aircraft and carriers was becoming increasingly difficult. Pan American, the major competitor for through traffic, had applied for a polar route between the US west coast and London that would enable them to provide London-Sydney services without change of carrier. Trans World Airlines were introducing, from November, a one-plane service between San Francisco and London that would be the fastest available. The Scandinavian airline, SAS, had announced their intention to increase frequency between Copenhagen and Los Angeles to once daily with the introduction of their DC7C aircraft and were advertising strenuously for Australian traffic. There was an urgent need for the Qantas-BOAC partnership to produce a service that was better than that available from these competitors. Hudson Fysh expressed serious concern to Turner about the growing impact of Pan American's Pacific operations on Qantas.

> Pan American receives greater Government assistance on the Pacific route than we do, their unadjusted mail receipts . . . being in the region of $14 million for last year. This advantage enables them to put further frequencies on the route which we cannot economically follow and it also enables them to operate at a profit on lower fares . . . Pan American operates under a straight out Bermuda type agreement which enables them to increase frequencies almost as they wish . . . As I see it, under existing conditions we are completely in the hands of Pan American and indeed our position could become untenable in a few years when straight jet competition commences.[67]

Apart from commercial considerations, Qantas saw the American route as strategically important to Australia. A draft joint paper prepared by BOAC and Qantas for presentation to their respective governments pointed out that:

> The existing Kangaroo route between London and Sydney passes through a large number of countries in the Middle East and South East Asia which are all susceptible to political unrest . . . Until now it has been possible to avoid any interruption of services but it would be dangerous to assume that this will always be the case. A major disturbance in the Middle East or in South East Asia could well make continued operation of a vital Commonwealth link virtually impossible. For this reason, it is our view that both partners should obtain operational experience on the alternative route so that, in the event of a major emergency on the route via India, traffic could be diverted without difficulty. This can only be achieved if BOAC and Qantas are both permitted to operate end-to-end services via North America.

The draft paper suggested that the Britannia 300LR should prove "eminently suitable" for the UK-Australia operation through America. It proposed that BOAC should inaugurate a twice-weekly service in April 1958 between London and Sydney via New York and San Francisco and that concurrently QEA should extend their trans-Pacific services to London at the same frequency, the whole operation to be in partnership. The implementation of such a plan, the paper concluded modestly, "would give adequate coverage for a round-the-world Commonwealth route."[68]

Though the Britannia received favourable mention in this draft paper, the number and variety of new aircraft types now becoming available from the world's aircraft manufacturers – all based on the gas turbine engine – provided a volatile and constantly changing situation for the airlines. They included the straight jets – the Douglas DC8, the Boeing 707, the de Havilland Comet IV, and the short-range French Caravelle – and the turboprops – the Lockheed Electra, Bristol Britannia, and Vickers Vanguard. Vickers, after their extraordinary success with the short-range Vickers Viscount, had met disaster because of domestic political decisions in their efforts to remain in the DC8 and 707 league. They had built to a very advanced stage a prototype of the V1000 pure jet transport, derived from the same basic technology and aerodynamics as the Valiant bomber. There was a contract for this prototype and for six production aircraft for RAF Transport Command. BOAC had been involved, specifying six-abreast seating and North Atlantic operation. The V1000 had nonstop trans-Atlantic capability,

43

which the Boeing 707 on entry-into-service lacked. But BOAC's minister, in the House of Commons in November 1955, made it clear that BOAC requirements for the 1960s would be met by the aircraft it already had on order. It considered that it could hold its own commercially on the North Atlantic with the Comet IV and the Britannia. The V1000 was cancelled six months before it was due to fly in what Sir George Edwards (who headed Vickers-Armstrongs [Aircraft] Limited and was to become chairman of British Aircraft Corporation) judged the biggest setback ever suffered by the British aircraft industry. "The loss of the V1000 effectively took us out of the big league", he wrote.[69] For Qantas, however, the V1000 was never even remotely considered as, in the closing months of 1955, the world airline industry gathered itself for the dramatic and concerted introduction of the jet era.

There was a rush by the major airlines to order the new jet equipment, sparked by a massive Pan American order for 25 Douglas DC8s and 20 Boeing 707s. By 21 November, in addition to the Pan American order, United Airlines had ordered 30 DC8s and National Airlines 6; American Airlines had ordered 20 Boeing 707s and 35 Lockheed Electras; Eastern Airlines ordered a massive 40 Electras, KLM 8 Boeings. In all this frenetic buying, only BOAC and British European Airways had

The last scheduled flight by a Qantas 749 Constellation left Sydney for Johannesburg on 20 October 1955. The aircraft was VH-EAD *Charles Kingsford Smith* which had flown the inaugural Qantas service from Sydney to London in December 1947. VH-EAD and VH-EAC were sold to the Mexican airline Aerovias Guest and their registration letters were reallocated to the eleventh and twelfth Super Constellations. A group of Qantas and Aerovias Guest executives are seen here inspecting VH-EAC in early October 1955. From left: Capt. E. Robinson, QEA; Carlos Colin, AG chief engineer; Capt. H. Thomas, AG chief pilot; John Mills, QEA chief inspector; Capt. R. J. Ritchie, QEA technical manager; and Capt. D. G. Richardson, AG operations manager.

supported the British industry with major orders. British
European Airways had ordered 20 Vickers Vanguard turboprops
and BOAC 33 Britannias and 20 Comet IVs. (Canadian Pacific
Airlines had placed a modest order for 3 Britannias.) In this
first round of buying, Douglas had come out on top with orders
for 69 DC8s. Boeing had orders for 40 of their 707s and Lockheed orders for 75 Electras.

Turner reported to the board on 23 November that "it would
appear that the large jet types, which will carry up to 120
passengers, are being purchased for the Atlantic and American
internal operations where traffic densities are high." The Comet
III, he said, was to visit Australia in December and Qantas would
have discussions with de Havillands on the Comet II and Comet
IV positions. "It might be possible to obtain delivery of Comet
IVs in 1959 if necessary, with BOAC's assistance, as the Comet
IV can operate on all our existing airports with practically full
load, including the Pacific route and San Francisco-New York.
If BOAC invest in DC8 aircraft, an excellent round-the-world
service could be provided in combination with Comet IVs."[70]
It was the Qantas view that the Pan American jets could not
compete on the Pacific before 1959-60 at the earliest.

Financially, Qantas faced the challenge of re-equipping to
enter the jet age as a seriously undercapitalised company.[71]
They had only just substantially completed their first major
aircraft replacement programme and the absorption of BCPA.
Turner considered it was time to review the capital position
generally and submit to the government a programme of capital
expenditure for 1956. Under the company's financial directive,
it was required as the year ended to inform the minister of
budgeted expenditure on capital projects for the coming year,
whereas requirements for additional share capital were needed
in May each year so that suitable provision could be made in
annual Treasury estimates.

Turner now proposed to the board that the Commonwealth's
approval be sought for the principles that recoveries by way
of aircraft obsolescence should be kept exclusively for reinvest-
ment in new aircraft; that additional capital should be subscribed
to finance all major buildings and plant requirements from 1
January 1956; that the overdraft available from the Commonwealth Bank to provide working funds should be extended from
the current £1 million limit to £4 million; and that insurance
and pension reserves should not be used in the business. Net
additional capital funds required by the following May were
estimated at £2 million. Provided the government agreed to the

principle that Qantas retain funds to cover the obsolescence of current aircraft, it was unlikely, he reported, that additional capital for new aircraft would be required for some years.

In the immediate future, one additional Lockheed 1049H, costing £1 million, was needed to stabilise the cargo fleet in early 1957 and five Otter aircraft at a cost of £275,000 were needed in 1956 for New Guinea. DC4 replacements could not, he said, be long delayed.

> We must also decide on our major replacement programme for trunk routes and reserve a position on the production line before the end of 1956 . . . We are currently examining the propeller turbine types such as the Lockheed Electra, Vickers Vanguard and also the straight jet types, such as the Comet IV and DC8. A conservative estimate of replacing passenger units of our present fleet would be £25 million and of this we might have approximately £19 million available from obsolescence recoveries and sales by 1960. We believe the balance of funds might be obtained from outside sources . . .[72]

This forward look at the central problem of fleet replacement had been forced on Qantas in a year in which the airline had only just stabilised its operations around the Lockheed Super Constellation. Eight of these aircraft had been delivered in 1955, bringing their number to twelve. Two more, designed for cargo carrying, had been ordered. At the end of 1955, Super Constellations were operating on all QEA's mainline routes. They had replaced the Constellations on the direct service to Tokyo in May and on the South African route in November (when this route was altered from via Perth to via Darwin, Cocos and Mauritius to Johannesburg). In that same year, the passenger mix had altered heavily towards tourist class, which had been extended to Hong Kong, Japan, South Africa, and New Caledonia. On the United Kingdom route, over forty-eight per cent of passengers carried travelled tourist class; on the route to North America it was forty per cent. Despite this consolidation around the Super Constellation, the DC4 Skymaster continued to play an important role in the Qantas fleet. They operated through Labuan and Hong Kong to southern Japan, where the requirements of the Australian forces had decreased substantially as commercial traffic increased; they were placed on the New Caledonia and Fiji routes in June to replace the Sandringham flying boats; and the Skymaster service to Norfolk Island was increased to once weekly and extended to Auckland as a charter operation for TEAL. Increasing traffic to Papua-New Guinea stabilised at five Skymaster return flights per week in November. DC3 services were operated from Lae to Hollandia and Honiara (while the internal Papua-New Guinea services and charter operations over a wide network continued and were entirely self-supporting).

Qantas personnel, in December 1955, stood at 5,535. The fleet consisted of twelve Super Constellations, six Skymasters (with two on order), eight DC3s, four Beaver DHC2s, one Drover DHA3, and two Catalinas. Four Constellation 749As had been sold during the year and three Sandringhams reduced to spares. Great changes lay ahead.

The jet engine, and the airliners built around it, were now commercial realities. The world's airlines were on the brink of a maturity that would influence the travel patterns of hundreds of millions of people. Qantas was reminded of its beginnings, however, with the death on Monday, 19 December of Sir Keith Smith. A director of Qantas, he had flown on the first flight ever between England and Australia thirty-five years before. Sir Keith, with his brother Ross and their engineers J. M.

Thousands of Sydney residents visited Sydney airport on Sunday 4 December 1955 to see the Comet 3. Flown by a de Havilland crew, it was the first jet airliner ever seen in Australia and its arrival had an extraordinary effect. Its first approach to land had to be abandoned when several hundred people ran onto the runway. When it came to a halt as shown, the Comet was surrounded by crowds up to fifty deep.

The Douglas DC7C made its first flight on 20 December 1955. It was built as an aircraft capable of flying nonstop from London to New York under all but the most adverse wind conditions. A 5-foot (1.5-metre) additional wing section was inserted between each wing root and inboard engine providing extra fuel storage areas. Because of the time saved by this relatively simple change, Douglas were able to beat Lockheed in the lucrative long-range market from 1956 to 1959. One hundred and twenty-one DC7Cs were sold compared to forty-three Lockheed L1649s, which featured a completely redesigned wing. Qantas resident engineers in the USA kept management fully informed on the DC7C and the L1649. The decision was made to remain with their L1049 fleet and wait for the Boeing 707 or the Douglas DC8 jet.

Bennett and W. H. Shiers, had flown their Vickers Vimy aircraft across the world to land in Darwin on 10 December 1919, where Hudson Fysh had been waiting to greet them. "Keith Smith and his companions", said Qantas in a tribute, "blazed that original trail for what is now a well-marked road, safely and comfortably plied by the airliners of today."[73]

British Links and
Boeing Jets
1956

Two issues of fundamental importance to Qantas dominated the opening months of 1956. One involved governments and required the negotiation of rights, the other the selection of aircraft for the jet age (and the intervening months) and required technical and commercial judgments. These judgments had to be made as the great American corporations who manufactured the big new jets began to apply their sophisticated, wily, and well-practised marketing pressures.

Edgar Johnston, in early January, proposed amendments to the future planning draft paper on the North American route to London for submission by BOAC and Qantas to their governments. He agreed that BOAC would have the Britannia 300LR available to inaugurate turboprop services to Australia through North America in April 1958. He also agreed that the joint objective should be to have parallel end-to-end services by both BOAC and Qantas operating by that date. But he pointed out that QEA already had a fleet of Super Constellation aircraft that were quite suitable for trans-America and trans-Atlantic operations, and that extension of the trans-Pacific service to London could be undertaken with little, if any, addition to this fleet. "In view of the competitive situation [wrote Johnston] . . . every endeavour should be made to establish a through service earlier than [April 1958] using QEA Super Constellation aircraft under rights already available to the UK, pending Australia obtaining the necessary rights. The aim should be to introduce this through service, if possible, during the coming summer in the Northern Hemisphere."[1]

2

The long-term strategy for the London link through North America was summarised for the board by C. O. Turner. "It would be unsatisfactory to have QEA's operations beyond San Francisco to Europe dependent on charter arrangements with BOAC and to protect long term interests for the Australian airline it is essential that Australia itself should have the rights to extend the Australian service beyond San Francisco to Europe." Despite this long-term view, Turner set off for London in January to seek BOAC agreement that it make use of Qantas aircraft under charter. He was going despite a cable from BOAC's chairman that little would be achieved unless the BOAC extension to San Francisco using QEA aircraft could be achieved on a satisfactory economic basis. Phillip Hood told BOAC that Turner believed that "BOAC ought to have known that the extension would involve a loss without waiting for QEA's official charter rate". Turner, wrote Hood, "is determined to sell you the San Francisco–New York charter . . . QEA has clearly over-bought aircraft and unless the trans-America – or extension to London – charter comes off, [QEA] utilisation will remain at about eight hours per day or less. This problem of utilisation would seriously increase when the two 1049Gs arrived towards the end of 1956. Behind all the arguments Mr Turner puts up is the ambition to operate a one-operator round-the-world service, and the decision to over-equip may well have been taken around the gamble that it might come off."[2] Turner did not succeed in London on the charter issue. Basil Smallpiece told him firmly that even on the basis of a reduced QEA quotation they could not contemplate chartering Qantas aircraft. It "would lead to a serious worsening of relations with BALPA [British Airline Pilots Association] and might well provoke a showdown". Smallpiece told Hood that Turner did not want a British case for a BOAC through service on its own account to go forward at that time because "the presentation of the case to the recently re-elected Liberal-Country Party Government, proposing a con-siderable extension in Qantas' sphere of influence, might provoke the Government into approving Britavia's route with a reciprocal service by an Australian private enterprise operator such as ANA".[3] Turner recommended on his return that QEA now press the Department of Civil Aviation, under its new director-general, Don Anderson, to have a fresh approach made to the US authorities for a routing through San Francisco (and Los Angeles) and New York to Europe.

On 2 February 1956, Turner put through a long-distance call to William Allen, president of Boeing since 1945 (and, before

that, Boeing's lawyer). It began: "Hello. This is C. O. Turner";
the reply was: "How are you, sir? Bill Allen". It was the
beginning of a long and intimate relationship between the big
American corporation and the modestly sized Australian airline.
Turner wanted a letter from Boeing setting out the Boeing 707
deliveries that Qantas could have if it ordered this aircraft.
"Then, if I could proceed further, I would let you know", said
Turner. "I don't know whether you're familiar with our set up
in Australia, and that we have to get authority from the government on aircraft. It will take many months for us to get it
through and get a decision." Qantas, said Turner, would have
to look at the engine situation. A team would have to go to
Hartford (Pratt & Whitney). But the new Rolls-Royce Conway
engine was also a contender.

Allen asked if Boeing should confine their letter to any
particular 707 model. "The intercontinental model, that's the
only one we're interested in," Turner replied. "With the J-75
(Pratt & Whitney engine). You haven't anything further on the
(Rolls-Royce) Conway, I suppose?"

Allen had not, but he said Boeing had made a study on
delivery dates with a Conway installation and felt they could
achieve the same delivery as they could with J75 engines. "We
don't know very much about the Conway either", said Turner.
He would, he said, have to send someone to make QEA's own
assessment about the stage of development and experience that
the engine would have by the time it was available.[4]

Boeing was prompt in responding to Turner's request. On
8 February a letter set down a basic price for the Boeing 707-320
Intercontinental airliner as $5,150,000 per aircraft. Delivery
was subject to the configuration of the aircraft selected and the
quantity being considered "and the expediency with which
negotiations can proceed".[5] It was the beginning of a long
process. Allen cabled proposals for the installation of Rolls-Royce
engines. Turner suggested the visit of a Qantas technical team
after Easter, but stressed that "any future business depends on
long term finance and advice as to what help, if any, Boeing
can give. [This] is our main concern."[6]

In February, the retiring chairman of Rolls-Royce, Lord
Hives, visited Australia on a farewell trip and took the
opportunity to urge the case with Qantas for the Conway engine.
Lockheed, in the meantime, was aware that Qantas could not
get delivery of jet aircraft for about three years and, in the words
of its senior sales executive at the time, Peter Mingrone, "put
on a hell of a sales campaign".[7] It was Lockheed's objective to

51

sell Qantas the Constellation 1649 as an interim aircraft and, to this end, they began to work hand in hand with Boeing.[8] Their competitor was the Douglas company, who urged their DC7C as an interim aircraft until the big DC8 jet was available.

The activities of these corporations in the early months of 1956 give some indication of the pressures placed on QEA's chief executive, and of the professional challenge that faced the senior Qantas people charged with the technical evaluation of individual aircraft and combinations of aircraft and aircraft engines. Boeing consultant Vernon Crudge was in Australia in April. He cabled Wellwood Beall, Boeing senior vice-president and a veteran who had joined the sales department as a young engineer in the early 1930s. "The Qantas position is fluid and requires much effort from us", he began. Constant contact at the technical level and renewed talks at management level were necessary if Boeing was to succeed. Douglas, he said, had made a good impression and achieved personal contacts on a private home basis. Their proposals included the lease of the DC7C as an interim type with a guarantee of return on delivery of the DC8. Qantas, however, was in the process of selecting from the Britannia, the Lockheed 1649, or the DC7C as interim types. Turner, he said, had refused to buy the Britannia even under BOAC pressure and envisaged only a lease or something similar. "You will therefore appreciate the importance of Ritchie and Yates visit to Seattle, as they are responsible for the selection of the interim type and the big jet, which two issues are interwoven." (Both R. J. Ritchie and R. J. Yates were to be future chief executives of Qantas.) The DC7C and DC8 combination could, Crudge said, "with a package financial deal cook our goose". He suggested that Beall immediately contact Lockheed on a possible package linking the Lockheed 1649 aircraft and the Boeing 707, which would also give him "the opportunity to smoke out Lockheed's lease and finance offering". The local Lockheed contact (Peter Mingrone) had been helpful. Crudge thought Lockheed would advise a similar proposition "which may offer much gain and little to lose". Turner had revealed to him that day, he said, that Qantas should have £10 million available by 1961 plus sums from existing fleet sales, and that he believed the Australian government would guarantee payment and dollar availability. Turner was to visit BOAC's new management as Qantas hoped their jet selection would conform with the ultimate BOAC choice. The outcome could "give Douglas a superb opportunity with both Qantas and BOAC, which appears to emphasise the need for speed for us to examine a Boeing-Lockheed liaison."[9] That such a liaison might contravene American antitrust laws concerned both Mingrone and Lockheed management, if the managements of both companies were involved. Instead, said Mingrone, "we got Boeing to sell our airplanes". Mingrone himself accompanied the Qantas evaluation team on its Boeing visit. In the demanding environment of the time he categorised C. O. Turner as "a very smart guy in financial areas who got on well with his people". He did not think as highly of the new Australian director-general of civil aviation. Anderson, he judged, was arrogant and egotistical.[10]

Lockheed's top management acted quickly. AT 1.55 p.m. on 30 April, Leonard K. Schwartz, commercial sales director, rang Wellwood Beall at Boeing. The conversation started playfully.

> Schwartz: Wellwood, this is an item of business. As you might guess, a lot of people ask us in a friendly way, what jet would you buy—the Boeing or the Douglas?
> Beall: The answer to that is easy!
> Schwartz: . . . Within the last week, three people have asked me that [question]. One of them was a Qantas fellow . . . We all [have] a selfish interest [in] the Qantas situation and . . . Qantas is an old customer of ours. We know the people very well and we know the situations in the country well, and we're trying to do some business with them for some of those old fashioned interim piston engine airplanes.

Schwartz summarised the Qantas position. Qantas had a lot of Lockheed 1049s but were trying to face up to the competition that Pan Am was going to give them on the Pacific with the DC7C. Lockheed had the 1649 Super Constellation which would "beat the pants off the DC7C".

> However, Wellwood, they have a peculiar political position . . . they are part of the British Commonwealth and they do have to operate, sometimes alongside and in pool, with BOAC. And the BOAC crowd and the British government crowd, of course, are always on their backs to buy British airplanes. The one in point at the moment is the Britannia.

He thought Qantas had four options. One, not to buy an interim aircraft and "take a helluva beating from Pan Am"; two, buy Britannias; three, buy DC7Cs; four, buy Lockheed's 1649s. But Douglas had come up with a solution which floored them, combining the DC7C with the DC8.

> I am calling you right now [Schwartz continued] because this is hot . . . This fellow Ritchie was here and he is a real good friend of ours. Well, they are all good friends of ours. They come crying

on our shoulders and tell us their troubles. Ritchie came through here last week and . . . he told me, when the door was locked, that it looked like they were going to have to buy DC8s and DC7Cs because it matched their political problem as well as their financing problem. They have plenty of money, but it is the dollar they are worried about . . . There is going to be a Commonwealth Prime Ministers' meeting in London on 1 June. They have to make the decision before that time because if they are not going to buy Britannias they have to brace their Prime Minister so that when he gets in and Eden says, "Why didn't you buy Britannias?" (and don't think those guys don't talk about that), he will have to tell them why.

Schwartz said he suggested to Ritchie that Qantas buy Lockheed's 1649s, then trade them in on Boeing 707s. Ritchie's reply was: "That would be dandy but Boeing doesn't own the 1649 and I don't think they are ready to make that kind of proposition." Schwartz responded: "Well, if they would . . .?"

The Lockheed and Boeing executives then discussed the possibilities of a trade-in deal between the two companies in general terms in which they would share the commercial risk. "You ought", Schwartz urged, "get in the picture down there real quick."

As this telephone conversation ended, Boeing consultant Vernon Crudge phoned from Sydney. Both Beall and sales manager Ralph Bell took his call. "I don't think", Crudge reported, "we are in a very secure position because the opposition has undoubtedly made one helluva lot of headway here." Beall told Crudge of his talk with Schwartz and the suggestion that Qantas buy Lockheed 1649s as interim aircraft but that Boeing would agreed to take them back: "It would be a Boeing deal". Crudge was delighted: "That's the most helpful thing you could have done", he said. "It is absolutely first rate and will stop them absolutely cold. They will be very impressed with that."

In the course of that telephone call, Crudge expressed the worry that Douglas had a full-time agent in Australia, while Boeing did not. He was acutely aware of the need to stay close to Qantas on a continuous basis, and was well informed about the movements of both Ritchie and Yates, who were crucial to the Qantas decision making. Boeing engineer Bob Hage was with Crudge in Sydney but planned to fly on with him to India, then to San Remo and London. He had booked to travel on the same service to New York as Ritchie and Yates. "We're going to lose Ritchie and Yates", Beall agreed, "unless we get someone travelling with them because they'll skip us if we don't look out." Crudge asked that Boeing send a cable to the Australian director-general of civil aviation, Don Anderson, who was to visit the United States in July, extending an invitation to visit Seattle. He had asked Anderson whether or not a decision on the jet order would be taken before this visit and Anderson had replied: "Yes, if we have sufficient information it is possible, in order to take advantage of delivery positions that we might make a decision before July". Qantas, said Crudge, had made it very clear that they were not going to make their jet decision without discussing it with BOAC. "They want to have the same type of airplanes but at the same time they are not going to be told what to do by BOAC . . . BOAC is going to try to say to them, 'Look, we'll get you enough Britannias for you to see your way through on the route between here and Australia until the Comet IV comes along'. It's true they might make a very good show on the Kangaroo route with the Britannia and the Comet IV but Qantas will lose their shirts on the Atlantic without a pure jet and on the Pacific."

One hour after receiving this call, Beall called Schwartz at Lockheed again. Crudge, he said, "reports exactly as you do. That the fat is in the fire for both Lockheed and Boeing unless we come up with something." Beall had his corporate controller, Clyde Skeen, on the line and the two companies now began to discuss figures. Summarised, they proposed to sell to Qantas four Lockheed 1649s for $2.5 million each and to buy them back after three years for $1,012,000 each. [11]

By the following day, when Schwartz spoke from Burbank to Skeen, at Seattle, he was able to say: "We have this DC7C deal and the follow-up DC8 deal effectively stopped, for a while at least". [12] On 2 May, Crudge wrote from Sydney to Wellwood Beall that Boeing had done a good job on the techical side but that it was too soon to know whether they had succeeded or failed.

> We will only know after Bob Hage has nursed the Ritchie-Yates team to New York . . . We can win this *in Seattle* if we try hard!! . . . So much for the technical attack. The focus is Scottie Allan, who will be persuaded (he doesn't need much) when Ritchie and Yates return here. He, Scottie Allan, takes the technical presentation to the Board. He is highly thought of by his Board and with the Government and was right about not having the Comet. I have just been invited to spend next weekend with him and his family and that will count for something I hope. He is a canny Scot but it's better to have you or me lose to him on the golf course than Bill or Bruce beating him. We bum golfers have our uses . . . Now for financing. They [Qantas] have been spoiled . . . they can today get 1649s at $40,000 per month flat

rental fee . . . Three years minimum rental is the only stipulation. This means that for a $2.4 million aeroplane, $1.4 million is paid off in three years – and the Lockheed boys have a good looking resale on their hands . . . Turner is a hard dealer and obviously wants the best he can get for Qantas. A good financial deal . . . would be used by him to soften the government to his choice. Sir Roland Wilson is a member of the Board and *Secretary to the Treasury of the Australian Government*!! . . . It's all good clean fun!! Ideally we should chum up with Lockheed and have a deal which says 1049s will be sucked in by Lockheed for 1649s, which will be sucked in for 707s . . . Qantas earning power is good and the Australian Government guarantee can (and will) be given independent of the UK government . . .[13]

Crudge had been busy.

I have been more than occupied with seeing those whose observations enable me to write this note. Of the Qantas directors I had an hour with Hudson Fysh, the chairman, yesterday; four hours in two separate sessions with C. O. Turner last week . . . Scottie Allan was present throughout. I spent last weekend with Scottie and his wife (old friends) and next weekend shall do the same. Bill Taylor, one of the toughest directors, I had an hour with last night. Sir Daniel McVey, another old friend, and I lunched at the Australia Club today. Hudson Fysh called me today and asked me to lunch tomorrow with him, Bill Taylor, Scottie Allan and some others – a sign of his enthusiasm and he is a kind guy to boot . . . We have therefore been covering the waterfront.[14]

On 11 May, Boeing cabled a formal offer to Qantas offering to sell seven Boeing 707-320s powered by Pratt & Whitney J75 engines at a price of $5,150,000 each. The same aircraft with Rolls-Royce Conway engines were offered at the same price. Delivery dates were set out in the cable from March to August 1960.

C. O. Turner had followed up QEA policy decisions on the proposed Qantas route across North America to Europe with a forceful letter to Don Anderson, director-general of civil aviation. "I believe", he began, less than diffidently, "that you are fully aware of the increasing tendency of passengers travelling between Australia and Europe to use the routing through North America instead of the Kangaroo route through India." Turner estimated that over half the traffic was, in fact, now using this route.

The growing nationalism of the countries along the Kangaroo route and the decline of the prestige of the white man in those areas, as well as the attraction of seeing the United States, are factors . . . The fare is substantially the same, although the distance via North

America is appreciably greater, and both Pan American Airways and Canadian Pacific Airways have been actively selling the routing via North America in competition with the Kangaroo route . . . Apart from the fact that the relative attractiveness of the North American routing will increase with time, particularly with an easing of the dollar restrictions, there is the real possibility of political unrest or emergency in South East Asia or in the Middle East disrupting or even severing completely the route to Europe. It is therefore essential as a protectionary measure that QEA should be in a position to provide service to the United Kingdom through North America . . . we are at a competitive disadvantage owing to the gap between New York and San Francisco over which US carriers have to be used. CPAL already provide a one-carrier service between Sydney and Amsterdam . . . Pan American Airways operates over both the Atlantic and Pacific . . .

Turner continued in a tone that would not have warmed the heart of the new director-general.

You will appreciate that for these reasons the Company has been greatly concerned at the lack of success that attended the Australian approach to the United States authorities about a year ago for rights to extend the Australian operations from San Francisco across the United States to Europe. Since that time we have re-examined the whole problem and are more than ever convinced that the reasonable routing for the Australian service . . . must be through New York . . . We have concluded that request for rights through New York to Europe should be processed further with the United States authorities . . . Capt. Johnston, from his contacts in Washington, believes that if the Australian request is appropriately presented again now it will receive sympathetic consideration . . . The QEA Board at its last meeting considered this question and endorsed the proposal . . .

Turner said he was hopeful that Anderson would appreciate the importance of this question to QEA and agree to the necessary action to be put in train. "If this is approved, I would like to suggest that the detailed case and the form of presentation should be worked out in consultation with the Company . . ."[15]

By 23 April Turner was able to write to Edgar Johnston, then in Switzerland, that Anderson had concurred with the minister that he should attend the Commonwealth Air Transport Council meetings early in June and then go on to Washington for unofficial talks "so that he can familiarise himself with the problem . . . I protested about the arrangements but the Department of Civil Aviation claims that there is nothing really new in our present application and that if we are to succeed the leader of the Australian delegation must have full knowledge of the circumstances and background of the problem. I think, too, as you yourself will realise, that there is a bit of jealousy on the part of Anderson . . . he realises that he does not know as much about the problem as we do."[16]

Cabinet now considered the question of a replacement on the Qantas board following the death of Sir Keith Smith. On 24 May the minister, Athol Townley, wrote to Hudson Fysh that W. C. Taylor, vice-chairman, and G. P. N. Watt, director, would be reappointed for a further three years from 1 July. As successor to Sir Keith, the government had appointed Robert Law-Smith as a director for the unexpired term of Sir Keith's term of office, ending on 30 June 1958. The minister concluded his formal note to Fysh: "He [Law-Smith] is a young man with extensive business and aviation interests whom I am sure will be of considerable assistance to you in your approach to the many problems which lie ahead of the company".[17]

Robert Law-Smith was then forty-one, an active private aircraft owner who had first obtained his pilot's licence in 1939 and had then gone on to serve in RAAF transport squadrons, ending the war as Director of Postings with the rank of squadron leader. The QEA board, with Hudson Fysh as chairman and Taylor vice chairman, now had Sir Daniel McVey, Sir Roland Wilson, and Law-Smith as directors. The company secretary and finance manager was F. C. Derham. There had been much bigger changes on the board of QEA's partner airline. On 7 March, Sir Miles Thomas had tendered his letter of resignation as chairman, irked by political interference. "You can either have an airline run as a competitive, keen, commercial concern using the best available equipment, or you can have it as a shop window for British aircraft you would not normally purchase", he commented later. His successor was forty-nine years old Gerard d'Erlanger.[18]

C. O. Turner had gathered around himself a group that he called the "head office executive". G. U. "Scottie" Allan was assistant general manager; A. A. Barlow, manager eastern division; W. H. Crowther, manager western division; C. W. Nielson,* commercial manager; and R. J. Ritchie, technical manager. But what Hudson Fysh described as "a key relationship of vital importance in any organisation", that between chairman and chief executive, was bad. "In the case of C. O. Turner and myself," wrote Fysh, "there existed an association of two

---

* There has been some confusion in the previous two volumes over the spelling of C. W. (Bill) Nielson's surname. The correct spelling is as it appears here.

key people . . . who were as poles apart in their outlook on many vital human feelings, yet obliged to work together for the common good of QEA."[19]

The men that Turner had gathered around him were intensely loyal to their chief executive and he, in his turn, never failed to support and if necessary protect them. But the bad feeling between chief executive and chairman quite naturally influenced his executive team. Turner's own brilliance was manifest and recognised both within Qantas and with all those outside the company with whom he dealt, even when his brusque and at times domineering manner alienated them. The members of his management team, all able and highly motivated and diverse in their skills, compounded and extended Turner's reach and influence. From all this, Hudson Fysh was increasingly isolated and his great contribution to Qantas over decades was often underrated or denigrated. Capt. Scottie Allan, as assistant general manager, worked closely with both men. Though he greatly admired Turner, he was also critical of him. Like Edgar Johnston, he recognised that in this period of complexity and expansion, Turner was the central strength of Qantas.[20] But he also had criticisms. He was, said Allan, remarkably selfish; he was incapable of dismissing anybody face-to-face, but from weakness, nor soft-heartedness. "He was nasty when there was nobody there but he would not be nasty to somebody to their face." He had no close friends. Captain Allan was as dispassionate in his criticisms of Hudson Fysh, but he never faltered in his regard for him.

> He was despised by some, held in contempt by some [said Allan]. But nevertheless he passed them all on the up-hill climb to fame and fortune . . . He was a nicer kind of human being . . . You've got to remember that Huddy had a bad education [but] he became managing director of Qantas, he became chairman of Qantas, he was knighted. Though the disabilities of men are obvious their abilities are sometimes obscure. You have to look for those obscure abilities of Hudson Fysh. Huddy started [the spirit of loyalty to Qantas] by *his* loyalty to Qantas, and sticking to Qantas all those many years . . . It did not happen by accident. Huddy was a character. He was determined. He produced an atmosphere at Qantas that made Qantas Qantas. I had barnies with him . . . trying to explain something that was beyond his comprehension and he'd say, "Don't bother me with detail". I knew exactly what he meant by that. The fact is that he didn't want to hear details because they were no use to him. He couldn't follow what it was all about . . . You can't give anybody the broad outline unless you give them the reasons, but he didn't want the reasons. It made it hard for me and made it hard for him . . . I'd walk out, and try again next day.[21]

In practice it was Turner and his management team that now provided the information, the analyses, and the recommendations to the board on which decisions were made. Turner's mind and style were evident in all the board papers that went forward as the pace of technological change in civil airliners now generated the single biggest pressure on him and his team. From these technological advances and their exploitation by the major aircraft manufacturers flowed commercial, financial, operational, and political implications for Qantas that had all to be resolved under the pressure of competitors' moves and of manufacturers' production line delivery date options. And, as Boeing had recognised, the two key men on whom the technical evaluation of the new aircraft depended were Ritchie and Yates.

On 17 May, Boeing's president, William Allen, and his top executives received a memorandum from Edward C. Wells, vice-president for development engineering (who had been with Boeing from the early 1930s). Lockheed had been advised by their representative in Australia, Peter Mingrone, who said that "Qantas – Turner et al – appear to be in the process of formulating a master plan for aircraft procurement. In its present form this master plan includes the purchase of up to eight Lockheed 1649As and for the trade-in of these airplanes on Boeing *or* Douglas jets. He further indicated the probable need for ten [Lockheed] Electras and for additional Lockheed 1049s . . . Lockheed believes that Mr Ritchie is a key figure in any negotiation with Qantas and that advantage should be taken of Mr Ritchie's visit [to Seattle] to impress him with the fact that our proposal involves only 1649s and Boeing 707s."[22] Boeing learned on the same day that unofficial information indicated that Roland Wilson was visiting the United States on a mission at government level. "Advice here is that Boeing should not approach Wilson directly regarding Qantas financing. Turner is attending the Prime Ministers' [London] meeting and every effort is being made to convince him to visit Seattle and New York prior to this meeting", said the cable from Boeing's representative in Sydney.[23] Boeing consultant Vernon Crudge cabled Wellwood Beall: "Presume you are aware that Roland Wilson is a most senior Australian government financial authority and actually signs their bank notes."[24] Boeing did, in fact, approach Sir Roland Wilson when he was in New York. But their vice-president controller J. O. Yeasting reported to Beall on 24 May that though he had offered to come to New York to discuss financing possibilities for Qantas aircraft, Wilson thought such a visit would be useless. He was, he said, exploring financial matters in a general way and not thinking in terms of any specific deal. He did, said Yeasting, indicate that he hoped to visit Seattle before returning to Australia.[25]

Boeing cabled Qantas on 25 May extending the expiration date of their Boeing 707 offer to the end of July. On 29 May, top Boeing technical man (later to become Boeing senior vice-president), Ken Holtby, wrote to Beall from Sydney: "If I remember correctly, you told me before I went on this junket that I was to be the guy to call the shots as I saw them. To call for technical aid, topside brass or whatever was needed to put this sale on ice. I think now is the time to make with the aid." Captain Ritchie's visit to New York and Seattle had, he said, been a success. "He feels this [the Boeing 707 prototype] is the finest machine he ever got his hot little hands on—and will talk for thirty minutes at a stretch given the slightest opportunity. Also, someone clued him into the fact that making one of these machines fly that way wasn't easy. Which, as you will recall, United [Airlines] took for granted." (Holtby was a top aerodynamicist.) The atmosphere at Qantas, he reported, had never been better. "Turner, who in his own way tends to be slightly stuffy, spent quite a bit of time with me. He was pleased that he now had a complete package to take with him to London and to the States . . . He now definitely intends to team up with Wilson, both in New York and on the trip to the West Coast." Turner had told him, he said, that a new committee had been formed in the UK to survey US equipment for intended purchase by BOAC. He wanted to know where Boeing stood with BOAC.

> Qantas will be heavily influenced by a BOAC decision. They are partners on the Empire route and equipment interchange is important . . . Furthermore, as he sees it, if BOAC goes for DC8s, Qantas would then be the only operator of Conway-powered Boeings. He feels this would be untenable. If BOAC buys DC8s, then if Qantas bought 707s it would be the -320 . . . The scene of the battle will shift tonight with Turner's departure to London. The key to the Qantas purchase lies with BOAC . . . It is your Australian representative's solid recommendation that you pack your bags and spend the next few weeks in London.

Holtby reported that technically Boeing had made their point with Qantas. "The enthusiasm on the technical level is already well established and I believe there is little more to be accomplished along this line."[26]

There were lighter matters among these major issues. Hudson Fysh reported to his chief executive the result of his talks with

Australia's minister for external affairs, R. G. Casey, in Canberra. Casey, said Fysh, "had only one criticism of the Qantas services, and that was a small one. It was that we should serve good French wines and not Australian wines, which can never come up to the French . . . I am inclined to think that, unless too expensive, we should serve the really best French wines on our Connoisseur Services."[27] A reply came from the assistant general manager, Scottie Allan: "The general feeling is that we should endeavour to serve the best Australian product available . . . Unfortunately, also, the French wines are difficult to obtain in sufficient quantities and to store at tropical out-stations."[28]

External Affairs had been concerned with other matters of more substance to Qantas and had advised the airline at the beginning of the year that the United Kingdom government had begun discussions with Malaya on a programme to lead up to full self-government, with similar but separate discussions starting with Singapore in April. The future of Malayan Airways had been part of these discussions. Though privately owned and operated, the three governments of Singapore, Federation of Malaya, and North Borneo all had an interest in it. Consideration was being given to a new organisation for MAL and BOAC had proposed that it should participate in it. Capt. Bill Crowther had made a similar suggestion on behalf of Qantas and T. K. Critchley, the Australian commissioner in Kuala Lumpur, had advised External Affairs on 20 April that Qantas participation would be favourably regarded by Federation ministers. In Singapore, however, BOAC reported that negotiations had reached a delicate stage. BOAC asked that Qantas cease their separate inquiries there. (QEA, however, felt that they needed to look after their own interests and persisted.)

On 18 June 1956, Athol Townley advised Casey that he agreed in principle that the Qantas acquisition of an interest in MAL would be beneficial not only to Australia's civil aviation interests but also to its broader political interests in the South East Asia area. He asked for Casey's support and for a message to Singapore's chief minister expressing the interest of the Australian government in the negotiations between Qantas and the Singapore authorities. Casey complied with this suggestion. By August, the Qantas board had judged that separate intervention by Qantas might tend to inflate the value of the MAL shares and it was agreed not to intervene further, on the understanding with BOAC that Qantas could obtain an equal shareholding with them. Qantas stood aside as these negotiations continued throughout the year. Fysh advised Townley that C. O. Turner had also been discussing with BOAC the problems of new aircraft and of finance, as well as the proposed new route across the United States. He was at pains to acknowledge the minister's authority in the matter of new jet aircraft and to prepare the ground for a Qantas order. Privately, he recorded in his diary that the tensions and unhappiness of recent years had eased. On 16 July he wrote:

> Anyone reading the various secret notes I have made from time to time – and if I do not live long enough to edit them – may think they are the ravings of an unbalanced mind. Please remember that they are the revelations of secret thoughts and difficulties which each of us has, but which are not often put down. Edited, they would read all right. Now – why have I not made many notes on the last four or five years? Firstly, I have had little time. Second, my health has been better – and fears and hates and unsettlement come a lot from poor health. This is a psychological fact. Thirdly, I have improved a little in reasonableness and in settlement of mind. My Dural place [Fysh had bought a small property on the outskirts of Sydney] has been a great thing. Fourthly, I have been enabled to lead a more balanced existence. These notes are in the heat of the moment, and not in the light of that lapse of time which must always be allowed to take place before a balanced (account) is written. [29]

The director-general of civil aviation, Don Anderson, had found in his discussions in the United States on rights for Qantas through New York to Europe what he reported as a genuinely sympathetic attitude, though there were difficulties because of the fear of creating a precedent. There would, he told Qantas, be no US objection to Qantas extending through New York under rights held by the United Kingdom. The conclusion reached after discussions between the director-general and Qantas was that formal discussions should be delayed until after the forthcoming US presidential elections. If rights were not obtainable through New York, trans-Canada rights would be acceptable. [30] There were other possible changes to the QEA operating environment from pending discussions on competing carriers' rights. The French airline, TAI, was investigating rights into New Zealand which would give them a competitive service to Europe. [31] The Indian government had designated Air India to commence operations under its air transport agreement with Australia in October 1956 (an agreement that had been concluded seven years before) and were pressing for changes to the capacity provisions under the agreement that threatened Qantas with an annual revenue loss of some £500,000. Anderson reported on 17 August: "A very serious view of the position which is developing is taken by this Department and by Qantas Empire Airways and the forthcoming discussions to be held in New Delhi are believed to be of fundamental importance to the future of the Australia-India Transport Agreement. In recent years the Indian Government has taken a strong protectionist stand in its negotiation of air transport matters."[32]

Qantas's decision on aircraft choice was now close, and although the details of financing the purchase remained of high importance, it was the technical team at Qantas who were ultimately to put this choice beyond question. In summary, Qantas had to consider the promising economics of the turbo-prop Britannia, from England, and the Comet; the improved Lockheed 1649 as an interim aircraft until the Boeing 707 was available in 1960; and the combination of Douglas DC7C and Douglas DC8 jet. In fact, another option was to present itself.

When Capt. Bert Ritchie had flown the Boeing 707 proto-type, Boeing had been quite accurate in assessing his enthusiastic reaction. "I was starry-eyed about it", said Ritchie. "I wouldn't talk about anything else. I said that while the turboprop formula was good, it had been superseded by events." Scottie Allan and Ron Yates supported this view. C. O. Turner, initially, favoured maintaining the Qantas relationship with Douglas who, Ritchie fully agreed, "had a score on the board, to say the least, as a very successful producer of commercial aeroplanes". There was a big argument between Ritchie and Turner. But the technical argument as it bore on the operational necessities of QEA, inexorably favoured a modified version of the Boeing 707. For Britain, this particular battle was over. "We finished with the Britannia", said Ritchie. It was the Qantas view that all the parameters set down in the Qantas letter of intent to buy six Britannias—empty weight, cruising speed, payload and range—had shifted adversely. After a final visit to Bristol with Ron Yates, Captain Ritchie recommended strongly against the Britannia. The letter of intent was withdrawn.[33]

Under Ritchie, at the head of the Qantas technical team, were the first two men to enter Qantas as professional engineers—products of Sydney University's school of aeronautical engineering and the degree course that it introduced in 1942—Ron Yates and Bob Walker. (It was a year and a course that was to produce graduates who came to fill the most senior positions in government, the services and other Australian airlines.) Bob Walker, who had done elementary flying train-

ing in the RAAF, graduated at the end of 1946 and joined de
Havillands in Australia. In 1948, Ron Yates rang and offered
him a job with Qantas at £6 per week, which he declined. Six
months later there was another offer, this time for £11 per week.
Bob Walker accepted. One week later, another graduate engineer
from Sydney University, Bill Hill (later to become director of
overhaul and maintenance), also joined. These two became the
Technical Development Department of Qantas, a department
that later was to grow to more than fifty professional engineers.
It was this department, under Ron Yates, that went through
the first full aircraft competition between the Super Constellation and the Douglas DC6B. Now the competition was
between Douglas and Boeing.

Boeing did not have a good reputation for civil airliners. Their
Stratocruiser, built in small numbers and burdened with an unsatisfactory Pratt & Whitney four-row radial engine, was
financially disastrous until a military version was ordered. More
than eight hundred military versions of the Stratocruiser were
built. Their main role was as tankers which were a necessity
for the military jet aircraft which lacked range. From this Boeing
role as providers of tanker aircraft emerged their jet tanker, the
KC135, and from this the civil Boeing 707. Bob Walker was

Although Qantas was operating
Lockheed aircraft in its
mainline fleet during the 1950s,
the company's executives
frequently visited other
manufacturers to keep abreast
of new types of aircraft or
equipment. C. O. Turner
visited Douglas Aircraft at
Santa Monica, California on
28 June 1956 to inspect the
mockup of their DC8. J. Clyne,
Douglas director of
international sales, is on the left
and Nat Paschall, Douglas vice-
president, is on the right.

C. O. Turner visited both the Douglas and Boeing factories in late June 1956 as the date for announcement of the Qantas jet airliner order drew nearer. He is seen here in the cockpit of the Boeing 707 prototype at Seattle, Washington.

stationed at Burbank when Qantas started its close assessment of the Douglas DC8 and Boeing 707.

Douglas was offering two versions of its jet – a continental (or domestic) version and an intercontinental. The principal difference was the smaller engine of the domestic model, the Pratt & Whitney J57 of some 10,000 pounds thrust. (The civil designation of this engine was the JT3C6.) For the intercontinental this was too small, in the Douglas view. They offered an identical aeroplane physically but with a new engine from Pratt & Whitney, of some 17,000 pounds thrust, called the J75. This aircraft had a higher gross weight, more thrust on take-off and a stronger structure. The new engine, a straight jet, was then unproven.

Boeing was also offering two physically similar versions of its new 707 jet – a domestic and an intercontinental version. This latter version had the same J75 engine as the longer range Douglas, and had a fuselage like the earlier 707 but lengthened by 10 feet. This earlier 707, 128 feet long, was what Boeing had originally meant to build but it proved too small for most of their customers.

For either the Boeing or the Douglas intercontinental versions, engine availability meant a considerable delay before Boeing

Burbank, 2 July 1956. Qantas was the first airline to order the L1049H model of the Lockheed Super Constellation. It was a freighter/passenger type with a strengthened floor and a large cargo door. The fuselage of the first of two Qantas L1049Hs, VH-EAM, is shown here as it was being moved into the Final Assembly building at Lockheed. Qantas resident engineer, Burbank, Bob Walker, gives scale to the door. Note the smaller passenger door integral with the freight door. Both Qantas L1049Hs were fitted out as passenger aircraft for the majority of the time prior to the introduction of the 707s in 1959.

could make delivery. It was, said Bob Walker, "hard to separate these two aircraft" and, also, Qantas did not want to wait.

A prime requirement for any jet ordered by Qantas was that it could fly the Fiji (Nadi) to Honolulu sector of the Pacific route. This long, overwater distance problem was compounded by the short length of the runway at Nadi (7,000 feet). Douglas did not want to alter their domestic aeroplane to increase its range, but Boeing were innovative. They suggested that Qantas consider their domestic aeroplane (the 100 series) with 10 feet taken out of the fuselage length. This, they said, merely went back to the original standard body of 128 feet 10 inches. It would save weight and give Qantas extra payload. To solve the problem of the Nadi runway length, Boeing now proposed a different engine, the military version of the Pratt & Whitney JT3C6

The announcement of Qantas's order for seven Boeing 707s was just five weeks away when this photo was taken on 31 July 1956 at the Douglas Aircraft Company's Santa Monica plant. The Qantas executives in this group are, from left: assistant general manager, Scottie Allan; chief engineer, Doug Hudson; projects-engineer, Ron Yates; and resident engineer, Burbank, Bob Walker. The aircraft behind them is a DC7C being prepared for delivery to Scandinavian Airlines.

which would give 500 pounds more thrust than the civil version. The military were willing to release this version in December 1958. With 10 feet taken from the 100 series fuselage and the higher thrust engine, it would be possible to fly Nadi-Honolulu.

On technical grounds this Boeing proposal shut out all other competition. When Boeing said that they could promise delivery of this version of the domestic 707 for 1959, it became clear that no interim aircraft of any kind would be necessary between the current fleet of Super Constellations and the Boeing 707. Qantas made its decision in favour of Boeing.[34]

On 6 September 1956, the minister for civil aviation, Athol Townley, announced that government approval had been given to Qantas for the purchase of seven Boeing 707-138 jet aircraft, with delivery beginning in May 1959, subject to the completion of the necessary negotiations with Boeing. "These aircraft", said the minister, "will cruise at 550 miles per hour, carrying more than eighty passengers and will operate over ranges up to 3,500 miles. They will be placed in operation on QEA's Kangaroo route to London and on the Pacific route to America late in 1959. They will reduce the present flying time from Sydney

68

to London from forty-eight hours to twenty-seven and from
Sydney to San Francisco from twenty-eight to sixteen." The
purchase, he said, meant a capital outlay of £18.8 million but
dollar commitments would be more than adequately covered
by QEA's own annual earnings in the dollar area and the resale
of some of the existing fleet for dollars (arrangements for which
had been satisfactorily completed).[35]

C. O. Turner, in his chief executive's bulletin to outstations,
commented on the ministerial announcement.

> The short version—the Boeing 707-138 of 128 feet 10 inches—is
> being specially built to fit our route requirements . . . The empty
> weight is 2,500 pounds less than the standard Boeing 707 and this,
> combined with a 5,500 pounds lower volumetric capacity, allows
> the aircraft to operate from all existing airfields on the Pacific run
> without any reduction in passenger capacity due to runway length
> restrictions. This is also true on the UK route . . . except Karachi,
> where the required extension will be available by 1960. Because
> of favourable delivery positions . . . it will not now be necessary
> to purchase new interim aircraft such as the Lockheed 1649A,
> Douglas DC7C or Bristol Britannia. This will avoid tremendous
> expense. Instead, we are going to keep our [Lockheed] 1049 fleet
> up to date by equipping all aircraft with radar noses for weather
> mapping, and fitting wingtip fuel tanks to five aircraft operating
> the Pacific route . . . which will enable us to guarantee non-stop
> flights between Nandi and Honolulu.

Two more Super G Constellations had, he said, been ordered
for October and November 1957 to bring the fleet to sixteen
of this type. Turner attached a report comparing the Super Constellation, Comet IV, Britannia 310, and Boeing 707-138 and
commented: "These comparisons readily illustrate why we were
unable to consider the Comet as an economic proposition for
our particular routes. The capacity of the Super Constellation
is rapidly becoming too limited for our traffic demands but the
Comet IV, although much faster, has an even smaller capacity
and payload—totally inadequate for operation in late 1959 . . .
The Britannia would be much too late to be competitive on
our Pacific service. Its speed is against it." Turner added that
although Qantas had decided against the Comet and Britannia,
"it should be clearly understood that in the interests of the British
Aviation Industry and because of our association with BOAC,
who have thirty-three Britannias and nineteen Comets on order,
we are most anxious for both these aircraft to be successful".[36]

This order for Boeing 707s was to make Qantas the first airline
in the world outside America to operate American jet airliners.
With it came the necessity for costly and far-reaching improve-

Burbank, 19 September 1956. Lockheed's last development of the Constellation series was the L1649. Qantas's first L1049H had been completed only days before and was to make its first test flight on 20 September. It was an ideal aircraft to use for a photographic comparison of the "old" wing and the "new" as used on the L1649. Copies of this photograph appeared in publications all around the world. The wingspan of the 1649 was 150 feet (45.7 metres) compared to 123 feet (37.5 metres) on the 1049. Other obvious differences are the longer engine nacelles, the engines mounted further outboard from the cabin, and the wing set further back on the fuselage. The primary reason for the 1649's huge wing was extra fuel capacity to give it the longest range of any airliner in service.

ments to the airline's plant and facilities at Mascot airport. A new engine test house had been finished at the end of 1954. The new building incorporating the precooked frozen food factory, catering, and cabin services needs was opened in 1956. But the test cell completed so recently was not adequate for the needs of the new jet engines. The decision to build a much more sophisticated test cell was helped by the major decision to reroute the railway that had bisected the Qantas area at Mascot. But it meant that the existing test cell would have to be demolished. In addition to these costly projects, the long-range plan to expand the engine overhaul workshop (prevented previously by the problem of flight clearances for aircraft on the new Mascot east-west runway) now became essential. The much enlarged workshop necessary for jet overhauls had now, by necessity, to be built in the new industrial area.

Aircrew training for the new jets required much larger and more sophisticated facilities. Link trainers in a hangar annexe were no longer sufficient. Crew training in ground simulators was required, instead of costly in-flight training. The increased freight capacity of the 707s brought with it the need for a new cargo building. Catering facilities had to be expanded. But the long-term plan for a new industrial area at Mascot had provided the logical place for all these facilities and helped justify the proposal to reroute the railway line around the northern perimeter of the Qantas area. Major earthworks were essential, with drainage, water and power supplies, new roads, and hard standing areas. These particular challenges for the new jet age faced QEA's general services superintendent, W. Hudson Shaw.[37] All these facilities were to be completed progressively from 1956 to 1960.

Qantas had pointed out in a submission to Cabinet, when approval was sought for the Boeing purchase, that the company would have to spend about £5 million during this period to provide the ground facilities needed. There were, however, other complications, arising from federal government policy laid down in 1949. Under that policy, all airport buildings and facilities erected on aerodromes for the use of carriers were to be owned and provided by the Commonwealth. In the years that followed, lack of finance in federal budgets had prevented the implementation of government policy. Operators were allowed to erect their own buildings subject to the right of the Commonwealth to acquire them at any time. In July 1956, the government advised that operators were to bear the cost not only of buildings but of all ground development work. "We understand", Fysh wrote, in a submission to the minister, "that the scheme contemplated that operators would be granted long term leases of the land areas on which they took responsibility for the ground development work." The directors, he said, had considered a proposal that Qantas "should obtain a long term lease of a large area of land at Mascot adjacent to and including our present hangars and other buildings, but also including an area to provide for future development over the years. The proposal involves the removal of the present Botany railway line which crosses the area near our hangars at a cost of £200,000 which, it is proposed, should be borne by the Company—as well as any cost required in levelling and paving the areas (estimated at £500,000 over the next five years) . . . It would allow for the concentration of Qantas facilities adjacent to one another in a most serviceable manner." The directors felt, he said, that "whilst the proposal appeared to solve many existing difficulties, they were unable to reach any conclusion on this important matter without being aware of the Commonwealth's planning for the

71

future development of Mascot Airport". He asked for a meeting with the minister. [38]

As the minister announced the order for the new Qantas jet fleet, Hudson Fysh also pressed him indirectly, from the other side of the world at the Edinburgh annual general meeting of IATA, to uphold the existing rate for the carriage of airmail. There was a threat to reduce the international rate from four gold francs to three, or even less, which, said Fysh, "the industry cannot afford, as it operates on a very small margin of profit". IATA members, he told the Edinburgh meeting, "spend great time and effort on fares and rates which they are responsible for fixing; but our governments are directly responsible for our mail rates, and it is to them that we must go individually and put our cases". In Australia, he said, moneys paid to the operators for airmail carriage were covered by receipts from the public. "Despite the great increase in passengers and cargo, the mails hold the right of way. They are primary." Reductions in postal payments and increased services, such as second class mail and air parcel post, had, said Fysh, only been made possible by the enterprise of the airline operators in building up their passenger services and minimising costs for airmail. What, he asked, would be the cost if the Post Office operated its own mail-only aircraft? [39] Qantas was strongly supported by the Australian government on both the issue of mail rates and that of the Britavia application to fly to Perth. Phillip Hood reported to BOAC's managing director that he had seen a copy of a letter personally signed by R. G. Menzies that left practically no loophole for reopening the Britavia issue. The Menzies letter, drafted by the Department of Civil Aviation, said it was necessary to give undivided support to the nationalised operators to meet the twin burdens of high capitalisation and low profit. If the Britavia proposal were agreed to, QEA's gross profit, estimated to be £570,000 on a revenue of £17 million, would be eliminated. Menzies also wrote that if the proposals for reducing the mail rate by the Universal Postal Union went through, QEA revenue might be reduced by £1 million.

In the same letter, Hood wrote that the financial implications of operating a competitive QEA-BOAC Pacific route had caused much sober thinking at Qantas. Fysh, he said, was particularly anxious for closer co-operation. "The Secretary of the Treasury [Sir Roland Wilson] and the Director-General [Don Anderson] devoted some time with me to this subject. This thinking is not, as you will imagine, altogether altruism but realisation that

QEA is not sufficiently strong without BOAC support to battle with the big air legions." Hood reported that "the new imposing QEA Sydney headquarters office will be ready for occupancy by September 1957".[40] These observations by Hood were given further substance by a letter from C. O. Turner to BOAC's commercial director, Keith Granville, on 16 November.

As far as we are concerned here, we still subscribe to the "principles" agreed with Sir Miles Thomas and Basil Smallpiece in July 1955, and we look forward to progressively developing a parallel partnership service via the US to the UK in conjunction with BOAC. The conception of using the best of our joint equipment and joint rights is clearly of advantage to both of us, and you can depend [on it] that Australia will not lightly give away rights on the Kangaroo route. Our present problem is to hold down the Pan American and Canadian Pacific services to the point where they are reasonable competition.

A look at our Kangaroo route problems surely highlights the necessity for the development of a partnership service via the North American Continent. At the moment, Djakarta has denied us refuelling, Singapore has just come through difficult rioting and it looks as though we will have more to come; India is demanding a new bilateral agreement with further restrictions on our fifth freedom rights; practically the whole of the Middle East area is closed to us, and we have lost quite valuable Cairo traffic . . . It appears to me that for both BOAC and QEA it is a matter of survival and we must get services operating via the US without delay.[41]

The L1649 made its first flight on 11 October 1956 but by that time Qantas had decided to standardise their fleet on the L1049. Two L1049Gs would be delivered in late 1957, bringing the Super Constellation fleet to sixteen. Eight of these aircraft would be traded back to Lockheed once the Boeing 707s entered service in late 1959.

In November 1956, Qantas carried the Olympic flame on a flight of 8,600 miles from Athens to Darwin as Australia played host

to the XVI Olympics in Melbourne. It was the longest flight ever made by this sporting symbol and the first time it had ever been carried south of the equator. Traffic generated by the Olympics pressed Qantas fleet resources hard. On more than a dozen occasions, the entire Super Constellation fleet was in the air at the same time. But the Olympic flame was carried across the Middle East, as Turner had indicated in his letter to Keith Granville, at a time of grave crisis. President Nasser of Egypt, against growing pressure from Britain and France, made his decision in July to nationalise the Suez Canal. Egypt, Jordan, and Syria announced a joint military command on 23 October. On 29 October Israeli forces invaded the Sinai. An ultimatum was sent by the British and French governments demanding that the Israeli and Egyptian armies each withdraw ten miles from the canal and, when this was rejected, the British and French military decided – with the support of the Australian prime minister and without the full backing of the United Nations – to use military force; the canal was blockaded. On 6 November Egypt severed diplomatic relations with Australia. (Canada proposed that the United Nations send an emergency force to the Suez area to secure and supervise the cessation of hostilities; Australia was one of nineteen countries that abstained from voting on this proposal.) On 25 September 1956, before the crisis itself, Menzies had made his view plain in Parliament, quoting from a speech by the British prime minister, Anthony Eden: "the industrial life of Western Europe literally depends upon the continuing free navigation of the Canal as one of the great international waterways of the world. No arrangements for the future . . . could be acceptable to Her Majesty's Government which would leave it in the unfettered control of a single power . . .". It was, as Alan Watt points out in *The Evolution of Australian Foreign Policy 1938-1965*, a policy of the prime minister himself, born of his long and intense loyalty to Britain, but it distanced Australia from the United States and isolated it from Afro-Asian nations.[42] There was rioting in Singapore and Malaya and Qantas passengers were taken to their hotels under the protection of armed convoys. Strike action in Indonesia stranded two Qantas aircraft for a time in Djakarta. Qantas had to reroute its flights through Iran, Turkey and Greece to avoid Cairo, instituting a sector from Basra to Istanbul over poor terrain and lengthening the journey by 200 miles. (Bahrein was later substituted for Basra.) Qantas aircraft were operating over the emergency route after a delay of only twenty-four hours. The swift Qantas action, in confused circumstances,

brought praise for Qantas from the new minister for civil aviation, Senator Shane Paltridge, in a letter to Fysh. (Paltridge succeeded Athol Townley on 24 October 1956.)

> The rearrangement of your services . . . went without a hitch and, from what I have heard, more smoothly than perhaps was the experience of many other airlines which had to divert . . . [It] is a tribute to your company and particularly to those most directly involved. I would like you to accept my heartiest congratulations on a job well done . . . You mentioned that the Board had commended Capt. P. W. Howson, your Operations Manager, and his staff for the reorganisation of your operations, effected in the face of considerable difficult. The Director-General has informed me that the liaison which Capt. Howson and other officers maintained with the International Relations Branch of this Department . . . was of the highest order and enabled the Department promptly to assess the rapidly changing situation, after full consultation with the Department of External Affairs . . . I understand that officers of your Company are now in close touch with the Department on the subject of planning alternative routings through the African Continent should developments make it necessary to use these routings . . .[43]

On 22 November, the Commonwealth Relations Office in Britain advised the Australian government through the British

Sir Hudson Fysh—fourth from right—at Seattle with a group of visiting executives from other airlines, in late 1956. The 707 prototype had been designed to replace the propeller-driven Boeing KC97 aerial refuelling tanker/transport used by the US Air Force. The $US16 million cost was a private venture by Boeing and it could have been a disaster if the air force had not ordered twenty-nine jet tankers, based on the prototype, in September 1954. In the left background of this photograph is a Boeing B52 jet bomber that had been involved in air refuelling trials with the 707 over the previous year.

High Commission in Canberra that a military air route across the south Indian Ocean was now necessary for routine movement of service personnel between the United Kingdom and the Far East and the carriage of freight, including some of a highly secret nature, to Australia and the Pacific for weapons tests, as well as the passage of combat aircraft and movement of emergency reinforcements. The memorandum stated:

> The routes normally taken involve staging in Pakistan and India or in Pakistan and Ceylon. Apart from difficulties which could arise over the portion of the route passing through the Middle East . . . the present route is susceptible of interruption [because] . . . annual agreements . . . have to be negotiated with India for the passage of men and combat aircraft . . . An emergency move would require special permission. This might be withheld . . . The attitude taken by the present Government of Ceylon over bases in Ceylon casts serious doubt on the value of these bases, particularly in an emergency . . . For these reasons, the Chiefs of Staff have recommended, and the United Kingdom Ministers approved, a proposal to develop a new South Indian Ocean air route which will be free from political interference. The proposal envisages the development of airfields in the Seychelles and the Maldive Islands . . .[44]

The uncertainties on the traditional Qantas route between England and Australia brought new urgency to the Australian application for rights across the United States. Fysh wrote to Paltridge on 27 November: " . . . it is so obvious that the routing between Australia and Europe through South East Asia and the Middle East can no longer be relied upon for the vital link between Australia and Europe. We are already prevented from landing in or flying over several countries along the route and it would not require very much more unrest in these key areas to make that route virtually inoperable as a practical proposition . . ." An alternative route through South Africa might, he said, be available in extreme emergency but it would be relatively costly and unattractive to passengers compared to a North American route. The Qantas board, said Fysh, considered this one of the most important and urgent problems facing the airline. The presidential elections in the United States were over, he said, and the board felt that a new approach should be made to the United States without delay.[45]

Financially, 1956 had been a good year for Qantas. Increasing world demand for air travel had seen revenue jump almost £4 million from the previous year to just under £20 million and passengers carried from 135,000 to over 161,000. Tourist class

Seattle, late 1956. Sir Hudson
Fysh and his son John, Qantas
manager, San Francisco, are
briefed by a Boeing engineer
during an inspection of the
Boeing cabin mockup. Qantas
engineer John Mills looks on
from the right.

services, introduced two years earlier, now carried forty-four
per cent of passengers on the Kangaroo Route, which had
passenger loadings up thirty per cent on 1955. Frequency on
this route had been increased from three to four services in
March and on the Pacific route from three to four in August.
Passenger traffic across the Pacific rose by fifty per cent. Though
the withdrawal of most of Australia's military forces in Japan
had seen the second weekly service by Skymasters through
Labuan and Hong Kong to Iwakuni terminated at Hong Kong
in April, revenue on Super Constellation services and a thirty-
five per cent increase in revenue almost counterbalanced the
effect of the reduced military loadings. The first full year of
Super Constellation services across the Indian Ocean to South
Africa brought a revenue increase of forty-two per cent. The
postwar pattern of substantial yearly increases in traffic was again
sustained. Two new Super Constellation 1049H aircraft,
strengthened for the carriage of heavy cargo (and convertible
from all-cargo to all-passenger configuration) were received
towards the end of the year, bringing the fleet strength to 14
Super Constellations, 5 Skymaster DC4s, 8 Douglas DC3s, 4
Beaver DHC2s, 1 Drover DHA3 and 2 Catalina flying boats.
On order were 2 more Super Constellations and the 7 big Boeing
707 jets which were to change radically the future of Qantas
operations.

Beyond America
1957

3   On 3 January 1957, Hudson Fysh wrote to C. O. Turner and congratulated him warmly on his achievements. He also used the occasion to remind Turner of his own requirements as full-time chairman.

> I wish to congratulate you on the splendid results achieved by the Company during the past year by you and the Management Group under your control and guidance [Fysh wrote]. As I have made it clear on all occasions when I have an opportunity, I feel Qantas has never before reached the high standard of efficiency and effectability [*sic*] that it has attained right now, and the major credit for this state of affairs goes to you as Chief Executive.
>
> During the coming year I wish to assure you of my continued sympathetic support, and I feel that this will be fully reciprocated by yourself. For the good of the organisation it is necessary that we should have the closest collaboration, especially in regard to big matters in the formulative stages, and the success of such collaboration lies mainly on you as Chief Executive. It is also necessary that I should continue to keep in the closest touch with the affairs of the Company and to know what is happening either through yourself or your officers.

Fysh then detailed his own priorities for the coming year. He wanted close and harmonious working with the minister and the department and strict adherence to the letter and spirit of the ministerial financial directive. "All matters which are my responsibility should be referred to me. When in doubt, in the case of borderline cases, consult me. Due time for consideration of important matters both by myself and the Board is very necessary . . . Matters like the annual budget should be seen by me at least some days before the Board meeting it is presented to." He referred to Turner's plans to appoint a public relations officer. "I feel that it will help a lot when you are able to make an appointment to this specialised job. I am hoping it can be someone from within the Company [who] already has a good knowledge of the Company, which is half the battle." He hoped for an early decision on whether Qantas was interested in holding the IATA annual general meeting in Australia in 1959. [1]

Two weeks later Fysh wrote to the new Qantas director, Robert Law-Smith, about Turner's salary: "I have had discussions in Canberra early in the week with various Ministers, when I pushed the idea that our Chief Executive was grossly underpaid and, while all agree that something must be done, no one seems willing to seriously take the matter up. All the top Civil Servants and heads of Government instrumentalities are in the same boat . . .". He went on to mention another matter that was as farcical as it was serious. "Rather a tragic happening has occurred here in that the eastern half of our new hangar, in the course of erection at Mascot, has collapsed. This will now have to be pulled down and rebuilt, with consequent delay and argument about who is to pay . . . the main steel truss holding the roof collapsed. Fortunately, the principal part of the building, the workshops, are undamaged, which means we can go ahead there, the disability being that our people will have to work on the aircraft out in the open till such time as the hangar itself is completed." [2]

In London, in his talks with BOAC, C. O. Turner had been trying to get agreement for an outline operating pattern both east and west-about for the next five years, including the introduction in 1957 of a Sydney-San Francisco-New York (or over-the-pole) route to London. BOAC, Keith Granville told Hood,

have not yet agreed the necessity of this operation in 1957, particularly as we are unable to mount such a service ourselves, due not only to shortage of equipment but shortage of flying staff . . . Cedric is still here until today week. It has been extremely difficult for everyone to give as much attention as we would wish to his problems . . . we really have a lot of things on our plate. However, it is all going quite smoothly and there is plenty of goodwill on both sides. I have just concluded a talk with Cedric and Sir George Cribbett about the Malayan Airways deal and . . . I think the outcome will be that we have arranged for the new Malayan Airways to represent both BOAC and Qantas in full, which I am sure will be a good thing for everyone. [3]

BOAC and QEA did reach agreement that BOAC should meet

Seattle, January 1957. Boeing liaison officer, Gil Stephenson (far right), speaking to members of the Qantas planning team visiting the factory to gain first-hand knowledge of the 707 and its systems. Note the row of airline badges painted on the nose of the prototype behind the group.

Qantas twice weekly from 2 April at San Francisco and that, subject to both partners obtaining the necessary US rights, they should operate after 1957-58 on a pool partnership basis. BOAC's chairman, Gerard d'Erlanger, in a briefing for talks in Sydney with Hudson Fysh on 13 February, was told that, on an operating level, QEA "has apparently informed BOAC that QEA would not object to BOAC operating right through from UK to Australia even if they were unable to obtain reciprocal rights. The UK Civil Air Attache in Melbourne has, however, approached the Director-General on this particular point and has been informed that Australia will eventually concede rights to BOAC, but only when QEA is in a position to operate similarly in the opposite direction. It looks, then, as if QEA, not wishing outwardly to deny a route to BOAC which might not be available to them, may have privately asked their own Government to over-ride their attitude to BOAC." The briefing said that following the joint talks in London there would be a growing habit between the two partners to look at the UK-Australia operation as a round-the-world one, both from a frequency and overall financial viewpoint. The only real point

80

of issue in partnership affairs was QEA's objection to BOAC operating nonpool services from UK to Malaya. D'Erlanger was reminded of the lack of hotel accommodation in Sydney and other places for tourists and that the advent of larger aircraft by 1959 would make the situation even more acute. In the event of discussions being possible with Australia's prime minister, the BOAC chairman was given a summary of Menzies' current activities and a few words about his wife: "Dame Pattie is a very intelligent but homely lady with diversified interests. Mrs d'Erlanger will find her anxious to talk about families, children, flowers, gardens . . .".[4]

On 11 February, discussions with India, which had been postponed from the previous September (when Air India International carried out a proving flight to Australia), opened in New Delhi. The Department of Civil Aviation described them in a letter to the Prime Minister's Department:

> [They] will be of the utmost importance to Australia . . . statistical and economic aspects will be very important and perhaps decisive . . . The discussions have major economic implications for Qantas Empire Airways since the proposals by the Indian Government for amendment of the capacity arrangements could, if they come into effect, reduce the volume of traffic picked up and set down in India by Qantas and result in a revenue loss to the company of between £400,000 and £500,000 per annum . . . There is a serious difference of opinion between Australia and India as to the interpretation of the provisions of the Australia-India Agreement affecting capacity. Moreover, since the inauguration of the service by Air India International, it has become apparent that fundamental differences could also arise in respect of the classification of traffic for which the Australian and Indian airlines may provide capacity.

The Australian delegation to New Delhi was led by the director-general, Don Anderson, and the assistant director-general (air transport policy), Dr H. W. Poulton.

The issues of the salary level of the chief executive, the hangar collapse, the Indian negotiations, the intensive preparations under way for the new jet fleet, and the battle to acquire rights across the United States to England were all to be overshadowed, from the beginning of 1957, by a serious and escalating dispute with the airline's pilots. On 25 January, the Australian Air Pilots' Association served a claim under the Commonwealth Conciliation and Arbitration Act, for substantial pay increases. Pilots' salaries had been the subject of conciliation procedures at the end of the previous year and the three major airlines (TAA,

Australian National Airways and QEA) had reached agreement with the association, granting increases, retrospective for some six months. (Senior overseas captains were granted an extra £325 per annum.) The airline operators did not at that time think that the association had justified the increases but agreed to settle the dispute to achieve a period of stability. The overseas branch of the association (only recently created) would not agree to the increases for Qantas pilots or that no further salary claims would be made before January 1958 and reserved the right to go before the Conciliation and Arbitration Commission. This they now did. Conciliation proceedings began in which the association sought rates that included, for senior overseas captains, a further increase of up to £1,333 per annum, bringing the total salary range of captains grade 1 to £4,446–£4,896 per annum (or up to £5,696 if certain licences and training duties were involved). Qantas issued a clear statement of its position on 20 February, after the proceedings had reopened which, combined with the equally clear attitude of the pilots, was to lead to a crippling strike. It was a problem of central importance to the airline. "At the outset of this conference," said the Qantas statement, "we desire it to be understood . . . that the Company's view is that we have exhausted conciliation on the subject of [pilots'] salaries and allowances." It was the Qantas position that the matter now had to go to arbitration.[5] There was a meeting of the parties before a conciliator which was ineffective. Turner advised the board on 25 February that the association had expressed its intention of not participating in arbitration proceedings. The pilots' association had, he said, advised its members that a twenty-four-hour stoppage would be held on 22 February. Qantas, in turn, notified the court of the threatened dispute and the matter came before the commissioner, G. A. Findlay. "The Commissioner told the Association that ordinarily, when a conference breaks down in regard to industrial matters and no agreement is reached, the matter should then proceed to arbitration. As this was an ordinary situation he asked the Association why it should not do so in this case", wrote Turner. "The pilots held a meeting (at which 112 pilots were present) . . . and it is understood that they unanimously decided by secret ballot to press their claims, if necessary by direct action." Referring to Australia's two domestic airlines, Turner added: "It is clearly the intention of the Association to continue putting one operator against another, and it is most essential that all the operators meet together in a common front".[6]

To Fysh, Turner wrote on 26 February:

While travelling overseas, our pilots are, of course, in regular contact with British and other international airline pilots . . . and they have convinced themselves that they should be paid international salaries, and not in accordance with Australian standards (. . . the Australian equivalent of pounds sterling paid to BOAC pilots). We are not alone in our troubles as the American Airline Pilots' Association is a most radical body and is endeavouring to force demands for very high salaries by singling out one operator at a time and threatening a strike if they don't capitulate. It seems that the Australian Airline Pilots' Association is endeavouring to follow the same procedure, and at this moment they have certainly succeeded in isolating Qantas, which we predicted would happen some months ago. I have informed the Director-General of Civil Aviation that I feel it is important that, in the event of the pilots endeavouring to avoid attendance at Arbitration proceedings, that the Minister should make a statement on behalf of the Government that the dispute must be decided by the Court in accordance with Government policy. I don't think this will make the pilots withdraw, nor will it avoid direct action, but at least it will let the pilots know that the Government is firmly behind the Court.[7]

Turner saw clearly what was coming: cessation of flying operations. He persisted, however, with his own very firm view. As the situation worsened, he advised the directors on 28 February: "It seems that an application for a penalty clause would probably be frustrated . . . but as there is no other means of preventing pilots from pressing their claims by direct action with impunity, then we must endeavour to obtain such a clause in the agreed Award . . . In view of the Pilots' Association's militant attitude, it will probably call a strike in any event and the Company must prepare itself for such an eventuality."[8]

The three airline employers, in the newly formed Australian Airline Operators' Association, now sought reductions in salaries and a prohibition on stop-work meetings and strikes.[9] An ugly development followed. A Qantas supervisory captain declared publicly at a meeting of the pilots that he would continue to fly the company's aircraft in the event of a strike. Similar commitments were made by four other supervisory captains. B. I. Crofts, manager of the pilots' association, warned them by letter that "while members are entitled to their own views upon any proposed course of action . . . once the decision is made it is incumbent on the individual to fully support the decision". If the supervisory pilots proceeded, said the letter, "the effects upon you personally would be far reaching . . . and would, no doubt, make it physically impossible for you to carry out efficiently the functions of your particular position . . . the resentment which your fellow pilots would bear would make

Qantas began fitting their Super Constellations with weather radar from early 1957. VH-EAM *Southern Spray* was the first to be fitted with the RCA-built AVQ 10 in January that year. The distinctive "radar nose" is clearly seen.

Capt. George Quinn (left) demonstrates the adjustments available on the newly fitted AVQ 10 radar aboard VH-EAM. First officer Geoff Rees looks on from the right-hand seat. The equipment could be adjusted in flight to give ranges of 150, 50, or 20 nautical miles.

your position an extremely difficult one. The Executive Committee has required me to seek from you a letter confirming or explaining your expressed attitude."[10]

C. O. Turner wrote a long and closely reasoned letter to all pilots on 9 April 1957 in which he summarised the history of past negotiations and said:

It is important that I should tell you that the Arbitration Court award made in 1954 firmly established that pilots' salaries must be related to Australian conditions . . . Your Association contended that pilots should enjoy remuneration in excess of that of General Medical Practitioners after many years of study and as a result of long hours of responsible work. It was claimed by your advocates that the average gross income of Medical Practitioners in Victoria, as a result of a very recent survey, was £4229 per annum (and this, of course, would mean a net income of less than £3000 after paying expenses). When, however, you stop to consider the benefits which you enjoy in comparison with a Medical Practitioner in relation to superannuation, long service leave, sick leave, annual leave, staff travel concessions and many other supplementary benefits you will see that . . . the most junior Captain flying with the Company is better off financially than the average Medical Practitioner in Australia.[11]

Qantas made an offer early in April offering maximum increases in flight pay of £200. It was rejected.

On Wednesday April 10, a special edition of the airline's in-house paper, *Qantas News*, was issued to all staff with a statement from Turner. It said: "Our pilots today threatened to go on strike from midnight tomorrow, Thursday 11 April. The pilots' threat was contained in a letter to the Company which their Association tabled in the Conciliation Commission in Melbourne this morning. This letter said that the latest Qantas offer of increased salaries and allowances was unacceptable . . . and they would go on strike for one week from midnight tomorrow."[12]

Acting prime minister Sir Arthur Fadden issued a statement on 11 April as the strike was implemented and Qantas operations were halted by the first-ever prolonged strike by Australia's pilots' association. It would mean, said Fadden, the complete disruption of the overseas air services operation by Qantas on behalf of the Commonwealth Government and the people of Australia and would directly and immediately imperil the employment of thousands of other employees of Qantas. "But the astounding thing is this. I am told that the pilots, having failed to achieve their full demands through the conciliation process, have point blank refused to submit their claim to arbitration . . . I find it completely baffling."[13] On the same day the commission acceded to a Qantas request to insert in the pilots' agreement a clause forbidding the association from striking.

The pilots, however, were clear in their objectives and attitudes. They wanted salary levels determined by international comparisons. They rejected, said the April-May issue of the *Australian Air Pilot*, the company attitude that "arbitration being the law of the land there is, consequently little or no place for negotiations between the parties . . . Eventually it must be accepted that unless both sides to a bargaining table understand the other's problems and accept their points of view as sincere, industrial peace is replaced by armed truce."[14] The association now pressed the government to set up a committee outside the court process. Senator Paltridge rejected the proposal, affirming government policy that normal procedures should operate. On 18 April the Commonwealth Industrial Court ordered the association to observe the award and dismissed its application for a further stay of proceedings. It issued a directive that left the pilots' association faced with possible fines of £500 per day. On 20 April, the strike ended. There was agreement between the association and the company that there would be no victimisation of association members of supervisory pilots and that the question of pilots' salaries would now go before Commissioner Portus for decision. Despite the association's view that the strike had shown its bargaining strength, the result was a victory for Turner. The pilots had been forced back to arbitration. Turner had won the battle, but the war itself was to continue for more than a decade.

Fysh wrote to Norman Watt on 23 April: "Mr Turner, backed up by his industrial experts and management staff, has been through an extremely trying time . . . and we will agree that they have all come through it with honour and skill". Privately, he considered that he himself could have done more. "My personal failure", he wrote later, "was in not being the very big man I would have needed to be in swinging the Board, Chief Executive and Government to realise the greater consideration which might have been given to the pilots' question before the 1957 strike, and after, and in forming a more realistic attitude towards the rather unique and peculiar body of men, the International Airline Pilots. As it was, an ever increasing attitude of perpetual warfare grew up on the part of the pilots . . ." The area of arbitration as written in law, said Fysh, could be understood but, in practice, it became difficult. "Negotiation and litigation [became] so obscure and necessarily devious in its ways that it horrified my simple mind. And then, of course, on top of it all would come from time to time . . . strikes and stoppages of essential public services." The pilots, he wrote, were amazed that he himself did not appear in discussions. Fysh had "wanted to become much closer to the problem in action, but the Chief Executive would lose face and lose credit if the Chairman had to step in . . . in any event I felt the Board had little confidence in my being able to procure a settlement – which I doubted myself. My methods were crude and rather unorthodox, if genuine in objective." (The association, some weeks after the conclusion of the strike, wrote directly to Fysh describing the extremely low state of morale among pilots. "[We] respectfully request an interview with you . . . personally, not only because of the office you hold but also in view of the esteem in which you are held, in particular by your pilots.")[15] On C. O. Turner's attitude, Fysh wrote: "No more unlikely person to deal effectively with the pilots, despite all his academic brilliance, could be imagined than the Chief Executive; not an ex-pilot, having seen no war service, and not a good negotiator when give and take and human understanding had to be brought to bear." His vice-chairman, W. C. Taylor, was, he wrote "one of the strongest supporters of the Chief Executive . . . an experienced industrialist and keen supporter of the arbitration system. These two had scant regard for the pilots and rather took the attitude of 'have them on' . . . This attitude was greatly [affected] by the fact that our airline pilots enjoyed a very high salary bracket in the company and enjoyed many privileges as compared with senior staff."[16]

Senior staff were, in fact, resentful of the special attention and high salaries paid to pilots. On the day before the conclusion of the strike, there was a voluntary meeting of representative senior staff attended by eight senior managers. They formally placed on record their opinion that pilots were already fairly paid and "recorded with disfavour that a section of the Company's staff who had been so favourably treated over a period of years should have shown such a callous disregard of the Company, having particular regard to the national service which it renders, and the welfare of its employees". They wanted penalties imposed on the strikers in any terms of settlement.[17] In fact, the outcome of the subsequent arbitration proceedings was that some justification existed for salary increases based on international comparisons but that pilots' salaries should be set having regard to the Australian community. The Qantas prestrike offer on salaries and conditions, not based on international comparisons, was accepted by the pilots' association.[18] Fysh was very affected by the conflict and made private rough notes about his sense of betrayal. "They [the pilots] have let me down . . . They have let down 6000 other people who depend for a living on them . . . Unity is strength . . . The pilots case made a mess of all along the line. What do I think of it? [I am] bitterly disappointed. [They] should apologise. Return to collective bargaining—get rid of conventions. They can't have it both ways."[19] In a public paper he made "a strong appeal to the flying staff of QEA to accept the principle of submitting any disagreement which cannot be settled with the Company to conciliation and arbitration, and then abide by the result—and thus conform to the law of the land . . . Great moral and financial damage has been done by the recent strike and the distressing feature is that although the pilots have agreed to submit their case to arbitration in accordance with the law . . . there is some irresponsible talk of pilots not abiding by the decision of the Court when it is given. This borders on anarchy . . .".[20]

On 24 April 1957, Hudson Fysh noted in his diary that it was Anzac Day eve. (Fysh had served at Gallipoli himself, though not in the initial landing.) He wrote:

BOAC commenced operations with their Bristol Britannias on the London-Sydney route in early March 1957. The Britannias used on the Australian route were Series 102s fitted with 42 tourist class seats forward and 30 first class slumberettes aft. Fifteen Series 102s were built for BOAC; they were registered G-ANBA to G-ANBO inclusive. G-ANBE is seen here taxiing up to the overseas terminal building at Sydney airport soon after regular services began.

> No note for many months . . . apparently I only resort to making notes when I am worried or disturbed—it is a means of letting off steam. I find I am able to let off steam to anyone less and less as the years pass and I become more and more isolated, and indeed out of touch with many in Qantas as the early ideals and usages in the Company become more and more obsolete in the [eyes] of the present-day regime . . . After a discussion with Turner on general matters this morning I realised what I have [known] for some years . . . One cannot totally [communicate]. When he flies into a temper . . . our ideals and things we believe in are utterly different. Mostly we are poles apart and antagonistic. Never once in all the years do I remember Turner responding to a suggestion by me . . . [He is] completely, absolutely money and power mad. Out of sympathy with me . . . out of touch with [those] lower down. Ruthlessly ambitious. On the other hand, his mind is brilliant. A great organiser and morally courageous. The great fault

is that [he was] never in the services. So one comes to a sad part of one's life—the unwanted stage, the stage when influence is waning and one sees old ideals and urges go, in the march of time . . . The old feeling will go. Not only the new management ideals but the very size of the show makes this so. All things pass. Times change. Ideals change—and my Qantas goes ahead under the new people to new victories. [21]

Turner was matched in ambition by the young director-general of civil aviation, D. G. Anderson. Whether, as Turner had written, Anderson was jealous of Qantas expertise in some matters, there was no hint of any underlying discord in the fulsome letter that Anderson wrote in April. "This is a short note", he said, "to say how much I appreciate what your organisation is doing to help my technical and operational staff to become familiarised with the Boeing jet aircraft project . . . the suggestion made by Mr Howson for a Boeing Committee consisting of Department of Civil Aviation and QEA staff is one which exemplifies very well the spirit of co-operation from your side . . . I feel certain that what you have done so willingly to help us will reap its reward in a smooth introduction into service of this new aircraft." [22]

As preparations for the introduction of the new jet airliners went ahead, Anderson led a four-man delegation to Washington to press for agreement on a route across the United States and on to Europe for Qantas. Edgar Johnston, as international

The Britannia was to suffer a spate of problems with its Proteus turboprop engines during its first year of service on the routes to Australia and South Africa. The Proteus used a reverse-flow intake system so as to reduce the length of the power plant; air entered an annular intake behind the propeller spinner and was drawn along ducts to a point halfway between the propeller and the wing where it turned through 180 degrees and flowed forward to the compressors. Ice was found to build up at the bend in the intake and then break away in slushy lumps, which could damage the compressor blades or cause the engine to flame out. The problem occurred only when flying through the intertropical fronts at altitudes of 16,000 feet (5,000 metres) and above. These conditions were not encountered on early flight tests in Europe and were first experienced in central Africa in mid-1956. Despite extensive flying in tropical areas testing modified engines, the problem was not completely solved until early 1958.

advisor to Qantas, and Neil Hay, Qantas legal advisor, were members of the delegation. It was to be one of the most important horse-trading deals in civil aviation rights ever effected by Australia.

Airline operations between countries are not possible without agreements between governments for the embarkation and dis-embarkation of passengers, cargo, and mail. These are made on the basis of self-interest and by weighing the benefits accruing to each side, often after the analysis of excruciatingly detailed statistics. The principle underlying the agreements is an equitable exchange of economic benefits. In some agreements, prior government approval on either side is necessary to vary the number of services provided. In others, service frequency is left to the judgment of the airlines under guiding principles governing capacity they are entitled to employ on the route. The Australian delegation to Washington was seeking amend-ments to the air transport agreement that had been reached between the two countries in 1946 and, as the Australian ambassador Sir Percy Spender put it in opening the discussions on 15 May, "to consider what amendments may be necessary to adjust any imbalance of benefits . . . arising from the present operations". Under the existing agreement, the US-designated airline (Pan American World Airways) was authorised to operate from the US to Sydney and, conditionally, to Melbourne. Qantas, as Australia's designated airline, was authorised to operate to San Francisco and, at its option, on to Vancouver. Both airlines were, in May 1957, operating four services each week in both directions.

Controversy and differences of opinion in negotiating air traffic agreements were always much more likely when they con-cerned the rights of airlines to carry traffic that neither had its origin nor its destination in the country to which the airline belonged (fifth freedom traffic). It was not disputed that an airline had the paramount right to traffic that had its origin or destination in its own country (third and fourth freedom traffic). Under the existing US-Australia agreement, involving primarily traffic between Australia and the US, only third and fourth freedom rights were involved. Now, however, Australia sought to carry its end-to-end traffic across the United States. Its argument was simple; it claimed its primary right to third and fourth freedom traffic between Australia and Europe, not simply between Australia and the United States, irrespective of whether that traffic travelled through the Middle East or across the Pacific. On the Middle East route, Australia argued, Qantas could carry this traffic from end to end; on the Pacific route it could carry it only about half way because the authorised route terminated on the west coast of the United States. By contrast, passengers could travel the whole distance on US flag airlines. It was, argued Australia, an anomalous position and gave rise to a serious imbalance of benefits between the two countries. Australia set out figures asserting that this imbalance of benefits for 1956 had been in excess of four to one in favour of the US airlines. What Australia saw as its third and fourth freedom traffic was carried as fifth freedom traffic by the US airlines.

Australia stressed its racial, cultural, and commercial ties with Western Europe and the United Kingdom. Trade between Australia and the UK approached in magnitude the trade between the United States and the UK. There had been a great flow of European migrants to Australia. Traditionally, air traffic had travelled along the Middle East route but Australia had calculated that for 1956 about forty-two per cent of the through traffic was using the Pacific route. Unsettled conditions in South East Asia and the Middle East had been a strong influence. So too had been the closing differential between the air fares for the two routes. Originally, with the North American route twenty per cent longer, fares had been appreciably higher across the Pacific. Now, there was a mere $28 difference in a total fare of almost $1,000.

Australia also pointed out that while it had only one gateway on the US west coast at San Francisco, the US airline had two, by providing separate direct services from both San Francisco and Los Angeles. It wanted Los Angeles added to the Australian route beyond the Pacific coast to New York and on to Europe and the UK.

Such was the essence of Australia's aviation case. Politically, the argument was that because of her position as the only European community, apart from New Zealand, in the South Pacific, Australia was of great strategic importance for western defence against communism in that part of the world. It was essential for Australia not only to have good communications with Europe and North America, but also to build up, maintain, and develop a substantial fleet of long-range aircraft. Such a fleet would be of the greatest importance in wartime as it was economically impracticable for Australia to maintain an adequate military fleet of transport aircraft for defence purposes. The United States, it was pointed out, was Australia's main source of civil aircraft, and Australia's continuation as a substantial customer of the US aircraft industry depended on the ability of Qantas to operate on a sound economic basis. All that Australia asked for from the United States was an equal opportunity to service traffic which, to Qantas, was third and fourth freedom traffic, but which to the US carriers was fifth freedom traffic. [23]

The Australian delegation was able to demonstrate statistically the volume and growth of the third and fourth freedom traffic moving between Australia and Europe via the United States and, eventually, the US delegation conceded that Australia had established a case for a route across the US. It was also agreed that rights would be conceded for the Australian airline at New York and beyond to Europe. Los Angeles was not conceded and the agreement was not clear on whether Tahiti could be included in any route across the Pacific flown by Qantas.

It was, in many ways, a remarkable achievement for the Australian delegation as no other country had ever been granted rights to fly across the United States. But Australia, in the time-honoured process of "equitable exchange of economic benefits" had, in its turn, to concede much. In exchange for the new route, Australia conceded rights at Melbourne, Darwin, and Perth and beyond to South East Asia (and beyond); to Africa and beyond; to Antarctica and beyond; and a new route to Australia via Japan. The Australian government accepted these American demands and the US-Australia air agreement was formally amended in August 1957. [24]

The director-general of civil aviation, Don Anderson, had also been heavily involved in the politically sensitive problems of Australian domestic aviation. The two main trunk operators reflected the political philosophies of the two political parties. Trans-Australia Airlines, government owned, had been established by the Labor Party in 1946 with the aim of running all internal services in Australia as a government monopoly. This Labor ambition had been frustrated by a decision of the High Court that ruled that such an interference with freedom of trade in interstate matters was unconstitutional. At that time, as Stanley Brogden points out in *Australia's Two Airline Policy*, only monopoly operation of interstate airline operations was contemplated. The conflict centred on whether this should be a private enterprise or a government monopoly. "The departmental policy until 1945", wrote Brogden, "was to grant operating licences only to one operator on any route; competition was at no stage permitted." The idea of a two-airline policy grew accidentally. Prevented by the High Court from establishing TAA as a monopoly, the Labor government was hardly sympathetic to ANA. "Employing the weapons of government control, Drakeford almost drove ANA [Australian National Airways] out of business in the late 1940s, the crisis actually breaking after his government was defeated [1949] in 1952."[25] After the defeat of the Labor government in 1949, similar accusations of unfair pressures, this time on TAA, were made against the Liberal-Country Party government. As David Corbett demonstrated in his *Politics and the Airlines*, the political structure of a country is usually reflected in the structure of its airline operations. Australia's closely matched two-party system was to become manifest in the continuing politics surrounding the evolution and maintenance of its domestic two-airline system. Throughout these political manoeuvres QEA, as a government-owned airline, watched the attitudes of the politicians carefully. As the Labor leader of the Senate was to ask in 1958, how could the Liberal and Country parties be committed to monopoly by a government airline on the overseas services and against it on the internal services?[26]

By mid-1957 the political debate on airline matters was again

Qantas House nearing completion, mid-1957.

at its height. Sir Ivan Holyman, chairman of ANA, had died on 18 January. His successor, P. W. Haddy, told Paltridge in May that ANA could not meet loan payments on its aircraft purchases. The private enterprise airline, under a private enterprise government, had in fact declared itself doomed without government intervention. ANA came forward with a proposal for a merger with TAA in which the government would hold a majority interest. Politically and commercially it was well outside the bounds of the possible. The government, however, was now under pressure to define its attitude. Should there be a monopoly of some kind? Should a two-airline policy continue? Should there be a multi-airline policy?

R. G. Menzies had written, as prime minister, on 28 March 1952 to Capt. Ivan Holyman in response to a much earlier proposal for a merger with TAA:

> We are opposed in principle to monopoly and will seek to avoid it wherever we can. We believe that competition between your own Company and TAA has produced advantages to the travelling public and has assisted in the creation of a remarkable technical efficiency of operation all-round. In these circumstances, the Government's strong desire is to retain both your own Company and TAA as major operators. I will go further and say that we would all regard it as a grave misfortune if ANA, whose long service to civil aviation is well known and appreciated, went out of business. But a merger as proposed by you would produce a monopoly. We have therefore decided to reject it.

Menzies went on to stress that in the light of that decision, his government had "most earnestly sought for ways and means of meeting what we recognise to be your current financial problems and prospective capital difficulties". Referring to the possible effects of ANA of any change in government, he wrote: "We are not unaware of the fact that so long as ANA has a precarious existence, dependent on current Government policy, it will have difficulty in raising the capital needed for the periodic re-equipment and modernisation of its fleet . . . I should perhaps add that we have discussed the future of the airlines in terms of two major operators because while we recognise and value the place of the smaller airlines, we believe that all experience indicates that in our present state of development there is no room for more than two major national operators if the necessary standards of efficiency are to be maintained." He outlined proposals that the government had adopted to ensure that each of the two major operators could "operate on a basis of solvency". They were, in essence, to give ANA a proper and substantial share of airmail; that government business, transacted on government voucher, be freely available to both airlines; that current air route charges be substantially reduced; that the government assist financially each operator to acquire new equipment by appropriate financial processes; that routes, timetables, fares, and freight rates be made the subject of rationalisation. "We therefore propose", wrote Menzies, "that if in point of principle you accept what I have set down . . . we should execute an agreement between the Commonwealth and your Company. Indeed, I would think it advantageous . . . that TAA should also be a party to the contract. If and when such a contract is executed, we propose that it be taken up and ratified by an Act of Parliament, thus achieving the maximum force for its provisions."[27] Holyman accepted these proposals in principle and the Civil Aviation Agreement Act was passed by Parliament on 30 October 1952. (Trans-Australia Airlines, the operating name for the Australian National Airlines Commission, was not a party in law to the enacted agreement but it was, of course, bound to observe government policy.) There was now a legislative basis for a two-airline policy of interstate operations within Australia.

Menzies's letter of 1952 was still, in substance, the government's attitude in 1957 but the government was now no longer totally reliant on ANA for avoidance of a government airline monopoly, should the two-airline system break down. Ironically, as Stanley Brogden has pointed out, the 1952 legislation and agreements "had not created a two-airline system, though they had announced a two-airline policy". Two smaller airlines, Butler Air Transport and Ansett Airways, continued to operate, with Ansett increasingly able to challenge the two big operators on their main routes. Ansett was now to provide the government with a solution to its dilemma, should ANA cease business. As it became more and more evident that this was inevitable, Ansett made an offer for ANA on 30 July of £3,300,000. Acceptable terms were negotiated and the offer was accepted on 23 August. (The agreement between Ansett Transport Industries Ltd and Australian National Airways was signed on 3 October.) R. M. Ansett had saved the private enterprise government potential major embarrassment and, in doing so, was to acquire and use continuing and strengthening influence in aviation matters. As his ambitions strengthened, he was to look with increasing interest at the possibility of breaking what he considered the Qantas monopoly on overseas operations by Australian airlines.

C. O. Turner was now viewed with hostility and suspicion

not only by the Qantas pilots but also by the managing director of QEA's partner airline on the Kangaroo Route, Basil Smallpiece. Fysh set down private handwritten notes on what he considered Turner's attitude to pilots and senior staff in June 1957. The whole attitude of QEA management to the pilots was, he wrote, dominated by Turner who in his judgment lacked "the human touch, the understanding touch", a fault that would have been tempered by good organisation. The pilots' position had been misunderstood by management, he thought. The general manager thought them overpaid in comparison with the rest of QEA staff. The assistant general manager, Scottie Allan, took the view that "anyone can be a pilot", thus belittling the importance of the job. "Staff", wrote Fysh, "are treated too much like pieces on a chequer board instead of like human beings." He had to stop the general manager dismissing older employees. Fysh criticised the shifting of senior staff at short notice and the continuous shuffling of staff—"like playing on a piano, the people the keys". Turner, he wrote, was "adamant and unyielding in discussions . . . will not listen to the other fellow and cannot convey the impression that he has some understanding and sympathy with staff in their problems". He was "resentful of the slightest suggestion from myself and unyielding and intolerant in discussion". He had, said Fysh, bad relations with BOAC and Anderson and no aptitude for relationships except on a dictatorial basis. Yet, despite these deeply felt feelings towards his chief executive, Fysh was able to allow that these were the "human problems of a brilliant man [who has] done great things for the Company and Australia." His notes ended resignedly: "If the pilots have had to put up with him, then so must I for the good of the Company".[28]

BOAC's managing director, Basil Smallpiece, had been far from satisfied with QEA's attitude to BOAC during the course of the negotiations in Washington for Australian traffic rights across the United States. He was blunt when he told Turner in a telephone conversation on 28 June just why it was that he doubted Turner's frankness. On the issue of QEA's future plans for operation across the United States, he believed he had been misled. "Cedric," he said, "Let me say at this stage that I take a poor view of your not having told us before now of the general terms of your negotiations. We have heard of them through our own people in Washington, we have heard of them through the Americans, we have heard of them through leakages in Australia, but we have heard nothing at all from Qantas as such,

and it is not the way I would like to be treated by a partner."
Turner excused his reticence on somewhat shaky grounds.

> I fully appreciate that, and that is why I am ringing you now [he
> answered]. We felt we were sort of tied by reason of the negotiations
> and that we had to get the endorsement of our own Cabinet. I
> have had to come back here to get the endorsement of the Cabinet
> for the negotiations. We did not have a clear brief in Washington
> and there was very little use us telling you how they were going
> or what we were intending to do if we did not have the support
> of our Government. That is the position we were in. We could
> not officially tell you anything, except we did indicate generally
> to MacCrindle that they were asking for everything when we made
> it clear we were asking for beyond America . . . Now the fat's in
> the fire again . . . The Cabinet released it yesterday . . . [it] was
> too premature . . . We had anticipated that it would go back to
> the Americans.

Turner switched the conversation from the issue of trust to
details of the negotiations. He asked Smallpiece not to get disturbed that America had insisted on Australia-and-beyond traffic
rights in exchange for agreement with QEA's request. To use
these rights, said Turner, the US would have to prove that there
was a flow of third and fourth freedom traffic.

> Smallpiece: Well, that is a good point. Is that in writing
> anywhere?
> Turner: Not in writing but it is clearly in all our negotiations.
> Smallpiece: Can you get it in writing, Cedric? It is terribly
> important . . . we know from experience of their method of
> operation Tokyo-Hong Kong that any protestations they make
> about basing a route on third and fourth freedom traffic do not
> get honoured when it comes to actual performance.

Turner reassured him. If Pan American wanted to operate
a route via Sydney to South East Asia they would, he said, first
have to get approval from their own Civil Aeronautics Board;
then they would have to show Australia the flow of third and
fourth freedom traffic.

> Smallpiece: . . . As long as the Australian Government will stand
> firmly with the United Kingdom in applying that sort of rule quite
> rigidly I think that would go some way to remove some part of
> our uneasiness about the whole thing.
> Turner: Our feeling is that there is very little fear of major com-
> petition . . . We have the assurance of our Government that they
> will take action . . . [that] assurance is not in writing . . . that they
> will take action to prevent unfair competition.
> Smallpiece: I think we shall have to ask from this end for that
> assurance to be given in writing. As time goes by, memories get
> dimmer . . .

Smallpiece summarised for Turner BOAC's own experience in negotiating with the United States for rights across the Pacific. "They are continuing to ask a quite fantastic price for our rights across the Pacific and we just cannot pay it . . . I believe the talks broke up last night . . . We are just not going to pay the price . . . They were hoping to force our hand by having negotiated with you this route through to London. I always saw that possibility."

> Turner: Did the Americans mention their agreement with us?
> Smallpiece: They told us about it the very day they arrived.

Turner told Smallpiece that Australia was prepared to give the United States the QEA section of the Tasman route and that, as a result of the premature Cabinet announcement, "Anderson has had to hare off quickly to New Zealand to try and apologise to them". Australia was, said Turner, "obliged to New Zealand under [the] Christchurch [agreement] in certain complicated ways to keep the Tasman closed for TEAL. But that is not forever . . .". Australia had a civil aviation minister who was not in Cabinet, said Turner, "and a fairly new Minister. And he made a press statement immediately and the result is everybody is embarrassed."[29]

Despite this telephone exchange, Smallpiece wrote formally to Turner a week later repeating his criticisms.

> I cannot but take a poor view of your not having told us . . . of the general trend of your negotiations in Washington and what you were proposing to give away that affected us . . . The general impression I get is that if it had not leaked . . . and got into the press of the world you would still not have told me what you were proposing to give to the Americans on the Kangaroo route and in other ways. At the end of our telephone conversation you expressed the hope that we would not allow this trouble to come between us in any way. I could not agree with you more in desiring this. But I think you must treat us differently if you want to avoid the risk of deterioration in our relations . . .[30]

Turner did not attempt to hide his anger when he replied but he also took great care to document in detail QEA's position, as he saw it.

> I am deeply concerned that, notwithstanding my telephone call and explanations to you . . . you still chose, some days later, to suggest that but for what you call leakages I would deliberately have withheld from you information which you were entitled to get . . . I have tried hard to find an explanation of your extraordinary outburst. I can only conclude that it was written under very severe mental stress . . . There is obviously something else

bothering you and I believe it arises from your having viewed the BOAC-QEA partnership for so very long from one end only. You have never been to Australia . . . Don't you think that it is high time that you, as Managing Director of BOAC, paid us a visit? There are many things that obviously need to be straightened out between us . . .

Turner pointed out that he himself had made four visits to the United Kingdom in the past eighteen months. He detailed the discussions that had taken place "for the record" and concluded:

There seems to me to be a complete lack of understanding on your part of the QEA problems of operating a Pacific service . . . Your letter seems to imply that Australia has no rights to complete air transport agreements affecting the Kangaroo route without your previous knowledge and endorsement. I would point out that the UK, as well as the Australian Government, has completed a large number of air transport agreements over the postwar years, many of which affect the traffic in varying degree – some quite seriously, and generally it is the UK agreements which have prejudiced the pool revenue most . . . It is clearly unreasonable and illogical to suggest as your letter does that Australia alone has let America into the Kangaroo route. The United Kingdom has done much more than Australia has . . . We here realise, of course, that the UK did so as the necessary price for rights which they needed vitally . . . When the revised Australia-US Air Transport Agreement is signed between the Governments we will deal with future plans, but for mutual planning to be effective it has become necessary to record the above views in the hope that by being frank our misunderstandings can be cleared away . . .[31]

Turner's strong letter drew a conciliatory letter from Smallpiece.

It is evident that you do not appreciate the depth of feeling and the shock caused here by your readiness to let the Americans in on the Kangaroo route [he wrote]. I do not think you should write of [my] letter as being written under stress; it was written more in sorrow than in anger. However, I do not believe the interests of the partnership, or of either of our two organisations, will be best served by pursuing a lengthy argument in correspondence. So I do not propose to take your letter point by point . . . I admit that I ought to have been out to Australia . . . and promise you that it will be the first major trip I make.[32]

While the Washington negotiations had produced this storm between BOAC and QEA, within Australia there was nothing but mutual congratulations. Fysh congratulated the minister and his department on the success of the negotiations and was fulsomely thanked by the director-general, Don Anderson. "I would like to make it clear", Anderson wrote, "that the job in Washington was essentially a team job and that your general

Flying training on the Super Constellations frequently used Narromine airport, about 205 miles (330 kilometres) north-west of Sydney. VH-EAK is seen here during a training session in mid-1957.

manager and colleagues made a particularly significant contribution to it. Mr Turner was ever ready to place the resources of the Qantas organisation behind our effort and his personal advice and counsel were at all times of great value to me . . . You will also know, of course, that one of your directors, Sir Roland Wilson, was in Washington at the same time and he also played a very significant part in the negotiations."[33]

By 22 July and in anticipation of the formal signing of the revised Air Transport Agreement with the United States, Turner was able to report to the QEA board that operations planning had been completed to begin twice weekly services across the United States and the Atlantic from December. "Although the Kangaroo route has been hit very badly this year, by a combination of the pilots' strike, re-routings from the Middle East crisis, and the early introduction of the [BOAC] Britannias, we can see our way forward to 1958 with reasonable prospects of making a substantial profit on the operation, and a combination of the routings both ways should mean we should more than break even. Much does, of course, depend on further planning with BOAC."[34] The partnership was, despite all, still intact and still essential.

The effect of the introduction by BOAC of Britannias on part of the Kangaroo Route and the QEA reaction to it illustrated the ever-present complexities and tensions in the resolution of detailed operational arrangements. Qantas had been notified that BOAC intended to run Britannias from London to Singapore, terminating there. It wanted these services to continue on to Sydney, making a fourth BOAC frequency to match the four frequencies by QEA. Turner told Smallpiece: "The introduction of the Britannias at very short notice, which coincided with our increase in Super Constellation frequencies to five per week, resulted in the financial return from the pool services being well below expectations . . . Being aware of the recognition within BOAC of QEA's assistance on operations during the arduous time of the failure of the Comet operation, and since then, we thought that you would be rather anxious to give some priority to assisting the Kangaroo pool services as Britannia time became available." Turner was also highly critical of BOAC's scheduling for future Britannia services that would continue on to Australia. Keith Granville, he wrote, had said it was extremely unlikely that BOAC would ever accept a schedule that called for BOAC passengers to be in the air for three nights when they needed only to be in the air for two nights. "The passengers he refers to are *pool* passengers", Turner emphasised. Granville's sentiments, however estimable, were not in the overall interests of the partnership unless applied to all pool services. "We strongly believe that the schedules should be changed and that they ought to be discussed between us as partners to achieve a sensible overall pattern, and that this should be done as quickly as possible to remove the atmosphere arising from this [Granville's] statement." Turner pointed out that with eight partnership schedules a week "we should at least be able to achieve a daily departure from London. The gap of one day in the present departures allows Air India to operate its scheduled services on that day to the detriment of us both." It was evident that the "atmosphere" between the partners, to which Turner had referred, was one of unpleasantness and mistrust. Turner was aware of the dangers of compounding their mutual lack of confidence by lumping all their disagreements under one disabling attitude of non-co-operation. "I do not think that our scheduling problems are in any way tied up with our trans-US trans-Atlantic problem, and we certainly request that they should be looked at as a separate problem," he wrote. [35]

Within days of this letter from Turner to Smallpiece, Fysh wrote to the Australian minister for civil aviation, Shane Paltridge, expressing the concern of the QEA board at British action restricting Qantas access to traffic on parts of the Kangaroo Route. "You may perhaps not be aware", wrote Fysh, "that on some recent occasions when it has been necessary to include additional stopping places on the Qantas route to London – specifically Istanbul and Bahrein – the UK authorities have imposed restrictions on the traffic which our service can pick up or set down at those centres . . . At Istanbul they have

[been] imposed to protect the interests of British European Airways . . . At Bahrein we have been denied traffic rights to all points on our route except Athens. Probably this ban has been imposed in the interests of BOAC non-pool services." (Qantas began landing at Athens in June 1957, making three calls weekly in each direction on the Sydney-London service.) The new restrictions, said Fysh, were quite contrary to the spirit of the partnership agreement. He requested that representations at the highest level be made to the United Kingdom "for the removal of these restrictions which prejudice the finances of the pool services, apparently in the interests of the UK non-pool services".[36] Quite clearly, while Smallpiece had no confidence in Turner's attitude towards BOAC, Qantas in its turn saw Britain as putting its own specific commercial advantage above that of the BOAC-QEA partnership whenever it suited them.

On 3 September 1957 the prime minister, R. G. Menzies, reported to Parliament on the comprehensive review of civil aviation that had been in progress during the year. By that date, of course, Ansett had not as yet concluded its takeover of Australian National Airways but Menzies was able to refer to Ansett Transport Industries as "the probable purchasers of ANA". The Ansett company, he said, "will automatically assume the financial obligations of ANA under the Civil Aviation Agreement Act if it purchases the shareholding of that company". Turning to international civil aviation, the prime minister referred to the government's intention to strengthen Australia's air links with both the United Kingdom and the United States.

> I am pleased to be able to report that early last month an agreement with the United States Government was signed in Washington which provides the necessary authority, as far as the United States is concerned, for the establishment of an Australian air service to the United Kingdom and Europe through the United States. In return, the United States has been granted approval for its airline to extend its services from Australia to Antarctica, South East Asia and Africa. The Government is conscious of the fact that a major political disturbance in the Middle East could easily disrupt the operation of our present air services to the United Kingdom . . .

Before Qantas could commence its new service, he said, it would be necessary to obtain the approval of the UK government for the necessary traffic rights at London. Commenting on Australia's agreement to grant a US carrier the right to take on and discharge in Australia trans-Tasman traffic, Menzies said the New Zealand government had raised no objection. "Air services between Australia and New Zealand are at present operated by Tasman Empire Airways, which is jointly owned by the Australian and New Zealand Governments. A conference at ministerial level has been arranged to discuss re-equipment plans for TEAL and to consider the possibility of closer association with Qantas." Menzies said that the government had been "taking a deep interest in the arrangement of air services in Malaya and Singapore which are in the process of important constitutional developments". Qantas had, he said, associated itself with BOAC in negotiations on the future arrangements for Malayan Airways services. It was proposed to authorise Qantas to make an investment in Malayan Airways equal to that made by BOAC.[37] (Qantas and BOAC each took up 32.9 per cent of the capital of the reconstructed Malayan Airways in 1957, representing a Qantas investment of £A339,554. The other shareholders were the Malayasian Federation government, the Singapore government, British North Borneo, Sarawak, Brunei, Ocean Steamships, Straits Steamship, and the general public.)

The prime minister showed his undoubted affection for QEA by opening the airline's impressive new head office building

The prime minister of Australia, Robert Gordon Menzies (centre), at the official opening of Qantas House, Sydney on 28 October 1957. The prime minister is standing in front of the boardroom mural on the ninth floor of the building. Sir Hudson Fysh is on the right and C. O. Turner on the left.

in Hunter Street on 28 October 1957. The building brought together, on its thirteen floors, staff who had been scattered through fourteen city buildings. It was a far cry from the small weatherboard structure that had served the pioneering Q.A.N.T.A.S. at Queensland's Longreach in 1922. Qantas was now the seventh largest international airline in the world. A packed passenger booking hall at street level heard the prime minister refer to the airline's humble beginnings and vast achievement. "The day will no doubt come," said R. G. Menzies, "when as well as having a statue to Burke and Wills and some of the ancient explorers, we will be having a statue to people like Hudson Fysh . . . Quite frankly," said the prime minister, "when I step into a Qantas plane, I feel I am coming back home. I'm in my own country, so to speak . . ."[38]

The atmosphere between the Kangaroo Route partners was improved by discussions in London between Smallpiece and Turner. Smallpiece told BOAC's regional representative in Sydney, Phillip Hood, that "things were going to be all right".[39] He sent Hood a copy of the BOAC board paper covering his talks with Turner which, he said, should form the basis of BOAC's relationship with Qantas for the future. "The

Arrival of VH-EAO *Southern Prodigal* on its delivery flight from Burbank, Sydney, 28 October 1957. It had flown Honolulu to Sydney nonstop, the first time this had been done by a commercial aircraft. VH-EAO was the first L1049 in Qantas service fitted with tip tanks. Before landing, Capt. A. A. E. Yates circled above Qantas House during the opening ceremony.

basic concept is that we are in partnership with Qantas on a fifty-fifty basis and anything which strengthens their position will also strengthen ours. Therefore there is no need for anyone in BOAC to fear they are stealing a march on us and getting ahead of us. I know that they have rights across the Pacific at the moment and we have not, but in all other respects we shall go ahead hand in hand on an equal footing . . ."[40] C. O. Turner, for his part, wrote amicably to Smallpiece setting out "how we might advise staff down the line of the policies agreed and how we might lay down some procedure to implement our agreement for the extension of the partnership to the Southern Cross route [via the Pacific]".[41]

The Lockheed Electra prototype made its first flight on 6 December 1957. When the Qantas round-the-world goodwill flight visited Burbank later that month, the Electra flew out to meet the Super Constellation. As the passengers left the goodwill flight, the Electra demonstrated its short runway capability by coming to a halt 330 yards (300 metres) after touchdown.

OPERATING CYCLE: Air is drawn in through an air inlet housing **(1)** and is directed to a 14 stage axial flow compressor **(2)**. The compressed air flows through a diffuser **(3)** to six combustion liners **(4)** where it is mixed with fuel and ignited. The maximum amount of energy is extracted from the hot gas to drive the turbine **(5)**. The power absorbed by the turbine is transmitted by a shaft forward to drive the compressor and also to the reduction gear **(6)** to drive the propeller.

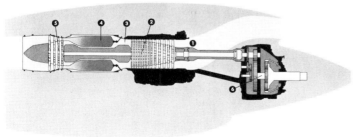

This drawing shows the location of the Allison 501 turboprop engine within the cowling of a Lockheed Electra airliner. The military derivative of the 501 engine was used on the Lockheed Hercules transport aircraft delivered to the Royal Australian Air Force in early 1958. From early 1960, Qantas serviced both types of engines at the Repair and Overhaul Shop. By 1972, when the last Qantas Electra was sold, Qantas was servicing engines from the RAAF Orion patrol plane which was based on the Electra and used an identical engine layout. Qantas continues to service Hercules and Orion engines into the late 1980s.

105

A second partnership arrangement for Qantas came into effect in November 1957 when South African Airways started a fortnightly service from Johannesburg to Perth, operating on alternate weeks to the existing Qantas fortnightly service. A revenue pooling arrangement had been agreed. The main Qantas fleet was strengthened, late in the year, by the delivery of two more Super Constellations, bringing the Constellation fleet to sixteen. Four de Havilland Otter aircraft were ordered for internal use in New Guinea. A proving flight with a Super Constellation was operated in November from San Francisco through New York to London and return in preparation for the trans-US and trans-Atlantic sectors of the new route to England. The company's new office in New York, which had been opened in July by Sir Percy Spender, was ready for business. A new office of impressive appearance and Australian character had been opened in London in October. Pilot training in America in association with Trans World Airlines had been under way. All was now in place for the introduction by Qantas of an airline service that circled the world.

Sydney, 20 December 1957. Sir Hudson Fysh and C. O. Turner watch Australia's minister for external affairs, R. G. Casey, as he farewells Capt. Ralph Bruce on Qantas's round-the-world goodwill flight.

With its planned ports of call painted down the fuselage, VH-EAO *Southern Aurora* departs Sydney on 20 December 1957.

Chief steward Syd Preece and flight hostess Pat Sparre during the goodwill flight around the world on Super Constellation VH-EAO, December 1957.

Capt. Ralph Bruce at the controls of VH-EAO during the goodwill flight, December 1957-January 1958.

On 20 December 1957 the Super Constellation *Southern Aurora*, with Capt. R. A. Bruce in command, left Sydney with thirty-two press, radio, and television representatives aboard on an extraordinary goodwill flight of 27,000 miles around the world. John Ulm, special assistant to management (later press relations manager), had arranged for them a succession of interviews en route on their twenty-day flight with presidents, prime ministers, church dignitaries, and others. Pope Pius XII and the Archbishop of Canterbury; the prime ministers of New Zealand, India, and Thailand; the presidents of Pakistan and India; Singapore's chief minister; a British cabinet minister and two junior ministers; America's undersecretary of state, State Department; and Lockheed's chairman and chief executive had all agreed to meet Australia's press on the QEA goodwill flight. It was the prelude to an even more spectacular demonstration of the reach of the Australian airline. The inaugural flight itself, in the new year, was to rival anything ever attempted before by any commercial airline.

Round the World 1958

Qantas inaugurated its round-the-world service from Melbourne on 14 January 1958 with the two Super Constellation aircraft, *Southern Aurora* and *Southern Zephyr*. One (*Aurora*) was to circle the world eastward, the other westward. Victoria's premier, H. E. Bolte, despatched the two aircraft in a blaze of publicity while Sir Hudson and Lady Fysh played host to three hundred guests at the official departure ceremony.

Both aircraft went north to Sydney for a second farewell function, then took off and flew in formation over the city before breaking away in opposite directions. *Southern Aurora*'s eastbound track (under Capt. M. Bamman) took it along the Southern Cross route through Fiji, Honolulu, San Francisco, and New York; *Southern Zephyr*, westbound (under Capt.

4

VH-EAP *Southern Zephyr* takes off from Melbourne's Essendon airport on the first leg of the inaugural round-the-world service, 14 January 1958.

Handing over special philatelic mails for the inaugural Qantas round-the-world service at Sydney, 14 January 1958. From left: Capt. Phil Howson, Qantas; J. J. Cahill, premier of NSW; Capt. M. Bamman; Capt. R. J. Davis; C. C. Smith, NSW director of posts & telegraphs; and Senator Shane Paltridge, federal minister for civil aviation.

R. J. Davis), flew through Djakarta, Singapore, Bangkok, Calcutta, Karachi, Bahrein, Athens, and Rome. Both arrived back in Sydney on 20 January. It was the beginning for Qantas of two complete round-the-world services weekly, one from Melbourne and one from Sydney. Two other Qantas flights connected with BOAC in San Francisco so that, between the partner airlines, there were four world services each week. Qantas was to begin flying the Atlantic as air traffic caught up with and passed sea traffic on that route; in 1957 the numbers using sea and air services were about equal at just over one million passengers each. In 1958 the airlines were to carry 1,292,000 passengers as sea passengers dropped to 964,000.

QEA and BOAC had reached an agreement by which both would sell the Qantas services from San Francisco to London and the parallel BOAC services. It was, in effect, an extension of the partnership agreement on the Kangaroo Route that had begun in 1934. For Qantas, it also marked a new emphasis on Melbourne as a major terminal port. For C. O. Turner, now fifty, it was a mighty achievement for the airline that he had

Queen Elizabeth, the Queen Mother, travelled on Qantas Super Constellation VH-EAA *Southern Sea* during her tour of Australia in February 1958.

Qantas earned an enviable reputation from the 1950s onwards for their superb aircraft maintenance, both mechanically and in appearance, inside and out. Typical of this attention to detail were the fittings specially made for the Super Constellation used by the Queen Mother during her Australian tour in February 1958.

joined when, twenty-three years before, its staff had numbered a mere thirty and it had made its first overseas flights from Australia. In the Queen's New Year's Honours List, Turner had been created a Commander of the Order of the British Empire.

Though the partnership talks in London between Turner and Smallpiece had done much to clear the air, there were still problems. A week before the Melbourne inaugural, Turner asked Smallpiece to give his personal attention to the issue of nonpool competition for pooled partnership traffic at Singapore. A planned new BOAC service terminating at Kuala Lumpur would, he said, make a second nonpool terminator to the Malayan area in competition with pool services. Recent traffic figures had, said Turner, shown a very serious fall on budget, mainly attributable to BOAC's nonpool Britannia services. He was disturbed, he said, that a directive had been given to the Kuala Lumpur office of Malayan Airways by BOAC that its nonpool services be given priority over pool services.[1]

Hudson Fysh was anxious, as the new year began, that Turner should ensure that close contact between management and chairman would continue. "On no account", he wrote to Turner, "should I be confronted with matters before the Board for their decision which have not been discussed by us beforehand . . . and in the event of new and important schemes and projects, well beforehand in the formulative stages. Our daily meetings", Fysh continued, "should continue, however brief . . ." He had noticed, he said, that less information had been coming to him than formerly from the press and publicity people.[2]

The extended partnership agreement between BOAC and Qantas had not been reflected in the attitude of Australian airlines to British airliners. Qantas and the two major Australian domestic carriers now pressed the government for permission to buy additional aircraft, but only Ansett-ANA included any British aircraft on their shopping list. Qantas had put forward to Shane Paltridge proposals for the purchase of five Lockheed Electra turboprops at an estimated cost of £8.035 million; Trans-Australia Airlines wanted to buy two of France's pure jet Caravelles for £3.218 million; Ansett-ANA sought permission to buy four Electras (for £5.418 million) and four Vickers Viscount 800 series turboprops (for £3 million). In all, the airlines sought approval to buy thirteen large turboprops and two jets for some £20 million.

Paltridge looked favourably on the Qantas proposal and considered the Electras ideal for use on QEA's secondary routes, with more capacity to make profits than competitive aircraft offering. Also, as Qantas had argued, the Electras could be delivered early enough in 1959 to make possible a very advantageous resale of almost the entire Qantas Super Constellation fleet. Their purchase would also, in Paltridge's view, enable the installation of special engine overhaul facilities for their Allison engines, engines that were used in the RAAF's C130 transport aircraft. The only aircraft competing against the Electra was Britain's Vickers Vanguard, powered by Rolls-Royce Tyne engines. Paltridge considered it a sturdy aircraft with fail-safe type construction. The Tyne engine he regarded as fully competitive with the Allison. But the Vanguard project in Britain, including its Rolls-Royce engine, had received no backing from the United Kingdom government by way of military orders. Development of the Vanguard would, he concluded, be completely dependent on civil demand, restricted to orders for forty aircraft from British European Airways and Trans Canada Airlines (compared with orders for 150 Electras by fifteen airlines). The Electras, in addition, had extensive military backing through US military orders for C130s. Qantas studies of the Electra and Vanguard were provided for the minister showing that the Vanguard, because it had been tailored to the unique operating specifications of British European Airways, was inferior in economic terms for Qantas purposes. Once more the British aircraft industry was to miss substantial Australian orders. The Qantas choice of the Electra for its shorter routes was to have consequences for TAA, Ansett-ANA, and TEAL and to overturn a Cabinet decision of 27 March under which, in an extraordinary intrusion into the management prerogatives of the domestic airlines, the Australian government dictated to TAA and Ansett-ANA the aircraft type on which their fleets were to standardise.

Cabinet issued a statement refusing Ansett-ANA's application to buy four Lockheed Electras and TAA's application to buy two French Caravelles. There was, said the government statement, an urgent need for a period of stability in domestic airline operations. The larger and faster aircraft requested by the domestic airlines would stimulate a competitive equipment race that could be disastrous for economic stability. Cabinet considered that a degree of equipment standardisation was desirable and that the 800 series Viscount should be the major unit of the two airlines' fleets. This dramatic government intervention in what was essentially a technical matter was motivated by political philosophy. The government was deeply committed to the continuance of a privately owned airline in competition with TAA but it was apprehensive about the financial consequences of a continuing equipment race. It was searching for a solution that would force stability on the two competitors and saw, quite correctly, that capacity was the key element in keeping them evenly matched. A much more elaborate structure, however, was to emerge to regulate the capacities of the competitors that did not involve dictating to them directly the type of airliner that they should purchase. The decision of 27 March was immediately challenged by Ansett. In taking over ANA and challenging the enormously successful TAA, Ansett did not want merely to follow in the footsteps of his rival by being forced to operate Viscounts. He pressed his case for Electras and, as the saviour of the private enterprise government's policy in Australia's domestic civil aviation, the government was in his debt and listened. Nevertheless, it was to be the influence of Qantas, pursuing its own interests and in no way concerned for Ansett, that enabled the government to reverse its decision on Viscount 800s in May. Qantas, which favoured the Electra for its own shorter routes, wanted to see it on the Tasman route, operated by TEAL, in which Qantas was part-owner. New Zealand, always far more closely tied to Britain than Australia, wanted the Comet IV for the Tasman. There was no possibility that Qantas would accept the Comet and, in the face of such pressure, New Zealand had no option but to give way. On the day that the decision in favour of the Electra was announced, the TEAL flag was flown at half mast over the airline's Auckland office. There was great bitterness in New Zealand and in Australia rumours abounded about the extent of Lockheed political influence and the manner in which it was exerted. (With the Electra choice there also came Australian and New Zealand decisions in favour of the Lockheed C130 military transport.) The Qantas choice swayed the Australian government and in May it decided in favour of the Electra for the two domestic airlines, restricting Ansett-ANA to an order for two of them and forcing two more on an unwilling TAA. TEAL was to have three Electras and Qantas four. (Both Ansett-ANA and TAA each then also ordered four Viscount 800s.)

Though the government had at least partially retreated from assuming the expertise necessary to dictate specifically the airlines' choice of equipment, it had made it absolutely clear that each domestic airline was to match the other in capacity and that each must match the other in fleet numbers. TAA, in effect, had been forced to abandon its own choice of aircraft and to accept that of Ansett. As Stanley Brogden comments in *Australia's Two-Airline Policy*, "the stage was set for the gradual erosion of true competition . . . The area for manoeuvre had been cut down to nothing."[3] The idea of a government-owned monopoly of civil aviation in Australia, so loathed by the Menzies government, was to become a government-backed duopoly. For the "private enterprise" arm of the duopoly, Ansett-ANA, it was (as R. M. Ansett himself acknowledged in the airline's 1962 annual report) to provide an effective government guarantee of the profits from half the domestic airline market.

Despite the conflict with New Zealand on airliner choice, the overriding importance of the QEA-BOAC partnership on the Kangaroo and Southern Cross routes was C. O. Turner's main preoccupation during 1958, as Qantas prepared to introduce jet aircraft into the fleet for the first time. There were, however, continuing issues of routes and traffic rights with other countries that had to be carefully weighed and argued. At the beginning of the year, the French authorities in Noumea adopted an unequivocal attitude of confrontation when they threatened to refuse permission for Qantas passengers to land there on the 16 January Qantas flight from Sydney. The French, following

By mid-1958, the problems with the Proteus engines on the Bristol Britannia had been overcome and the aircraft settled into service with BOAC on its trans-Atlantic, South African, and South East Asian services. The delays due to engine changes after ice damage gave the aircraft a poor reputation with the world press in 1957. The situation was not helped by one of the Series 102s on the London-Sydney service having the registration G-ANBG; the letters NBG are a well known acronym for "No b----y good!" in both the United Kingdom and Australia. On another type of aircraft at another time, this would not have drawn attention but BOAC felt that re-registration was called for and they changed G-ANBG to G-APLL in March 1958. Often referred to as GAPPLE by Qantas ground staff, it is shown taking off from Singapore in June 1959.

Taken about April 1958, this aerial photograph of Sydney (Kingsford Smith) airport shows some of the major building projects being undertaken in readiness for the Boeing 707 fleet due in late 1959. Starting from the area of light-coloured concrete at the centre, the following buildings and features can be distinguished: The new Hangar 96, with space for two 707s and its associated offices and support area at the rear, dominates all other buildings in the foreground. To the right of Hangar 96 are Hangars 20, 58, and 85 and two nose hangars built in late 1954 for the Super Constellations. Behind the row of parked aircraft opposite the QEA hangars, the Sydenham to Botany railway line can be seen. The long, narrow shape of the Engine Test House can be seen on the far side of the line and the new jet engine overhaul workshop is nearing completion. To the right of the engine workshop are the new aircraft kitchens.

long argument, wanted Qantas to have the flight authorised as a nonscheduled service, operating with special clearance; Qantas considered that, under existing agreements, they were entitled to operate the flight as a scheduled service. The satisfactory resolution of such conflicts about traffic rights was, of course, as central to the commercial success of the airline as choice of airliners.

Qantas had operated to Noumea under a temporary arrangement with France from November 1950 under which they exercised the five traffic freedoms between Australia and New Caledonia, and onwards to and from Fiji. A fortnightly service was increased to weekly in April 1951, without comment from the French. Since that date Qantas had varied its frequencies, discontinuing the Fiji extension in November 1955. In October 1957, in one of the various changes, the airline was authorised by the Australian government to revert to a weekly Sydney-Noumea service from an existing frequency of three services a month. The French director of civil aviation in Noumea claimed now that Qantas was not entitled to increase its frequency.[4] The battle continued through the first six months of the year, with Qantas operating on a provisional basis until the French high commissioner in Noumea, under instruction

from the French minister of Overseas France, granted Qantas special temporary authorisation for three months to operate on a weekly basis. France was not behaving whimsically; it was exerting pressure on Australia to further the operations through Australia of the French airline, TAI.

Qantas also considered in some depth in 1958 its bilateral agreement with Canada. The Australia-Canada air transport agreement, signed in June 1946, was the first postwar agreement negotiated by Australia. It came under the category of a "Commonwealth-type" or "pre-determination" type agreement and authorised the carriage of third and fourth freedom traffic. The two governments determined the capacity allowed on the route, which was shared equally between Canada and Australia, but the two airlines were authorised to determine the actual flight frequencies, subject to government approvals. However, when Australia began operating into Canada in 1947, an informal agreement was reached allowing BCPA to carry fifth freedom traffic and when, two years later, Canadian Pacific commenced operations, it too was authorised informally to carry fifth freedom traffic to and from Australia. This informal arrangement served until January 1954, when a Canadian delegation visited Australia seeking to replace the Commonwealth-type agreement with a Bermuda-type agreement, with the objective of enabling the Canadian airline to share formally and freely in the traffic between Australia and UK-Europe. Australia responded by requesting that its service be authorised to extend from Vancouver through Montreal to London. Canada was unable to agree. From 1954 notes were exchanged between Australia and Canada at six-monthly intervals authorising CPAL to operate weekly and Qantas to operate three times fortnightly. By mid-1958 Edgar Johnston advised Turner that Canada appeared agreeable to Qantas extending across Canada, but without rights to the traffic between Canada and UK-Europe, rights which CPAL itself exercised. If Australia, as it had at one stage suggested, were to prohibit CPAL access to the Australia-Europe traffic then, said Johnston, it was likely that Canada would terminate the existing agreement. "With that position in mind," he told Turner, "we can examine whether we should press the Australian authorities to take any further action with the Canadians in the interests of Qantas." He concluded that a routing through Montreal was unlikely to provide any substantial volume of traffic while the shorter routing over the pole, even if rights were given by Canada, would provide only extremely low load factors. Canada, said Johnston, can give us nothing of any real value; the only real value of the Australia-Canada agreement was the ability it gave Qantas to run a service to North America in the most unlikely event of the loss of traffic rights in the United States. In this situation, the Canadian airline was carrying traffic to and from Australia that could otherwise be expected to travel on Qantas. "Financially, therefore," he wrote, "it would be to Qantas' advantage if the Australia-Canada agreement were cancelled, even though we would lose the revenue we now earn from traffic between Honolulu and Vancouver." That point made, Johnston turned from financial to political realities. "The termination of this agreement by either party", he said, "would be an event of major political importance with bearing on Commonwealth relations, and I can see no case that we could advance that would induce our Government to take such a step." Even supported by the most rigorous logic and the most justifiable of commercial stances, Qantas could not avoid the constraints imposed on its interests and its competitive thrust by political considerations.

June 1958. Four Otter aircraft replaced the Qantas Beavers on the New Guinea internal services. Built by de Havilland Aircraft of Canada, the Otters could carry up to fourteen passengers. One of the Otters was an amphibian model. It was able to continue services to villages on the Catalina route while retaining the capability to use sealed runways such as those at Lae and Port Moresby.

That it had to compete vigorously for international traffic that it once shared only with BOAC was increasingly evident. In 1958–59, as a short, severe recession in the United States in 1958 caused world airline traffic to decline, nine airlines were operating into Australia—Air India International, BOAC, Canadian Pacific Airlines, KLM Royal Dutch Airlines, Pan American World Airways, Qantas itself, South African Airways, TAI (the French airline), and Tasman Empire Airways. In that year, they flew a total of 4,520 flights in and out and carried

a total of 144,075 passengers, plus 4,966 short tons of mail and freight. Of this total, Qantas flew 1,783 flights, to the UK via the Middle East and United States, to Hong Kong, Japan, South Africa, New Caledonia, Dutch New Guinea, the Solomon Islands, and Fiji. Of the 144,075 passengers carried by all the airlines, Qantas carried 42,557 plus almost half the freight and mail. Competitive pressures were compounded by the ebb and flow of political events. Although landings at Cairo, which had been suspended since the Suez crisis of 1956, had resumed in February 1958, operations into Djakarta were suspended in April following the promulgation of prohibited areas by the Indonesian government as an emergency measure of the civil war in that country. The reported presence of Indonesian rebel aircraft in the Celebes area, near the normal track of the Qantas Sydney-Singapore Skymaster route, affected operations. In May, the company decided in the interests of safety to withdraw its fortnightly service into Labuan. The Indonesian prohibited areas to Australia's north caused a costly diversion of 378 miles from the normal route between Darwin and Manila on the Hong Kong and Japan services. (The new 8,000-foot runway at Hong Kong's Kai Tak airport, however, opened in September 1958 and had a positive impact, ending the difficult operational problems associated with the old runway.) Overall, Qantas saw traffic volume increase through 1958 but the proportional increase in the airline's fleet capacity was greater and, as a result, load factors declined.

Qantas's last Catalina flight took place on 27 August 1958 when VH-EBD flew from Port Moresby to Lae. The retirement of the "Old Cat" marked the end of a seventeen-year association between Qantas and the famous American flying boat that began with the ferry flights for the RAAF from San Diego to Sydney in 1941. VH-EBD is shown here being pulled ashore for maintenance at Lae in June 1957.

119

Although Qantas had bought the Wentworth Hotel in Lang Street in 1950, motivated by the chronic shortage of first class accommodation in Sydney, it became evident that it could not hope to satisfy the airline's needs as airline passenger traffic, on Qantas and its competitors, continued to grow strongly from year to year. The Wentworth had 113 rooms and beds for 161 people and because Qantas Wentworth Holdings (the company that, registered on 17 November 1950, owned it) invested heavily in upgrading it, it steadily increased its profits each year. In 1953 the adjoining block of land was bought, with extension of the hotel in mind. As Sydney's accommodation shortage continued, the Qantas Wentworth Holdings board considered replacing the old hotel with a new one on the same site but were restrained by memories of the political difficulties that had accompanied the original purchase of the Wentworth. C. O. Turner, strongly backed by W. C. Taylor, were prime movers in 1955 in steps that were to lead to a new Wentworth Hotel on a new site. The site of the Union Club in Elizabeth Street, fronting Bligh Street, became available when the club instituted rebuilding plans. It was next door to the new Qantas headquarters building and, as a site for future expansion and a city passenger terminal, its purchase was approved on 13 April 1955 by the minister, Athol Townley, for £515,000. In June, Cabinet rejected a proposal by the Wentworth board to build a new hotel next door to the existing one. When the Union Club site was finally purchased in 1956, Qantas began planning to erect its new hotel on this land, next door to the airline's headquarters. On 29 July 1958, Turner put forward a proposal to build a modern, 400-room tourist hotel. "With the introduction of modern jet airliners on the Company's international services in 1959," he wrote, "allied with the operation of similar types by competing airlines and the addition of several new large ships on the overseas shipping routes between Australia, Europe and the United States, the limited hotel accommodation in Sydney will be entirely inadequate to meet the demand." The cost of the proposed hotel, said Turner, would be £3,900,000, excluding land cost.

It is proposed to finance this project by equity capital from a share issue by Qantas Wentworth Holdings Ltd to Qantas Empire Airways Ltd, other overseas travel interests and private shareholdings to the amount of £500,000 and by the utilisation of £400,000 of funds from the Wentworth Hotel Ltd. The cost of the building is to be borrowed on long term loan from an Australian finance house . . . The land site will be leased by QEA Ltd to

Qantas Wentworth Holdings Ltd for a 100-year term . . . The hotel will make an important contribution to the Australian economy. It is estimated that dollar expenditure in the hotel by US tourists will be $1.5 million per year.[5]

It was an ambitious proposal that was to encounter much political and hotel industry opposition before its final approval in August 1961.

The many complex issues that were now increasingly taxing the Qantas board and management led C. O. Turner to put forward proposals to the board for its reorganisation. Turner, as chief executive and general manager, now saw it as appropriate that he be designated managing director. These were matters of the highest importance, of course, but Turner chose not to bring them first to the attention of his chairman, as Fysh had specifically requested him to do in his new year letter. Fysh noted on 19 August 1958 under the heading "Board Discussion in Private Session on Company Organisation" that the board should discuss the action of the chief executive in making a recommendation to the board for its reorganisation without prior discussion with the chairman. "Does the Board wish to recommend to the Minister that the Chief Executive be made Managing Director?", wrote Fysh. "If yes, then [it must] consider the Chairman's position as to his functions. The Management has requested more assistance from the Board. How can this be effected?" Fysh canvassed the possibility of more board members or more frequent board meetings. "Before anything is done," he wrote, "it should be shown that at present the Board is not clearing Management matters quickly enough".[6]

These matters were discussed at a private session of the board on 21 August, but as the full board was not present no decision was reached. The members who were present—W. C. Taylor, Norman Watt, and Robert Law-Smith—"decisively agreed that the recommendations [from Turner] should never have come forward without the prior knowledge and agreement of the Chairman of the Board". In formal notes circulated by Fysh he wrote: "It was agreed that in future the Chairman should see and agree Board submissions of importance by the Management before they are put up, and that it is his responsibility to see that this is done". The directors agreed that the board might well be increased by two outside members, making a board of eight "which would still not be large by airline standards abroad". Fysh noted that "Board members felt opposed to recommending to the Minister that the Chief Executive and General Manager be made Managing Director but would be willing to consider recommending at a further Board meeting that the C.E. and G.M. have a seat on the Board, but to carry only his present titles . . . it has not been the practice in Australian Government Instrumentalities for the Chief Executive to have a seat on the Board, except in the case of the Commonwealth Bank". Board members agreed that they did not favour other members of the QEA executive "being elevated to the Board" but would welcome their attendance at board meetings if desired by the chief executive and agreed by the chairman. The board also discussed how it could assist the chief executive and his management group in easing their burden but nothing conclusive was decided. "Board members thought it would be very difficult to meet more often and there was no evidence to show that the Board at any time had retarded business or been in any way a retarding influence. The opinion was expressed", wrote Fysh, "that the Chief Executive should not normally serve on Boards of subsidiary or associated Companies and that the Chief Executive might be wise to retire from the Boards of Malayan Airways and Fiji Airways at an appropriate time. This should assist the Chief Executive."

Despite this apparent setback for Turner, the recommendations by Fysh to the September board were conciliatory to him. Fysh proposed that the board recommend to the minister that Turner have a seat on the board, with his titles and other duties unchanged. "The Board's recommendations, however, should be subject to the position being explained to Mr Turner, his co-operation being sought and obtained to make the set up work, and that he feels satisfied with the recommendation." Fysh referred to the issue of other members of the executive joining the board and commented: "I would like to say that I, for one, already regard Capt. Allan, as we do Mr Turner, as a 'member of the Board' and I would be happy to see him on the Board if this could be secured in some way. Perhaps this can happen on his retirement from his present position." The issue of more appropriate titles for senior QEA executives was also raised. There was, Fysh noted, a good deal of board objection to the title of "director". "I agree with one of the suggestions put up by the Chief Executive and General Manager, which is that there should be a series of Assistant General Managers — Assistant General Manager Commercial; Assistant General Manager Technical, and so on . . ."[7] (Turner was never, in fact, to be appointed to the Qantas board.)

Reaction against Australia and Qantas by employees of TEAL,

following the forced acquisition of the Electra, had been so bitter and so strong that New Zealand's minister-in-charge of civil aviation, J. Mathison, made a long speech of explanation and justification to the New Zealand House of Representatives. TEAL distributed it to staff in September 1958. Mathison stressed the importance to New Zealand of continuing operation of overseas air services for economic, political, and military reasons. "Tasman Empire Airways is our instrument in achieving these advantages and carrying out these obligations", he said. "It is an instrument half of which belongs to New Zealand and half to Australia." Co-operation with Australia "whatever others may say to the contrary" was, he said, a vital and inescapable factor in New Zealand's external aviation policy. "Some day New Zealand MAY want to operate independently its own external airline . . . but it is quite irresponsible to suggest that this can be done today." If it tried it would have to find a capital outlay of some £5 million in overseas exchange for fleet re-equipment. Commercially, independent operation would mean, he said, that New Zealand would have to share the trans-Tasman traffic monopoly with Australia.

> The position would be even worse if we wished to go further afield and take advantage of our reciprocal rights to operate, shall we say, to the North American mainland. To do this we should have to buy the latest long-range jets . . . We should also have to compete with large operators such as Qantas, Pan American and Canadian Pacific, with their widespread operations, big fleets and extensive financial resources. And compete for what? . . . The available traffic is not sufficient to make present trans-Pacific services a paying proposition and the advent of TEAL as a Pacific carrier would make the position worse.

Mathison referred to the conflict on aircraft choice.

> TEAL's directors recommended the de Havilland Comet – with the Lockheed Electra their second choice – and the Government supported this. The Australian Government and Qantas were in favour of the Electra, which they regarded as the best commercial proposition for TEAL and Qantas. There are good arguments for both aircraft . . . the New Zealand Government recognised that the Electra is a fine aircraft. It has been said that New Zealand gave way on the choice of aircraft under pressure from Australia, who forced the decision on us. This is absurd. The choice of aircraft was only one of many problems facing us . . . But the fact that Qantas will be operating Electras had a considerable bearing on the desirability of buying Electras for TEAL.

Mathison pointed out:

> At any time in recent years it would have been more profitable

for Australia if the Tasman traffic were handled by two separate airlines, one Australian and one New Zealand . . . TEAL is small. Its overhead costs are high relative to the hours flown, and Australia has in effect been contributing to meet these higher costs . . . I would like to take this opportunity of stressing that we have received very fair and in certain respects very generous treatment from our Australian partners.[8]

In November, Australia's minister for civil aviation, Shane Paltridge, thanked Hudson Fysh for his message of congratulations on the government's victory at the general elections. It meant for Qantas that the political environment at home, under a supportive prime minister and an able civil aviation minister, would continue as the airline entered the year in which it was to become the first non-American airline to operate international services with the new American jet airliners. The QEA Boeing 707-138s ordered would have payloads of 34,500 pounds, compared with the Super Constellation 1049G's 20,900 pounds. In an averaged mixed class seating arrangement they could take eighty-four instead of fifty-five passengers. Though each type had the same 3,500-mile range, the Boeings could cruise at 550 miles per hour, almost twice the speed of the 282 miles per hour of the Constellation. At the main QEA base at Sydney's Kingsford Smith airport, the £5 million development programme required for the jets was well under way. Work had begun on the diversion of the railway line; filling, drainage, sewerage, roads and water, and power reticulation were fifty per cent complete by year's end. The main structure of the repair and overhaul shop had been finished and occupation by engineering sections had begun in October. Building work on the jet engine test house and fuel tank farm had been completed in September. A Boeing flight simulator was due for installation in the completed technical training centre in April 1959. (In May 1958 a Redifon flight trainer had been installed.) Throughout the year, the airline's chain of sales offices throughout the world had been extended, with new offices opened in San Francisco, Honolulu, Bangkok, Osaka, and Perth. In March QEA had acquired its interest in the reorganised Malayan Airways (which had a fleet of eleven Dakotas plus smaller aircraft) and in the same month had completed the purchase of Fiji Airways, whose main service with de Havilland Drover aircraft was between the capital of the colony, Suva, and Nadi international airport. (The Qantas aim was to extend Fiji Airways services to nearby islands and feed traffic into the main trunk route at Nadi.) There were, at the end of 1958, 6,049 staff employed by Qantas and their average wage per week was £22.

The year also ended with a question mark over Australia's future relationship with India on civil aviation matters as discussions between the two countries broke down on service frequencies for Air India and Qantas. At the same time there were renewed pressures from England for reconsideration of the Comet airliner along with allegations that there were deficiencies in the performance of the Boeing 707.

India, on the Kangaroo Route between Sydney and London, was in a strategic position to pressure Australia for additional frequencies between the two countries for Air India. It was the view of Edgar Johnston and Turner that reasonable balance in economic benefits to the two airlines would be maintained on the basis of three Qantas services transiting India and one Air India service flying to Sydney each week, a stand that the director-general of civil aviation, Don Anderson, also supported. India rejected this position and demanded parity of frequency at two services weekly for each airline. "This is entirely unacceptable to us so the discussions broke down", Turner recorded in his December report to the board. "But we achieved our objective of having included with the Record of Meetings a concise statement of the Australian attitude designed to convince higher authorities in India that there may be some merit in the Australian case—and so deter any precipitate action." Qantas, said Turner, had no inside information about the discussions between their partner, BOAC, and Air India. The Indian attitude was no surprise. In May 1956 Turner had told the board:

> We know that the Indians for some time past have felt that the rights conferred on QEA under the bilateral negotiated in 1949 were too liberal, at the expense of Air India International and [that they] have been considering proposing consultations for the purpose of reviewing the bilateral . . . While the statistics which the Indians have supplied indicate that on two of the sectors concerned, between London and India and between India and Rome, the traffic carried has on occasions come very close to the limit authorised, DCA and ourselves believe that on a reasonable interpretation of the bilateral provisions it has not exceeded that limit . . .[9]

Britain had by no means given up the battle to persuade Australia to buy and operate the Comet IV airliner. Turner wrote to Fysh on 28 November: "As you are aware there has been quite a deal of controversy as to the respective merits of

125

the Boeing and the Comet. A good deal of propaganda has emanated from England, some of it from the de Havilland people, mentioning possible deficiencies in the performance of the Boeings. I believe you will be interested in the attached factual technical comparison which has been prepared by our Technical Department. In view of the reference to de Havilland's past history it must, of course, be kept strictly confidential."

The report, dealing as it did with a subject that had generated wide debate within Australia between the pro-British and pro-American camps as well as political pressures on the Australian government from London, provides an excellent case history of QEA's objectiveness and expertise in airliner analysis. It demonstrated a strength within the airline's management structure of central importance in the airline's history and, together with its intrinsic interest – dealing as it did in depth with one of the greatest dramas of postwar civil aviation – deserves recording in some detail. QEA's capacity for analysis had been boosted by the addition to the Technical Department of Dr R. R. (Dick) Shaw, formerly superintendent of aeronautical engineering of the Department of Civil Aviation. Dr Shaw, in August 1957, had been considering a move from the department to the position of professor of mechanical engineering at the University of Western Australia, which had been offered to him. Even so, there were political niceties that had to be observed if the government-owned Qantas were to tempt him away from the government's Department of Civil Aviation. Hudson Fysh wrote circumspectly to the minister, Shane Paltridge, asking for his approval to offer Shaw the new position of technical adviser in Qantas.

> The introduction of Boeing jet airliners and the increasing complexity of the technical problems of the industry makes it essential that we have the best possible talent in this field [he write]. As a result of discussions between your Director-General and our Chief Executive we have agreed to offer a position to Dr. Shaw . . . we have offered a salary of £3,400 per annum, which compares with his present salary of £3,150 from the Department and is about equivalent to that he would receive in salary and benefits from the University of Western Australia. It compares with the salary of £3,500 per annum at present being paid to our Technical Manager, Captain Ritchie . . . Under Section 30A of our Financial Directive, salaries in excess of £2,500 per annum must be approved by the Minister and we would therefore greatly appreciate your agreement so that the posting can proceed.[10]

The minister agreed and Dr Dick Shaw joined Qantas. In addition to his considerable qualifications, he had the great gift of lucidity and was to be widely recognised in the industry for his ability to communicate complex technical matters to non-technical people. That ability is evident in the analysis he prepared, in November 1958, of the relative merits of the Comet 4 and the Boeing 707. It was a paper, he wrote, that "is a frank but, so far as possible, objective analysis of the current status of the Comet 4 and the Boeing 707, seen from the airline point of view. [It] covers briefly the history of the two types and discusses the strengths and weaknesses of each as they now appear to stand. Since a very genuine attempt has been made to present the good and bad features of both types impartially, the picture presented is not a wholly one-sided one."

The Comet 4, Shaw wrote, had to be seen against the background of the Comet 1, which was in airline service from 1952 to 1954, and the "so-called Comet disasters" that terminated that service. "Having carefully analysed these events, and seen them against the long and consistent de Havilland record of lack of structural integrity, it is difficult to avoid the conclusion that the Comet disasters, far from being the result of a courageous step into the unknown, were the product of a consistent policy of excessively light structural design. While the de Havilland Company has made strenuous efforts to retrieve this situation since 1954, their prior record is such that it seems prudent to wait and see the results of their reformation proved in service."

These were comments that, if they had been leaked and publicised in the climate of the time, would have created an unprecedented political storm between Britain and Australia. Dick Shaw was, however, just as frank in his appraisal of the Boeing 707. "The performance of the Boeing jet," he wrote, "at least in the aircraft delivered to Pan American, is seriously below the anticipated figures. These performance deficiencies, together with the discriminatory anti-noise restrictions imposed at New York, have reduced (though not eliminated) the range and speed advantage of the Boeing over the Comet in the North Atlantic area. From the performance point of view, therefore, the Comet is at present in better shape than the Boeing."

Design of the Comet had started in 1946, for a 44-passenger, 2,200-mile aeroplane, conceived around four 5,000-pounds thrust de Havilland Ghost engines, with an all-up weight of 107,000 pounds. The prototype first flew in July 1949 and commercial services began in May 1952. In April 1954, following the two accidents off Italy, the certificates of airworthiness of all Comets were suspended. At that time the "oldest"

Comet in service had flown a little over 3,500 hours; seventeen civil Comets had been delivered to four airlines and there had been a total of four fatal Comet accidents. An improved Comet version, the Series 2 fitted with Rolls-Royce Avon engines, was in production at that time and a further development, the Series 3, with more powerful Avon engines and an extended fuselage was in prototype form. Following the revelation of design deficiencies by the investigation of the Comet accidents, production of Comet 1s and 2s was stopped. Most of the Comet 1s then in existence were used in research and testing and the bulk of the Comet 2s were substantially modified and ultimately delivered to the Air Force. After the Comet accidents, plans were immediately laid for the Comet 4, aerodynamically identical to the Comet 3, but with a redesigned structure and new engines. After a gap of over four years, the Comet 4 received its certificate of airworthiness in September 1958 and commercial Comet services recommenced in the same month.

With great clarity, Shaw set out the deficiencies of the Comet 1 in its brief operating history. They fell into three groups: miscellaneous mechanical and systems defects including numerous minor service defects, high control forces ("break-out" forces), and proneness to fuel tank damage in refuelling; aerodynamic and performance deficiencies, including "ground stall" in take-off and marginal landing performance; and fatigue deficiencies, in the pressure cabin and wing structure.

Shaw conceded that the miscellaneous mechanical and systems defects were probably inevitable in such an advanced design and that any manufacturer would probably have run into similar, though not identical, problems. He also allowed that the first of the aerodynamic deficiencies, "ground stall", was understandable in retrospect. It arose from the limitations of the then state of the art rather than any particular oversight by de Havillands. "It was nevertheless", he wrote, "the direct cause of two major accidents, including the CPA accident at Karachi, that killed everybody onboard." The marginal landing performance of the Comet 1, which caused several nonfatal accidents, he thought less forgiveable. The basic responsibility here, however, lay with Britain's Air Registration Board, which "adopted some dubious landing performance standards in 1951, probably with the motive of fitting the Comet into existing airports". These standards were quite out of line with contemporary standards of safety in the USA and elsewhere.

"The two most highly publicised accidents in aviation history", wrote Shaw, "are undoubtedly the in-flight disintegration of the two BOAC Comets off the Italian coast in January and April 1954." It was, he said, common knowledge that they were caused by the explosive propagation of fatigue cracks in the pressure cabin but the public understanding of the nature of the design weaknesses tended to have the wrong emphasis. "The basic error was not that which led to the early development of fatigue cracks. Nearly all pressurised aircraft have experienced fatigue cracking . . . What was basically wrong with the Comet fuselage was that the cracks developed in areas of very high and unrelieved stress. In this circumstance, after a very short development on a slow, progressive basis, the cracks reached a stage where further propagation was rapid and disastrous." (Shaw also noted that, contrary to the findings of the Indian court of enquiry, it was widely believed in technical circles that the in-flight disintegration of the third BOAC Comet near Calcutta in May 1953 also had its basic cause in fatigue cracks in the fuselage, though the progression of these cracks to failure was due to flight loads rather than to pressure loads.)

If the cracks had been solely due to the high pressure differential (between cabin interior and atmosphere) then, said Shaw, "it could fairly be claimed that the disasters were the unfortunate (but forgiveable) concomitant of a bold design step into the unknown. In fact, this is not the explanation." The analysis that followed was damning to de Havillands. Even in the light of the state of knowledge in the 1946–50 era it was, he said, difficult to understand the design of the Comet fuselage. There had been a considerable amount of experience of pressure cabin design in the USA at that time which, if followed, would have prevented the Comet disasters. "Compared with American practice, the Comet design raised pressure differential to roughly double the then current service figures. Yet at the same time the designers used a skin which was very little thicker at any point, and in many critical areas was substantially thinner than the skin in contemporary American aircraft. In effect, they applied very much larger loads to a structure which, on the whole, was less strong. The result was inevitable."

The Comet situation, he wrote, had to be considered against "the long record of structural failure which aircraft from the de Havilland stable have experienced . . . the de Havilland record of structural integrity is unimpressive. Of the eight series of aircraft with DH numbers of 100 and above which have flown, examples of at least four of the series have suffered in-flight disintegrations (killing all onboard in each case). A fifth series, the Heron, narrowly escaped the same fate, solely due to the extreme vigilance of a ground engineer of Butler Airlines." If the Comet 1 fuselage had not given trouble then, said Shaw, serious difficulties would have arisen due to fatigue of the wing structure. "Whether this would have led to in-flight failure or merely early grounding for spar replacement will never be known."

These observations on de Havillands and the Comet 1 were, of course, an integral part of the total Qantas process of evaluating the new Comet 4 series and its relationship to the Boeing 707. "Whatever one may think of the de Havilland company for its policies and practices prior to 1954," wrote Dick Shaw, "there can be no doubt that it has spared no trouble or expense to ensure that the Comet 4 Series is free from structural troubles . . . It is my considered view that . . . de Havillands have succeeded in achieving these aims." He nevertheless qualified this statement. "The integrity of an aircraft design depends not only on the philosophies and objectives of the Chief Designer and his section leaders. It also vitally depends on the integrity, ability and outlook of all the design staff, down to the most junior design draughtsmen. It is quite impossible for an outsider, no matter how technical, to assess a large firm for the integrity of its design detail on a new and unproven project. In this respect the common and prudent practice is to judge each manufacturer on its past record."

Shaw pondered whether "the de Havilland leopard [had] really changed its spots" and decided that he thought it "very likely, but one can't be sure." It was necessary to wait until the company established a record for design integrity by successful service of the Comet 4 before a positive answer could be given. Dick Shaw also had reservations about the buried engines of the Comet (unlike the Boeing 707, where the engines hung in pods). He thought the buried engines limited the level of safety because this layout "inevitably involves the use of concentrated wing spars, precluding a fully 'fail-safe' design in the engine area. It must also remain more prone to serious structural damage in the event of engine disintegration or engine fire than is a podded engine design."

Shaw's assessment of the merits of the new Comet 4 was more brief. The new series, he said, undoubtedly had a number of advantages when compared at that date with the American jets, and particularly the Boeing 707-120 series. "Because it has an appreciably better ratio of thrust to weight, and a lower wing loading, it demands appreciably less runway for take-off and has a much steeper climb-out than the Boeing. It consequently is better able to meet current anti-noise restrictions on jet operations. The relative runway requirements and noise characteristics of the Comet seem likely to offset the potential range advantage of the Boeing in certain areas, notably the North Atlantic." He also thought that the Comet's margin of thrust available when cruising would make it more flexible than the Boeing 707-120 as it then stood in fitting into air traffic control restrictions along congested air routes. His final comment on the Comet 4 was that because of the great amount of test flying done during its development, it was probable that it would comfortably meet its nominal performance figures. "The Boeing, on the other hand, seems likely to be delivered rather below nominal performance, even if it is within guarantees. This will decrease (but will not eliminate) the Boeing advantage in speed and range over the Comet."

Shaw next turned to the Boeing 707 in an analysis that was as rigorous and impartial as that of the Comet. Boeing, unlike de Havillands, had started with the design of large multijet aircraft for military use when, in 1945, they began design studies for a six-jet, swept-wing bomber (which ultimately became the B47). It first flew in December 1947 and in the years that followed Boeing delivered 1,200 of them to the US Air Force and hundreds more were built by other contractors. In 1948, Boeing began the design of a much larger and more advanced swept-wing, eight-jet bomber, which was to become the B52. The prototype flew in April 1952, and at the time that Shaw wrote, over three hundred had been delivered to the Air Force.

Paralleling the development of jet bombers, though trailing it slightly, Boeing had made studies of turbine-powered transport aircraft and had examined a very large number of configurations. In 1951 the first design study closely resembling the 707 was put together. In mid-1952 detail design on the 707 prototype started. Boeing embarked on that prototype with the double objective of getting a US Air Force contract for a jet tanker and, at the same time, entering the civil jet airliner field. The prototype flew in July 1954 and, soon after, Boeing was awarded its contract for the jet tanker version, the KC135. As Shaw wrote, 175 of the KC135 tankers had actually been delivered. Civil orders for the Boeing 707 followed in 1955 and regular airline services started in October 1958.

Despite this impressive record of military jet production, Dick Shaw commented: "At this point in time the general integrity of the 707 design, like that of the Comet 4, must be regarded as yet to be proven. However, it may be forecast with much more confidence." Boeing's vast experience with the B47 and B52 was in itself substantial grounds for confidence. "One can see in many engineering sections at Boeing detailed evidence of a progressive mastery of the problems of analysing and predicting the aerodynamic and structural performance of large swept-wing jet aircraft."

Shaw continued that compared with the Comet 4, "the 707-138 [the Qantas version of the 707] is larger, more advanced aerodynamically (and consequently a good deal faster) and has more range. Mainly because of these three factors it is also much more economical on a per seat-mile basis. All other things being equal, the speed and economy are absolutely decisive advantages."

The Boeing did, however, have deficiences and Shaw noted that the problems of performance were real ones. But there were some public myths. "It has also been thought necessary to discuss two other 'problems' which have been bandied about in certain British circles as defects of the Boeing series. They are not defects at all . . ."

On brochure performance Shaw noted that the 707 had barely enough engine thrust. Its thrust loading (maximum weight divided by maximum total engine thrust) was nearer the early Comets than was the Comet 4. As a consequence the Boeing tended to make runway demands that were near or at the maximum available. In cruise in hot weather it tended to be limited in its ability to attain an efficient cruising altitude or an economical cruising speed, or both. Yet it appeared certain that the Boeing 707-138 would have an actual performance appreciably below this nominal brochure performance in respect of both take-off and cruise. Guarantees, however, were likely to be met by the time of Qantas deliveries, though these were appreciably below the nominal performance.

Shaw had no doubt, nevertheless, that this situation would be a temporary one.

> Since the performance deliveries are so serious mainly because the thrust available from the engines is barely adequate, it is clear that they will be largely relieved by increases in engine thrust. Thrust increases are already being negotiated and some relief is certain by the time QEA gets deliveries. Moreover, the history of commercial gas turbines has been one of extremely rapid increases in power as experience accumulates . . . Continuing relief from engine development is probable as time goes by . . . However it is only realistic to face up to the fact that for the time being we must concede that some of the advantage of the Boeing over the Comet in respect of speed and range has been lost.

132

On the issue of wing strength, Shaw praised Boeing's excellent wind-tunnel resources and their advanced and accurate methods of estimating flight stresses in swept wings in flight. "The de Havilland Company, having less experience of large swept wing aircraft, and poorer technical facilities, has had to deal with similar problems in the Comet by making certain assumptions . . . [which] include appreciable 'margins of ignorance'." These margins of strength on the Comet had led to ignorant comment. "It is inevitable that the refined Boeing design, when checked by the relatively crude de Havilland methods, appears under strength. This is the origin of the press allegations on this point." Shaw commented acidly that this situation reflected "a deficiency not in the Boeing wing, but in the British analysis". It had also been alleged that at least on one point the Boeing wing did not qualify as fail-safe. "We in Qantas", wrote Shaw, "have been as sceptical on this feature of the Boeing as anyone could be, and we are now in a position to categorically deny this allegation."

The quantum jump in speed of the new airliners, made possible by the thrust of the jet engine, had required the design and development of new high-speed wing sections. These had inherent problems in loss of efficiency at high angles of attack (the angle at which the airflow meets the wing). Such high angles of attack came about as the aircraft reduced its speed and had to lift the nose to maintain appropriate lift over the wing. As a consequence all modern aircraft showed loss of performance on take-off if the nose of the aircraft was lifted too high too early in the take-off run.

"While the Comet 1 had this feature to a very marked degree, many other aircraft will exhibit this phenomenon", wrote Shaw. "For example, the Convair 240 is quite critical in this respect . . . The development of the picturesque title 'ground stall' for this phenomenon during the Comet program has the implication that it is a matter of black or white – an aircraft either has the ground stall or is free from it. This is quite misleading. The question is one of degree, not of absolutes." The Boeing designers, profiting from Comet experience, took precautions to minimise this problem in the basic 707 wing design, said Shaw. "Even in its basic form the 707 cannot be said to have had 'ground stall' in the same sense as the Comet 1." However, in the precertification flight trials it had been decided by Boeing that the basic 707 wing was not yet good enough. A leading-edge flap was developed and incorporated in the civil series, which according to Shaw was "product improvement"; the cer-

133

The first Boeing 707-138 for Qantas nearing completion at Boeing's Seattle factory in early January 1959.

tificated 707 was even less sensitive to attitude on take-off than the prototype.

Shaw summarised his comparison between the Comet 4 and the 707-138. "The overall balance is one overwhelmingly in favour of the Boeing as things now stand, and one which shows every prospect of changing in favour of the Boeing as the performance problems are overcome."[11] It was clear that Qantas, though remote from the world centres of aircraft design and manufacture and exposed to intense and continuing arguments and pressures at home and from abroad, meant to choose aircraft for their fleet on the strictest criteria of technical and commercial merit. It was also clear, as the date for acquisition of their new jets approached, that they were confident in their ability to make such choices with complete independence.

Higher and Faster
1959

Dick Shaw's comments that the Boeing 707 had barely enough engine thrust and therefore tended to make runway demands that were at or near the maximum were no airchair comparisons. Qantas, to its embarrassment, was forced to ask the minister for civil aviation, Shane Paltridge, that the runway length at Sydney's Kingsford Smith airport be extended before the Boeings were introduced. The minister was less than friendly:

> The first request made by your Company for extension of the runway, which was then 7,900 feet long, was made in December 1958 [Paltridge wrote to Sir Hudson Fysh]. This was based on your anticipation at that time that your Boeing 707 would require longer runways at Sydney than you had originally foreseen as being necessary. The north-east end of the runway was already then only about 1,200 feet from the boundary fence and it was pointed out . . . that my Department considered that any extension which would bring it closer to the boundary fence at General Holmes Drive would be unsatisfactory airport design practice . . . Nowhere in the world today is any major airport authority willingly designing or constructing runways for large jet aircraft with their ends closer than 1,200 feet from public areas[1]

Paltridge was ruffled on a second matter. Two days before Christmas, he had received a letter from Qantas requesting approval to give notice to Lockheed Aircraft Corporation of QEA's intention to sell six Super Constellations. "Approval is granted", Paltridge cabled Fysh from Perth. "But I take this opportunity of again, repeat again, indicating my annoyance that a request of this nature should be submitted to me a matter of hours before deadline. It would appear that this practice is regarded at your organisation as being pretty good tactics but I have completely different views."[2]

Fysh, in private notes for the board, commented that some doubts existed in Qantas as to whether the matter should have gone to the minister at all. He had been kept fully informed that the deadline for taking up the option with Lockheeds to trade in Constellations for Electras was 31 December. The Qantas letter of 23 December was purely formal "and indeed . . . despatched in pursuance of a desire to keep the Minister informed and in touch. No conceivable advantage would have been gained by deliberately withholding our request to the last moment as the trade-in deal had already been agreed, and in any event heavily benefited Qantas and the Commonwealth."[3]

As many important matters affecting Qantas depended on ministerial approval, an irritated minister was clearly not in the interests of the company. Fysh, always sensitive to ministerial attitudes, took up the matter with Turner on 5 January. "In reference to the complaint of our Minister that he is often not given sufficient time to consider important matters put forward by us for his agreement before an early deadline, we should take extreme care that we give no cause for complaint in the future – whether or not the Minister has had cause for complaint in the past."[4]

An issue of more substance involving the minister in the opening weeks of 1959 was that of salary levels for senior executive Qantas staff and the salaries of the chief executive, Turner, and his deputy, Scottie Allan. On 22 January the Qantas board approved increases in salaries for senior executive staff and, in accordance with the company's financial directive, submitted them to Paltridge on 6 February. Previous reviews, in July 1953, January 1955, and January 1956 had all been largely of a marginal nature. The board told Paltridge that in approving the present salary increases they had had regard for the very substantial increase in responsibilities over the past five years and the further responsibilities being placed on senior executives with current staff reorganisation moves. It was a reorganisation designed primarily to strengthen the top administration of the company to meet the pressures and requirements that would come with the introduction of Boeing 707s and Lockheed Electras during the year. That extra strength was being provided, in particular, by the creation of three senior positions: director of technical services, director of commercial services, and secretary and director of finance. (The board had overcome its objections to the title of "director".) A new position of engineering manager had been created under the director of technical services with responsibility for all aspects of engineering. Under the director of commercial services, provision had been made for two commercial managers, one for traffic and sales and one for planning. Fysh told Paltridge:

> The Board feels strongly that if the operations of Qantas are to be conducted successfully as a commercial enterprise, it is essential that adequate remuneration be paid to senior executives, and particularly to top management . . . Consequently the Board feels that the salaries of its senior executives should be examined and determined in relation to the salaries paid in commercial undertakings and that it may be quite unsound, in principle, and unfair to its personnel to continue to rely on comparisons within the Commonwealth Public Service, or even with salaries paid to quasi-Governmental authorities. Qantas is a highly specialised organisation competing against the world's best in similar organisations.

After full consideration, he said, the board had decided to recommend that the salary of the chief executive and general manager should be at least £7,500 per annum and that of the deputy £5,500. Fysh explained that the directors, "some of whom have wide experience of many types of business in Australia, feel very strongly that the Qantas executives are gravely underpaid". He reminded his minister of the present size and ramifications of the Qantas organisation.

> International air transport is an industry in which rapid growth and radical changes have been the normal and not the exception. Today we are on the threshold of jet airline operations in competition with the major airlines of the world. Few top executives in other industries in Australia have had to cope with such complex and rapidly changing problems of administration and finance as have the top executive management of Qantas; and since the operations of Qantas are international in character involving the maintenance of good relations in other countries the world over, there is a political flavour to everything we do. All of this calls for personal qualities in our chief executive of an exceptional kind . . .

Turner's present salary of £6,000, considered conservative when it had been implemented in July 1957, did not reflect the company's growth. Revenue had increased from £15.9 million in 1955 to £23.6 million in 1958. Assets, in the same period, had increased from £22.6 million to £47.6 million. "The great growth in the complexity of the technicalities," wrote Fysh "as well as the increased importance to Australia, both economically and politically, of these international air services, demands not only that we should have the very best in top management, but also that their work should be adequately remunerated."[5] On the salary levels of senior executives, Paltridge was reminded that Qantas was one of the largest business undertakings in Australia. Compared with Trans-Australia Airlines it had, 6,073 staff to TAA's 3,812 and, at £24 million, double its revenue. It was far more complex, dealing with bilateral agreements with other countries (there were 42 outstations in 23 countries); intense competition; effects on its operations from military and political disturbances; problems related to partnership commitments; the complications of inter-national fare structures; and interests in subsidiary companies such as Malayan Airways, Fiji Airways, and the Wentworth Hotel. Even within Qantas itself, it was pointed out, the senior executive staff were at a serious disadvantage compared with pilots. In January 1956 a senior, first-grade pilot received £3,305 per annum plus an overseas allowance of £200, compared with £3,350 for the operations manager. In 1959 the senior pilot received £4,095 plus £250 while the operations manager received £3,415.

Fysh paid Turner a high compliment when he set down the attributes needed for the airline's chief executive in his letter to the minister. He also wrote supportively and without any overtones of authority to Turner on 10 February in a general letter looking to the future. "I . . . congratulate you on all the achievements of 1958 and on your leadership as Chief Executive which has once again been the major factor in the success of the Company." Qantas was getting bigger and more complex all the time, he wrote, and so international that any major happening in the world could affect it. He expressed the wish "that we were not operating on such a dicey financial margin", and then said he wanted to discuss various matters "from my point of view as Chairman of the Board and with my liaison with the Minister and in maintaining a normal Chairman-Chief Executive contact". Fysh referred again to the minister's annoy-ance that he was not given sufficient time to consider important decisions. "Will you please watch this matter carefully?" Fysh wrote. "If we fail in this I expect to be asked to submit a weekly report on Company affairs."

Fysh also returned to his theme of the previous year that Turner should maintain a close liaison with him on all company matters, particularly those affecting the board. "I am anxious that such matters never come up at the last minute when there is no time for discussion or possible alteration before submission to the Board", he wrote. It was an echo of the minister's problem.

"All good wishes for the year, Cedric," he concluded, "and for the tremendous job of ushering in the Boeing 707 and the Electra services. I do wish to assure you that myself and the Board are right behind you. The great thing to watch is that Qantas continues to fully enjoy the confidence of the Commonwealth Cabinet, our Minister and the Director-General of Civil Aviation."[6] It was clear from Fysh's response to the minister's irritation over the minor matter of the authorisation of the Constellation trade-in deal, as well as his emphasis to Turner on the airline's need to maintain the confidence of its political masters, that the Qantas board and management (unlike their privately owned competitors) would have to direct energy and time to the satisfaction of Cabinet, ministerial, and departmental perceptions of proper performance.

The tone of Hudson Fysh's letter to Turner was conciliatory. That he longed for some small element of personal rapport with his chief executive is very clear from his personal writings and notes. He was never to have it. Blame for this extraordinary situation, when at times the chief executive of the national airline would not even speak to his chairman and at others would exhibit flashes of ill-temper and aggression, is not easy to apportion. John Fysh, son of Sir Hudson and certainly no apologist for C. O. Turner, experienced their conflict both as a senior executive within the airline and as an intensely loyal and devoted son. Yet he did not by any means simply condemn Turner. On the disastrous relationship between the two men he commented: "I think it went wrong because he [Turner] was able and he was ambitious. He would have liked to have ended taking my father's position. My father was not a clever man; he was much more wise than clever. I think a lot of people could not understand how he succeeded when he was not a wheeler-dealer, with clever argument. This frustrated people who were clever, like Turner." John Fysh, nevertheless, had a good deal of regard for Turner. "A lot of people had an affection for him. He always stuck up for his staff. Always. He defended them at board level and as a result he gained a lot of loyalty from his staff." He was, said John Fysh, reluctant to discipline those below him but, by contrast, could not get on well with his peers and his seniors. He fought with Don Anderson, the director-general, and "was completely mistrusted in Canberra", according to John Fysh. Fysh quoted one Australian prime minister, Sir William McMahon. "Billy McMahon said to me once: 'Your father is a great man, but if I may say to you, the problem we see down in Canberra is his inability to control his general manager." Turner, by his exceptional abilities, knew how to keep particular board members on side. "I think if it hadn't been for those board members," said John Fysh, "my father would on several occasions have had him dismissed. But he was supported by the board."

Possible grounds for the dismissal of such an able chief executive did, in fact, exist. C. O. Turner had a problem with drinking. He was not, when compared with others, a heavy drinker of alcohol and he was not an alcoholic. But, increasingly, from the time of the company's move to its new headquarters at Hunter Street, Turner was a consistent drinker. Colin Porter, who was his assistant for more than a decade and worked more closely with him on a day-to-day basis than any other executive, thought he drank far less than the majority of his executives but that his system simply did not tolerate alcohol well. "He was affected by alcohol in limited quantity but affected in a peculiar way", said Porter. Turner would fall asleep at public functions, sometimes for only a matter of ten minutes. When he woke, apparently oblivious to what had happened, he would continue talking. However badly he seemed affected, however, he remembered in precise detail next morning all that had been said to him. Turner had a room with a bar, known to all as "913", set up next to his office. It was open every night and senior Qantas people as well as outside guests dropped in to talk. It was not merely a personal indulgence for Turner. The talk with his executives was almost entirely Qantas talk. Turner ferreted out information long before it surfaced in formal reports, retained it with impressive accuracy, and used it. It was Porter's view that Turner drank because of the loneliness of his position as chief executive and the great demands made on him over long hours each day. "Everyone worked hard and long hours", said Porter. "It was the fashion to have a drink at the end of the day. Those sessions always started off as working sessions." Turner, he said, was always thought of as a tough, unforgiving character. "That was a facade; he was a shy man and a very compassionate man." When Qantas staff were in trouble from family accidents or tragedies, Turner involved himself personally in ensuring that their financial pressures were minimised. "Being a shy man [he] dodged as many official functions as he could [Porter said]. C.O. was best around a negotiating table when there was hard bargaining going on. On the other hand, Sir Hudson Fysh loved to socialise; he loved being in the public eye. So we saw develop a situation where both people tolerated each other and Sir Hudson became the public "image" and was seen publicly, whereas the man behind the scenes getting things done was Cedric Turner."

The two men became resentful of one another. "Huddy was chairman of the board . . . finding himself more and more resentful of C.O. and the ideas that C.O. was coming up with. Perhaps more importantly, he was resentful of the team that C.O. was building up around him. There were many things happening and, really, Hudson Fysh had extreme difficulty in keeping up with what was happening . . . Hudson Fysh had this difficulty, and for a long period of time." John Fysh, in his foreword to Sir Hudson Fysh's account of his childhood, early years, and involvement in the beginnings of Qantas, *Qantas Rising*, wrote: "Later my father confessed to the fault of having allowed himself too much personal publicity. He felt this had been unfair to some of his hardworking colleagues. This, together with his high moral stance about personal behaviour, led, he believed, to his being placed at some distance from his beloved Company in his retirement."[7] This "high moral stance about personal behaviour" was evident in, amongst other matters, Hudson Fysh's repugnance towards Turner's drinking habits. (It was also evident in his attitude towards propriety in marital relationships, though this was not directed at Turner.) But Colin Porter thought that C. O. Turner's drinking, for which criticism within and outside Qantas was to mount over the years, was overrated.[8]

By contrast, Capt. Scottie Allan (deputy chief executive and general manager), who admired Turner greatly, thought there was no doubt that Turner began to drink more than was good for him. "There's no doubt he became an alcoholic. You couldn't communicate with him. He wasn't maudlin but he was not comprehensible." He was not drunk during the day, said Scottie Allan, but "come night time, especially when he went away on trips in an aeroplane . . . there was nothing else to do. There are lots of people like that. You don't give them enough to do and they just get drunk. You've got to keep their nose to the grindstone, out of the way of the bottle. C.O. [Turner] was a worker and the work he did for Qantas . . . was remarkable." Turner inspired respect but was, said Allan, remarkably selfish; he had no friends.[9] Capt. R. J. (Bert) Ritchie, director of technical services in 1959 and later to become the airline's chief executive, saw Turner as a man of consuming passion, "a man of great dominance and, coupled with that dominance, dictatorial and pretty sweeping in everything. Also, a brain." Ritchie described the relationship between Fysh and Turner bluntly.

141

"There was a great deal of animosity, in fact enmity, between Turner and Fysh. Turner regarded Fysh as a fool . . . I regarded Fysh as a sincere, well-meaning, highly ethical man, but a simple man. Not able to match it with scheming people like Turner—and I don't mean that in a derogatory way. Turner was a general, seeing his way ahead. The grand strategy in Qantas was for many years, and certainly the important years, the brainchild of Cedric Oban Turner. That's the only way to state it." Ritchie, quoting W. C. Taylor (Chifley's able appointment to the QEA board), said that Fysh almost destroyed himself once a year in Canberra. "But he managed to hang on somehow in his simplistic, dogmatic, stupid, irrational way. But hang on. As the knives would start to go in, always he had the ability to pull his head back . . . I've seen him do that three or four times."[10] Capt. Edgar Johnston, who had known Hudson Fysh from the very first years of Qantas and who was to become deputy director-general of civil aviation (and was in 1959 international relations consultant to Qantas), saw C. O. Turner as the outstanding man in Qantas. "C. O. Turner was", he said, "the brains of Qantas . . . a strong man, a bit difficult, a bit outspoken. Other people didn't get on with him, but I always did . . . I can see him storming up and down the room." Johnston acknowledged the long contribution of Hudson Fysh to the airline but thought that in later years "he was an unnecessary cog there. He wasn't even trying to keep up with everything, but he wanted to be kept informed."[11]

In practice, in 1959, C. O. Turner attended board meetings of Qantas not as a director, but by invitation. He had no vote at such meetings. Colin Porter commented: "He was smart enough to know that when you are in that situation, if you are going to have a slanging match you don't have it at a board meeting. You have it outside the boardroom." In general terms, as chief executive, the board delegated authority to Turner to run the airline. But in those matters of policy in which authority was not delegated, it was Turner's role to go to the board with recommendations. For these, the board's endorsement was necessary, but on particular issues the chain of authority did not stop with the board. The terms of the government's financial directive to the airline constrained the board too, so that often the recommendations put forward by Turner to the board had to be sent on for final acceptance to Canberra. It was a measure of Turner's abilities and those of the executives supporting him that rarely were his recommendations not accepted. His management team resented Turner's exclusion from the board and

identified Hudson Fysh as the prime cause of this exclusion.
Fysh, however, always won the loyalty of those not in the
immediate hierarchy of top executives. Turner was seldom seen
at Mascot or on the floors of Qantas House. Fysh, said Porter,
"had the happy knack of going out to Mascot and greeting the
fellows in a way that Turner couldn't do. Two schools developed
in the company."[12]

C. O. Turner was well aware of his pivotal role in Qantas.
In a radio interview with an American journalist, he was asked
to define it. "I set policy", Turner responded bluntly. It was
a reply that infuriated his board, and none more so than Hudson
Fysh.[13] "Turner", said John Fysh, "used to usurp the
prerogatives of those above him if he could. My father saw him
as a threat. My father, by reasonableness and rational argument
could persuade people . . . but with C. O. Turner he could never
get to the basis of an understanding." There was, said John Fysh,
a campaign to try to embarrass his father at board meetings,
with Turner enlisting the aid of W. C. Taylor and Sir Daniel
McVey. "I think that C. O. Turner was the only person that
my father disliked to the extent of becoming a little irrational
about it."[14]

These considerable and tragic tensions between the two most
senior men in the airline had no noticeable effect on its
performance and accelerating success. Hudson Fysh, in the
public arena, was strongly identified with the pioneer struggles
of the airline and as the man who had headed it through almost
four decades of challenge and development. There is little doubt

The first Boeing 707 for Qantas
is towed out of the factory on
16 February 1959.

that, in that role, he met every criterion necessary to personify the organisation. Fysh had fought at Gallipoli, been decorated as an airman, flown as one of the airline's first two pilots, and had, to the best of his ability, been its administrative head in peace and war. He was regarded with great affection by his peers in the international airline industry and by the great majority of Qantas employees. Turner had been neither a serviceman nor an aviator and was little known to the general public. Yet, without any doubt, the success of Qantas, in the postwar years and in 1959 as it faced the great technological leap into the age of jet airliners, was due in large measure to the energy and particular gifts of Cedric Turner.

How did Qantas, under C. O. Turner, compare with existing major international airlines in efficiency? The yardstick used for comparative purposes within the airline was the cost of its basic "product", capacity-ton-miles, or the total load lifting capacity of the fleet in tons multiplied by the total route miles flown. While this was the test of efficiency in the final analysis, there were other tests. The number of capacity-ton-miles produced by each employee was one; so was revenue produced per employee. But these were not considered reliable enough as comparative measures. Even the raw cost per capacity-ton-mile had statistical shortcomings because of differing labour costs and productivity in the home countries of each carrier. In measuring itself against other major international carriers, Qantas attempted to adjust its raw costs to obtain truly comparable figures and did so by expressing the costs of other carriers as if those carriers operated with wage levels current in Qantas.

An analysis of Pan American, Trans World Airlines (international division), KLM, Scandinavian Airlines System, Swissair, Air France, and BOAC in 1959 showed that, in broad terms, labour costs at the carrier's home base was one-third of the total of service expenditure. In a comparison with these airlines, Qantas isolated this element of the total cost per capacity-ton-mile and adjusted it to reflect the Australian forty-hour week and Australian salary levels to place each airline on the same basis as itself. (These home base labour costs included maintenance labour, traffic handling, crew salaries, administration, selling, and passenger service.) All the carriers under comparison used predominantly American equipment, not affected by labour costs in the home country. Fuel costs, landing charges, and crew expenses, operating as they did on worldwide networks, did not differ materially between carriers. Labour cost at the home base was the only significant item requiring adjustment, though there were two other factors to be considered – the effect of short-haul expensive European networks on the costs of KLM, Swissair, and Air France and the high staff productivity of the United States carriers.

This 1959 comparative analysis underlined substantial differences in the costs structures of the international airlines. Expressed in Australian pence, the raw cost of producing a capacity-ton-mile was, for example, 39 pence for Qantas, Pan American, and KLM but rose to 48 pence for BOAC, 50 for TWA, and 55 for Air France. The average number of hours worked by employees each week was forty for Qantas, Pan American, and TWA; forty-eight for KLM, SAS, and Swissair; forty-five for Air France; and forty-six for BOAC. Weekly salaries expressed in Australian pounds varied from fifteen for Qantas to thirty-seven for the US carriers. On the basis of adjusting the other carriers' costs to Australian home base wage rates for estimating the cost per capacity-ton-mile, Qantas was among the best. (Air France was worst.) The Qantas cost in Australian pence was 39. Only Pan American was lower at 31 pence. TWA was 40, KLM 56, BOAC 51, and Air France 73.

Swissair and SAS had manhour costs much the same as Australia. KLM had wage levels less than half those of Qantas and one-sixth of the wage levels of US operators. Air France, despite very high load factors, required a subsidy to operate. BOAC, despite manhour rates close to those of Qantas, had costs about twenty per cent higher. The astonishing fact to emerge from the analysis was that the two American carriers, with wage levels two and a half times greater than those of Qantas, were still able to compete with other international carriers. The secret, in the Qantas view, was their remarkable productivity resulting in great measure from higher frequencies, dense traffic flows, and consequent much higher utilisation of both air and ground equipment. Qantas concluded that its position lay between the long hours/low wages European extreme and the high labour cost/efficient American extreme. Apart from the American carriers, favoured by size and high frequencies, Qantas compared more than favourably with the other international carriers. "Our non-labour expenditure per capacity-ton-mile is the same as that of the most efficient international carriers in the world even without making allowances for our relative smallness and low frequency of operation", the analysis concluded.[15]

The pressures to match competitors in strict commercial terms

The first of Qantas's seven Boeing 707-138s made its first flight on 20 March 1959. Because the Qantas 707s were built 10 feet (3 metres) shorter than any previous 707 model, the first -138 had to undergo tests by the US government's Federal Aviation Administration (FAA) to ensure that its handling characteristics had not been affected by the reduction in its length. The aircraft was flown with the US registration N31239 during these tests. Boeing allocated a two-digit code to each new airline ordering 707s. Qantas was given "38" and this code continued as new types were ordered. The figure "1" indicated that the first Qantas 707s were derived from the -120 series aircraft.

were no less severe than those in the operational and technical fields, in which Qantas excelled, and those where negotiations for routes and rights involved politics and governments. Canada was now expressing "serious concern" at the Australian attitude to its traffic rights across the Pacific, while Qantas fought to prevent what it regarded as substantial encroachment by Canadian Pacific Airlines into Australia-Europe traffic, an encroachment that threatened QEA revenue and was in every way considered prejudicial to the interests of the Australian airline.

The Australia-Canada Air Transport Agreement had been concluded in 1946 and, though it then exchanged only the first four freedoms, was subsequently amended so that the airlines of both countries could carry fifth freedom traffic (traffic that neither originated nor terminated in the country of the airline). The agreement provided that the capacity to be operated should be closely related to the traffic offering. For each airline the route in question was between Vancouver and Sydney but for CPAL, which also operated between Vancouver and Europe, the agreement made possible a direct service between Europe and Australia through Canada.

Qantas had tried to persuade Canada, in 1954 and 1955, that it too should be allowed to carry traffic through Canada to and from Europe, but in 1955 Canadian Deputy Prime Minister C. D. Howe told the Australian minister for civil aviation, Athol Townley, that Canada would not authorise this extension. It was then that Australia turned its attention to extend the Qantas route through the United States. Australia reacted to the Canadian attitude by examining the frequency of Canadian flights allowed into Australia. In March 1953, without the permission of the Australian authorities, CPAL had increased its fortnightly frequency to a weekly one. Australia had at once protested but, following strong representations from the Canadian high commissioner's office, CPAL was allowed to continue this weekly frequency on a temporary basis, requiring temporary permits at six-monthly intervals. For five years this ad hoc arrangement was allowed to continue but in December 1958 the Canadian high commissioner was warned that CPAL would have to revert to a fortnightly frequency from 11 December. The importance of these details is evident from the involvement of both the Australian and Canadian prime ministers. CPAL was given a brief extension to 11 February 1959 to enable adjustment of passenger bookings. In early January the Canadian high commissioner asked whether the Australian government would be interested in discussing a new pattern of air routes and a new bilateral air agreement. Australia replied promptly that it was not interested as the Australian airline had no plans for operations to Canada other than those currently authorised. By now, as Canada expressed its serious concern, this seeming detail of airline commercial self-interest acquired political overtones. The Australian Department of External Affairs emphasised that apart from civil aviation, "there were broader aspects to be considered" and it expressed the hope that some solution could be found that would be acceptable to the Canadians. Australia gave CPAL a further extension to 11 March to enable talks to be held and then extended this extension to 11 May. All this political activity at the highest level was hardly critical in financial terms to either airline. Each carried an average of eighteen passengers a week in both directions and no substantial growth in traffic was predicted. Qantas, however, saw the Canadian pressure as directed primarily at traffic between Australia and Europe and therefore in competition with both its trans-American services and those on the traditional Kangaroo Route.[16]

QEA's difficulties with BOAC on the BOAC approach to non-pool traffic on the Kangaroo Route, as well as misunderstandings with BOAC on the operations of Malayan Airways, paralleled the tensions with Canada. On 18 March, Fysh referred in a letter to Turner to the inherent difficulties of Malayan Airways and his fear that QEA-BOAC good relations could be affected. "Matters", he wrote, "have not improved and at present are critical."[17] In April, however, an important meeting between BOAC and QEA at San Francisco, attended by both Smallpiece and Turner, cleared away the doubts and misunderstandings between the two airlines and set the QEA-BOAC partnership course for the years ahead. In the opinion of BOAC's Sydney representative Phillip Hood, it did "more good than the meetings, at all levels, over the last few years".[18] The partners recognised the importance to each of the whole Far East region and that any policies either of them pursued in the area must stem from the policies of their respective governments. "They are agreed", the meeting recorded, "that they should always act as partners in relation to Far Eastern affairs and not as competitors."[19] The role of Malayan Airways was defined as that of a regional operator based at Singapore, a separate entity from Cathay Pacific Airways (in which BOAC held a fifteen per cent interest), but having a special relationship with it. The partners agreed that they would place no restriction on the desire of the governments of Singapore and Malaya to operate any services politically or economically important to them, but that uneconomic services should be operated at the cost of the governments. (They also agreed as general policy that they would not encourage a regional operator to acquire equipment suitable for trunk route operations.) "In participating in Malayan Airways," the meeting recorded, "the partners had agreed to promote Malayanisation as rapidly as possible. They are agreed that the rate of Malayanisation must be dependent upon the educational standards and training of Malayans employed by the company . . . The partners agreed that there should be a constructive policy towards maximum Malayanisation." On the issue of BOAC's nonpool services to the area, BOAC indicated that under the negotiations that were under way between BOAC, QEA, and Air India—"the Indian pool negotiations"—these nonpool services would be brought into the pool. BOAC "hoped that this would remove a long-standing source of grievance which had been felt by Qantas".[20]

As the Canadian, Malayan, and Indian matters proceeded, the nagging conflict on QEA's right to fly to Noumea was again brought forward. At the same time the more substantial issue of QEA's operations to and within New Guinea was receiving the attention of the Australian government.

An understanding on Noumea had been reached in November 1958 between the director-general of civil aviation, Don Anderson, and the authorities in France (later confirmed in correspondence) that pending the outcome of negotiations, there would be no further need for periodic applications to be made to the French authorities at Noumea for Qantas to operate flights there at frequencies greater than fortnightly. However, on 4 April the Australian Consultate in Noumea advised that the authorities there had received no instructions along these lines from Paris. They would, therefore, said the Australian Department of External Affairs in a cable to the Australian embassy in Paris, "insist that an application be made if Qantas wishes to retain such rights". The department said it did not intend to make such an application. They asked the French authorities in Paris to take urgent action to inform the Noumean authorities. [21] (Negotiations for a permanent air agreement with France broke down in December 1959 and the French cancelled the arrangements under which they operated from Brisbane to Noumea and Qantas operated from Sydney to Noumea.)

While these international matters were ongoing and forever subject to debate and change, the question of QEA's future on the route to Port Moresby and its operations within New Guinea involved government decisions that would permanently affect the airline's operations. From April 1945 Qantas had operated a weekly service between Sydney, Port Moresby and Lae (later increased to three times weekly). In July 1946, following a request from the administrator, Colonel J. K. Murray, Hudson Fysh visited New Guinea to assess prospects and on 20 November the first QEA Dragon aircraft left Brisbane, to be stationed at Lae. In 1948 Qantas accepted the responsibility of operating all air transport services for the Administration in Papua New Guinea, from centres at Lae, Madang, and Port Moresby. By mid-1952 the airline had 174 European staff in New Guinea. In that year Qantas had fourteen aircraft flying from its three centres to over one hundred places, either on regular services or on charters. Twenty-six pilots flew more than 35,000 passengers and almost a million and a half ton-miles of freight. Though the airline received a subsidy from the government, the operations were not profitable that year. "We never", wrote Hudson Fysh, "made much out of the New Guinea services and directors were still anxious about the poor security of tenure from the Department of Civil Aviation, our capital stake in our Territories organisation having become large, with half a million pounds invested." The QEA security of tenure, in 1959, came under serious threat.

There had been pressure on the Australian government from

Ansett for access to New Guinea, with Ansett arguing that the route from the mainland and the internal operations were not international services, but domestic. Ansett-ANA had inherited, with the takeover of ANA by Ansett, a shareholding in the Hong Kong-based Cathay Pacific Airlines. It was Ansett's ambition not only to fly to and within New Guinea, but to extend internationally and link up with Cathay. In 1958 the newly formed Ansett-ANA, having saved the federal government from the domestic airline monopoly that threatened after the collapse of ANA, applied for a licence to serve New Guinea. The government-owned Trans-Australia Airlines responded immediately with a similar application.

Qantas was now earning £1.86 million annually, or about eight per cent of its total revenue, from its New Guinea operations. Of this total, £1.25 million came from the trunk route to the mainland and £610,000 from internal services. Overall it more or less broke even in financial terms on the total operation, after charging £460,000 of its general overhead against revenue earned. In April 1959, it was the assessment of the government that a Qantas withdrawal from all New Guinea air services would involve a loss of £300,000 to £400,000. The government, at that date, recognised that the New Guinea services were an essential part of the Qantas financial structure and that any substantial reduction in the revenue earned from them would seriously affect the general economic position of the airline, particularly in view of the large sums committed to the purchase of its new jet fleet.

The government, however, had other considerations in mind. Qantas received each year a total mail payment of £4.8 million

The first Qantas jet engine test cell at Sydney airport was completed in mid-1959.

The 707 flight simulator in place at the new Technical Training Centre at the jet base. It was officially commissioned on 13 April 1959.

and, as long ago as 1954, the treasurer had indicated concern at the effect of this payment on consolidated revenue (as revenue from international airmail postage fees was not equivalent to mail payments). It was decided in 1954 that rather than reduce the mail payments to Qantas, the mail rate of 3.99 gold francs should be continued on the Hong Kong route and be increased on other routes to the same rate. As a quid pro quo, Qantas agreed to forgo its subsidy payments totalling £150,000 on its New Guinea and Pacific Island services and continue to bear the losses it incurred on the South African service. In mid-1958, however, international airmail postage fees were adjusted so that the gap was closed between the net postal revenue to the government and the mail payments to Qantas, so eliminating the call on consolidated revenue. In effect, the government benefited while Qantas continued to forgo the New Guinea and Pacific Island subsidies and absorb the South African service losses. At the same time, the costs of developing its round-the-world jet operations placed heavy new demands on its finances.

Despite government realisation of the Qantas financial position, it was firmly of the opinion, in mid-1958, that internal operations in New Guinea were essentially domestic in nature. It saw the trunk route between Sydney and Port Moresby as a domestic route. The minister, Senator Paltridge, held the opinion that if it were not for the financial effects of a New Guinea withdrawal and the loss of a valuable aircrew training ground, the Qantas board could have no real objection to a take-over of the New Guinea operation by Trans-Australia Airlines. While proceeding on the assumption that Qantas would for the present stay in New Guinea, he urged that steps be taken to change the situation in New Guinea to one in which two large airlines, one private and the other government, should compete. It was to be the beginning of the end for Qantas in New Guinea.

While all these matters of substance were in train, the over-riding preoccupation of Qantas in mid-1959 was its preparation for the introduction of new jet airliners on its world services. A joint Qantas-departmental Boeing 707 survey group was assigned the task of surveying and assessing the main airports on the Kangaroo Route for jet operations and left Sydney on 13 May. Over a period of six weeks, the group conferred with ministries and departments of civil aviation in ten countries and inspected thirteen airports before returning on 28 June. The mission was a fact-finding one but the group found that, with the exception of European countries, very little was known or appreciated about the problems peculiar to large jet aircraft. The group found it necessary to advise and make specific recommendations on many aspects of airport construction, operational techniques, and ground handling of both aircraft and passengers. Despite this lack of knowledge, the group concluded that jet operations along the Kangaroo Route could be conducted into all the airports that were surveyed, though with some restrictions. There was lack of air space at Djakarta, Singapore, and Karachi; runway length problems at Karachi and possibly Calcutta; and the general unsuitability of Ciampino airport, at Rome, for jet operations. Athens and Djakarta were found to be of poor standard and not recommended for Boeing 707 operation unless the level of communication and air traffic control was improved. The group found that parking positions agreed for the Boeing 707s would be at a considerable distance from terminal buildings, necessitating the use of tarmac transport. Refuelling would be of an acceptable standard but because of delays caused by air traffic control restrictions, ground air conditioning units should be provided at all tropical stations.[22]

On 2 July 1959, the first of QEA's seven Boeing 707-138 jet airlines, the *City of Canberra*, arrived on its delivery flight at Sydney's Kingsford Smith airport. This 707-138 was the Qantas version of the standard Boeing 707-120 but was faster and had improved all-round performance, particularly on take-off. A water injection system used on its Pratt & Whitney JT3C6 engines used 2,500 to 5,000 pounds of water on take-off, depending on conditions, and added about seven per cent take-off power. (Not all operations used water but it was needed for heavy loads over long ranges.) Its length, at 134 feet 6 inches, was only 18 feet more than that of QEA's Constellation L1049s and its wingspan, at 130 feet 10 inches, was a mere 7 feet longer. Both range (3,500 miles) and payload (34,000 pounds) were almost exactly equal to the Constellation. It was in speed that the new Boeings excelled. Cruising speed of the piston-engined Constellation was 275 miles per hour; for the 707-138 it leaped to 550 miles per hour (top speed was 595). Flying time between Australia and the United Kingdom through the Middle East was reduced from just over fifty hours to just under thirty-one hours. The Constellation cruised at 20,000 feet, where clouds and turbulence were a constant handicap; the Boeing cruised

San Francisco, 29 June 1959. Delivery flight of the first Boeing 707. From left: Mr W. Allen (president of Boeing), the Misses Allen, Mrs Allen, Mrs Howard Beale, Lady Fysh, Hon. Howard Beale, Sir Hudson Fysh, Mrs H. Birch, Mrs Ritchie, Capt. Birch and Capt. Ritchie.

above most of the weather in the still air at 35,000 to 40,000 feet. The new jet fitted perfectly into the Qantas traffic pattern, its capacity permitting the airline to maintain its high service frequency.[23] The existing Qantas fleet, when the *City of Canberra* arrived, consisted of sixteen Lockheed 1049s, five Douglas DC4s, eight Douglas DC3s and smaller aircraft. (Qantas vice-chairman Robert Law-Smith later recalled that Pan American had been ready to start jet operations to Australia six months earlier. It was not a move that Qantas wanted as the competitive effect would have been devastating. "I suggested to Don Anderson", said Law-Smith, "that perhaps we should make absolutely certain that the runway strength at Sydney would be adequate for Boeing 707 operations and that a departmental study should be undertaken". The director-general readily agreed with him. "The study", said Law-Smith, "took six months".)[24]

The *City of Canberra* took sixteen hours ten minutes actual flying time for the delivery flight from San Francisco to Sydney. The previous best flying time, by a Pan American DC7C, had been twenty-seven hours thirty minutes. There was a red carpet welcome in Sydney headed by the minister for defence, Athol

The arrival of the first Boeing 707 in Australia, 2 July 1959. A guard of honour of twenty-four Qantas staff representing more than six thousand staff worldwide waits for the passengers to disembark.

Townley, but press and public were wary of the noise level of the new jet and critical of the black fumes that issued from its engines when, on 5 July, it took off for Avalon in Victoria for crew training. Criticism by local council representatives was intense. But on 29 July 1959 the new jet left Sydney under the command of Capt. Ian Ralphe to inaugurate the first Qantas jet service with the minister for civil aviation, Shane Paltridge; the minister for air, F. M. Osborne; and the post-master general, C. W. Davidson, in attendance. Qantas was the first international airline in the world outside the United States to bring into operation the new jets, but there were forty-one Boeing 707s in service with American operators that had logged 30,000 hours in eight months of commercial operations, confirming QEA's

The crew of the *City of Canberra* pose with their aircraft before departure of the first Qantas jet service, Sydney to San Francisco, 29 July 1959.

The early Pratt and Whitney engines on the 707 produced very conspicuous trails of smoke on take-off. The aircraft shown here is VH-EBG, the last aircraft built under Qantas's initial order. Seen leaving Seattle on its delivery flight to Australia in late September 1959, VH-EBG has a spare engine fitted with streamlined covers under its left wing. This "fifth pod" capability of the 707 was carried over to the 747.

assessments of the aircraft's technical capabilities and passenger appeal. Fysh cabled Boeing senior vice-president Wellwood Beall that the send-off had been most successful. "Even the newspapers now being silent on smoke and noise", he added. [25]

Discussions with BOAC now followed to finalise planning for the introduction of Comet and Boeing aircraft on the Kangaroo Route but these were interim talks. The proposed tripartite partnership on the Kangaroo Route with Air India and a forthcoming IATA meeting in Honolulu precluded detailed planning before March 1960 but agreements up to that date were reached. BOAC agreed that it would not operate Britannias or Comets through Perth until the airport was suitable for QEA's 707s and Qantas, as a result of this decision, planned continuing operation of Constellation 1049s from Sydney through Perth and Djakarta to Singapore, shuttling back through Perth to Sydney. BOAC undertook to provide Qantas with a "wet" Comet charter from 1 November to serve points on the Kangaroo Route below 707 standard and to connect with this 1049 shuttle. This Comet charter was to operate with Qantas markings, with the Qantas logo being taped over the BOAC Comet markings. BOAC was to supply the Comet crews. The Comet, though never bought by Qantas, was at least to fly with Qantas markings for a brief period.

In September, the jet service to San Francisco was extended through New York to London. On 15 October, as a result of the QEA-BOAC planning meeting, three Qantas Boeing 707 services were introduced on the Kangaroo Route, supplemented by one Constellation 1049 service and a Constellation cargo service. BOAC, from that date, operated four Britannia 102 services on the Kangaroo Route via Darwin plus a Constellation cargo service. These were intermediate arrangements only, pending the introduction between November and the following March by BOAC of five Comet 4 services on the route. Qantas, in this period from November, retained their three Boeing and single Constellation services but these were to be supplemented by the BOAC Comet charter and the Constellation Perth-Singapore shuttle. In all these complex arrangements, the two partners agreed to continue to share revenue on an equal basis on the passenger services. The arrangements were now in place for Qantas to operate its round-the-world service with the new jets. (They became effective when, on 27 October, the Boeing 707 *City of Perth* operated the first Qantas jet service through the Middle East to London.)

Soon after the euphoria of the 2 July jet inaugural to San

Francisco, Qantas found its minister, Shane Paltridge, once again at odds with the airline. This time the issue was the operation of international charter flights, providing fares for common interest groups at lower levels than those approved for scheduled operations. Paltridge had made a statement to the Senate on 22 April setting out the circumstances in which international charter flights would be approved. He reminded Hudson Fysh, in an angry letter on 28 July, of his statement and pointed out that the only justification for the government's restrictive policy was to protect the legitimate economic interests of the regular airline operators in general, and of Qantas in particular. He had had, he said, since that date numerous representations from responsible and influential organisations for a substantial liberalisation of the government's policy.

"I am, therefore, surprised to find that the regular operators are the only operators currently seeking approvals to operate charter flights", wrote Paltridge. "A typical example is the recent submission by Qantas on behalf of the Australian Dental Association. The public impression is that Qantas is willing, if not anxious, to conduct the charter but that the Government has refused permission. In view of the growing public opinion in favour of charter flights this is an intolerable situation." Paltridge asked whether Qantas had fully explored the usefulness of IATA machinery to set up some sort of excursion fare. "You might please inform me whether this subject is likely to be discussed at the next IATA Conference, and if so what policy your company proposes to follow."[26]

Paltridge had cause to feel aggrieved. His statement to the Senate on 22 April had strongly defended the fare levels of Qantas as a scheduled international carrier.

The rights which Qantas exercises in overseas countries on its world-wide network [he told the Senate] are dependent on agreements which the Government has negotiated with these countries . . . These services perform an essential function . . . On the other hand, charter operations are by nature only supplementary to regular services. In some respects, charter services have unfair advantages over regular services. The charter operator has no obligation to perform a flight unless it is commercially attractive, whereas the regular operator is obliged to fulfil his advertised schedules whether individual flights are profitable or not. Moreover, the tariffs of regular operators are at fixed levels whereas the charter operator aims to set his tariffs well below those which the regular operator is obliged to charge by international agreement.

Extensive intrusion of charter operators into the legitimate business of regular services could, said Paltridge, "be most injurious to the maintenance of those services and is therefore not in the public interest".[27] To Hudson Fysh Paltridge wrote tersely: "I now find myself in the position where it will be necessary to make a further statement on Government policy to the Senate as soon as possible during the next session of Parliament. I would, therefore, like to have almost immediately a definitive statement from Qantas as to whether the announced policy has its unqualified support and if not, what variations it would recommend."[28]

The engines on the new Boeing 707s were pure jet engines. Put simply, all the air drawn into the front of the engine was compressed by rotating compressor blades, fed into combustion chambers where the fuel was ignited, and then passed at high velocity from the rear of the engine. Apart from the handicap of noise, the process was inefficient in providing the necessary thrust because relatively small volumes of air passed through the narrow engine at very high speeds. Within months of the introduction of QEA's 707-138s, new jet engine technology became available capable of passing larger volumes of air through the engine at lower speeds. It was called the fan jet (the British called it a bypass engine) and in it some of the first stages of the compressor blades were lengthened to make a mini-propeller inside the cowling. A proportion of the air entering the front of the engine now bypassed the combustion process, passed round the main engine core, and mixed with the hot exhaust effluent to pass rearward. (The early fan engines had a relatively low bypass ratio but the main thrust from modern fan engines comes from the large fan, or ungeared propeller, which is locked to the very front end of the engine's compressor shaft. The fan blades near the core of their diameter pump air into the other compressor stages of the engine but further out on the fan diameter they act like a propeller and the air they accelerate here passes round the engine.) Pratt & Whitney, in late 1959, were now able to offer fanned versions of their pure jet engines that not only provided substantial increase in thrust (from 13,500 to 17,000 pounds) but markedly reduced fuel consumption. The necessary airframe modifications cost per aircraft was approximately $1 million. Qantas was one of two airlines in the world (the other was American Airlines) to recognise immediately the wisdom of retrofitting their new jets with fan engines. Negotiations for modifying the old engines on the seven Boeing jets began in September 1959, barely three months after the introduction of the Boeing 707s. (Four additional aircraft ordered later were fitted from the outset with the fan engine. Altogether Qantas would acquire thirteen of the Boeing 707-138s, which, with the fan engine, were designated the 138B.)

Air India had, like Qantas, ordered Boeing 707 aircraft and, under the leadership of Indian industrialist J. R. D. Tata, planned to expand. It was in a powerful bargaining position with both Qantas and BOAC. The minister for civil aviation, Shane Paltridge, described the situation in a letter to the prime minister, R. G. Menzies:

> For some years now the United Kingdom and Australia, as well as a number of other countries including the USA, have had extreme difficulty with the Indians on bilateral air transport agreements. Because of its geographical situation India can exercise very powerful sanctions over those airlines operating along either the Kangaroo route to Australia or the route through Singapore and Bangkok to the Far East. In addition, India itself generates a very big flow of international air traffic, especially to Europe . . . The Indians are very conscious of their strength in this matter of traffic rights but fortunately have some appreciation of the heavy capital and other costs involved in jet aircraft operation which make desirable the reduction of these costs through pooling arrangements with other international airlines. They have already made a highly satisfactory deal of this type with the Russians on the route Delhi-Moscow.
>   It must also be admitted that the Indians operate a very successful international airline themselves which is presenting increasingly serious competition to all other airlines . . . The British reaction to this threat was to propose a pooling arrangement with Air India and discussions on this reached a fairly advanced stage before an alert Australian diplomat in New Delhi informed us of the situation . . . We took the opportunity of suggesting that pooling arrangements between British Commonwealth countries should be extended as widely as possible to combat the potential threat of the powerful airline blocs developing in Europe and the USA . . . The Indians have for some time been pressing us to reduce our frequencies through India and at the same time asking for approval to increase theirs . . . We have so far managed to withstand this pressure but with the impending introduction by Qantas of Boeing jets on the Kangaroo route, the Indians recently made a fairly peremptory demand for an increase in their Australian frequency . . . We accept in principle, of course, the desirability of negotiating a pooling arrangement with Air India.

Paltridge suggested that Menzies might find time, in impending talks with the Indian prime minister Jawaharlal Nehru in London, to mention the proposed pooling talks so that he might use his influence to have these convened before any further

The second Lockheed Electra built for Qantas, VH-ECB *Pacific Enterprise*, in flight off the Californian coast in October 1959. VH-ECB arrived in Sydney from Burbank on 7 November.

bilateral bargaining ("commercial haggling") took place. The Indians, he said, had in the past cancelled their bilateral agreement with the USA and had recently made one or two veiled threats to do the same to Australia.

For Qantas, whose main commercial artery was the Kangaroo Route, the negotiations that lay ahead with India were of the utmost importance. C. O. Turner and his team were thorough in their preparations.

At a preliminary meeting in Sydney with BOAC on 29 October 1959, Turner stressed the importance of agreement between the two airlines on all major issues before going to Bombay the following month for tripartite pooling talks. At the heart of such issues were traffic statistics and airline traffic rights. Air India had valuable traffic rights in Europe with, in particular, rights to Paris and beyond, Geneva and beyond, and Cairo and beyond. The airline also proposed to operate three flights weekly across the Atlantic and to build this to a daily frequency. Air India, BOAC pointed out, had made it quite clear that the Atlantic services must be included in the tripartite pool. Both airlines agreed that the Air India requirements would need careful consideration because of the favourable rights enjoyed by the airline. Turner pointed out that it would be difficult to argue with Air India without being in possession of the Atlantic traffic figures and Air India's entitlements. They agreed to ask the airline to make available all relevant information. The meeting ended appropriate with discussions on forthcoming arrangements to celebrate the twenty-fifty anniversary of the BOAC-QEA partnership at functions in London and Sydney on 10 December.[29]

In November, in Bombay, the three airline chief executives and their teams met formally to agree on the mechanism for bringing Air India into the long-established QEA-BOAC pool. C. O. Turner for Qantas, Basil Smallpiece for BOAC, and B. R. Patel, vice-chairman and general manager of Air India, had a task of daunting complexity. One prime object, set down in the preamble to the agreement, was "to attract more revenue than the total otherwise obtainable by the partners separately". Fysh wrote that the calculations for annual financial adjustment of the pool, and who got how much, were "most complicated and, indeed, difficult of comprehension by the ordinary man". The difficultly worded agreement, Fysh commented, "led to the employment of quite a large expert staff to unravel and execute its mechanics . . . Examinations of some of the final interpretations led to some difficult and heated discussions in the boardroom at Qantas House." Air India, Fysh judged, did well out of it, though there were some advantages for all. The agreement was formally signed on 4 December 1959 and later ratified by the boards of the three airlines and their respective governments.[30] Much simplified, the entitlements of each partner to participate in the pool were calculated mainly on national third and fourth freedom traffic (traffic originating or ending in the country of the airline concerned), with the figures based on actual traffic carried in the year preceding the partnership year. The total revenue traffic of the pool was then divided in this way, regardless of the amount of traffic actually carried by each partner. Expenses were not consolidated, each company bearing the cost of its own flights. It was agreed that the tripartite pool would be nullified if any of its three members authorised a second national airline to operate on a major segment of the route, thus effectively preventing intrusion by

On 14 October 1959, *Southern Aurora*, the second-last L1049G Super Constellation delivered to Qantas, becomes the first of eight L1049s to be traded back to Lockheed. The US registration N9722C was allocated to *Southern Aurora* for the return to Burbank. Ten months later, this same aircraft was back in Qantas service, providing capacity while the four L188C Electras were returned to Lockheed for modifications. To commemorate its return to the fold, Qantas engineers renamed VH-EAO *Southern Prodigal*.

161

the so-called independent airlines of the United Kingdom. Fysh pointed out that as some £60 million sterling was in the pool in the first year, a few decimal points could make a great deal of difference to the amounts received. (When the pooling arrangements were implemented, QEA services were well ahead of those of Air India and BOAC in performance and public appeal. The QEA board had reservations about the fairness of the pool agreement but felt, on balance, that they could not reject what had been agreed at so senior a level by the three airlines.)

Hudson Fysh later commented: "Perhaps what we paid out was worth the price. But for Air India it was magnificent. It set them on their feet in a big way and enabled them to go on through the years ahead and expand in a way they would never have been able to otherwise, and far in excess of their third and fourth freedom traffic entitlements."[31] The Qantas board had, in fact, little option but to agree to the document signed on their behalf by C. O. Turner in Bombay. Fysh told G. P. N. Watt (a director of QEA and chairman of the Australian National Airlines Commission that operated as Trans-Australia Airlines): "I have been placed in rather an embarrassing position in regard to this [tripartite pool] matter as no report has been received from Mr Turner on the several outstanding matters, and also in regard to the attitude of BOAC and Air India – who more or less conclude that an agreement is now sewn up, whereas no final information on the contents of the Agreement has come to me or the Board".[32]

The tripartite pool agreement with India was more than a complex commercial arrangement. Shane Paltridge took pains to set out its implications to the prime minister, R. G. Menzies. "In essence," he wrote, "it provides for all the services, with minor exceptions, operated by the three airlines in the triangle Europe-Australia-Japan across the Indian sub-continent as well as trans-Atlantic services to be operated in partnership. All revenue will be pooled and shared according to the capacity which each airline provides on the various services."

There was, he stressed, a clear acceptance of the principle that there must be no loss of identity by any partner and that each partner, while it had an obligation to operate competitive aircraft, preserved its freedom of choice of aircraft.

The new agreement leaves unaffected the existing partnership between Qantas and BOAC so that these partners can make adjustments between themselves if they so wish within the framework of their existing agreement and the historic Kangaroo route partnership may continue as before if ever the tripartite partnership dissolves . . . If approved the partnership arrangements will come into effect on 1 April 1960, except in the case of the Atlantic services when the pool commences on the date upon which Air India commences Atlantic services.

Paltridge told his prime minister that the agreement would undoubtedly have considerable commercial advantages for Qantas, and that the alignment of Air India in the pool alongside Australia and the United Kingdom also had important political significance. He took the opportunity to remind Menzies of other Qantas arrangements.

Of course we already have our association with New Zealand in our joint ownership of TEAL, but I have hopes for an even closer association between Qantas and TEAL by an arrangement now being considered under which the two companies will operate certain trans-Tasman services in pool. In the Pacific we have just finalised arrangements for joint UK-Australia-New Zealand ownership of Fiji Airways, which is the local Fiji airline purchased as a going concern by Qantas in 1958. We offered equal shares in the Company to New Zealand and the United Kingdom which have been taken up by both countries. Qantas still maintains its financial interest in Malayan Airways along with BOAC and the local Governments and local public . . . As to our relations with Canada, we have been advised within the last few days that the Canadian Government accepts the principles of Commonwealth co-operation which were developed in March and discussed with them in London in July. This is a most important advance by Canada away from its previous position of "splendid isolation" . . . [33]

In November and December 1959, Qantas received the four Lockheed Electra International prop-jet airliners it had ordered in May 1958. Domestic versions of the Electra had been operating within Australia since April 1959 and, worldwide, Lockheed had already received orders for 166 Electras from fifteen airlines. From QEA's point of view, the prop-jet (in which a turbine engine drove a conventional propeller) was an economical, high performance aircraft, well suited for its medium-stage operations to the Far East, New Guinea, and the Pacific Islands, and as a supplement to its Boeings on other routes. (The QEA aircraft, four Lockheed Electra L188C Mark IIs, were 104 feet 6 inches long with a 99-foot wingspan. They were powered by four Allison 501-D13 turboprop engines rated at 3,750 horsepower each. Passenger capacity could be varied between 50 and 75 and average cruising speed was 375 miles per hour.) Qantas Electra services were inaugurated on the

Departure scene at Sydney airport in late December 1959. Qantas Electra services to Hong Kong began on 18 December and to Tokyo on 21 December.

Sydney-Hong Kong route with *Pacific Explorer* on 18 December and, a few days later, Electras began operating on the Sydney-Tokyo service.

Technical and commercial studies by Qantas during 1959 had led not only to the decision to retrofit the new Boeings with fan engines but also to order three more Boeing 707s. Unlike its commercial counterparts in international airline operations, Qantas had to justify these decisions to the government. The minister, Shane Paltridge, responded cautiously on 8 December. It was, he said, an important matter needing careful examination and there was no possibility that Cabinet could deal with it before the end of the year. Despite Qantas advice that the airline did not expect any difficulty in financing the projects while still paying dividends to the Commonwealth, Paltridge requested assurances that the company's assessment was not over-optimistic. "The increase in loan capital", he commented, "also raises in my mind the question of whether the ratio of borrowings to shareholders' funds will be an acceptable one in the peak years." Lastly, he wrote, "I am advised that the Rolls-Royce Company is developing a new engine designated as the RB 141-11 which is expected to be available by 1962, and which might suit your purposes. I would appreciate advice whether you have investigated this possibility and if so what conclusions you have reached".[34]

Qantas responded promptly. It gave Paltridge comparative details of the Rolls-Royce RB141-11 bypass engine (later to be called the Conway) and the Pratt & Whitney JT3D1 ducted fan. Thrust take-off from Rolls-Royce was 15,400 pounds and from Pratt & Whitney 17,000 pounds (the latter using water injection); cruise specific fuel consumption was 0.814 for the British engine and 0.790 for the American. The RB141 weighed 3,560 pounds as against the JT3D's 4,025 pounds and the British engine was about twelve inches less in diameter. Delivery date for Qantas aircraft was October 1962 for Rolls-Royce equipped engines and July 1961 for aircraft with Pratt & Whitney engines.

These were the bare facts, on which Qantas commented: "It can be seen that the Rolls-Royce will be an attractive engine, though so far not sold. To ensure that it has received every consideration, visits have been made to both Rolls-Royce and to Boeing to endeavour to advance their co-operative effort in installing the RB141-11 at reasonable cost in our aircraft and at the earliest delivery date. The integrity of either engine is not questioned . . . We have no reason to expect the aeroplane's economic performance overall would be very appreciably different using either engine."

The Qantas arguments against the Rolls-Royce engine were neither technical nor operational, but financial. Boeing, said QEA, had no indication that any other operator was showing interest in installing the Rolls-Royce engine in the Boeing 120 series aircraft except Qantas "who therefore would be forced to bear the entire costs of design engineering and certification". These particular additional costs spread over ten aeroplanes for the British rather than the US engine would, said Qantas, amount to $1.5 million per aircraft. There would be, however, other more substantial costs involved.

Qantas provided details of the comparative costs for converting the initial fleet of seven aircraft and for installing new engines on three additional aircraft to make a total fleet of ten aircraft: for the Pratt & Whitney engine they were $31,610,000 and for the Rolls-Royce engine $50,219,000. Qantas put other arguments favouring continuity with the American engines. There would be less redundancy of spares and no redundancy of engines; a continuation of spares supply procedures; and continued use of expensive fixtures, test apparatus, and tooling. "It seems", Qantas told the minister, "that neither Rolls-Royce nor Boeing appear to be in a position to participate in a Rolls-Royce RB141-Boeing programme and, owing to the prohibitive cost to us, we cannot justify further effort in this direction."[35]

Qantas also reassured the minister on the financial implications of its re-equipment programme. Its projected profit of £1.185 million for 1960 was not considered unrealistic because for a great part of the year jet competition, particularly on the

Kangaroo Route, would be relatively small. Also, despite a natural growth each year in international air traffic of about fifteen per cent, Qantas had not reckoned on any improvement in profit in 1961 over 1960 because of additional jet capacity operated then by competitors. Progressive growth in revenue, estimated at £31 million for 1960 and £43 million for 1965, was considered reasonably conservative, though the main factor in the improving profit position in those years would come from the lower operating costs of the Boeing aircraft compared with piston-engined aircraft. Qantas financial projections were also, it pointed out, based on the relatively low load factor of fifty-eight per cent.

On the ratio of loan funds to capital, Qantas told Paltridge that by the end of 1961 there would be outstanding aircraft loans of £24.8 million compared with a capital of £17 million, or a ratio of 1.5 to 1. "In the airline industry, where funds invested in aircraft are recovered by way of obsolesence over such a relatively short period, loan funds are, as a general rule, the most satisfactory method of financing the purchase of new equipment, a particular advantage being that repayment of the loans can be made progressively out of obsolescence recoveries." Qantas compared its loan-capital relationship with Pan American, at 2 to 1; Air France, at 4.1 to 1; TWA at 0.8 to 1; KLM at 1.3 to 1; and Sabena at 3.7 to 1. These comparative figures, it pointed out, were based on past periods and would move markedly upwards. [36]

Fysh wrote to the minister on 1 December on the delicate subject of airport policy and runway lengths at major Australian airports. At Brisbane, though additional length would be needed using the existing 707's engines, none would be necessary with the new fan engines; at Perth, additional runway length was needed using either engine; at Melbourne, the restrictive nature of the Essendon aerodrome made the Tullamarine airport project the best solution. At Sydney, Fysh wrote, the 400-feet extension to the 07/25 runway approved by the government would only benefit Qantas financially for one summer in 1960–61 if permission was given to install the modified Pratt & Whitney fan engines. Qantas, said Fysh diplomatically, "is reluctant to offer opinions on the priorities of work to be done on runways as we recognise that this and the question of how Government money for this purpose should be spent, are entirely matters for the Government to decide". [37]

Paltridge replied angrily: "In an endeavour to help your Company, my Department did agree to construct a 400-feet extension [to Sydney's 07/25 runway], which brought the runway within 900 feet of the boundary . . . It is now apparent that the 8,300 feet provided will be sufficiently long for all the other types of large jet aircraft expected to use Sydney in the near future except your Boeing 707-138A [the QEA aircraft with the original pure jet engine], and that any further extension of this runway is something which is required by your Company alone." Paltridge reminded Fysh that on 23 November, Fysh had told him that because of the impending improvements to engine thrust from the new fan-jet engines, QEA could not justify incurring from its own resources the cost of runway extensions. He rejected Fysh's suggestion that the Commonwealth should extend the runway "from the point of view of overall airport policy" on the grounds that only Qantas required it. If Qantas was not justified in itself incurring the cost of runway extensions, he concluded, "I would think that the Department would be even less justified in incurring any such expenditure".[38] The extension, he said, had been contemplated only as a means of enabling Qantas to meet a situation in which its Boeing 707s could not operate from existing Mascot pavements with satisfactory payloads.

The year had been one of unparalleled complexity and pressure for Qantas management and staff. Despite the effects on revenue in the first half of the year from the aftermath of the 1958 recession in world air travel, revenue had risen from £23,871,102 in 1958 to £29,257,563 in 1959 and net profit had more than doubled from £419,097 to £853,963, though load factor had remained constant at fifty-six per cent. Staff strength had increased appreciably from 6,049 to 6,737 in a year which had seen the introduction of both jet and prop-jet aircraft. Fysh wrote to Turner on the last day of the year: "We can all agree it has been a hectic and eventful and, above all, a successful year. A tremendous amount of the credit for the great advancement made . . . is due to yourself and the great amount of energy and thought that you have put into it all." It had, he said, been a difficult feat to introduce two new types virtually simultaneously, and "some people said it could not be done". After discussing operational matters, Fysh concluded with a matter that was always close to his heart. "In regard to the Minister, he looks to me to keep him informed and . . . specifically asks for written information. The Minister is still talking about demanding to see our Board Minutes." The minister must, he said, be informed in advance on public matters affecting Qantas. "I realise that the Director-General keeps the Minister informed to a great extent", continued Fysh. "The other channel is through me, or yourself when you see him and this, in turn, depends on you and your officers keeping me carefully informed and not bringing new matters up out of the blue. All good wishes for 1960."[39]

Pilots, Politicians, Pools; Qantas Loses New Guinea 1960

While Hudson Fysh sent his good wishes as chairman to his chief executive in formal correspondence, his private feelings towards Turner were less amiable. He wrote:

> Turner gradually built up for himself a reputation for ruthless aloofness, later to develop into a form of egomania and an attitude of absolutism which I found it impossible to deal with effectively. In all the years of our relationship and daily meetings, I fail to remember even one single instance in which this self-concentrative Chief Executive expressed personal approval of any matter initiated or expressed by myself . . . How different it would have been, and how less painful over the years, if he had extended a few warm words of loyal support, and how I then would have flown to his side in an anxiety to help in his problems.

Fysh set down his thoughts on Turner's drinking habits.

> At this time when a pattern of difficulty was building up with the Chief Executive, not only as regards myself, but with the Board, a most unhappy and unfortunate innovation gathered force at Qantas House in the establishment of what I called a "drinking den", in the annexe to the Chief Executive's office. At nightly gatherings, the spirits often flowed freely with the top staff and visitors, and far too much was drunk. This was particularly unfortunate as the Chief Executive was constitutionally unable to drink without showing the effects of it. For instance, there was the occasion in Wellington, New Zealand, when our Chief Executive had to be led away from Senator Paltridge's table in a stupor, he having slumped forward on the table. The good name of the Company suffered, to my critical annoyance, and at times the Chief Executive so worried the Board that, on a number of occasions, members were detailed to see him, and curb his actions,

which were offsetting the good work he was doing for the Company in other directions. Despite bringing these things to the notice of my Board, they took no effective action . . . My view was that however academically good a Company head was, behaviour by him could not be condoned which, in the case of a lesser employee, would have occasioned dismissal.

In this atmosphere of internal difficulties we were having our other troubles. Trouble with tradesmen at Mascot. Grave rumblings from the pilots. Restlessness of top Management over salary increase delays. There were troubles between the Chief Executive and BOAC and TEAL. Senator Paltridge was our Minister and an almost perpetual state of warfare seemed to exist with him . . . the Board Room often being blue with attacks on the Minister and the Department of Civil Aviation.[1]

Industrial problems with pilots, which always posed the possibility of a rapid and complete cessation of airline operations and revenue generation, had become an increasing preoccupation of management as the new year began. The pilots had, over the years, become increasingly disenchanted with Australia's conciliation and arbitration system and the high cost of its legalistic rituals. They had, with ingenuity and thoroughness, investigated ways of escaping from this system and had, on 14 July 1959, dissolved the Australian Air Pilots Association, which had been registered with the Arbitration Commission. In its place, and simultaneously, they had created the unregistered Australian Federation of Air Pilots (AFAP). There were, as a consequence, now no agreed procedures for the settlement of disputes. The pilots took the view that they were now outside the jurisdiction of the act, while the operators resisted this view. The pilots asked the operators to recognise the new body and put forward proposals that were meant to reassure the operators by setting out specific restrictions that limited the strike process. TAA, in October 1959, proposed to the secretary of the Department of Labour and National Service, Henry A. Bland, that a trial of strength should immediately be initiated. Bland disagreed and proposed immediate recognition of the new AFAP. Qantas, on 23 November, asked for advice from the minister for labour and national service, William McMahon. On 8 January 1960, McMahon advised Qantas to accept the reality of the AFAP. By February the operators had agreed that this was the only course available. Concurrently with these pilot pressures in the new year, C. O. Turner received a formal letter from C. E. Oliver, QEA's manager Far East and Pacific Islands, advising him that at a meeting of senior staff, it had been determined to proceed with the formation of a Qantas Senior

Staff Association. "We thought you might be interested to know," Oliver wrote on behalf of the new association, "that as of today's date, of the total eligible staff, i.e. those not covered by the Company's grading scheme and with a salary of £2,000 per annum or more, all have now joined the association with the exception of one outstation manager from whom we have not yet received a reply." It had been decided, he told Turner, that the new association would seek an interview directly with the minister for civil aviation.

Oliver enclosed a copy of a letter sent by the association to the minister. "Over the past few years," the letter said, "there has been growing a deep and disturbing feeling of injustice amongst Qantas senior staff in relation to salaries." It gave details of increases paid to members of the public service, Qantas graded staff, and, particularly, pilots, which were not paid to senior staff members. "The expansion of the Company over the past few years, especially in connection with the Boeing and Electra, has led to marked increases in the responsibilities and duties of all our members since the general level of senior salaries was last fixed in 1956 on a standard related to December 1954", the letter continued. The minister was told that the senior staff were loyal and responsible but that they had "observed with growing concern the practical fact that the loyal and devoted service, in itself, has not brought commensurate financial return and that the largest and most immediate rewards have gone to those who have been prepared to use all the tools of militant unionism".[2] The new Senior Staff Association requested and was granted a meeting with the board of Qantas, with C. O. Turner, Scottie Allan, and Capt. R. J. Ritchie in attendance. There they repeated that there was "a deep sense of injustice felt by the Company's senior staff in regard to salary matters". Senior staff considered it inequitable that pilots and certain other sections of the company's staff enjoyed the privilege of salary adjustments as determined by the board, but that an entirely different procedure applied to senior staff. Senior staff expressed concern that the pilots were contemplating another strike. In regard to the salary increases granted to pilots since their previous strike, members of the association "could not help but feel that militancy had been rewarded". Because of this, the board was told, "it would be difficult in the event of another strike, to expect the same degree of loyalty and determination from senior staff". Hudson Fysh told the delegation that, following advice that Cabinet had the previous night decided on new procedures for salary reviews in Commonwealth instru-

In late January 1960, Super Constellation VH-EAA was returned to Lockheed for modification to a cargo aircraft. The conversion was carried out by Lockheed's subsidiary company, Lockheed Aircraft Service Inc., where this photograph was taken. Qantas supervising engineer, Clem Allen (right) checks the cargo door fittings with an LAS technician. On return to Australia, VH-EAA was to join the two L1049H aircraft, VH-EAM and VH-EAN, on the Sydney-London express cargo service.

mentalities that would be implemented immediately, he was hopeful that their problems could be resolved without delay.[3]

These mounting pressures from Qantas pilots and senior staff were no easy matters for the government, whose responsibility it was to co-ordinate and review salary levels in the Commonwealth public service and the various statutory authorities. There was, for example, a committee from the permanent heads of government departments (the Permanent Heads Committee) that met to review the salaries of particular positions in the statutory authorities, as well as a Cabinet Higher Salaries Committee for reviewing salaries at the highest levels. By March 1960 it had been agreed by these bodies that, while there should no longer be any necessary equality of salaries between similarly named positions in Qantas and Trans-Australia Airlines, both should retain their existing freedom to fix staff salaries, but up to a limit of £3,000 per annum. All proposals to determine salaries above this were to be submitted for approval to a committee of review whose members included the chairman of the Public Service Board, the secretary of the Prime Minister's Department and the secretary or deputy secretary of the Treasury. However, the salaries of the general manager and assistant general manager of both airlines were to be a matter for the Cabinet Higher Salaries Committee.

To a large extent the many pressures accumulating on Qantas, its minister, and the Department of Civil Aviation flowed directly from the technological leap to jet and turboprop aircraft. There were powerful effects on airline productivity that influenced bargaining for traffic rights; on pilots' attitudes to what they considered their new responsibilities and increased productivity; on senior staff attitudes to the salary increases of pilots; on airport and air traffic control changes; and on the all-pervasive increase in tempo and intensity of everything concerned with civil aviation. Fysh wrote to Turner on 11 February:

> With the bank up of unresolved matters between us and the Minister and Director-General, an atmosphere of some tension, which is not surprising, seems to now be apparent, and is much to be lamented. I wish to make it clear that I feel the Board and Management has acted correctly in all matters but at the same time I would like also to make it clear that it is our duty to do everything possible to relieve the position and to be careful not to unwittingly in any way fan the flames. The Minister is our constituted Authority and this accordingly is a governing factor in our actions.[4]

March 1960 was a busy month for both the minister and Qantas. On 3 March, the *Australian Financial Review* reported that the minister had been obliged to make considerable concessions to both the French and Italians in exchange for Australian traffic rights. The existing temporary rights for Rome had been firmed on a permanent basis, allowing Qantas three frequencies a week on an unrestricted basis in relation to Frankfurt, London, Damascus, Beirut, and Athens traffic. Alitalia was granted rights into Australia. With the French, Australia now conceded rights for the French international airline, TAI, into Sydney as part of its round-the-world service. In return, Qantas rights were restored in Noumea and the French agreed that Qantas could operate through Tahiti if, at some time in the future, it wished to do so. The *Review* reported: "It is estimated that the concession to TAI could cost Qantas something like one million pounds worth of business a year, in return for which Qantas gets a mythical benefit in Tahiti, transit rights into Marseilles and terminating rights into Paris. It is reckoned in Qantas that these latter two concessions have a very small value indeed to Australia." It added: "Civil aviation agreements these days are very often — perhaps too often for the

London Airport, 27 February 1960. Capt. Lewis Ambrose, Qantas regional director, farewells Senator Shane Paltridge, Australian minister for civil aviation. Accompanying the minister are Mrs Paltridge and Don Anderson, director-general of civil aviation.

health of the industry – settled on the level of top politics rather than of strict business."[5] These public criticisms of both ministerial and departmental achievements that appeared inspired by leaks from within Qantas could only have been initiated by Turner.

On 4 March Paltridge announced Cabinet approval of the tripartite pooling agreement between Australia, the United Kingdom and India. The three airlines, he said, would each sell the services of the others, and operations and reservations systems would be co-ordinated. The agreement would provide important commercial advantages to the airlines of the three Commonwealth countries.[6]

On 15 March Cabinet approval for the purchase by Qantas of three additional Boeing 707s with turbofan engines and the modification of engines in the existing fleet was announced. The total cost of the new aircraft and engine modifications was $41 million. It was a financial commitment that the federal government considered a very large one. It prompted a review of the policy question of whether the government's attitude to the future role of Qantas in international operations should continue the attitude of past years. When approval had been given in 1956 for the purchase of the initial fleet of seven Boeings, the government had explicitly recognised the economic and defence value accruing from Australian ownership and operation of a modern jet fleet. Qantas expansion since then had made it the tenth largest international airline in the world in terms of annual miles flown and its revenue, since 1955, had increased from £16 million to £28 million in 1959. In that period there had been traffic growth of sixty-five per cent. It was clear that the early confidence in the potential of Qantas had been clearly justified. The government, with its approval to modify and expand the Qantas fleet, now gave clear support for its international carrier in its future role. As it did so, however, it was considering in principle that TAA and Ansett-ANA should operate the existing Qantas route between the mainland and New Guinea and that TAA should assume responsibility for all the New Guinea services operated by Qantas and purchase all Qantas assets necessary in New Guinea to do this.

Qantas was quick to hear of these ministerial discussions. On 24 March Fysh wrote to Paltridge:

> We understand you are again giving attention to the matter of air services to and within New Guinea with the object of securing an early policy decision by the Government upon this problem. Over several years during which this matter has been under consideration, I have several times written to you expressing my Board's concern at the effect which the proposed changes of policy could have on Qantas . . . As you are aware, the Qantas operations to New Guinea and within New Guinea have never been really profitable to Qantas though they do provide a not inconsiderable contribution to our overhead costs and are most valuable to the Company in other directions . . .

Fysh gave an updated assessment of the financial consequences to Qantas if it was required to withdraw from New Guinea. Over a five-year period the loss to Qantas would, he said, be not less than £3 million "made up of loss of contributions to overhead and fixed costs, diversion of New Guinea traffic to other international carriers and costs which the company would have to incur in the provision of alternate means for training junior pilots to the stage where they could be transferred to our mainline aircraft". He emphasised the board's concern over this possible £3 million adverse effect on Qantas finances, in view of the commitments arising from existing dollar loans for airliners: "In arranging these loans we had counted on the continuance of our New Guinea operations . . . The Board naturally feels that if in fact Qantas's financial position is to be so adversely affected by Government direction, then the Government should compensate Qantas either directly or in other directions." Fysh summarised the importance of New Guinea as a training ground for pilots. "At present our practice is to process our juniors through New Guinea internal operations and, in fact, approximately half of our current Boeing commanders have graduated through that sphere." Without the New Guinea operations it would be difficult and more expensive, Fysh said, for Qantas to fulfil its role as Australia's international carrier in the Pacific Islands.[7]

Though the Prime Minister's Department did not believe that the existing policy on New Guinea should be changed in the way proposed by Paltridge, the minister's view prevailed. "It seemed," wrote Fysh, "as in other instances, the Government was determined to do something for Ansett-ANA . . . However, Ansett-ANA could not go to New Guinea unless TAA did the same".[8] In April the government finally announced that air services operated by Qantas between Australia and New Guinea and within Papua and New Guinea were to be included in the Australian domestic transport network. On 8 May 1960, TAA formally took over the Qantas services between the mainland and New Guinea and Qantas operated its last services to New Guinea on 9 July 1960. On 31 August, TAA took over the internal Qantas operations. C. O. Turner, who had the habit of writing notes for his own use on small cards, commented

In early 1960, Qantas chartered one of its four Lockheed Electras to Trans-Australia Airlines, which required extra capacity to match Ansett-ANA. TAA had ordered three Electras after Ansett had secured early positions on the production line. By March 1960, Ansett had three Electras in operation but TAA would not receive its third aircraft until September. The charter was arranged to cover that period and VH-ECD *Pacific Enterprise* was repainted in TAA markings. It was renamed *Charles Sturt* by TAA; the name was passed on to their third Electra when it was delivered.

Goroka airstrip in the New Guinea highlands, April 1960. At the direction of the Australian government, Qantas services in New Guinea and the Australian Territories were taken over by TAA on 31 August 1960.

under the heading of "Great Fysh Myth" that Hudson Fysh "did not oppose the New Guinea take-over, which was a disaster for Qantas".[9]

In April 1960, Qantas again faced the threat of a strike by its pilots. On 1 April, Fysh told Qantas director W. C. Taylor: "I had a telephone chat with the Minister who . . . is most anxious to avoid a strike but will not advise what our attitude should be in this difficult matter. He says that it is a matter for the Board and the Department of Labour and Industry and that we should carefully consult with Mr McMahon and/or Mr Bland before our Board meeting on Tuesday."[10] On the afternoon of the same day, Fysh received a personal message from the president of the AFAP, Captain Dick Holt: "It is my duty as President of the Federation to request an audience with the chairman of the Board so that he is in no doubt of the gravity of the situation".[11] Fysh, though he was strongly critical of what he considered Turner's legalistic and authoritarian attitude to the pilots and believed that he himself had a far better rapport with them than Turner, replied: "Sir Hudson regrets that he does not feel it proper to see you at this juncture . . . Sir Hudson looks forward to having a drink with you and any others as soon as a settlement is reached."[12]

On the same day, Turner summed up the issues in a memorandum to Fysh headed "Significant Principles Involved in Pilots' Margins Dispute". The Australian Federation of Air Pilots, he said, is now an unregistered body under the Commonwealth Conciliation and Arbitration Act, but "they are still, of course, expecting to receive the benefits which accrue to other groups". Under threat of strike, TAA had guaranteed increases related broadly to twenty per cent of current margins. Other domestic operators were forced to follow TAA. "The pressure tactics of the pilots in recent years has resulted in extraordinarily high gains since their salaries were fixed in relation to the Fitter in 1954. These increases amount to £2,324 per annum for a top captain and £541 for the most junior first officer (including £104 per annum cost of living allowance)." Qantas, said Turner, "is now isolated on this issue. The Pilots Federation has strength because they are no longer a registered body, whilst the Company . . . if it stood firm, could be faced with a lengthy stoppage from which it could only extricate itself after lengthy legal proceedings. In yielding to pressure the other operators, through no fault of their own, struck a serious blow at the Conciliation and Arbitration system . . ." Turner said Qantas had already been approached unofficially by the secretaries of two moderate trade unions "who have virtually pleaded with the Company not to accede to the pilots' demands under threat of direct action . . . or they will have difficulty in restraining their members from emulating the pilots". The new pilots' federation, said Turner, believed itself to be the spearhead in the introduction to Australia of the American system of collective bargaining in industrial relations. "If therefore in their first major issue they have complete success by forcing Qantas to submit to their demands, the position of other major employers in the community will also be threatened. The issue at stake in this dispute is whether the Arbitration system should be made to function or be abandoned. Qantas as a Government instrumentality has always strongly supported the Conciliation and Arbitration system and any departure from this policy should be by Government direction."[13]

The *Sydney Morning Herald* commented on 1 April:

Very important matters of principle are involved . . . As things stand, Qantas pilots have called off their threatened stoppage, have accepted the Company's £400 offer [the pilots had asked for more than double this amount] pending negotiations, but threaten to decide by secret ballot whether to strike if the new negotiations break down. Should Qantas yield to them? . . . In the first place they [the pilots] argue that there shall be no fixed base for their claims but only the last agreed figure. If that principle were applied to all wage fixing, the result would be economic chaos. In the second place, by threatening direct action if direct negotiations do not give them their claim, they are stepping outside the nation's arbitration system . . . The Government has a duty now to back its instrumentality to the hilt. [14]

As with the comments by the *Australian Financial Review* on the government's part in negotiating overseas traffic rights, the press again seemed extraordinarily well briefed, this time on a course that C. O. Turner favoured. Turner advised the board on 4 April: "The Company's stand has been one of principle and the Management does not believe that that principle should lightly be violated because of a threat of a stoppage." [15] There were, however, differing but considerable pressures on the board. Hudson Fysh telephoned Qantas legal counsel, Sir Garfield Barwick, on 5 April and told him: "My point in ringing you is that Bland, [secretary] of the Department of Labour and National Service, has indicated to the Qantas Management that we should meet their demands. This would be a shock to the Arbitration Commission and we feel we cannot go along with that . . ." [16] It was the Bland view that prevailed. On 11 May, in the face of strike threats, Qantas agreed to the AFAP demands. It was by no means the end of pressures from the AFAP. On 6 June, the federation served a long and complex claim on Qantas relating to the salary structure of pilots. These pressures came in April 1960, when a depression period of some fifteen months began during which there was to be no traffic expansion. The Qantas pilot strength was 320 and the airline carried surplus pilots during a period in which the extra capacity provided by its jet and turboprop fleet was underutilised.

Turner flew to Canada in May with the director-general, Don Anderson, for talks that included possible joint arrangements, including pooling, between the two countries and the United Kingdom on services between Australia and Europe through Canada. He reported to Fysh by letter on 9 May: "In the broad consideration of this whole problem, I think it should be stated that the introduction of Canadian Pacific services into any pooling arrangement on the Pacific and beyond to the UK could substantially strengthen Qantas in future. The UK ambition is, of course, to establish a Commonwealth airline based in

London . . ." In fact, the Australian High Commission in London had briefed the Department of External Affairs in Canberra as far back as September 1959 that Britain denied any official sponsorship of a Commonwealth airline concept. Press reports had stemmed from a speech by Britain's minister for transport and civil aviation, H. A. Watkinson, in the House of Commons early in July, in which he had stated that close Commonwealth airline co-operation, including pool partnership, was United Kingdom government policy. He referred to the economic and political advantages of such Commonwealth airline partnership arrangements with standardised aircraft fleets and the improved market created thereby for the sale of United Kingdom aircraft. Britain's Ministry of Transport and Civil Aviation told the High Commission that they were embarrassed by newspaper guessing that had linked this Watkinson speech with recent meetings of the United Kingdom, Australian, and Canadian government aviation representatives and the subsequent UK-India air agreement talks.[17] The Australian prime minister, Robert Menzies, answering a question in the House of Representatives on 15 September 1959 as to whether his government had been approached by the UK government with a proposal for a merger of British Commonwealth airlines, replied that he had "heard of no proposal that would affect the independent existence of Qantas, which I regard as one of the outstanding airlines of the world".[18] Senator Paltridge was somewhat more explicit in a press release when he said: "The proposed Commonwealth Airline as reported in the London press has not been considered at an official level".[19] Neither the prime minister's nor the minister's statements denied that, as Turner put it, the UK ambition was, in the interests of BOAC and the British aircraft manufacturers, the establishment of a Commonwealth airline.

Turner was concerned that New Zealand's secretary for Air had arrived in Ottawa and that New Zealand apparently intended to offer rights across the Tasman to Pan American in exchange for a terminating service for TEAL at Honolulu, through Tahiti. This, said Turner, would make it impossible for Australia to deny BOAC the rights to extend from Sydney to Auckland, and "the present monopoly would disappear. The Indians and the Canadians would want to operate too." Turner commented: "In the long run, it might suit Australia to bust up the present New Zealand monopoly of the Tasman but it would not suit us at this time to have TEAL extending beyond Tahiti to Honolulu (or beyond). I have told Anderson that

180

TEAL should disappear altogether and that if New Zealand wanted to enter into international operations, they should do so on their own account and at their own cost."[20] Canada and New Zealand comprised, of course, only a small sector of the international horizon that Qantas had now continuously to survey. Since 1946 Australia had negotiated permanent air agreements with Canada, Ceylon, Egypt, West Germany, India, Ireland, Italy, Japan, Lebanon, Federation of Malaya, New Zealand, the Netherlands, Pakistan, South Africa, Thailand, Turkey, the United Kingdom, and the United States. In addition there had been temporary agreements with France, Greece, Indonesia, Iran, Iraq, the Philippines, and Saudi Arabia. As new routes and different countries became involved, the negotiations were always complex and detailed, particularly when Australia's pool partners had to be taken into account, or when matters of high government policy were involved. Turner, for example, wrote to BOAC managing director Basil Smallpiece on 25 June about talks with Japan in which Japan Airlines had indicated that they would welcome a closer relationship, possibly involving pooling. "It appears that our Government would look favourably on a closer relationship between ourselves and JAL", wrote Turner. "Australia has recently entered into a trade agreement with Japan and in the whole complex political situation of South East Asia, it seems that Australian policy is directed towards closer friendship with Japan as one of the few strong influences against the spread of Communism in the area."[21]

Turner reported to Qantas employees, in the June issue of *Qantas News*, on a quite different challenge that was emerging. Supersonic airliners, he said, would on present indications be in general use in the 1970s, enabling Australians to have breakfast in Sydney and lunch in London on the same day.[22] So rapid had been the advance in civil airliner technology in little more than a decade that the notion of air travel at supersonic speeds seemed, in 1960, not merely the next logical step but a step that was, with effort, attainable in practical terms. In a paper delivered before the Adelaide branch of the Royal Aeronautical Society in April 1960, the director-general of civil aviation, Don Anderson, remarked that a commercial aircraft capable of flying at a speed at least three times the speed of sound (i.e. at about 2,000 miles per hour) could be built without the need for any major technological breakthrough. He quoted authorities saying that such supersonic civil airliners could

181

provide excellent returns on investments, that they were desirable and even inevitable. An operational supersonic airliner was possible, technically, as early as 1965.

For Qantas, having in fifteen years survived the postwar use of crudely modified bombers on the reopened London route, assimilated a modern fleet of sixteen Constellation airliners, and then, with continuing excellence in technical judgment, having led the world's international airlines outside the United States into the Boeing 707 era, the appraisal of this next likely leap in technology was now a matter that had to be addressed in commercial and operational terms.

There were some heady possibilities for air travellers in the decade ahead. At a speed of Mach 3 (three times the speed of sound at sea level under standard conditions), the supersonic airliner would, said Don Anderson, always outdistance the sun on any westbound flight. "There would be nothing to prevent the Australian Prime Minister from accepting a Friday evening dinner engagement with Mr Macmillan [the British prime minister] in London, yet remain in his office in Canberra until 5 p.m. the same day and still arrive in London in plenty of time to don a black tie before going to No 10 Downing Street." Anderson, however, found United Kingdom and United States manufacturers

> obsessed with the idea, as they so often have been in the past, that any new aircraft's maximum range capability must simply be the 3,000 odd nautical miles necessary for a non-stop crossing of the blue ribbon North Atlantic air route. The probable size of the supersonic aircraft – somewhere in the 300,000 to 600,000 pound and 200 passenger category – is also markedly influenced by the North Atlantic philosophy. From the Australian viewpoint I think this is all wrong. An aircraft capable of carrying 100 passengers up to 5,000 miles and possibly beyond, would seem to meet our needs best.

Anderson asked what the likely effects of supersonic airliners would be on Australia's participation in international civil aviation.

> A supersonic aircraft costing about £7 million is a very expensive piece of equipment. A fleet of such aircraft – three I think would be an economic minimum – would cost in the vicinity of £28 million. This should represent no insuperable difficulty for Qantas for it has built up a magnificent record in recent years in the financing of its own aircraft re-equipment purchases. Between 1956 and 1961 Qantas will, without any direct Government support, have financed a £48 million jet re-equipment programme.[23]

QEA director and secretary to the Treasury, Sir Roland Wilson, had, like Turner, also been in North America making arrangements with the United States Eximbank and Boeing to finance the airline's new aircraft and engine modification programme. The Australian treasurer, William McMahon, announced the successful outcome of these negotiations in June for loan funds totalling $30 million. Fysh wrote to Wilson: "Your colleagues on the Board and I myself greatly value what you have done to assist the Company again on this occasion".[24]

Hudson Fysh attended the executive committee meeting of the International Air Transport Association in Holland early in June. What would normally have been a routine matter ended with Fysh coming under severe criticism from his board and chief executive. In his report on the meeting, Fysh referred at some length to flagrant breaches of the traffic rules of IATA, which had given the committee and IATA's director-general great concern. They had, he said, come close to undermining the main function of the association in fixing fares and rates and conditions of carriage. In fact, said Fysh, "its continuing existence has been threatened". This evil had, he said, been caused in the main by a very heavy overprovision by the world's airlines of capacity, described by the director-general as "a rat race of members with 7,000 seats a month chasing the odd 3,000 who can be persuaded to fly". The main trouble area had been South America but, reported Fysh, "the position in the near East threatened to become as bad, with flagrant and deliberate breaches . . . My own observations in Cairo showed that the position had been very bad there with flagrant 'catch-me-if-you-can' breaches." Fysh, returning through Cairo heard allegations against three airlines and made public references to Air India's attitude in such alleged breaches and to the existence of "slush funds" in certain airlines, used to bribe travel agents and others. "This was the sort of thing I felt very hot about", he wrote. "I hated what was freely called cheating".[25] In a report on his trip that was printed and circulated, Fysh wrote that Cairo had been an acute trouble centre for illegal fare rebating and other traffic infringements.

> Swissair and Air India, together with Miscair, are named as the main offenders. The practice has been for passengers, after shopping around, going to one of these airlines, taking out and fully paying for a ticket in the front office, and then walking round to the back office and receiving a rebate in cash. Air India in Italy were observed in Milan paying cash to an agent representing bonus commission and Swissair were accused of flying a load of watches

to Cairo for distribution to agents there. A current joke in Cairo is: "Will Air India continue to pay out on passenger bookings because if they do, they will be subsidising their partners BOAC and Qantas".

His board thought that Fysh had been extremely indiscreet in his comments. W. C. Taylor told the board he doubted whether Fysh should be allowed to go to Copenhagen for the IATA annual general meeting, where Fysh expected to be declared president-elect of the association. "Air India was dragged into the discussion", wrote Fysh. "It was then, at this time, that I considered tendering my resignation and so informed the Minister. But if I did, I would ask for a full enquiry into the now rather ridiculous Air India affair." It was not, he said, a happy time on the board. "I was in bad standing with McVey, Taylor and Turner yet enjoyed the full confidence of the Government and my Minister, with the Company going from strength to strength in effectiveness and profitability and enjoying great public acclaim." In his diary he scribbled a note: "Who has this system [of slush funds]? Feel so far that I was perfectly right reference A.I. in what I did, and no need to be taken up in the way it was by touchy, chipping people. The trouble is I had no backing, especially by the Chief Executive."[26] In fact,

From November 1960 to April 1961, Qantas leased one of the L1049s that had been traded to Lockheed in 1959. The aircraft was VH-EAI and it was brought back to Sydney while the four Qantas L188C Electras were returned to Burbank for modifications. With its new name *Southern Boomerang* painted on the nose, VH-EAI stands behind Ron Yates, Clem Allen, and Bob Stevens as they check the paperwork before accepting delivery at Portland on 24 October 1960.

Fysh did attend the September 1960 IATA meeting in Copenhagen and was voted president-elect of IATA, to take office at
the following IATA annual general meeting, planned for Sydney
in October 1961.

C. O. Turner, at this time, was also having problems. "There
was some general uneasiness about top QEA affairs," wrote Fysh,
"and my Minister, Shane Paltridge, overworked, was in a critical
mood. Turner was in trouble with the Minister in regard to
an over-expansive article in the *Sunday Telegraph* on 3 July 1960,
and I was in trouble with McVey and Taylor in my comment
on it to the Minister, when he wrote complaining."[27] In more
general terms, Fysh wrote:

> As these tensions mounted, so did the lack of conformity and a
> proper personal attitude on the part of our Chief Executive . . .
> Reports of unusual happenings drifted in . . . capped by a letter
> from a New Zealand passenger complaining of the behaviour of
> Turner on a BOAC jet at Tokyo. Turner objected to the New
> Zealander being seated beside him, [Turner] wanting a spare seat.
> A row developed on the plane, which left late. Copies of the letter
> to me had been sent to Sir Giles Guthrie, Chairman of BOAC,
> and to Sir William Hildred, Director-General of IATA. I had no
> option but to take the matter up. This was done and Turner, after
> failing to attend a Board meeting without leave, was firmly dealt
> with by a Board sub-committee, of which I was not a member.

Turner was, in fact, in the habit of insisting on two seats for
himself when he travelled. Fysh wrote:

> Some time after this unhappy [Tokyo] incident came the "Perth
> seating case". The Chief Executive, on his way to South Africa,
> had been granted a spare seat alongside his own seat, despite the
> turning down of a passenger from Melbourne to Johannesburg.
> A QEA first officer had to be off-loaded and remained in Perth.
> An accumulation of these sorts of things over the years seriously
> compromised the reputation and organisation of QEA.[28]

The main preoccupations of the Qantas board in its relationship with government in mid-1960 are indicated in notes
prepared by Fysh for a meeting between the board and QEA's
minister, Shane Paltridge. Heading them was still the problem
of providing information to the minister well ahead of actual
official requests. It would no doubt, wrote Fysh, be an issue
raised by the minister. The minister, he wrote, would like to
receive "information letters" but he had explained that written
information about matters not fully developed by the chief
executive and board might be very misleading. Personal con-

tacts were preferable. There was also, Fysh noted, "a feeling on the part of the Minister and, at least, some Cabinet Ministers, of 'what is Qantas going to ask for next now they have got that one through' ". He thought the minister would have in mind the issue of the Electra replacement and the possible order of cargo aircraft, while the chief executive was considering the introduction of another Boeing 707. On financial matters, the minister should be informed that while the introduction of the Boeings had been spectacularly successful, the balance of the financial year using the last of the Constellations had not been profitable. Progressive introduction of large jet aircraft by competitors would make it harder to secure good payloads. There was a worldwide move for lower air fares; particularly competitors (Pan American, TAI, KLM, JAL) were exercising air route rights that affected Qantas. In meeting the minister, Fysh wrote, further issues for discussion were the financial effects on Qantas of the New Guinea decision; the alarming rise in the cost of operating because of cost rises in wages, salaries, and improved conditions of service; the unprofitability of the politically valuable South African service; and the desirability for a uniform attitude by Qantas and TAA in adhering to the industrial laws of the nation.[29]

The political pressures on the Qantas board and management were varied but were always a continuing part of the Qantas environment. Civil aviation was, in the sixties, a matter of intense public interest and the government, in recognition of this interest, had formed a Government Members Civil Aviation Committee in 1960 with D. E. Fairbairn as its convenor. Paltridge wrote to Fysh on 28 July: "It is perhaps unnecessary for me to emphasise that this Committee will have a very important function in relation to civil aviation policy". Paltridge enclosed for Fysh's confidential information a copy of a letter he had received from Fairbairn requesting that arrangements be made for Qantas to address the committee on 24 August. Fairbairn's letter said:

> Incidentally, during the past week, two Press statements about future equipment of Qantas have made me gather that the airline is looking, as usual, towards American manufacturers without any consideration of suitable types from England. I see that Mr Turner has commented that "the next immediate move in Qantas's master plan is to supplement its Super Constellation freighter fleet with jet cargo planes, several types of which are well advanced in the US". Is it not a fact that several types of cargo planes are more than advanced in the United Kingdom? Also, I see that *The Aeroplane* mentions that Qantas is interested in a Boeing which

will not be flying until 1964. Could you give me further details
of this plane and where it is expected to be superior to the Vickers
VC 10?[30]

Paltridge commented to Fysh:

You will perhaps know that Mr Fairbairn has, over the years, been
a constant advocate of the use of British aircraft by Australian
operators . . . He has given considerable time to a discussion of
technical matters (by the committee) which I suspect is based on
his Air Force experience during the last war; and, although he
appears to be able to speak authoritatively, I have always thought
that his post-war knowledge has been gained from aircraft
magazines and similar literature rather than from actual and
practical knowledge . . . In addition, he is always well briefed by
the British aircraft manufacturers.[31]

Qantas prepared a careful brief for its meeting, on 24 August,
with the new Government Members Civil Aviation Committee.
"Contrary to popular belief," the airline's evidence began, "the
only reason we purchase new types of aircraft is economics in
its broadest and most cold-blooded sense." In real money terms,
Qantas told the committee, it was operating a service with
effectively a decreasing fare structure. "Although Qantas is one
of the very few airlines of the world that has consistently shown
a profit since the early 1920s, our economic life remains finely
balanced. Since the war, our profits before tax have averaged
about 4 per cent of turnover. Quite small percentage differences
in costs and revenue are therefore absolutely vital to our
economic survival." Some two-thirds of total expenditure went,
said Qantas, in the direct operating costs of its aircraft fleet.
"We therefore regard the problem of the selection of new aircraft
types as a matter of the utmost importance to the company's
future. It is a subject on which we cannot possibly afford the
luxury of sentiment or prejudice." With that direct and unsubtle
serve at Fairbairn, the Qantas evidence summarised the way
in which data on new aircraft was analysed, and set down the
steps involved in the 1956 decision to order Boeing 707s. It
explained why the relatively late delivery of the British Vickers
Vanguard had proved an insuperable objection to its selection
in competition with the US Lockheed Electra. "With the
extensive delivery of pure jet and turbo-prop aircraft to the
airliners of the world during 1959 it was expected that by the
end of 1959 the market for second-hand piston-engined aircraft
would have collapsed and that by the first half of 1960 they
would have little more than scrap value. We therefore considered
it absolutely vital to complete our new aircraft deliveries in 1959

so that our Super Constellations could be sold before the market collapsed. Therefore we could not wait till late 1960 for the Vanguard."

The decision between the Electra and the Comet 4, as support aircraft for the Boeing 707s, had been, the committee was told, more difficult. The economic advantages of the Electra over the Comet did point fairly clearly to the Electra as first choice. When Lockheed agreed, as part of the contract for the Electra purchase, to buy back six of the Qantas Constellations at a price close to book value, "this offer was decisive". Qantas did, however, concede in its evidence that "Committee members will know that the Lockheed Electra has been subject to certain speed restrictions as a result of structural difficulties with the engine nacelles and, as a consequence, the economics of the Electra at present are only slightly better than the Super Constellation". When those restrictions were removed, said Qantas, the economics of the Electra would be as predicted. "We have recently contracted with Lockheed to have the modifications necessary to remove speed restrictions done to our Electra fleet on a free-of-charge basis at the end of this year and early next year."[32]

While Qantas had constantly to look over its shoulder towards Canberra to assess or anticipate the political climate for its decision making, pressures and problems in the strictly commercial world of international airline operations grew steadily in scale and complexity. Service revenue in the first five months of 1960 had increased by an encouraging 15.7 per cent to £13.5 million, of which the Kangaroo Route had provided £6.75 million and the Pacific route £3.41 million. The company had an overdraft with the Commonwealth Trading Bank of £1.6 million and was seeking a capital subscription of £200,000 from the government in the 1960–61 budget, additional advances from the bank of £2 million, and £780,000 from TAA for the purchase of its New Guinea assets to finance commitments for the aircraft programme in 1960. There was, though, a difference of opinion with TAA. The domestic airline took the view that it should select only those assets that it wanted. Qantas thought this unreasonable and impracticable as its complete withdrawal from New Guinea was involved. By mid-year the first fan-engined Boeing 707 had flown successfully at Seattle, with the target date for completion of the certification programme December. The introduction of Boeing 707s on the Far East route in 1960 had been put off because competition on the Pacific had forced the airline to use all its available 707 capacity

there, leaving it vulnerable to KLM's DC8 jet service between
Tokyo and Sydney, scheduled for October. The additional
Pacific frequencies had also meant the introduction of more aircrews while at the same time reducing the jet aircraft time
available for crew training. There were, however, two particular
matters that dominated board and management thinking in the
second half of 1960: one was the future of the Tasman route,
linked with the expansion of New Zealand's overseas air services;
the other was a mounting disagreement with BOAC on the
application of the Kangaroo Route partnership principles to
the tripartite pool with Air India.

In early July 1960 discussions took place in Melbourne on
civil aviation matters between Australia and New Zealand. New
Zealand's existing route pattern involved a fortnightly flying
boat service to Tahiti, trans-Tasman services, and services
between New Zealand and Fiji. Senator Paltridge told Prime
Minister R. G. Menzies on 28 July that "in essence the New
Zealand thinking was that TEAL should not permanently
remain on branch lines". In response to the pressure of tourist
and trade interests, there would have to be a more liberal policy
towards overseas operators and a gradual expansion of TEAL
services; "public opinion would not allow the Government [of
New Zealand] to keep the Tasman sea closed for very much
longer". Two recent negotiations had forced the pace for New
Zealand. The French had asked for rights in New Zealand to
provide four connections each week to Europe. In return they
offered New Zealand a weekly service beyond Tahiti to
Honolulu. The Americans, in exchange for giving New Zealand
rights to put Tahiti on a route to the US west coast, wanted
trans-Tasman rights. Paltridge commented: "It has never been
our view that any TEAL expansion should involve a breach
of the Tasman monopoly and it is for this reason that we do
not favour any arrangements which the New Zealanders might
enter into with France or the United States which would have
this effect". In the financial year 1959–60 Tasman traffic had
comprised eighty-three per cent of total TEAL revenue. Even
with its monopoly, the company had made a net profit of only
four per cent on turnover.

> It will be necessary to consider the replacement of TEAL's Electra
> aircraft about 1965 and it is about this time that the infiltration
> of the Tasman would be likely to occur [wrote Paltridge]. To re-
> equip TEAL with jet aircraft at that time would, if TEAL wished
> to extend services across the Pacific and on to London, involve
> the purchase of up to four long range jet aircraft at a very high

capital cost. The Australian Government would have to decide whether in this set of circumstances it would be willing to accept the responsibility of bearing half the cost of financing long range jets for TEAL, having in mind the commitments it would already have in supporting Qantas, which would have at least ten or more long range jets by then. In essence, having taken steps which will destroy the profitable financial basis of our alliance with them—that is, the Tasman monopoly—New Zealand asks whether we would be prepared to continue as joint owners of TEAL, involving the financing of long range jet aircraft which would compete with those of Australia's own carrier on routes of doubtful profitability, while various foreign carriers are permitted to intrude extensively into Tasman traffic . . . From a civil aviation point of view I see no basis upon which we could continue as joint owners in TEAL.

Paltridge recognised, however, "that there could well be political considerations which would need to be weighed alongside the civil aviation factors". He felt that the New Zealanders, through their prime minister, Walter Nash, "may well try to exploit these political factors to get our agreement to a very poor civil aviation arrangement".[33]

New Zealand's prime minister did not, in fact, bear strongly on wider political factors when he wrote to Menzies on 5 August. "While I am writing to you because I greatly hope that you can ensure that our civil aviation plans are assessed in the larger framework of our overall relations and common interests, I think you would prefer to think first about the matter from the more narrow civil aviation viewpoint", he said. Both countries had long recognised, wrote Nash, that the monopoly of the trans-Tasman traffic enjoyed by TEAL could not endure forever. There was very strong public demand in New Zealand that national development in all fields should be accelerated:

Just as public opinion here will not tolerate the thought of New Zealand as an economic backwater, so it will not tolerate a negative or restrictive aviation policy . . . My colleagues and I have considered the situation and have concluded that when the New Zealand jet airport at Mangere is completed (about 1965) it will no longer be in New Zealand's developmental or strategic interests to maintain rigorously the Tasman monopoly and leave New Zealand on a branch line . . . We are also convinced of the strategic, defence and economic importance to New Zealand of an increasing participation in overseas aviation. We have therefore decided firmly that New Zealand must plan now for the expansion of its air services beyond Tahiti in order to provide an adequate base for airline operations when the Tasman monopoly is eroded and to underpin our political and economic interests. This means that we must plan to re-equip with a fleet of modern jet aircraft by 1965 and must be prepared to grant the Americans, Australia, the

United Kingdom and possibly others trans-Tasman rights on services through New Zealand, to come into operation when Mangere is capable of receiving jets. [34]

Menzies received a memorandum from his own department criticising the Department of Civil Aviation. "Our Civil Aviation people talk angrily of double dealing by the New Zealanders and by the French . . . We come to the conclusion that the faults are not all on one side and that the rather loose way in which the matter has been handled between the Civil Aviation Departments of the two countries has probably contributed to misunderstandings." [35] The prime minister responded to Nash's letter on 31 August, taking pains to express the Australian position in the friendliest terms. It ignored Paltridge's attitude to maintenance of the Tasman monopoly.

You may [Menzies wrote] count on our continued goodwill and cooperation in assisting to achieve the results you have in mind . . . Certainly we have never, during the whole of our twenty years association with New Zealand in trans-Tasman operations, looked at any of your aviation problems only from the strictly commercial viewpoint of an airline operator and there is no intention of doing so now . . . We share enthusiastically the view which you have expressed on the overall interests of Australia and New Zealand. We admire the enterprise which encourages your Government to seek a pattern of development for your international airline, TEAL, similar to that which we have been able to achieve in respect of Qantas.

Menzies suggested ministerial talks to discuss arrangements, adding "for reasons which I shall explain it seems to us that our withdrawal from ownership of TEAL is a necessary part of these arrangements". That, he said, did not preclude a continuing close relationship in the form of a pool partnership on the Tasman. The Australian government had, he explained, already been committed to a very large capital investment on the account of Qantas and for Australia's domestic airlines. It could not, on budget if no other grounds, share in the re-equipment of TEAL. On the matter of traffic rights, Menzies welcomed a position in which Australia would itself be able more freely to concede the Tasman to obtain rights urgently needed for the development of Qantas. The Australian experience, he said, of endeavouring to negotiate traffic rights for the jointly owned TEAL "clearly points to the fact that in the negotiation of traffic rights a sovereign State can do infinitely better without the involvement of another country in the ownership of its airline. In our view this is a decisive argument.

For these reasons we have therefore come to the conclusion that the best course in the circumstances is that you should assume complete ownership of TEAL."[36]

The issues of the Tasman and TEAL were argued diplomatically, if firmly, by prime ministers. The disagreement between Qantas and BOAC was more bluntly discussed between the chief executives of the two airlines. Basil Smallpiece wrote to Turner on 15 July 1960 saying: "Our Board agreed to accept the tripartite pool on the repeated assurances that I gave them after consultation with you, that the Kangaroo route partnership between BOAC and Qantas took precedence over the tripartite pool . . . I feel we should commence by isolating the Kangaroo route service revenue and subject to adjustments for sale of capacity as between BOAC and QEA should split the resulting figure on a 50-50 basis in accordance with our previous partnership arrangements."[37] Turner replied:

> It seems clear to me now that you and I have different interpretations of what is meant by giving priority to the principles of the Kangaroo partnership . . . As I understand it, you consider that the higher load factors which the Kangaroo route has often enjoyed compared with other routes should continue to accrue to Qantas and BOAC. In my view, the whole essence of entering a tripartite agreement, or in fact any pooling agreement, is to pool load factors. We cannot put a route into the pool and arrange with the other partner (i.e. Air India) for common selling of that route with all the others, and then afterwards claim to have a separate pool among ourselves in respect of that particular route to our own advantage and not theirs.

Turner agreed that load factors on the Kangaroo Route had certainly been much higher than on other routes in the first three months of the tripartite pool, but argued that it was always dangerous to base arguments on figures covering a short period.

> It is quite impossible to prove what would have happened to the Kangaroo load factors had no tripartite agreement existed. I am personally certain, although you may not agree with me, that the load factors on the Kangaroo route, particularly west of Singapore, are much higher than they would have been had there been no tripartite [pool] . . . As I see it, we stand by our assurances that nothing in the tripartite agreement over-rides the fundamental and long-established basis of the Kangaroo partnership that Qantas and BOAC share the Kangaroo route equally. But, having jointly agreed to put that route into the tripartite partnership pool, we share equally in the results of the route after pooling with Air India.[38]

Fysh described the argument between Smallpiece and Turner

as "a bitter bone of contention". Qantas, he wrote, was increasingly successful and fears as to how the tripartite pool would work were soon realised when it was estimated that payments to Air India by BOAC and QEA for the year would be £1,064,000 sterling more than the revenue actually earned operationally by Air India. "The QEA hand-over of revenue it had earned in its own carriages was estimated as £960,000 sterling. This seemed an extraordinarily high price to pay and, indeed, contravened the wording of the agreement which stated inter alia: ' . . . and thus to achieve an improvement in the financial results of each Partner'. The agreement was entirely without any safety valve such as would alleviate any budgetary miscalculation . . ."[39]

BOAC's regional representative in the south-west Pacific, Phillip Hood, told Smallpiece: "C. O. Turner drafted a very long letter to me on the subject we are arguing about, but it is still not easy to find out what is really in his mind except a general desire to have more money out of the pool than he is in fact getting".[40] Turner, writing again directly to Smallpiece, was conciliatory in general expressions of goodwill but adamant in his view of the Kangaroo Route arrangements.

> I have expressed the view to you on many occasions that without complete goodwill and understanding between you and us, a pool of the magnitude of our present one cannot be made to work . . . It is not too much to say that the Kangaroo route pooling, which has taken many forms over the last twenty-five years, has been successful because of our close understanding with BOAC at all levels, despite the fact that there has been no formal written agreement between us over this long time. In accepting the heavy responsibility to my Board and Government of leading Qantas into a tripartite pool I was concerned, as I told you so often, that Qantas' position under that pool should not place us at a disadvantage in relation to our position under the Kangaroo route pool . . . You did agree that the Kangaroo route principles should be preserved and that to that end, irrespective of what was agreed with Air India under the tripartite pool, we should have a separate adjustment between us.

Turner quoted the provision in the tripartite agreement that existing partnership agreements "shall be unaffected" and commented: "If at the time the agreement was signed this particular provision was meant to be construed in a more restricted sense than its plain words bear, the qualification was not made known to me". He summarised the basic principles of the Kangaroo Route partnership: "There is to be maintained an equal provision by each of the partners of the end-to-end capacity agreed between the UK and Europe on the one hand and Australia and New Zealand on the other hand . . . In relation to the services as so agreed and equally shared as to capacity, there is to be an equal sharing of the revenue derived from the traffic carried." Turner set down the projected results of the tripartite pool for the first year, which had broadly been agreed with BOAC in March, in which Air India would gain £1,064,000 more from the pool than their services earned, with Qantas losing £960,000 and BOAC losing £104,000. "Expressed in another way, the Qantas loss of revenue represents transfers to other services as follows—Air India, £552,000; BOAC's non Kangaroo services, £408,000. It is the Qantas view that this does not represent an equitable adjustment nor does it reflect a just application between Qantas and BOAC of Kangaroo route principles." Turner's letter was long and technical but concluded: "I do agree that none of us contemplated a payment to Air India of this magnitude and I feel this is a matter requiring the most serious consideration . . . Since we are presumably committed to this result vis-a-vis the third partner I am therefore prepared to share this burden for this year on an equitable basis and there are numerous avenues by which this can be achieved." Turner's proposal, in essence, was to adjust the revenue shares between BOAC and Qantas by £440,000 in Qantas's favour, "the remaining loss of revenue to Qantas of £520,000 [being] roughly half the assessed Air India loss. In all circumstances we submit that this is an equitable method of adjustment."[41]

Smallpiece responded with both logical argument and obvious exasperation.

> What you are trying to argue [he said in a letter as long and as detailed as Turner's letter to him] is that while the Kangaroo route must (as long as it has a higher than average load factor) pay the resulting higher than average revenue into the tripartite pool, Qantas is to be insulated from the effect of doing so and excused the obligation to contribute your 50 per cent share, leaving the whole 100 per cent to be put in by BOAC on our own. What a suggestion for one equal partner to make to another! Where is our long-established 50-50 partnership in this proposal? Nowhere. It is inconceivable to me that you would let our long-standing partnership, or the new tripartite one with Air India, founder on the financial difficulty it seems you find yourself in at the moment. But when you come to Bombay [for talks in November] it will only be deluding yourself if you think that we are at all likely to shift off the basic principles of pool operations as they have evolved over the years . . . I entirely agree with you. . . . None of us contemplated a payment to Air India of the magnitude that has arisen.

194

Smallpiece affirmed the generalities of goodwill and cooperation but added: "We must not blind ourselves to the fact that our primary loyalties must always be to our respective Boards; and I am sure I do not need to point out that I too have 'the heavy responsibility' of ensuring that the tripartite pool does not work out to the detriment of BOAC . . .". It was clear that the emotional temperature was high. "You seem to have come to think", wrote Smallpiece, "that our undertaking to preserve for you the Kangaroo route *principles* amounted to an undertaking to preserve intact for you the Kangaroo route *revenues*. This is a manifest impossibility – not to say absurdity . . . To have sought to give Qantas this protection would have made a mockery of the basic philosophy of a pool." Smallpiece disputed Turner's figures in which he claimed that Qantas was threatened with a loss of £960,000. "In effect, you are asking me to agree, solely to relieve Qantas, that BOAC will cough up another £440,000 beyond what we have to pay anyway under the terms of the Bombay agreement . . . Your argument seeks to take the Kangaroo route right outside the tripartite pool, leaving BOAC to bear the brunt of almost the whole burden of any settlement with Air India."[42]

Smallpiece sent copies of this correspondence to the secretary of the UK Ministry of Aviation, Sir Henry Hardman. "I am frankly staggered at the way Cedric is behaving", came the reply. He detected desperation on Turner's part. "I cannot believe that he will carry his difference with you to the point of letting BOAC break their partnership with Qantas . . . Cedric must realise that Qantas is in no position to stand alone on the Kangaroo route and that without a partnership with Air India they have no hope of maintaining their present level of fifth freedom rights through India."[43]

The seriousness of the dispute between the two chief executives had so escalated by the end of October that Turner informed Smallpiece he had decided to seek advice from the Qantas board. All Qantas directors were present when Turner raised the matter and the discussion took more than five hours. "They consider", wrote Turner, "that a further exchange of letters is unlikely to help . . . Accordingly, they instructed me to seek further talks with you after the tripartite meeting in Bombay next month and if we should then still fail to agree, they have requested me to state that they would greatly appreciate it if you could return home through Sydney to provide them with an opportunity of personally reviewing the problem with you."[44]

It was very clear that the original agreement made by Qantas with BOAC and Air India had been a faulty one and that in accepting it, Qantas had, at the very least, allowed the possibility of costly misinterpretations of its intent. BOAC, just as clearly, was convinced that Turner now wished to distort what to them had been specifically agreed upon. Whatever the niceties of fact and interpretation, there was no denying that Qantas faced massive payments and that the figures involved, regardless of the terms of the agreement, showed an inequity in the actual workings of the new pool.

There was to be no quick agreement between Turner and Smallpiece and BOAC's managing director flew to Sydney in the last week of November to meet the Qantas board. He summarised his views on this meeting in a letter to Turner on 30 November. Much more dramatic than the meeting with the board, however, was the outcome of a talk he had with Turner in Turner's office the day after this meeting. Turner, in no way reflecting the views expressed by the Qantas board, told Smallpiece that the long partnership between Qantas and BOAC would be terminated at the end of March 1961.

Smallpiece wrote that BOAC maintained that their reading of the tripartite pool agreement was the correct one. The future, he said, was dependent on the Qantas board's answer to his question: "Do the board of Qantas regard the Kangaroo route as having been put into the tripartite pool in December 1959 or not?". If they did, he said, then the Kangaroo Route must be subject – the Qantas half of it as well as the BOAC half – to a pool adjustment with Air India and BOAC's non-Kangaroo services before BOAC and Qantas could share between them on an equal basis the revenue after pool adjustment. If the Qantas board considered Qantas did not intend to put the Kangaroo Route into the tripartite pool, "then it would seem we have reached a critical point". It was agreed at the meeting that these main issues would be left unanswered for a month so that Qantas directors could have time to consider them.

However [write Smallpiece], the morning after the Board meeting, you and I had a talk in your office in the course of which you told me that, if BOAC did not modify its attitude, it would be necessary for Qantas to terminate the partnership on 31 March next. As I mentioned at the time, this was not in accordance with what was said at the Board meeting on the previous day. But to make certain that I was not misunderstanding the position, I asked you if you were, in effect, giving me notice of terminating the partnership. You replied that that was so, unless I were to change my attitude to these pool issues. You added, in response to my question, that in that event Qantas would go it alone; and that you had felt for some time that that is what Qantas ought to do.

Now, Cedric, this is not just a question of attitudes, capable of being changed under pressure. It is a question of what is right and what is wrong. I sincerely believe that the proposals you have put forward are wrongly based and that you are claiming for Qantas a financial position that they are simply not entitled to . . . The issue of whether we continue the partnership or not is a matter of high policy, on which I assume the Board is the ultimate authority in Qantas. I did not get the impression on Tuesday last week that the Board had any desire at all to terminate the partnership, but rather that they wished to clear up a matter of dispute within it. However, in view of what you said to me on Wednesday, I think it is essential that we have the main issue – of whether we go on in partnership or not – out in the open, and settle it one way or the other.

The position is that I have now had notice from you, as General Manager and Chief Executive, of possible termination of the partnership on 31 March next. In the circumstances, I would be grateful if you could let me have your Board's decision, not only on whether they regard the Kangaroo route as having been put into the tripartite pool, but also on this question of whether we and you go on in partnership or not, by about the end of this year . . .

I should like to add that I personally – and everyone in BOAC – would regret very much a decision by Qantas to abandon a partnership which we have had together for so many years. It would certainly not be our wish that this should happen. On the other hand, if it is true that you have felt for some time – and your Board agrees with you – that it would be better for Qantas to go it alone, then it might well be best to face that issue now rather than to continue unwillingly a partnership with which you are not in sympathy, however much we in BOAC would regret such an outcome.[45]

BOAC's chairman, Rear Admiral Sir Matthew Slattery, cabled Fysh on 8 December that on his return from an overseas tour he had been told by Smallpiece of Turner's verbal intimation that Qantas might wish to terminate the partnership. "I write to ask you whether this is in fact in the mind of your Board? I need hardly add that all of us in BOAC, not the least myself, would be very sad if this were to come about."[46]

New tensions, this time amongst Qantas board members, arose from a handwritten letter sent by Smallpiece to QEA director Dan McVey from San Francisco, when Smallpiece was on his way back to London. McVey had had a long and well-documented attitude as a supporter of Empire and Commonwealth, which had, naturally, influenced his attitude over the years to disputes and possible rifts between Qantas and BOAC, as well as his underlying support for the use of British civil airliners. McVey had also had a long and close relationship with Phillip Hood, BOAC's regional representative in Sydney. It was therefore not unusual that Smallpiece should confide in McVey, who immediately informed Fysh. "Although Basil's letter to me is in manuscript and marked 'personal' and is, therefore, written throughout in the frank language which men use in correspondence who have implicit confidence in one another, the whole of the subject matter of his letter cannot be regarded as other than official, and also of prime importance to Qantas . . . My colleagues, I am sure – as well as I – would wish to hear what Cedric has to say before coming to any conclusions." The Smallpiece letter, in fact, expressed no more in substance than his later letter to Fysh, setting out his understanding of the boardroom discussions and Turner's verbal intimation the following day that he was giving notice of termination of the partnership. To McVey, he described this as "an extraordinary discussion with Cedric, the gist of which I must tell you".[47] McVey suggested that Fysh circulate copies of his letter to all directors and to Turner prior to a board meeting at which the whole matter was to be discussed. Fysh, in a letter to Law-Smith, commented: "It is apparent that the dispute has developed more and more into one of a personal nature between Messrs Smallpiece and Turner . . . both Chief Executives have been working on a difficult problem under great stress".[48] There were, however, other repercussions which Phillip Hood described in a letter to Smallpiece.

> I feel you would like a report on the question of your letter to Dan McVey as the whole thing must have seemed very strange to you . . . It seems that, on receipt of your letter, Dan McVey felt very strongly about the matter under dispute and in particular to C. O. Turner's general behaviour and he felt that something had to be done urgently. Unfortunately he met Law-Smith and, wishing to have somebody else on his side as it were, he showed Law-Smith your letter. This was, of course, the worst thing he could have done because, as you know, Law-Smith is tipped to be next Chairman of Qantas. He saw a golden chance to hit at C. O. Turner so he either told or showed Don Anderson a copy of your letter. Anderson then rang Ritchie and asked him to let C. O. Turner know that the copy was on its way to him.
> In the meantime, McVey had told W. C. Taylor [QEA vice-chairman] of the letter and also what he had done with it (not knowing Law-Smith had told Anderson) and Taylor tried very hard to get hold of it but failed to do so. By this time McVey had realised what he had triggered off and, as most of the Board had got to know of the letter, it was decided to circulate it to the Board . . .

Taylor came to my house to see me and told me all this. He was
very upset about the whole thing but particularly about what he
called Dan McVey's stupidity in letting Law-Smith see it at all,
and he feared that the Board might use this letter in some way
against you personally (or at least some of the Board) . . . There
has been a complete ban on any information regarding the Board
meeting and also a definite move by top level people to avoid
me . . . It was decided to keep the matter between the two
Chairmen and a letter of reply to Sir Matthew's letter . . . is in
state of preparation largely, I think, being drafted by Turner who
has not been seen since the Board. Nielsen told me that the Board
had firmly said that there was no question of Qantas leaving the
partnership and also added that he understood Turner had been
warned in no uncertain terms to mend his ways . . . I realise only
too well that you will feel that I ought to have got more detail
of the Board meeting for you but there has been so much secrecy
about it that it has been impossible, short of asking a member of
the Board outright, which would be bad tactics from my point
of view for the future . . . It would be wise to suggest to you not
to write again to McVey or anybody else, although I felt you knew
of this already. [49]

This crisis in the relationship between Qantas and BOAC,
who had been partners in varying ways since 1934, was resolved
in a letter from Fysh, on behalf of Qantas, to Sir Matthew
Slattery on 29 December.

Our Board [wrote Fysh] believes strongly that our association with
BOAC in the Kangaroo partnership has worked admirably in the
past, and to the great benefit of BOAC and Qantas, and it would
be the last thought in our minds that this long-standing partnership should in any way be disturbed. However, they are not nearly
so satisfied that the new tripartite pool arrangement . . . will give,
not only to Qantas but to BOAC and Air India, a result that will
be satisfactory and equitable as between the three partners. They
have been disturbed firstly by the financial outcome during the
first year of operation which has been quite different from what
they believed likely when the arrangements were entered into.
Secondly, an attitude appears to have developed that no important
amendments or modifications can be considered even if one partner
in the pool believes the results are working out strongly to his disadvantage . . . We are most anxious to remain in the tripartite pool
and to help make it work to the benefit of all parties . . .
   I mention this merely in order that I may put in its proper light
any misunderstanding that might have arisen between Smallpiece
and Turner . . . Future activities and exchanges particularly
between Smallpiece and Turner should be directed to seeking out
satisfactory arrangements for the future within the broad pooling
idea which offers so much for all of us. Accordingly, our Board
has reached the conclusion that we should tell both BOAC and
Air India that we are ready to go along with the tripartite pool
arrangements for 1961–62 in the hope that further experience will

elucidate and clarify the problems . . . It has decided to ask BOAC and Air India to concur in its view that the existing arrangements will possibly need review from time to time in the light of actual experience of the pool operations . . .[50]

While this disagreement was in course of temporary resolution, the Qantas vice-chairman, W. C. Taylor, stunned the board by accepting the chairmanship of the Australian subsidiary of a large British manufacturer of civil and military aircraft. Fysh wrote:

I opened my paper one morning in December 1960 to read that Bill Taylor had been appointed Chairman of Hawker-Siddeley (Australia) Pty Ltd. I refused to believe it, but it was indeed a fact. Bill, without reference to his Minister who appointed him to QEA, and to his Chairman, had taken the top position in a company manufacturing aircraft in which Qantas, Malayan Airways and Fiji Airways were interested. This action caused a crisis in relations with Government, which resulted in him leaving the Board. The press reported a Board squabble between myself and Taylor.

The reports, said Fysh were accurate. There had been argument about Taylor's action, which Fysh considered questionable.

It was not the only board shock. Another big British manufacturer of aircraft, British Aircraft Corporation, had been in process of forming an Australian subsidiary and seeking a suitable chairman. Fysh was himself sounded out by one of BAC's directors, Sir Reginald Verdon Smith. "Of course, I was unable to consider such a position", wrote Fysh. "I was then (as the Taylor affair was still unresolved) shocked to receive a telephone call from Dan McVey, while I was trout fishing . . . to inform me as his QEA chairman that he was taking the job on. He had always wanted to do something for the British aircraft manufacturing industry in Australia, and here was his chance."

Fysh commented: "This similar action by the two QEA Directors firmly sealed the fate of each in regard to their positions with us. How could we properly operate as a Board when a choice of aircraft came up? Would the two Directors be asked to leave the room? Comets were involved, Viscounts, Tridents and even the supersonic Concorde. All we would want to complete the fun would have been a Boeing and a Lockheed Director on our Board."[51] (W. C. Taylor's appointment as a Qantas director and vice-chairman terminated on 2 August 1961; Sir Daniel McVey's appointment as a director terminated on 15 June 1961. Both had been on the QEA board since 1947.)

There was no reference in the Qantas annual report covering the 1960 year to the dispute about the tripartite pool, which had come into operation on 1 April. (The twenty-seventh annual report covered a period of fifteen months, from 1 January 1960 to 31 March 1961, as the company's balance date was changed from 31 December to 31 March to coincide with that of its pool partners.) "The main object of the tripartite agreement", said the report, "is the economic co-ordination of schedules, reservation systems and sales efforts of the three operators." There was a net operating profit for this fifteen-month period of £671,892 after charging £952,942 for interest on loans and a net capital profit from the sale of aircraft and other assets of £455,466, used (with an additional £325,440 from revenue) to help write off training and pre-operational costs for the Boeing 707 and Electra aircraft. Total training and pre-operational costs were capitalised in the balance sheet at £2,095,296 to be written off against future operations. The operational profit, lower than in 1959, indicated the significance of increasing jet competition and the depressed economic conditions internationally.

In 1960, on 16 November, Qantas had celebrated its fortieth anniversary. It had grown, since the formation of the company

During Qantas's fortieth anniversary celebrations in late 1960, this replica of the 1921 Longreach office was built opposite Qantas House in Sydney.

Qantas House in Sydney
decorated for the fortieth
anniversary in 1960.

in Queensland in 1920 and its beginnings with two small single-engined aeroplanes costing £1,950, into an international carrier with round-the-world services, a staff of 6,600, and a fleet of twenty-one four-engined airliners (including eleven large jets) costing £27 million.

This Remarkable Position
1961

In 1960 there had been seventy thousand overseas visitors to Australia yet Sydney, the nation's biggest city, had a total of only 1,800 first class hotel rooms and, of these, many were second rate or worse when compared with overseas hotels. Qantas saw in these figures a clear case for their proposal to the government that the company should build its own first class hotel on the site it had acquired next door to Qantas House. For the Menzies government the dilemma was whether or not the government-owned airline should be allowed to extend into what had always been a private enterprise field.

Qantas had argued that their competitors, Pan American, KLM, SAS, Japan Airlines, and others, were building hotels but the government had received strong opposition from Australian hotel interests. In May 1959 the Qantas project had been approved in principle; in 1960 it had been twice turned down by Cabinet. Paltridge had called together opponents of the Qantas plan and Qantas in a "Hotel Investigating Committee" under the chairmanship of QEA director Dan McVey. By 17 January 1961, Paltridge was able to write to the prime minister once more on the proposal: "Initially, some delay was caused by the necessity for making a very full study of the results of the meetings with the various hoteliers of the McVey Committee", he wrote. "I am now in a position to report to Cabinet." He highlighted Qantas's activities in earning foreign currency for Australia.

It is estimated for 1960 that net foreign currency earnings will represent an invisible export of the value of £1.8 million and that

203

for 1961 the figure will exceed £2 million. These amounts are not great, but I think they are certainly useful. It is part of the Qantas argument in favour of the hotel project that unless they can guarantee first class hotel accommodation to their passengers they must expect a check in their traffic growth rates and, as you know, I accept this argument . . . Foreign passengers who enter Australia not only contribute to Qantas' foreign earnings but – obviously – spend money while they are here. In the Qantas estimates for a new hotel, an 80 per cent occupancy rate and an average stay of three days suggests an annual turnover of some 45,000 guests. If, as we anticipate, 30,000 of these are overseas visitors, and each spends a total of £200 in Australia, the earnings in foreign currency will be of the order of £6 million. This is by no means an exaggerated figure . . . I also propose to emphasise to Cabinet the importance of the Qantas hotel project in relation to our recent decision to promote tourists as a means of earning foreign currency.[1]

The positive tone of this ministerial letter was severely modified only weeks later when Paltridge was forced to tell his prime minister: "It so happens that Qantas are at present experiencing some cash difficulties which I am attempting to resolve with my colleague, the Treasurer. Until this is done, I feel that it would not be politic to bring forward the hotel proposal. I intend, therefore, to defer it at present."[2] (Qantas had earned a profit of £283,968 in the first three months of 1960 but only £387,924 was earned in the following twelve months to 31 March 1961, mainly because other international competitors had by then introduced jet equipment.) Qantas was not to receive official approval for its long-sought hotel until 11 August 1961.

As 1961 began, there were renewed signs of industrial trouble from pilots, a bid by Ansett to buy TEAL, a review of migrant passenger traffic, and moves by Pan American to force the filing, in the United States, of details of airline pooling agreements.

It was the view of the pilots, expressed by the executive committee of the Australian Federation of Air Pilots on 22 January, that Qantas negotiations throughout the past eighteen months had not been carried on in good faith. Qantas, it considered, had been solely concerned with forcing the unregistered AFAP and its members back under the control of the Arbitration Commission. C. O. Turner was held to be the main architect of this Qantas policy and the federation now exerted its influence to attempt to force the government to create an independent committee of enquiry to investigate Qantas staff management.[3]

Ansett's bid to buy Tasman Empire Airways Limited received wide publicity in the Australian press. On 7 March, the Australian and New Zealand governments had announced agreement on a new plan for the ownership and operation of TEAL, but did not give details. Paltridge and New Zealand's minister of transport, J. K. McAlpine, made a brief statement: "We have agreed to recommend certain action on the future ownership and operation of TEAL. Until this action is approved it is not possible to release any details."[4] R. M. Ansett, with three of his executive directors, flew to Wellington where he had discussions with New Zealand's acting prime minister, J. R. Marshall, and the civil aviation minister, McAlpine. Ansett told the press that Ansett Transport Industries Ltd had offered to buy TEAL for £2 million. TEAL, he said, would remain in New Zealand and its executives, staff, aircraft, workshops, and related facilities would continue to operate as before. TEAL's propjet Electra aircraft would, he said, be interchangeable with Ansett-ANA's. Most of the finance for the purchase would be raised in New Zealand. New Zealand, said Ansett, already had two thousand shareholders in Ansett Transport Industries.[5]

The day following press reports of the Ansett offer, Paltridge told Parliament that he had no knowledge "of a purported offer by Mr R. Ansett to the New Zealand government. No offer has been made to the Federal Government." The Australian and New Zealand civil aviation departments had, he said, recommended against the sale of TEAL "to an outside concern".[6] In fact, two weeks before, Paltridge and McAlpine had reached agreement on the details on the future of Australia-New Zealand civil aviation relations, subject to the approval of the two governments. Australia was to sell its shareholding in TEAL to the New Zealand government for £NZ811,400, the par value of the shares, with effect from 1 April 1961, with payment to be made on or before 31 March 1965.

Paltridge told Menzies that recommendations to the governments were that they should conclude air service agreements giving Australia air routes to Christchurch (on New Zealand's south island), Wellington, Auckland, and beyond; and giving New Zealand air routes to Sydney, Brisbane, Melbourne, and beyond. These agreements were to be supplemented by a revenue pooling arrangement from 1 October 1961 covering trans-Tasman services, services between New Zealand and Fiji, and services beyond Fiji to Tahiti and Honolulu. The agreement envisaged future participation by BOAC in the pooling arrangements. "I am very satisfied with the outcome", Paltridge reported. "While we are being generous in regard to the proportion of revenue we are permitting TEAL to have, nevertheless the new arrangements will have commercial advantages for

Qantas and will help their revenue position appreciably."[7] (From 1 October 1961 TEAL share of the Tasman revenue was to be seventy per cent, decreasing to sixty per cent on 1 April 1963.) The arrangements were made public on 27 April. The agreement ended Fysh's long service on the TEAL board.

> It was my lot [Fysh wrote] ceaselessly . . . to plead for understanding and to moderate, as far as I could, that hostile QEA higher management which would have liked to see TEAL go out of business. Management could scarcely be blamed for this as TEAL was carrying trans-Tasman traffic, half of which in a strict sense, should have been carried by QEA. On the other hand, QEA was carrying much of New Zealand's third and fourth freedom traffic to far places, and most of this would have been lost when TEAL operated to its full strength. The circumstances caused a lack of trust in us by the New Zealanders . . .[8]

The TEAL monopoly of the Tasman had, because of the high air fares charged, been much criticised in Australia. It had also, of course, been under constant pressure from the United States, which saw it, like the operation of pooling arrangements by international airlines, as contrary to its preferred free market philosophy. On 14 February 1961, Pan American moved against the operation of pools by filing a motion with the United States Civil Aeronautics Board to broaden the scope of a CAB investigation that had been instituted on foreign air carrier permits. Pan American wanted the CAB, in cases where air transport involved traffic to or from the United States, to call on foreign carriers to file, for US approval, interairline agreements entered into for "pooling or apportioned earnings, losses, traffic, service or equipment or for regulating stops, schedules and character of service or for other co-operative working arrangements affecting air transportation to or from the United States". Australia rejected these moves. In advice to the Australian High Commission in London, the Department of External Affairs said:

> It is the policy of the Australian Government that, in appropriate circumstances, its overseas airline, Qantas, should associate with other airlines of the Commonwealth in co-operative arrangements . . . Any arrangements so made are of a commercial nature and concern only airlines directly involved and their governments. The suggestion made in the motion by Pan American that such arrangements could radically affect air transportation by producing a marked impact on the activities of United States carriers is emphatically refuted. An essential feature of the arrangements is the retention by each airline of its individual identity . . . The Australian Government recognises its obligations to ensure that

Qantas, as the Australian designated airline, operates air services to and through United States territory in conformity with the provisions of the Australia-United States Air Transport Agreement.[9]

The Pan American move was not solely aimed at the Qantas-BOAC-Air India pool; on 20 May 1959, Air France, Lufthansa, Alitalia, and Sabena agreed on a partnership scheme, called Air Union, under which traffic was to be shared on fixed quotas.

Although the fifteen months ending with the new balance date of 31 March 1961 had been eventful ones, there had been (apart from the termination of the New Guinea route and internal services) only minor changes to the Qantas route system. The frequency of the Melbourne-Auckland-Nadi Super Constellation service (operated under charter to TEAL) doubled to twice weekly in October 1960; the Sydney-Hong Kong via Port Moresby Electra service frequency had, in March 1960, also gone from once to twice weekly; the Sydney-Noumea service had resumed in March 1960, after two and a half months suspension pending negotiation of the air transport agreement with France. (Electras were introduced in May.) The company's withdrawal from New Guinea was reflected in the very modest 1.5 per cent overall increase in the total number of passengers carried on the airline's network, but air cargo loads showed an annual rate of increase of 48 per cent. (A new air cargo building was commenced in February 1961 at Mascot to provide for an anticipated heavy expansion in air cargo business.) There were four weekly round-the-world services operated in conjunction with the Sydney-London services through India and the United States.

Qantas was, in the maturing world airline environment of 1960, one of about three hundred international and domestic airlines in one hundred nations, operating a total of more than seven thousand aircraft.[10] The international airlines were all invariably recording either very small profit margins or losses. Qantas, though its profit was small as a percentage of capital, was relatively large. Fysh was not quite certain how to treat the budgeted profit of £1.8 million for the current year and wrote to Qantas director and secretary of the Treasury, Sir Roland Wilson.

> There has been some difference of opinion here and . . . we have appealed to you for your opinion . . . Since this [profit] was struck and communicated to the Minister, international air traffic carried in comparison with the seats offered has taken a serious turn for the worse. We must rebudget without delay. On what I know I

would say we would be extremely fortunate to break even this financial year . . . It may be that Qantas will be obliged to retrench quite large numbers of staff later on this year and this will indeed be in a bad atmosphere if we have made what appears to be a handsome profit. We might strike real trouble in this . . . While C. O. Turner is undecided, Fred Derham [director of finance] is in favour of the figures and recommendations as presented. Your advice is valuable to us . . .[11]

In the event, the annual report for the twelve months to 31 March 1961 recorded a modest net profit of £408,817 and a recommended dividend of only three per cent. In mid-year, Turner advised Fysh from London that the main tripartite pool group was running at £3 million below projections with no evidence of immediate recovery. BOAC revenue was running at a rate of £8 million per annum below targets on all services, with the Atlantic particularly bad. The Qantas share of the Southern Cross pool, he advised, could be £500,000 below target. Turner attributed the revenue loss to a "worldwide loss of confidence affecting political and economic stability". A review of the airline's planning, he said, had found it to be sound. "I believe that the Qantas position is relatively sound compared with other operators as we have the right equipment and have not over-stretched ourselves but immediate action must be aimed at disposing of our Super Constellations – which will mean some further staff redundancies in all departments. BOAC is in serious industrial trouble due to efforts to rationalise the staff position . . ."[12]

Qantas's first turbofan-engined 707, VH-EBH *City of Darwin*, about to take off on its first flight, 13 April 1961. Because it was the first of a new model, it had to undergo testing by the FAA before they would issue a certificate of airworthiness.

At 31 March 1961, the company's aircrew totalled 319 pilots, 133 flight engineers, 69 navigators, and 5 radio officers. There were 208 flight stewards and 71 flight hostesses. Flight training was carried out for the Boeing 707s and Electras at Avalon,

near Melbourne, and supplemented in the flight simulators at Sydney. (There were three simulators from July 1960, for the Boeing, the Electra, and the Constellation.) The main Qantas jet base at Sydney had, by now, become a completely self-contained organisation handling every phase of aircraft, engine, and instrument overhaul and modification. Reflecting the airline's consciousness of its role in projecting Australia's national identity, in all of the company's principal sales offices overseas a section had been set aside as an Australian centre. Called Corroboree Rooms, they provided a meeting place and reading room for Australians and, with special displays and exhibitions planned and a wide selection of books, were being developed to interest non-Australians in matters Australian.[13]

The Qantas fleet of Boeing 707 aircraft, in service and on order, were to be the real basis for its continued ability to operate profitably in depressed world economic conditions that were to cause the international air transport industry as a whole heavy losses in the forthcoming year. There had, of course, been major efforts by Britain to sell its VC10 airliner to Qantas and there were still some hopes remaining that Qantas could be persuaded to buy it. In a tour of Australia in early 1961, BOAC's chairman, Slattery, took pains at press conferences to publicise its merits. The wisdom of the Qantas choice of Boeing 707s and the professionalism of the senior engineers in its technical development department were evident from BOAC's real, in-house, and con-

Lockheed Electra VH-ECB and Boeing 707s VH-EBF and VH-EBA at Sydney airport, March 1961. They are parked on the area where Qantas's four major aircraft maintenance hangars were built during the sixties and seventies. The international terminal at Sydney now stands in the area beyond the Electra's tail.

fidential attitude to the VC10. As QEA's partner on its main route, the BOAC approach to ordering major items of equipment in this period is worth recounting. Rear Admiral Slattery set down its main elements in a confidential report to Britain's minister for aviation, Peter Thorneycroft, in April 1961.

"We, and your officials," he wrote, "have for some time been aware that the economics of the VC10-Super VC10 are not so good, on paper, as those actually being experienced with the Boeing 707, which is available for purchase as and when we would want it." Slattery told the minister that he had been repeatedly asked at press conferences in Australia whether BOAC had ordered VC10s purely to support the British aircraft industry. "My reply was on the lines that the VC10 would be a more flexible aeroplane and better suited to the Corporation's worldwide routes – as it has been our official policy at all times not to show any dissatisfaction with the VC10 in public." Slattery said that this was sound commercial policy and commonsense. "BOAC is committed in the broad national interest to buying and operating a fleet of British-made VC10s and it makes no kind of commercial sense to allow the aircraft to build up a bad reputation before it goes into service . . . If it were publicly to gain credence that BOAC did not like the aeroplane, it would have a very damaging effect . . . and, in addition, ruin the chances (albeit slender) of the manufacturers selling it to other operators." Slattery said that there were some factors, incapable of precise evaluation (better field performance and passenger appeal), that might operate in BOAC's favour but "by no stretch of the imagination can they outweigh the basic economic disadvantages".

He quantified these for his minister. "I should not like you to be under any misapprehension as to the extent and effect of the basic operating cost differential. In a full year of operation of VC10s, the same seating capacity could be provided by Boeing 707s at an annual cost of some £11 million less than that of the VC10s." On the basis of frequency of service rather than equivalent seating capacity on some routes (the two aircraft were different in size), Slattery said that this annual penalty might be reduced from £11 to £7 million. "It has been the practice, quite understandably, to attempt to compare the Corporation's financial results with other international operators. These operators will be using mainly 707s and although the Corporation will have eighteen of these aircraft out of a total jet fleet of sixty-three, nevertheless a built-in disability of £7 million a year would be quite sufficient to put the Corporation's activities in an unfavourable light." He was, he said, loath to bring these facts to light publicly in the current year but there would come a time when it would be his duty to do so. "I have to consider the morale of all those who work so devotedly for the Corporation and who are so often discouraged by the constant criticism in Parliament and elsewhere of the Corporation's financial results; criticism that might be tempered if the true facts of what the Corporation is doing to sustain the British aircraft industry were more widely known."[14] In a background summary for Thorneycroft, BOAC's chairman reminded him that the original BOAC contract for the VC10, signed with Vickers in 1958, was "very hastily drawn up . . . because BOAC were told by Ministry that if they did not get something started quickly they might not be able to get Government approval for more aircraft". In 1960, he said, the Boeing 707 had come into service in BOAC and proved a remarkably efficient aeroplane. In that same year "ten Super VC10s were prematurely ordered by the Corporation under pressure from H.M. Minister. This was connected with the re-organisation of the aircraft industry and HMG undertaking to give some financial support to Vickers with the Super VC10 programme [and] Vickers' threat that they could not continue with the thirty-five standard VC10s without this aid." These were facts, of course, that were not known in Australia to the Government Members Committee on Civil Aviation, whose chairman, David Fairbairn, so staunchly supported the use of British airliners and who had queried the Qantas preference for Boeings.

Dr R. R. (Dick) Shaw, Qantas's technical development controller, gave some indication of the meticulous approach given to the airline's operating procedures for their 707-138As in a report outlining the many and varied efforts made since their introduction to improve their performance in terms of both speed and fuel consumption. "Individually these efforts have had only minor results—we have chipped away at mere fractions of a percent at times. Collectively the results are very significant." The results of these detailed changes to operating procedures were a saving of over a million gallons a year in fuel, worth £88,000, and a total saving in block times (from the roll-out of the aircraft to its final halt at the destination) of 751 hours a year, which, at £220 per hour, represented monetary savings of £165,000 yearly. The total annual rate of savings from the painstakingly modified operational procedures of the 707s was, therefore, at least £253,000. "This", said Shaw, "is a substantial achievement and reflects great credit on our performance engineers and development flying group in establishing new procedures and flight plannings methods, on the flight crews in applying them and on our overhaul and maintenance engineering groups in keeping the aircraft and engines at a high level of performance."[15]

In 1960, the Australian government was still led by a prime minister whose traditions and culture were devotedly Anglo-Saxon. Robert Gordon Menzies was a man "largely untouched by non-European cultural traditions".[16] Australian immigration policy mirrored his views. Anxious as Australia was for immigrants, there was no move to look to non-European sources until Menzies announced his retirement. The government had formed an Inter-governmental Committee for European Migration (ICEM) and was operating an assisted passage scheme. Qantas met with the Department of Immigration and the Department of Civil Aviation in April 1960 to discuss Qantas proposals for carriage of migrants both on special flights and as fill-up loadings. In a report on activities for the year, Qantas noted that it had been hoped to establish in mid-1960 a regular weekly service between Europe and Australia for the carriage of migrants in Constellation 1049s, but that difficulties following the introduction of the Electras as well as aircrew shortages had delayed the project. Instead, migrants

April 1961. A Lockheed Electra of Tasman Empire Airways Ltd and a Qantas 707 at Sydney. The round markings on the Electra's tail fin and near the cockpit windows were badges commemorating twenty-one years of service.

212

were carried at a low fare (£130 sterling from the United Kingdom) on a fill-up basis and on charter flights. For the year, 938 British adults and 15 children were carried as fill-up traffic by the pool partners for a total revenue of £152,425. Under the government's General Assisted Passage Scheme, migrants from countries included in the scheme received a grant of £71 per head toward the cost of travel to Australia, but the travel arrangements were a matter for the individual migrants. Under the ICEM, Qantas carried migrants from Europe at a directed fare on a fill-up basis. The numbers carried were small as most migrants came to Australia by air on special ICEM charter flights. Qantas could not provide its own aircraft for such charters but made arrangements with BOAC for the use of Britannia aircraft. In 1960, using these Britannias, Qantas operated thirty-one charter flights for ICEM but did so at an overall loss of £17,670 because of the low fares involved. (Other airlines also operated charter flights. In 1960 KLM provided twenty-two, the French airline TAI four, and other airlines among them a further three.)

Hudson Fysh left Sydney in May for an executive committee meeting of IATA in New York. His notes on the trip show his preoccupations. Overprovision of airliner capacity by international carriers was a major worry. "The South Pacific is an area which could become a trouble area and a sink for profits", he wrote. "The Atlantic is now over-provided . . . even in peak periods." Australia and New Zealand, he noted, must be most careful not to grant rights to any other operator under any circumstances unless they received as much as they gave. The impact of the French TAI and of Alitalia on Qantas would, he thought, severely affect the revenues of Qantas, possibly even critically. Pan American were expected to exercise extensive Australian rights in the future. Fysh felt the test should be whether Qantas was "obtaining traffic from the other country equal to what they take from ours". Though Qantas progress overseas was striking, Fysh stressed the need for a moratorium on all spending abroad. He made a brief reference to the coming supersonic era. "A 300,000-pound supersonic plane at 40,000 feet will break every window over an area of thirty miles." Of their Kangaroo Route partner, he wrote: "Sadly for BOAC it was confirmed that the VC10, at least in its present form . . . will not be as good an aeroplane as our fan-type 707s. BOAC are worried about the aeroplane."[17]

On 1 June 1961, the Australian Federation of Air Pilots signalled an intensification of its ongoing conflict with Qantas and the domestic airlines in a circular to all its members. "The Federation is facing a critical phase in its relations with Airline Operators . . . a firm stand is now necessary. The problems arise in Western Australia [MacRobertson Miller Airlines], in Qantas and collectively with TAA and the ATI Group. In Qantas the Federation is confronted with that Company's imperative [*sic*] decision to continue the expansion of 'Executive Pilot' ranks, with the associated enforcement of their resignation from the Federation. Additionally, pilots are being selected (irrespective of seniority) for dismissal on the grounds of 'lack of potential' – a Company term." The AFAP circular said there should be a limited number of executive positions – three in Qantas – and those holding such positions should be ineligible for membership of the Federation. "Supervisory positions", it commented, "can no longer be said to be filled on ability alone. The prime requisite now is the agreement to resign [from the AFAP]. Little confidence can thus be held, by virtue of the appointment alone, in the integrity or ability of the office holder."[18] At that time Qantas had eighteen supervisory captains, four senior training captains (and one DC3 training captain), sixteen senior check captains, and fourteen check captains. The eighteen supervisory captains comprised the executive pilot group.[19] In the April 1957 pilots' strike, the entire supervisory pilot strength (eight in total and all members of the AFAP) had refused to accept the strike directive and remained on duty. Following resumption of work by the pilots, the association had threatened disciplinary action against them and the supervisory pilots had voluntarily resigned their membership of the AFAP on the basis of incompatibility of loyalties. It was the management view in June 1961 that supervisory pilots should not be members of the federation because, in management's view, the federation paid regard to safety but accepted no responsibility for it. The Qantas Senior Staff Association strongly objected to the pilots' pressure for a government investigation into the management of Qantas. The association wrote directly to Paltridge on 21 June describing the situation as of serious concern to its members.

> While the Chief Executive and General Manager of Qantas is responsible for the Company position on this matter we believe that Mr Turner has acted on and entirely consistent with advice given him by officers who are members of our Association. Any demands to investigate Company Management therefore directly reflects on our members. We therefore respectfully advise you that

Mr Turner has the complete support of the Association in the current dispute and that we feel bitter resentment of the slur cast by the pilots' demand for an investigation. [20]

Feelings were running high.

The company's administration of its pilots and their duties came under the Flight Operations Department, which controlled all flying operations, including the standard of operational discipline and all technical flight staff. To control particular route operations, flight captains and assistant flight captains were appointed for each aircraft type. For the Boeings, for example, there was one flight captain for the Kangaroo Route and one for the Pacific route, plus one flight captain and two assistant flight captains in charge of the forty-seven technical flight staff based in London. (In this London group were eleven supervisory pilots.) The flight captains, who each had an average of forty-five pilots under their direct control, co-ordinated the rostering of their pilots, ensured their standard of safety, and kept abreast of changes in airfield development and lighting, instrument approach, and en route navigational facilities and instrument let-down patterns. They administered the requirements for route qualification, tours of duty, rest facilities at slip points, and verification that fuel reserves for various route ports were adequate. They were also responsible for the general discipline and behaviour of all technical air crew.

In the Training Section there were seventeen senior check captains. The training organisation ensured that all pilot licencing requirements were met and that pilots met all departmental and Qantas flying standards. A separate group headed by a development flying controller analysed aircraft performance standards and worked with the technical development controller on optimum flight performance techniques, aircraft modifications, and flight acceptance of new aircraft. (The same principles of control applied to navigators and flight engineers.) [21]

The problem of redundancies for aircrew had arisen because of a reduction in flying hours for the L1049 Constellations, which had necessitated the inhibiting of two aircraft (and one DC4). The company had drawn up a retrenchment programme affecting pilots, flight engineers, and ground maintenance personnel. Also, the company had for some time been reviewing the overall position of its first and second officers. A management memorandum on 15 June said: "Many have not shown the potential capacity to increase their pilot qualifications, or have been slow in assimilating the techniques associated with jet aircraft, and therefore fall in the category of permanent first

The Qantas area at Sydney airport, mid-1961. A BOAC Comet 4 stands between Boeing 707 VH-EBG and L1049 VH-EAA. Note that the windows on VH-EAA are covered; it was withdrawn from service following a downturn in air cargo traffic. Construction of the air cargo terminal is underway in the left background.

and second officers. As the Company acquires additional jet aircraft, these pilots will become more difficult to utilise, and the increase in number of such people is blocking the advancement of younger pilots with greater potential who are our future captains of the supersonic age. The situation is becoming unmanageable." The company had, said the memo, made decisions on terminations on the basis of weeding out the least efficient of its pilots.[22]

Paltridge had made it plain to Fysh that he did not want a strike by pilots and had, Fysh told the board, put the onus on Qantas to prevent it.[23] Fysh told the minister:

> These issues [supervisory pilots and redundancy] are clearly not strike issues and the Company will do all in its power to find a satisfactory solution . . . Since the pilots' strike in 1957 the Company has been repeatedly harassed by the threat of further stoppages . . . The Pilots' Federation adheres to what they term a policy of collective bargaining. The Company does not object to such a procedure but insists that this policy be developed within the machinery of Conciliation and Arbitration as laid down by Parliament. This impasse must be resolved. The consequences of a failure to invoke the authority of the Arbitration Commission can be catastrophic. It will be recalled that ground staff at Mascot struck last week on the issue of redundancy, and after a march on the Company's Head Office and a conference with Management, returned to work to await the outcome of the pilots' dispute.

The pilots, Fysh reminded the minister, had all resigned from the body registered with the commission, the Australian Air Pilots' Association, and had become members of a trade union known as the Australian Federation of Air Pilots "which remains

216

to this day unregistered. The pilots regard themselves as being outside the system of conciliation and arbitration." The AFAP, he said, being an unregistered trade union, was not a body corporate. "The parties to the current dispute are therefore the Company and the individual pilots . . . The AFAP might well seek to legalise its impending strike by advising its members to attend proceedings as individual parties, either all together or in large groups."[24]

Fysh called an emergency board meeting and assured Paltridge that he would put his views to the board and that every reasonable measure for conciliation and discussion would be taken. The pressures from above on Fysh were considerable, but they were equalled by those from his chief executive. In a personal, handwritten note at the board meeting dated 21 June, he wrote:

> At the beginning of the pilots' discussion Turner flew into a rage and was rude to me when I said "Could there be any accusation that we were building up a strike-breaking force with supervisory pilots?" . . . I told Turner we must do everything to talk with the Association and not have a strike and that the Minister and Anderson [the director-general] were determined about the strike question. He flew into a white heat – furious – and accused me of wanting to give everything away. He said there could be no strike. I sat quietly. I am unable to get along with Turner. He just rages and will not listen. I never even thought of giving everything away.

Fysh was critical of Turner's approach to the conflict:

> There has never been any air of conciliation about our approach. Too much stress [has been] put on getting the Association into court, however desirable this is . . . All pilots I talk to stress there should be some way of the Company Chief, Turner, seeing more of pilots, and making them feel they are in it. With the heaviest regret I have to report to Board members that the Chief Executive and General Manager is quite incapable of talking rationally or receptively in listening to me in regard to the pilots' strike. I do not feel I have to go into details to the Board, but last week Mr Turner was most insulting to me and disloyal in his duty to me as Chairman. This is one of the reasons for my calling this special meeting. If I am unable to talk to the Chief Executive on important matters [the only alternative] is to call the Directors in. I do not wish to have this matter resolved at this Board but when we get past this present trouble I will call a future session of the Board to discuss the present insufferable position.

If, said Fysh, Turner behaved before others in negotiations or discussions as he behaved to himself, then he was completely unsuited to handling the pilots. The board, wrote Fysh, was to treat Turner firmly.[25]

Turner had an official bulletin issued on 22 June, under the heading "Staff Retrenchments", which read: "In the event of it becoming necessary to retrench members of the Company's staff, employees will be retrenched in the following order: (a) employees who are the least efficient (b) employees who have reached or are beyond normal retiring age [50 for technical air-crew and 60 for ground staff] (c) all other things being equal, the employee with the shortest service."[26] (An interesting comparison in attitudes to staff retrenchment at the time can be found in the Commonwealth Public Service General Orders setting out the order of discharge to be followed for temporary employees. In order of discharge they were: married women, women over compulsory retiring age (65), males over compulsory retiring age (65), single women and widows, female persons qualified for permanent appointment, relatives of deceased soldiers, female members of the Forces, and, only then, various categories of men.)[27]

Fysh had further trouble with his chief executive a few days after the first explosion. He described it in a "highly confidential" letter to R. R. Law-Smith and Sir Roland Wilson.

> Again, on Wednesday last, Mr Turner made a violent scene in my office, accusing me of wanting to give everything away. Again he was insulting. This kind of thing cannot be let to go on and at the appropriate time I will bring the matter up for discussion at a private session of the Board. The present critical situation has long been working up. I had hoped it would improve but it has now come to a head, finally culminating in the scene in the Board Room at the end of our special meeting, and when directors could do nothing else but obtain a clear picture of the position.[28]

The directors were by no means united in sympathy for Hudson Fysh. He met with Qantas director W. C. Taylor and Turner on 27 June and made handwritten notes:

> Turner was anxious all the time to get the words right, and I agree this most important and that he is a big help here. However he wants to do this, as he says, because "Melbourne [the Department of Civil Aviation] blame Qantas for the strike threat". Taylor finds no favour in what we have done and stands right behind Turner and his staff, even after what he raised in the Board about Turner's attitude. A complete about-face. Taylor gave the impression that QEA is lily-white on the pilots strike threat issue. If this is so and the Board takes the same view, this whole matter could turn out as another personal triumph for Turner. This would be fatal.[29]

It was neither the Qantas board, Turner, nor the pilots' Federation that determined the next important and extraordinary turn of events. On 15 August 1961, the High Court handed down its decision on the AFAP's case that it was outside the jurisdiction of the arbitration commissioner. The High Court found, in effect, that although the AFAP was not a registered body, its individual members could become involved in a dispute with the airline and that such a dispute could be the subject of arbitration. Qantas could insist on arbitration, even though the federation was not, as a body, party to the dispute. Turner had a different perspective on the High Court finding. In a memorandum to all pilots on 31 August he wrote: "This judgement is regarded by Industry and Government as a most important one in industrial law because it eliminates any doubt about the genuineness of an unregistered Trade Union's ability to create a dispute on behalf of its members—a body such as the AFAP can create a dispute and the Commission is bound under the Conciliation and Arbitration Act to deal with that dispute."

The AFAP was later to make clever use of the situation created by the High Court finding by advising its members that in any dispute with Qantas, each individual pilot would be required to take separate action in any proceedings. The court's decision effectively changed the rules for disputes involving arbitration and led both to intense legal manoeuvring by both sides in the years that lay ahead, escalation of ill feeling, and increasing involvement by government.[30] In the meantime, the AFAP continued to press for independent negotiations while Qantas sought a new hearing before the commission. There was no implementation of the pilots' strike threat, though Turner advised the pilots: "The Company is now facing a most critical financial recession brought about by a worldwide fall in travel. Already the pattern of Constellation 1049 operations has been reduced and further changes are imminent. The effect of these changes will be felt by the pilots and other members of the staff."[31]

On 1 July 1961, with the retirement of its deputy chief executive and general manager, Capt. Scottie Allan, Qantas lost its most famous airman. His flying career started in 1916 when he joined the Royal Flying Corps in England. From 1922 (when he re-joined the services) to 1929 he served in the Royal Air Force and flew all current aircraft types. He came to Australia in 1929 and joined the select band of great aviation pioneers, flying with Kingsford Smith and Ulm on many of their famous flights. He joined Qantas in 1934 from the original Australian National

Airways, where he had been chief pilot, and was (with Lester Brain) the guiding influence in developing and administering the sound flying procedures of the infant Qantas Empire Airways as it introduced on its new overseas routes the four-engined DH86 biplanes and, in 1938, the revolutionary and handsome flying boats. Scottie Allan used his flying boat experience with the Royal Australian Air Force in World War II and was, as a member of the RAAF, part of the Qantas crew that ferried the first of the Catalina flying boats from the United States to Australia in 1941 (on what was only the third ever direct crossing by air of the Pacific). He returned to Qantas after the war, first as London manager and then as controller of technical development before coming, in 1952, assistant general manager and the airline's chief adviser on new aircraft types. Fysh wrote:

> It was always the practice for the Assistant General Manager [Scottie Allan] to attend Board Meetings in support of the Chief Executive, who was lacking in technical experience . . . [He] was retired on 30 June 1961 having reached retiring age and his place was taken by Capt. R. J. Ritchie, who proved a good choice. Scottie, after his retirement, continued to give valuable service in an advisory capacity, and also as Chairman of Fiji Airways and with a seat on Malayan Airways Board. [32]

Qantas director W. C. Taylor's departure from the board was greeted with front page headlines in Sydney's *Daily Mirror* on 2 August under the banner "Top Man Quits in Qantas Row". His resignation, said the story, was the sequel to a bitter personal row with Hudson Fysh. Fysh asked Turner to let it be known to all staff, particularly management staff, that the story was without foundation. "I have just spoken to Bill Taylor on the phone", he wrote. "He is most upset that the reason for his resignation has been misconstrued. He also made it abundantly clear to the QEA Board and to Senator Paltridge that his resignation was on account of his Chairmanship of Hawker Siddeley in Australia. Bill Taylor remains a friend of myself and the Board and of his host of friends in the Company." [33] The *Mirror* inferred that Taylor had also been "jettisoned" by the Menzies government happily enough because he had had "a lifetime association with the late Mr Chifley" and had been trouble-shooter for the Labor prime minister in the 1949 federal election campaign. Taylor had been appointed to the Qantas board by Chifley in 1947 and had served it well. Fysh wrote later: "Whatever differences I had with McVey and Taylor, they were minor in comparison with the great work they did for QEA during their terms of office". [34] With the departure of McVey and

Taylor, Sir Norman Knock was appointed to the board on 16 June and James N. Kirby on 3 August. Law-Smith, a director since 1956, was appointed vice-chairman on 3 August. Fysh commented to TAA chairman and Qantas director G. P. N. Watt:

With Bill Taylor and Dan McVey out . . . we have lost a great deal of strength and it will take us some time to recover from the effects. In addition, we have lost Scottie Allan from the Board table. I am very happy about the replacements as far as I know them and I feel we will have great strength in the company, but just at the moment perhaps, it can be said that we are going through a difficult reformative period . . . You are now our mainstay on the Board and your ideas and opinions will, I think, make more of an impact than perhaps was possible before. You are due for re-election as from June 30 of next year and I wanted to let you know that I am most anxious for you to continue . . . [35]

Fysh was, in fact, grateful to Watt and to the new vice-chairman, Law-Smith, on a matter of particular importance. Both had been concerned at Turner's escalating outbursts of rage towards Fysh and had undertaken to speak to Turner about them. Norman Watt was able to tell Fysh on 2 August:

The interview last Friday between Bob Law-Smith and myself and Turner went very satisfactorily. Turner was quick to express regret that he had lost his temper and had said things to you which he was sorry for, and I am sure that he is going to try to be less emotional in the future and to work harmoniously with you. By now you will have had your chat with him and I trust that your personal and official relations will now have been restored to the level on which you have worked amicably, if sometimes with

The second of Qantas's new turbofan-engined 707-138Bs at Boeing's Renton plant near Seattle, August 1961. The colour scheme shown was changed soon after VH-EBI arrived in Australia. The photograph also shows some of the aerodynamic changes introduced on the B model 707; note the increased height of the tail and the change of angle on the leading edge of the wing between the fuselage and the inner engine.

difficulty, over the years, with so much benefit to Qantas and its development. [36]

Fysh declared himself satisfied with the outcome and told Watt: "You did a good job well handled, and relationships between Turner and myself are already back on a good footing". [37]

The first of the fan-engined 707-138B aircraft, *City of Darwin*, reached Sydney on 6 August 1961, with the fourth of the new aircraft arriving on 1 September. The remainder of the 707 fleet, the 138As, progressively returned to the United States for replacement of the three forward compression stages of the engines with two fan discs, were all modified by January 1962. The turboprop Electras, which had suffered from speed restrictions imposed by the Department of Civil Aviation in March 1960, had also been flown back to the United States for modification of engine mountings and wing structure but all had returned to service by March 1961 without interruption to Qantas schedules. They were introduced on Tasman services on October 1961 when Qantas began operating the route in its own right. (The Electras were already being operated, in the interests of long-range economy, at speeds within the temporary limits imposed, so that there were only minor variations to time-tables.) The operational highlight of 1961, however, was the introduction in November of Boeing V-jet services on the Hong Kong and Japan routes, reducing the total journey time by five hours twenty minutes to just under seventeen hours. (The

The Qantas Board, August 1961. From left: F. C. Derham, secretary; C. O. Turner, chief executive and general manager; Sir Norman Nock, director; R. R. Law-Smith, vice-chairman; Sir Hudson Fysh, chairman; G. P. N. Watt, director; Sir Roland Wilson, director; Sir James Kirby, director; Capt. R. J. Ritchie, deputy chief executive and deputy general manager.

Electras were withdrawn on 14 January 1962, when the jet service was increased to three times weekly on the Tokyo route.) The Boeings also replaced the Electras on the weekly Noumea service in December 1961.

With their turbine-powered fleet fully modernised, Qantas now received official approval from Paltridge for their proposal to build a 400-room hotel on the site adjoining Qantas House. In a public announcement, Paltridge said that the project would cost £5 million but it was not expected that any funds would come from government sources. A new company, which was to arrange for a loan of £3 million against a security of a first mortgage on the hotel, would be floated and the public would be invited to subscribe a further £2 million in equity capital. The subscription made by Qantas would, he said, be from their own resources and would involve capitalisation of the current value of the hotel site. To Fysh, Paltridge wrote: "I think it best that your Board should now obtain a clear understanding for the availability of the loan funds and communicate to me the precise terms. I can then clear these with the Treasurer . . . You have at all times, and very properly, emphasised the necessity for protecting the public investment in Qantas Wentworth Holdings Limited."[38] Fysh wrote a personal note to Menzies, expressing his satisfaction. "The confidence placed in Qantas by you personally and by your colleagues has been terrific . . . For some time back I have realised that the real issue lay in regard to whether Qantas was to go ahead in enterprise

Two of the early model Boeing 707-138s being converted to 707-138B specifications at Seattle in late 1961. By 1962 all seven of the early aircraft delivered in 1959 had been rebuilt to the new turbofan standard.

223

Departure of the first Qantas service to New Zealand, 3 October 1961. Sir Hudson Fysh and S. C. Johnston, New Zealand's high commissioner, pose for photographs at the foot of the aircraft steps.

and competition with its competitors, or whether it had reached a high water mark from which it would inevitably recede."[39]

Representatives of world airlines, including Qantas competitors, met in Sydney in October 1961 for the seventeenth annual general meeting of the International Air Transport Association. In all, including the wives of the most senior, there were 400 delegates and guests representing 92 international airlines from 57 countries. Getting them all to Australia was, in itself, a challenge as only by 1961 had there been enough international flights to provide sufficient capacity for this sudden influx. Hotel accommodation, too, was strained and was sufficient only because Sydney's newest hotel, the Chevron Hilton, had been completed. Guests stayed at the Wentworth and the Hilton, and the conference was held in its new and glamorous public rooms.

Annual general meetings of IATA traditionally included lavish and carefully planned entertainments. To the cynical, these came under the well-tried process of "duchessing"; to the practical, they were a unique opportunity to demonstrate to one of the most influential travel bodies in the world the attractions, character, and abilities of the host country. The first of the air transport leaders and their wives to arrive were entertained in Canberra by Lord De L'Isle, the governor-general. They visited the War Memorial, played golf, and were taken to a fine sheep station to watch shearing, crop dusting, buck jumping, and cattle droving, as well as passing kangaroos crossing the road and seeing black snakes killed casually and hung on the fence.

Back in Sydney, the prime minister, Sir Robert Menzies, gave the address of welcome and then, in a proud moment for Sir Hudson Fysh, he was handed the gavel of office to become, for a year, the IATA president. Its members (at the end of 1960) had among them 3,339 aircraft (382 jets, 480 turboprops, and 2,477 piston-engined), but had on order a total of 900 jets. The vast increase in capacity that they represented was, however, creating massive strains between many of the association's ninety-three member airlines. Their financial outlook was unpromising. "It was", wrote Fysh, "a case of acute aerial indigestion, resulting from the rapid absorption of the new jet fleets. The airlines had not been able to dispose of, without loss, the old piston-engined equipment . . . It was a horrifying situation which QEA had avoided by careful planning."[40]

The International Air Transport Association was an unusual body for its time. Every airline member, whatever the size of its fleet, had an equal vote in the association's proceedings. (Size varied from small inter-city helicopter operators to the great world airlines.) In its deliberations, on committees that covered finance, law, technical matters, medical matters, facilitation (customs, immigration, and other procedures), and traffic, IATA worked on the rule of unanimity. Any one of the carriers represented could withhold agreement on any issue; each had the power of veto. It was a power that was at its most valuable in the proceedings of the true problem child of IATA, the traffic conferences. In the two years leading to the 1961 annual general meeting, IATA traffic conferences had faced problems so severe that the very roots of the system had been badly shaken. It had not failed because of the general recognition that a collapse of the traffic conference system would mean the end of the power of IATA in civil aviation and the loss, by airlines, of their right to set fare levels, rates, and conditions. In 1961, IATA

225

resolutions covered a series of interairline agreements for all phases of passenger, baggage, and cargo handling, and reservation codes. Some seven hundred resolutions included agreement on a standard IATA ticket, baggage check and air waybills, as well as 30,000 agreed fares and rates, and the rules for constructing others. In a system involving almost one hundred airlines from around the world, each with a veto power, it was a unique international body.

The main theme of the 1961 meeting was the substantial operating losses that had been sustained, diminishing load factors, and the consequent cheating and fare rebating to entice passengers that threatened the existence of the association. It was a year in which BOAC had lost £15 million, Lufthansa over £13 million. KLM, SAS, and TWA had lost heavily. Qantas, Pan American, Air India, Swissair, Philippine Air Lines, and Aer Lingus were the only international carriers to operate profitably, though the profits were small. IATA's director-general, Sir William Hildred, estimated that illegal fare rebating had taken $400 million from the total revenues of the operators and, in doing so, had turned profit into loss for the industry.

The Sydney annual general meeting of IATA began on the Monday morning of 23 October with its plenary session. The normal business of receiving and adopting reports from standing committees and discussion of agenda subjects followed through the week. But the atmosphere and the memories of IATA annual general meetings came from other events. Qantas

Taken from the Latin word "vannus", which meant "fan", the V-jet designation was introduced in late 1961 by Qantas to advertise the fact that their 707s were the new turbofan models, superior in performance to the aircraft of all other international airlines serving the Australian market. This striking photograph of VH-EBL taken by a Boeing photographer near Mount Ranier in August 1964 emphasises the symbol that meant Qantas to millions of travellers until it was phased out in the mid-seventies.

had spent months of preparation for the one single event that was to dominate the week. In an outdoor setting of gum trees and wattles by the Lane Cove river (christened "Kangaroo Flat" for the occasion), the overseas guests were shown shearers at work, sheep dogs working and yarding sheep, tree felling, stockwhip displays, boomerang throwing, and even swagmen boiling their billies. Ned Kelly's armour had been borrowed from Victoria and two uniformed policemen led someone playing the Australian folk hero through the crowd. Australian birds and reptiles were on display and the sound of kookaburras (recorded) issued from the surrounding bush. When the record was stopped, the sound continued. It had attracted local kookaburras to the site. The occasion had impressed. The world's best-known aviation journalist, American publisher Wayne Parrish, reported: "It was generally agreed that Qantas had performed the best organisation task in IATA history".[41]

Hudson Fysh wrote with more than usual deference to his minister, Shane Paltridge:

> I attach an extract from IATA documentation for the Sydney AGM which shows the position of Qantas amongst the international airlines in respect of revenue tonne miles flown. We came from 11th last year to 7th, to now lie next to the few very big operators.
> I do not know whether you specially engineered this position in your various negotiations, and in the authorisation for the purchase of our new jets—which enabled us to achieve this remarkable position so that it could happen in my presidential year. I cannot tell you how very proud I was to read the list of 84 international operators and to realise the big part you had played in it.[42]

The inaugural 707 service at Noumea, 7 December 1961.

A Sort of Milch Cow
1962

8 As 1962 began, Hudson Fysh turned to his diary, after a long period during which he had put it aside.

> It is five years since I wrote an entry [he began]. A most eventful five years and here I am, sixty-seven not out, and still going strong – having ridden through troublesome times . . . many storms, risks and difficulties. [There have been] no entries because I have been too busy. Except for some difficult periods [I have] achieved more peace of mind and better health – my health is improving through a better life. With Board appointments I am now in a better position than ever in regard to loyalty to me and support of my Board, my Minister and my Government.
>
> IATA in Australia has come and gone and left a great impression. I am now the President of IATA and the World Airline organisation. This is a pinnacle of honour, if nothing else, and I suppose shows one has managed to make the grade . . .

Commenting on the departure from the board of Taylor and McVey, Fysh noted:

> I wrote in one of my personal crises last year: "The battle is on . . . some may die". And some months later: "Yes, and now the battle is now won". Indeed more than one bit the dust, the Boss coming out with a higher rating than ever. It was this, or resignation.[1]

To Turner, who had figured so largely in those personal crises of 1961, Fysh wrote a cordial new year letter. The previous year, he said, had left Qantas in a good position as one of the few international airlines not in great difficulties.

> The prestige of the Company, finally capped by the IATA AGM in Australia, was never higher. This position is indeed a matter for congratulation for the whole of the Qantas organisation, led

by you as Chief Executive. With us, while some difficulties disappear others soon loom up to take their place and 1962 will, no doubt, be no exception. As an Australian National Instrument operating far and wide overseas, we must expect difficulties and that in some cases profitability will have to be sacrificed to national needs. We are politically vulnerable both domestically and internationally.

Fysh listed "a few of the multitude of considerations which beset us . . . only what occur to me at the moment". There is no documented evidence of Turner's reaction to such discursive reminders from his chairman but there is little doubt that they fuelled his irritation. On all the matters raised in such an ad hoc manner, Turner and his closely knit management team not only monitored them closely and quantified them but were, of course, the source of the information that made it possible for Fysh to make his generalised comments. Indeed, the circular nature of their exchange is evident in Fysh's words: "Your attack on costs from what you have told me will be vigorously maintained". He then advised: "The main thing is to eliminate where possible all unproductive costs". It was hardly advice that his stormy general manager would have considered helpful. It was, too, immediately tempered with: "I realise in regard to the implementation of some major savings, political and kindred considerations can be a bar to the quick action which you would otherwise like". More pertinently, Fysh asked that "the top bracket of Qantas, including myself and the Board, should set an example and watch such matters as travelling expenses . . . and that sort of thing". On costs, he concluded with an uncertain platitude: "Finally in regard to costs, I suppose the position really is one in which you are cutting costs to wherever point this is possible so long as it does not interfere with maintaining and increasing our revenue . . . In some places added costs will be necessary in order to increase revenue."

Fysh urged the importance of membership of clubs and organisations.

> In Sydney I belong to the Australian Club, Royal Sydney and other organisations. We are well represented at the Australian Club but not at the Union. As suggested, you should join the Union and I want to put Ritchie up as a second member at Rotary, as I cannot see you attending their luncheons or other functions in a way they demand. Nielson should regularly attend and fraternise with members at the New South Wales Club. The Lions Club is also important and Golf Clubs help . . . The expense of these clubs will amply repay us in added bookings.

He reminded Turner of traffic leaks. "Firstly, there is the problem of empty seats where, theoretically, they should have been filled." Qantas representatives at en route ports sometimes turned away passengers on advice that all seats were filled only to find, when an aircraft arrived, that there were vacant seats. There was the perennial problem of the "no show", when a booked passenger did not turn up to travel. Grave leakages came from some competitors and agents who gave passengers rebates on correct passage money. Also, commissions were split, giving extra money to agents. Fysh wrote of hearing of "an agent in Darwin not booking Qantas whenever possible as we would not agree to irregular procedures. We should do our best to catch offenders and report them to IATA."

After stressing the importance of the tripartite pool with BOAC and Air India and the great political significance for Australia and New Zealand of the Qantas-TEAL partnership, Fysh wrote: "The pilots' position remains one of our key problems. The whole set up at its very basis seems to have no stability or firm footing on either side . . . We should approach the whole thing as sympathetically as possible and carefully watch for the success of our own day by day relationships with our people."

As always, in these now annual letters, Fysh tactfully raised the matter of communications with the chief executive. "Any thing you and Management can do to keep myself and the Board in contact with affairs would be appreciated . . . A number of instances have occurred during last year where I have not been informed beforehand. You have the support of the Board and the more you take us into your confidence in planning ahead, the more satisfactory it is."[2] It was, from any point of view, extraordinary that the chief executive of a large and government-owned organisation should have to be cajoled to take the board into his confidence.

Though communication between chief executive and chairman was always uncertain, management procedures for the preparation of board papers were thorough and professional. They were, however, in their content and the timing of their submission, firmly under the control of C. O. Turner, a factor that greatly contributed to Fysh's growing sense of isolation in his last years with Qantas. Fysh was, though, an important as well as a formal link with government through the minister, with whom his relations were friendly. Paltridge wrote a personal note to him on 8 January: "Dear Huddy: Am looking forward to discussing some of the matters raised by you. Use of Con-

Perth, 1 February 1962. The first Qantas jet service from Perth to London was operated by VH-EBE *City of Perth*, one of the original seven 707-138s recently converted to -138B (V-jet) specification. Note the early style dark fuselage band along the windows and the lighter colour on the tail. By late 1962, all of the early aircraft had been fully repainted with the new markings.

stellations will, of course, involve Government decisions on policy. The relationship with the Air Pilots' Association, quite frankly, worries me considerably and I regret that no real progress appears to have been made."[3]

Fysh had written to his minister on 21 December about the future use of the airline's remaining Super Constellations "with particular reference to their value to Australia as a reserve defence unit". Qantas had eight Super Constellations left from an original fleet of sixteen. Two were full cargo aircraft, two mixed cargo-passenger versions, and four in full passenger configuration. Their book value at the end of 1961 was about £2 million, including spare engines and parts.

"Unfortunately," wrote Fysh, "due to the failure of certain projects to develop, the effective utilisation of these aircraft after 31 March 1963 will fall to the extent that we will only have full utilisation for at most two of the units. It was earlier considered that it would be to the best advantage of the Company and Australia to dispose of these aircraft, but the prices on the world-wide market have fallen to such an extent that they would have to be practically given away." The Constellations, he said, "would provide an essential addition to Australia's defence position . . . Also, since Qantas have been operating the aircraft to many points around the world and to the Far East, they offer an immediate and worldwide transport facility in the event of war." The Boeing 707 fleet, said Fysh, would be required, in the event of war, to keep open vital commercial communications with the United States, the United Kingdom, and Europe "and we could not depend on using these aircraft exclusively for emergency military work". He asked for government financial support to cover the costs of maintaining and operating the Constellations over and above the revenue received from possible services in trade and immigration programmes. There was, he said, a further important problem. "We have a large number of fully trained aircrew who have been operating the Super Constellation fleet and if the aircraft are grounded at the end of March we will have a serious redundancy problem involving about 100 aircrew personnel, 50 of whom are highly qualified pilots. In addition, there will be a considerable surplus of engineering staff." Their redundancy, he said, could lead to serious industrial disputes. [4]

Paltridge took up the suggestion of retaining the Super Constellations with Athol Townley, the minister for defence. Townley replied that he was advised that the Boeings would be more efficient for the movement of military personnel in the event of a limited war in South East Asia, and found little merit in the argument that the Constellations were more flexible in their airfield demands. "In view of the extent of the task to be met, however," Townley wrote, "in initial deployment and subsequent maintenance, the Super Constellations would provide a valuable lift capability." He had examined the possible use of the aircraft for the movement of overseas service personnel in peacetime. "During the last two calendar years movements between Australia and Malaya totalled 9,800 persons. Of these, 5,600 were moved by sea and 4,200 by civil airline." As a maximum in the two-year period ahead, Townley said that there could be some 9,800 movements between Australia and Malaya that could possibly be made by chartered Qantas Constellation aircraft, though these included about 4,200 already moving by normal services. He wanted to know the cost involved for any proposed Qantas charters. [5]

The secretary of the Defence Department advised (in a memorandum to the Defence Committee) that Qantas could make use of three of their Super Constellations on South African migration flights, air movement of service personnel (if this were obtained), and some limited ordinary commercial charters. "There will thus remain five of these aircraft for which there is no prospect of utilisation and, failing some special arrangements, I cannot see that the Qantas Board will have any alternative but to dispose of the aircraft for what they will bring. A capital loss would result, of course, but this would have to be accepted . . . Quite frankly, I should regard the availability of the present Super Constellation fleet as the key to any successful rapid deployment of a properly equipped and sizeable force." It was possible, he said, that five aircraft could be retained as a special reserve at no great cost. An annual charge of about £150,000 would "allow for the retention of the aircraft and the continued employment of the small number of engineers needed to make the aircraft operational in an emergency". The minister for defence, he concluded, "would appreciate an early report from the Defence Committee on these matters".[6]

As this problem of the disposal of the remaining Constellation fleet, made obsolescent by the arrival of jet aircraft, occupied Qantas, the beginnings of a new and extraordinary push to extend the technological horizons of civil aviation were emerging. In England, amidst great concern by BOAC, there were strong moves for the development (in partnership with France) of a new airliner that would fly at over twice the speed of sound and make even the new Boeing jets seem slow. On 26 January 1962, BOAC's managing director, Basil Smallpiece, wrote to his chairman, Sir Matthew Slattery:

> I went down to Weybridge on Tuesday evening to see how the VC10 was getting along and Sir George Edwards [BAC managing director] told me that agreement had been reached the night before between BAC [British Aircraft Corporation] and the French Company on a combined submission to be made to the British and French Governments for the development and production of an Anglo-French supersonic airliner capable in different versions of medium range and of long range operation.

It would, he said, be a Mach 2.2 aircraft, of alloy and titanium, with about one hundred seats and a Paris-New York range capability. The suggested date for achievement of its certificate of airworthiness was 1969.

> All this is apparently regarded as practicable by the French and British teams, though we have not had any opportunity of seeing or even checking the detailed estimates on payload and range. But, apart from having achieved agreement on feasibility, the other major point that emerged is that the French Government are going to pay for the whole cost of the development of this aircraft and it is felt that it will be very difficult for the British Government, with their desire to get into the Common Market, not to follow suit. If so, then George Edwards believes the aircraft could be offered for sale at about £2.5 million, and the seat-mile cost would

233

work out at within 10 per cent above the Boeing 707 seat-mile cost. Moreover, as there would be no development cost to be recovered, he would only need an order for about eight aircraft in order to commit himself to start production.

All this, he said, had been told him privately by George Edwards.

> But today we have been told of this by the Ministry who have warned us that the aircraft side of the Ministry may well try and rush the thing through as part of what Britain will commit itself to in the process of going into the Common Market. If this is so, then there is a strong likelihood that we shall be asked . . . for an indication of our degree of interest in the project. Frankly, I am sceptical as to the range and operating cost possibilities of the aircraft, among other things. But I have a feeling that if it did come off we ought not to be out of it – and there is just a possibility that it might be a winner . . .[7]

Slattery replied forcibly:

> We cannot contemplate placing an order until we have had ample time (at least six months) to study the project . . . Any order which we might be prepared to place, with the approval of HM Treasury, would be subject to the aircraft meeting performance estimates. George Edwards has made it clear to me that BAC would not be prepared to accept an order based on a guaranteed performance as he does not regard this as a commercial risk . . . The whole of this is a tremendous issue both to the Corporation, BAC and the Ministry and I cannot believe that any major decision can be taken for several months, at least as regards an order. The only decision that can be taken is to go ahead with the French.[8]

For Slattery it was yet another government shotgun aimed at BOAC. He was later to write to Hudson Fysh about his feelings on the ambivalent role that BOAC was sometimes forced to play.

> I have had a bit of a showdown with Her Majesty's Government, firstly insisting on revealing the true state of the finances over the whole period since the end of the war and, secondly, making the point that HMG must make it clear whether we are supposed to be an instrument of national policy or a commercial organisation . . . Ministers have interfered outrageously with the Corporation's policy over the years and are now declining to accept responsibility for what they did and are trying to put the blame on my unfortunate predecessors, but they are not going to get away with it.[9]

Though possible sale of the surplus Constellation aircraft in the Qantas fleet threatened a capital loss, Qantas was now operating with great cost efficiency relative to most of the world's international airlines. In its scale of operations, it was, in terms of capacity ton miles performed, seventh among the world's airlines. In its cost of operating each unit of capacity, only Pan American and TWA had lower figures. (The Qantas cost per capacity ton mile was 35.2 Australian pence. The costs for Pan American and TWA were 34.2 and 34.1 pence.)[10] Competition on the airline's main Kangaroo Route was, however, increased with the entry of the French airline TAI and Italy's Alitalia, which now, with KLM, carried traffic into and out of Australia. There was, as TAI extended into the Pacific to Los Angeles through Noumea, Fiji, and Tahiti, a severe diversion of revenue. Total revenue earnings of Qantas competitors in and out of Australia in 1961 had been £3 million, with KLM taking £1.5 million, Alitalia £0.4 million, and TAI £1.1 million.[11]

Qantas had, in fact, been outstandingly successful in the years that had just passed and had expanded at a rate well in excess of world averages. It had maintained its profitability at all times, even during the 1961 crisis when other international airlines had suffered crippling losses. The immediate future, also, looked bright. But beyond that, there were powerful external and internal factors that were turning against Qantas interests. Recent talks with BOAC on the future of the Kangaroo partnership had failed to reach agreement on some important aspects of future operations. Their partner was suffering from the increasing support given by the United Kingdom's conservative government for the operation of the privately owned, independent airlines. British United Airways and Cunard Eagle were now both powerful airlines with ambitions to extend worldwide and were making increasing inroads into the routes of BOAC and BEA. Turner thought that these pressures alone could force a revision of the existing tripartite pool within a few years. "Perhaps", he told Fysh, "BOAC can see this coming and it is the reason for their present restrictive attitude to any proposal that looks like giving Qantas an increase in operations or new routes – for instance, their refusal of a Qantas service over Hong Kong."[12] Turner set out to identify the technical, economic, and political long-term trends and to adapt Qantas planning to them. He issued a strictly confidential memorandum to the board on future policy that he described to Fysh as pessimistic, but realistic.

Turner expressed pride in the airline's profitability, achieved with a load factor of only forty-nine per cent, by prudent aircraft procurement and advances in efficiency of operations at all levels.

"However," he wrote, "the very lowness of the figure is indicative of the onset of a law of diminishing returns . . . We are already lean economically and cannot expect our profitable load factor to continue to drop at the past rate." Turner told the board that the next major technical development in the industry was the advent of the supersonic transport (SST), "which is likely to be available for commercial use in the next decade". There were active programmes in Britain and the United States, all of which shared three characteristics. Costs per seat-mile would be no better and could be worse than those for existing jets and might therefore lead to a rise in the Qantas break-even load factor. No SSTs would be suitable for short stage operations and, therefore, these would continue to be performed by current aircraft types. This would mean the operation of two types of aircraft on current Qantas routes. Finally, each SST would have a very large traffic-producing potential with the consequence that the minimum practical fleet of supersonic airliners would produce a passenger-carrying capacity greater than many small airlines could command. "These factors will tend to force the grouping or amalgamation of airlines into larger units", wrote Turner.

General economic pressures, he said, also contributed to the undoubted trend throughout the world of strengthening airlines either through pooling or take-over to exploit the greater efficiency obtainable by large organisations. He quoted a report to the US president on national aviation goals that said: "The proliferation of pools among foreign airlines makes it necessary to search for effective ways to deal with the resulting shifts in competitive relationships".

Turner listed the countries on the Kangaroo Route with which Australia had signed bilateral aviation agreements since the end of World War II. It was an impressive list: Ceylon, Germany, India, Iran, Ireland, Italy, Lebanon, Malaya, the Netherlands, Pakistan, Thailand, Turkey, the United Kingdom, and the United Arab Republic. There were, in addition, interim agreements with France, Greece, and Indonesia.

With a few notable exceptions [he commented], these agreements have, on paper, been based on roughly an equal exchange of rights. In practice, however, the rights have been exercised mainly by Australia and the reciprocal rights have been dormant. There is now a marked trend for the other parties to these agreements to start exercising their rights and it is only prudent to expect this trend to continue into the future. Even though the exercise of rights to Australia by many of the foreign carriers appears uneconomic, foreign Governments seem willing for their national airlines to sustain losses on such routes in the interests of prestige. There

236

is therefore no guarantee that we can drive these airlines off our routes by the mere success of our commercial competition.

Turner was also concerned at the implications of the British move towards joining the European Common Market, and he remarked that such a move seemed inevitable. There were two views on the outcome. The optimistic view, he said, was that there would be no effect on BOAC or its relationship with Qantas and other pool partners. "On the other hand the Rome Treaty which sets up the European Economic Community is clearly directed far beyond the mere lowering of trade barriers between members. In the long run it is directed towards a total economic and even political union." With British European Airways extending its operations into the Middle East, Turner saw the dividing line between this corporation and BOAC becoming increasingly hazy. "There seems a probability that a union of the two Corporations will take place at sometime in the future." He thought a combined British corporation might ultimately enter the Air Union grouping and that the existing tripartite pool with India would then be broken.

This external political hazard was matched by internal political attitudes. Turner wrote forcefully:

> The outstanding success of Qantas over the postwar years has undoubtedly led the Australian Government, and more particularly its advisors in recent years, to regard Qantas as a sort of "milch cow", capable of making endless sacrifices to sustain the Australian domestic aviation industry, and even Australian trade policy in its broadest sense. Indications of this trend are (i) the handover of the New Guinea operations to the domestics, which was not only costly to us at the time but will continue to be an economic burden into the indefinite future (ii) the denial of cabotage rights between remote Australian centres such as Port Moresby and Perth served by our international services and our main base – purely in the interests of the domestic operators (iii) the disastrous French bilateral agreement which, if it can be rationalised at all, can only be done so as a major sacrifice of Qantas interests in support of general Australian trade with France.

The French bilateral agreement was, together with the Dutch bilateral, responsible for the main Qantas loss of revenue. Turner considered the route exchange with the French, agreed in 1960, to be most unequal. If the United States, he said, refused to allow Qantas to include Tahiti on its permit for US services, Qantas should urge the government to reopen negotiations with the United States. In general, the prospect that within a few years additional foreign carriers would probably commence competitive operations into Australia made it essential, he said, to impress upon the government the necessity for the most careful review of all Australian bilateral agreements.

On Australian developmental routes, Turner wanted to make it clear to government that, although Qantas had to date had the economic reserves to carry their losses in the interests of national policy (a notable example being the South African route), it could not continue to do so indefinitely. "We must ask for direct subsidy to the extent of our losses or must, alternatively, cease such operations", Turner wrote.

Finally he addressed what at that time seemed an enormous strategic threat to Qantas.

> The development of Air Union and the possible or even probable ultimate inclusion of the British corporations in this group, plus the discernible trend in the US towards recognising the desirability of pooling or amalgamation, faces us with the probability of ultimately having to compete with a single European and a single North American block of airlines, both of immense power and resources. We should therefore give very careful consideration to the possibility by pooling or possibly even ultimate integration into an "Air Asia". [He listed Pakistan, India, Malaya, Thailand, Japan, Formosa, the Philippines, Indonesia, and New Zealand as countries for possible inclusion in such an arrangement.] There are tremendous practical and political problems in this proposal and we would need the fullest support from the Government. However it may well prove in the long run the only way to re-establish a balance of power in international aviation.[13]

It was clear that the Qantas chief executive had, with supersonic airliners on the horizon, internal political problems from the pressures of the Australian domestic airlines, and international developmental possibilities of unprecedented scope — concerns that fully stretched even his remarkable talents.

The BOAC perspective on Air Union was, however, at odds with C. O. Turner's apprehensions. It was summarised in a letter from Basil Smallpiece to Air India's general manager, B. R. Patel, on 12 June 1962, when Smallpiece responded to Air India's plan for pooling arrangements with Japan Air Lines.

> I hope I can take it [Smallpiece wrote] that your going into pool with JAL between India and Japan will not have any adverse financial effect on your tripartite pool partners. I am glad to have this opportunity of telling you something of our attitude to Air Union in relation to the discussions that are going on about the United Kingdom's possible admission to the European Common Market . . . There seems to us to be no necessary connection between our joining the ECM and our joining Air Union . . . What joining the Common Market does is to increase the size of the area in which free trade and therefore greater competition is

possible. Our reaction to the UK joining the Common Market would be along the lines of wanting to make our existing pool agreements stronger so that we could better meet European competition and could take greater advantages of any openings that arose in Europe.[14]

The domestic political pressures that Turner had referred to with acrimony had not stopped with the transfer to TAA and Ansett of the New Guinea route. Ansett's ambition to operate internationally was unabated and he had continued to press what he saw as an opportunity in New Zealand to gain access to international routes through the purchase of Tasman Empire Airways Limited. His powers of persuasion, political acumen, and aggressive record were more than sufficient to unsettle TEAL's chairman, Leonard Isitt. He wrote to Fysh:

> The present [New Zealand] Government have a catch-cry "private enterprise" and it is getting increasingly more and more difficult to operate national organisations under the private enterprise Government. However, I cannot for the life of me believe that they will wreck our organisation and jeopardise the whole of the Tasman concept for the sake of a few promised overseas pounds. You ask: "Can't TEAL match this fellow?" We have endeavoured to show the Government that we have done and are doing more than Ansett promises, but he is a hard man to combat. He promises everything, and even his past history is not taken as evidence against him. Very confidentially, and for you only, one of our problems is that the solicitor for the [Ansett] company who is urging this matter is a business partner of the Deputy Prime Minister. I have done everything I can short of knocking on doors of Cabinet members and pleading with them, and this I am not prepared to do.[15]

The commercial performance of Qantas, excellent as it had been, was increasingly constrained by political pressures and events far beyond its direct control. The right to fly to Tahiti, acquired at such cost from the French, was an example. In itself, Tahiti was of no commercial significance to Qantas in terms of traffic potential. Tahiti was commercially promising only as an alternative route between Australia and the United States. This issue of Australia's right to operate to operate through Tahiti to the United States was now to be argued at the highest level between the two countries and to involve the Australian prime minister and the US president.

Turner was told by the director-general of civil aviation, Don Anderson, on 7 June that the United States Civil Aeronautics Board (CAB) had turned down the formal application by Qantas to fly through Tahiti to and from the United States, finding that the bilateral agreement between the two countries could not "properly be interpreted as authorising Tahiti as an intermediate point". He wrote formally to Anderson the following day: "It is clear that the decision is not subject to appeal by way of legal process but we feel this is a case calling for a strong protest and is of sufficient importance to suggest that the protest might come from the Prime Minister". It had been obvious for some time, he wrote, that in an endeavour to stem the increasing diversion of traffic from US carriers to foreign carriers now competitively equipped, the CAB was adopting a policy reflecting a highly protective attitude towards its own and an aggressively restrictive attitude towards foreign carriers. "The US decision means that Tahiti has now lost what was its main value to us, namely as a staging point on trans-Pacific services between Australia and the USA . . . For economic reasons we could not contemplate operating a service from Sydney to terminate at Tahiti . . . In our opinion the imbalance in the value of the rights exchanged under the Australia-France arrangements has now become so great as to justify fully a reopening of negotiations."[16] In an internal report from Edgar Johnston, Qantas international affairs advisor, Johnston commented: "This is a difficult and delicate subject, particularly at this time while Australia is so vitally interested in the moves for Britain's entry into the European Common Market but . . . in the interests of Qantas, it is only reasonable that some major change must be made in the agreement".[17]

Shane Paltridge took up the matter with the prime minister on 14 June.

> I believe that you have been informed of a decision which has been made by President Kennedy to reject an application by Qantas for the inclusion of Tahiti on its air service through the United States. This decision has been conveyed in confidence by the State Department to our Embassy in Washington to which they made the suggestion that they would withhold promulgation of it until after you had a chance to raise the matter in Washington during your visit if you wished to do so. Although I am most reluctant to divert your attention from the other important matters which will be occupying you during your short visit to Washington I felt obliged to provide you with the necessary background on this matter so that you can decide what action you should take . . . The crucial point is that in the Australian view Qantas is entitled, under the terms of the Australia-United States Air Transport Agreement, to operate services 'via intermediate points' on the air routes to and through the United States . . . The State Department has agreed with the Australian view, has never wavered from this position, and is on record. It has come therefore as a considerable

shock to us that the President, acting apparently on the advice of the Civil Aeronautics Board and possibly the Justice Department, has overruled the State Department's view . . . It seems to me that this decision has been taken in an atmosphere affected deeply by domestic pressures in the United States aimed at ensuring greater protection for their own airlines.[18]

Paltridge followed this letter with a cable to Menzies through the Australian embassy in Washington suggesting it might well be practicable to get the president to defer his final decision until further representations had been made through diplomatic channels.

Very simply, we have on the civil aviation side a case where the United States, apparently for irrelevant commercial reasons, is denying what we believe and our legal authorities confirm is a legal right under a formal air transport agreement negotiated at Government level by its own State Department. Moreover it is an agreement to which effect has already been given by Australia by the approval in 1958 of Pan American's request for the addition of Tahiti to its Australian permit . . . We have taken the precaution of not finalising our agreement with the French until this matter is finally resolved . . . On the commercial side, there is little doubt that the United States-Australia Air Agreement confers substantial benefit on the Australian airline in giving it access to a round-the-world route through San Francisco and New York. I have no doubt, however, that the United States Government carefully weighed the balance of the Agreement when conceding it to us . . . We have been one of the best customers in the world for United States aircraft equipment. We have purchased Lockheed, Douglas, Convair and Boeing aircraft since the war to a total value of something near the £100 million mark.[19]

President Kennedy went a very small distance with Prime Minister Menzies during his Washington visit and agreed to postpone the announcement of his final decision on the Qantas application for Tahiti until 1 July. The prime minister, on his return to Australia, sent a detailed and carefully argued cable to the president on the Australian case and concluded: "In these circumstances, I would be most grateful if you could see your way clear to have another look at the decision you had proposed to make".[20] It was to no avail.

President John Kennedy wrote to Menzies on 15 July 1962: "I have reviewed the points you raise most carefully, but I regret that it is necessary to find that there is no over-riding basis for reversing the recommendation made to me by the Civil Aeronautics Board. I have therefore approved the Board's recommendation and will release this decision within a week. I realise that you will receive this decision with disappointment, but I

241

hope you will understand it was reached only after intensive consideration of all aspects of the question."[21]

Paltridge commented on the decision to his prime minister that the United States had decided against giving Australia Tahiti presumably because they felt it was already getting a very good deal out of the agreement. "There is room to doubt, as I do, whether this is the proper way to discharge obligations under an agreement but as the alternative method of redressing any economic imbalance could well involve re-negotiation of the whole deal, we will have to live with the President's decision for the present", he said. He saw two important issues flowing from the president's decision. One was whether Australia should withdraw Pan American's rights to fly through Tahiti on its Australian services. The other was whether the US denial of the intermediate points formula in the bilateral agreement would prevent Qantas from including New Zealand as an intermediate point on the Pacific route. He suggested that, as the agreement provided for consultation between the parties when such matters arose, it would be valuable to have such consultation. "We might be able to get some long term understanding about a reciprocal exchange of Tahiti rights when the US are ready for their trunk operator to Australia to include Tahiti, and about the inclusion of New Zealand on our Pacific route. Paltridge thanked the prime minister for his intervention and suggested that Sir Garfield Barwick see the US ambassador to point out that Australia would not like the impression given to the world that there had been any serious misunderstanding between the two governments, and that withholding of the president's decision until consultations had been held might make it easier for joint announcements to be made.[22]

The inability of Qantas to fly through Tahiti on its services to the US west coast was already a cause of revenue loss because the French airline, TAI, automatically drained off some Qantas trans-Pacific traffic on its services. On their round-the-world service through Tahiti, TAI had cut heavily into the Qantas traffic without any compensating gain for Qantas. There had also been traffic losses to Alitalia, but with some compensating advantages for Qantas through Rome. Fysh characterised Alitalia's competition, in its efforts to get established without heavy losses, as apparent systematic defiance of IATA rules in the provision of attractions to passengers with consequent losses not only to the tripartite pool, but also to the industry. In addition to the new pressures from the French and Italian airlines, the German airline, Lufthansa, was spending heavily to establish itself and was making spectacular advances. Their cabin service was already spoken of as superb and lavish and only rivalled by that of Qantas. If, said Fysh in notes on his attendance at an IATA executive meeting, Lufthansa opened an office in Sydney they too would cut into Qantas traffic. Australia would, he said, need action to limit the fast growing competition, and "if the tide of competition is not turned back, deficit operations seem certain". [23]

Already, in the financial year that had ended on 31 March, Qantas had seen revenue well below expectations and load factor fall over four points on the previous year to only 47.9 per cent. (Revenue was only marginally above that for the previous year but capacity had risen by 14.6 per cent.) With its tripartite partners BOAC and Air India, Qantas had increased services out of Australia by the end of March to twelve frequencies a week (to the United Kingdom through India) and three per week to Hong Kong and Japan. Qantas itself operated six weekly services to the United States, two of which extended to the United Kingdom. There was a weekly service to Johannesburg in pool with South African Airways and thirty-one services each week to New Zealand in pool with TEAL. (Qantas also operated a weekly service to both Noumea and Norfolk Island.) Altogether Qantas and its associates operated fifty-five services each week from Australia. There had been a swing from first class to economy class travel with first class accounting for 27 per cent and economy for 73 per cent of the total, on the basis of passenger miles flown. The calendar year 1962 had seen the main Qantas jet fleet of eleven identical Boeing 707-138B fan jets in operation from January. [24]

The commercial importance of pooling arrangements to Qantas was evident. It was one of two forms of interairline co-operation in which it was involved. The other, investment in another airline, was in operation with Fiji and Malayan Airways. By far the most important arrangement was pooling, a system that had been expressly permitted by the authority on most international aviation matters, the Chicago Convention of 1944. A postwar phenomenon, it was now spreading rapidly throughout the world except for the United States which neither officially recognised the existence of pools nor allowed US airlines to participate in them. Pooling did not constitute either a merger or a true partnership as no joint contribution of capital was involved. Each party to a pool operated as an entity, bearing the losses and keeping the profits severally. Their main object was to provide, against competition, co-ordinated selling of frequencies, ports of call, and departure times to attract to the pool more revenue than would otherwise be obtainable by the parties separately. Pooling completely eliminated competition among the participants and at the same time increased their combined strength against other carriers.

Under the general principles of pooling, the revenue earned from carriage of passengers or cargo and mail on pooled routes (sometimes after deduction of directly related costs such as commission) was shared according to an agreed formula. Each party had a responsibility to provide services in return for revenue share, but its costs of doing so were its own responsibility. With only two parties to a pool using the same aircraft along the same route, the problems involved were simple and this was, in essence, the position with the Qantas-BOAC parallel partnership on the Kangaroo Route from December 1947 until the start of the tripartite pool with Air India in April 1960.

In the Qantas-TEAL pool it was recognised that as more New Zealanders crossed the Tasman than Australians, TEAL should be entitled to sixty per cent of the revenue share on that route. Both operated Lockheed Electra aircraft and each was responsible for its own costs incurred in providing its share of the annual frequencies in the same proportion to the revenue share. In the Qantas pool with South African Airways, only a fortnightly service by the national carrier of each country was justified. Although SAA operated a DC7C between Johannesburg and Perth and Qantas operated a Lockheed 1049 between Sydney and Johannesburg, there was no great imbalance in national traffic flows and, in a commercial agreement, revenue was shared equally (with Qantas invoicing SAA for half the extra cost difference between the two that arose from the extra cost to Qantas of flying a larger aircraft further). With BOAC, when Qantas extended its Pacific service across the United States and the Atlantic in January 1958, it was agreed that Qantas would operate in parallel partnership. In July 1962, Qantas operated three Boeing 138B services weekly and BOAC matched this capacity in the total number of flights operated by them between London and San Francisco.

The Qantas-BOAC-Air India tripartite pool was, however, quite different in character to all these other pools and was, in world terms, unique. The area of the main pool (called Group 1) was not confined to a single route but covered the network of all three partners stretching from the United Kingdom to Australia via Europe, the Middle East, India, and the Far East.

244

Also, the tripartite pool was based on a much closer application of traffic rights conferred by bilateral agreements than existed in all other Qantas pools.

The basic principle of the tripartite pool was that each country (and therefore the national carrier) was entitled to an equal share of the traffic moving between its respective partner countries, regardless of their population or any other considerations, plus 100 per cent of the traffic from the carrier's country to any other country (and vice versa), plus one-third of all traffic both picked up and set down outside the countries of the three partners. (Because the Australian government had previously used the origin and destination principle in bilateral negotiations, Qantas had insisted on this method of determining traffic entitlements in the tripartite pool.) The pool entitlement statistics could, of course, only be prepared on a historical basis and could therefore only be applied in the period subsequent to that used for their preparation. The past, in fact, was used to determine the present.

The pool partners had, however, to determine in advance for each period the capacity to be provided by each member. Prolonged negotiations were necessary to then obtain an optimum scheduling pattern for the pool and lay down for each partner its aircraft frequencies through particular ports on particular routes. In 1962, for example, Qantas was required under the pool (in order to draw its share of the total pool revenue of £70 million) to operate five Boeings per week between Sydney and London, with an additional twenty flights between November and April, plus three Boeings per week between Sydney and Hong Kong. Any failure to do so brought the necessity to purchase capacity from the other partners. To preserve a competitive stimulus, a limitation was imposed (in the 1961–62 year only) on the difference between what a partner took from the pool and the total revenue earned from his own carriage of traffic. (Apart from the main tripartite pool, Group 1, there were two other sections that were quite different in character involving London–New York and Hong Kong–Tokyo.)

The basic philosophy behind all the revenue pooling agreements was the sharing of traffic rights. The old Kangaroo Route parallel partnership involved an equal responsibility for capacity and equal sharing of resultant revenue. One of the conditions of the Qantas entry into the tripartite pool was an acknowledgment by BOAC that the Kangaroo Route principles would be maintained by separate arrangement between BOAC and Qantas. In practice, however, the complete preservation of these principles proved incompatible with tripartite pool requirements and the inevitable compromises that resulted had proved very restrictive for Qantas planning. Those Kangaroo Route principles as applied in 1959 (when the tripartite agreement was drawn up) no longer, in 1962, met the changing situation on the route. Traffic was beginning to show a decided preference for a route to Australia through Hong Kong instead of through Singapore. The necessary effort to maintain equity now involved variation of those principles or their suspension.[25]

By mid-1962 Australia was achieving prominence in the international airline community of a particular and unwelcome kind. After London, its fees for navigation and landing charges for airliners were believed to be the highest in the world. Fees had been increased three times in the preceding five years and it now cost £173 to land a Boeing 138B at Sydney. Most elements of airline expenditure had fallen per unit with the introduction of jet aircraft; landing fees were a striking exception. For the first time in Qantas history, the annual cost of landing fees and air navigation charges was to exceed £1 million.

In all other countries of importance to civil aviation except Australia and New Zealand, landing charges at airports were quite distinct from air navigation charges (for the use of en route facilities). Landing charges were assessed on the maximum permitted take-off weight of the aircraft (except for a few cases when actual aircraft weight was used). They were introduced generally in the late 1940s and by the mid-1950s all countries were charging them. Air navigation charges were a newer concept by which some governments charged airlines that communicated with their territory (but did not land there) a fee for the use of the navigational aids provided. As heavier aircraft came into existence, landing charges rose broadly in accordance with weight increases but remained an acceptable proportion of total airline costs. In 1959 and 1960, however, when jet airliners were introduced, landing fees jumped steeply. For Qantas, the cost of landing fees and air navigation facilities in 1957 totalled £215,000; by 1959 this had doubled; by 1961–62 it had risen to £885,000. In terms of cost per capacity ton mile the rise was from 0.45 pence in 1957 to 0.90 pence in 1961–62, a doubling of cost per unit of production in four years. The £885,000 cost in 1961–62 was substantial in all ways for Qantas, and equalled 2.9 per cent of total airline expenditure.

Australia had introduced what it called 'air navigation charges' ten years before, in 1952. The method of assessing these charges was unique, combining the landing fee with a charge for use of navigation facilities, and reflected a practical approach to airline usage of facilities spread across the country's large continental land mass. For aircraft weighing more than 100,000 pounds, a rate was nominated per 1,000 pounds of take-off weight. This rate was then multiplied by a flight factor related to the sector distance. Sydney-Perth, for example, was thirteen units. An additional charge of eight units was made for arriving and departing Australia. At £11.4.0 per unit, a Boeing 138B flying Sydney-Perth and beyond attracted a total of twenty-one units and a charge of £235. By contrast, Sydney-Nadi (Fiji) attracted no flight factor charge at all, not flying over the continent, but paid only the eight units for departing – a total of only £90. From the point of view of the Australian government, the cost of providing air navigation facilities in Australia (according to the 1962–63 budget papers) was £7.6 million per year; the total recovery from airlines was only £1.7 million. The cost of providing the facilities was increasing at an estimated £600,000 per year. It took little vision to predict that there would be further increases in airline charges. Worldwide, the big new jets were more and more able to overfly the airports of countries that they traversed, with a consequent loss of revenue to governments from landing charges. Governments began responding by charging for en route user facilities. (Egypt, for example, charged a fee of seventy-five per cent of the landing fee when an aircraft overflew Cairo but did not land; Canada, from January 1960, introduced a charge of $64 for the use of Gander navigational aids by all aircraft crossing the Atlantic, though the airlines collectively refused to pay and instituted litigation.) Landing fees and navigation charges were to remain a painful issue between airlines and governments.[26]

High as the costs were for these necessary facilities, they in no way matched the huge costs to the world's international airlines of the excess airliner capacity that the advent of the new jet fleets had provided. For many operators, six out of every ten seats that took off on each flight were, on average, empty. The industry nightmare of 1961–62 was load factor. To squeeze any revenue at all from those empty seats, whether or not in flagrant violation of IATA agreements, was seen by many airlines as commercial pragmatism rather than illegal rate cutting. Hudson Fysh, as IATA's president, was appalled at the effects of such practices. He expressed his feelings about the increase in serious infringements of IATA rules in strong language to IATA's director-general, Sir William Hildred.

They are business destroying and soul destroying and the time
has now arrived when the evil is striking at the existence of IATA
itself and is making the organisation a laughing stock in that it
has lost control of its members [he wrote]. I now find that things
are . . . worse and, indeed, heading for an increase in the evils and
a general collapse of the main function of IATA – rate fixing. We
are in the midst of a crime wave, like prohibition, and we must
tackle it as such by vigorous and exacting measures . . . The Middle
East is rampant and serious infringements are now evident on a
world-wide basis. Even under the nose of IATA in the city of
Montreal I am informed the position is bad.

He advocated the employement of enforcement officers with
good detective experience.

Enforcement men are cops and their main training should be as
cops . . . If we do not do the job, governments obviously must.
The quicker we can bring in fare reductions where this can be
done the better. This will help enormously not only the enforcement position but will assist us against non-IATA competition and
in the eyes of the public. However, no airline in my opinion should
budget for a loss, and should not lower fares simply to minimise
losses. Once down we will never get them up again.[27]

Fysh spoke publicly on the issue in his retiring presidential
address at IATA's annual general meeting in Dublin in September. His term of office, he said, had been from a business point
of view the worst in the history of the industry, with record
financial losses and the lowest seat occupancy yet recorded. "Of
course," he said, "there is a bright side to the picture. Our one
hundred million passengers have never had it so good, with
handsome illegal discounts available worldwide . . . The airline
passenger, the non-IATA operators and, I regret, some of the
agents and IATA members have had their hands in the industry's
till during the year." In 1961, said Fysh, the industry had
absorbed a further 326 jets and propjets into their fleets. A
worldwide overprovision of capacity had brought with it a
certain state of anarchy, illegal rate cutting, loss, and disruption.
Fysh posed the question: "How did we come to lose £50
million?".

In fact, the industry was to be saved by an unpredicted upsurge
in traffic and a normal resumption of its traditional growth
pattern by 1963. Qantas itself had not suffered in the great airline
recession year of 1961–62 but had managed to achieve an
increase in revenue passenger miles of 8.6 per cent over the
previous year. By December 1962, C. O. Turner was able to
advise the board that even better growth was expected in the
current year. An increase of at least 15 per cent over 1961–62

was anticipated. The traffic carried by Qantas's pool partners had not grown at the same rate, however, and restrained Qantas from the immediate application of additional airliner capacity. The mechanics of the pool held back Qantas growth in another way. Because of the historical method of apportioning shares in pool traffic, the 1961–62 recession in the Australian economy had resulted in statistics that limited Qantas entitlement for 1962–63. In its real time commercial performance as well in its forward planning, Qantas was constrained by the results of its pool partners. The future, though, looked healthy. Recovery of the Australian economy was reflected in pool statistics that governed Qantas entitlement for 1964–65 and promised an increase in the Qantas pool share. Traffic growth, both pool and nonpool, was expected to increase through 1964–65 and 1965–66. Turner was confident that utilisation of the airline's eleven Boeing 138Bs could be increased to accommodate anticipated growth for 1963–64, but that by 1964–65 traffic growth would have overtaken the capacity of the existing fleet. "We regard daily aircraft utilisations of 10 to 10.5 hours as a practical maximum, leaving virtually no reserve to cater for lost or damaged aircraft", he wrote.[28] In fact, despite the general gloom that had pervaded the industry from the onset of the 1961 depression, Qantas had increased its jet services on the Kangaroo Route from four to five weekly in April 1962 and to six weekly in October. These were augmented by a Comet aircraft operating once weekly throughout the year as a Qantas service under charter from BOAC. The Southern Cross route services to London through San Francisco had been increased from two to three weekly in April, with a twofold effect. Qantas round-the-world services increased to six per week (three through India and three through the United States) and the service between Sydney and San Francisco became a daily one. (Qantas had purchased its leased eleventh Boeing aircraft in September.) At the company's jet base at Sydney's Kingsford Smith airport, which now covered 110 acres, the volume of engineering work handled had increased by over 20 per cent with an increase in engineering personnel of less than 1 per cent.

In reviewing anticipated developments in and beyond the second half of the decade, Turner foresaw a significant growth in cargo, as well as passenger traffic. Although overall load factors in the capacious holds of the Boeing 707s was not high, the airline was already being offered cargo loads beyond its capacity on individual services at peak times. Demand for cargo capacity was, in the long run, expected to exceed the capacity available in the holds of passenger aircraft. It was a problem whose solution lay, in Qantas's view, in the use of jet aircraft designed for composite cargo-passenger loads in the aircraft cabin. "We expect", he told the board, "that we will need a minimum fleet of three such aircraft by about 1966-67." It was a prediction influenced by the expected arrival of supersonic passenger airliners. "We are supported in this view", wrote Turner, "by our very long term plans ultimately to purchase supersonic transports. The SST has little or no hold capacity beyond passengers' baggage and mail and will need support by subsonic cargo aircraft."

Projected traffic figures showed, at the end of 1962, that two new Boeing 138B aircraft would be needed by the end of 1964 to meet traffic commitments. The year's end also saw Qantas prepare for the construction of its large new hotel in Sydney with the formation of a new company, Kenmaster Holdings Limited, which purchased the paid-up capital of Qantas Wentworth Holdings Limited. The problems that lay ahead for C. O. Turner, his management team, and the airline's staff of almost seven thousand were, with some notable exceptions, to be the problems of growth.

Fodder for Government Barter 1963

In the seventeen years since the end of World War II, Qantas had grown rapidly and continuously. Australia's overseas air routes in 1945 totalled only some 16,000 miles; fewer than 15,000 passengers a year were flown; and freight, under 100 tons, was one-third of mail carriage. By 1962–63, the route network was four and a half times longer, numbers of passengers had increased twenty-fold, freight carried was sixty-eight times greater, and overseas mail nine times. In 1945, however, there had been no competition. By January 1963, it had grown formidably and was continuing to grow.

Qantas had reacted to these changing circumstances by its pool arrangements with BOAC, Air India, TEAL, and SAA as well as its investments in Malayan and Fijian airways. Its competition in the home market came from Alitalia, TAI, KLM, and Pan American. It did not regard Canadian Pacific Air Lines as significant competition as it usually carried only about thirteen passengers out of Sydney on each fortnightly service. ("Why do they bother?" was the expressive attitude from Qantas.) Similarly, Cathay Pacific could be ignored; they had opened a service to Australia in July 1959, and, in the words of a Qantas report, "retired to lick their economic wounds in October 1961".[1]

Italy's national carrier, Alitalia (ninety-six per cent government-owned), had not only grown at a faster rate than Qantas in the previous five years (pushing Qantas from seventh to ninth largest international operator) but since June 1961 had been providing keen competition on the Kangaroo Route. Its inter-

9

251

continental network linked Italy with North, Central, and South America, all Africa, the Far East, and Australia; in addition it maintained a European and domestic network. By the beginning of 1963, Alitalia's fleet consisted of nine DC8 jets, fourteen Caravelle jets, fourteen turboprop Viscounts, and nine other piston-engined aircraft. A decision had already been taken to add a further five DC8s and twelve Caravelles to the fleet by 1965.

Alitalia's initial service to Australia had been run by TAI under charter but Alitalia had taken over its operation on 6 April 1962. Load factors had not been high (42 per cent into Australia and 28 per cent out, compared with 55 per cent in and 58 per cent out for Qantas) and mail and cargo loads out of Australia had been poor. Despite what Qantas judged to be unprofitable operations, the airline was regarded as an aggressive carrier, prepared to spend much more on selling than Qantas was. By January 1963, Alitalia had carved out 7 per cent of the Australian passenger market for themselves and were a competitor that Qantas had to watch closely.

The French airline TAI (Compagnie de Transports Aeriens Intercontinentaux) had been formed as a charter operation in 1946 by a group of private French investors. In 1955, a government-inspired agreement was signed by the three French airlines, Air France, UAT, and TAI, that established distribution of French long-haul traffic whereby Air France shared traffic originating in France to all sectors of the French community equally with TAI and UAT. TAI routes included West Africa, Somaliland, and the area east of Calcutta and south of Saigon. In 1956 TAI took over Air France services to Noumea through Brisbane and in 1958 a side route to New Zealand was started. At the beginning of 1953, this French competitor to Qantas operated DC8s weekly to Djakarta and weekly from Paris to Los Angeles via Vietnam, Australia, New Caledonia, Fiji, and Tahiti. There were side legs from Noumea to New Zealand and from Tahiti to Honolulu. Its fleet consisted of three DC8s, two DC7s, five DC6s, two DC4s, and one DC3. Its staff was about one-third that of Qantas. High utilisation of aircraft had been a feature of their operations and they had made a profit (about two per cent on turnover) in every year from 1946 to 1959, breaking even exactly in 1960. Qantas estimated that TAI was depriving them of about £600,000 in revenue on the Kangaroo Route. Firm figures were not available for the Pacific traffic but the drain on Qantas was worsening.

The remaining competitor on the Kangaroo Route, KLM,

was formed the year before Qantas, in October 1919. At the end of 1962 it was, in terms of capacity offered annually, twice as big as Qantas and, with unduplicated route mileage of 170,000 miles, had a network more than twice the size as that of Qantas, serving sixty countries. Its fleet, as a consequence of its mixed long and short-haul operations, was mixed. Among its seventy aircraft were thirteen DC8s, eleven Electras, fourteen DC7Cs, six DC6s, four DC3s, four Constellations 1049Gs, nine Viscounts, and ten Convair 340s. At the end of 1961 ("that wretched year for airlines" as a Qantas report described it) its staff numbered more than 18,000.

KLM was seventy per cent government-owned, the remaining thirty per cent being held by private shareholders. Modest profits had been earned until 1960 but there was a substantial loss in 1961 and KLM was forced to get government help to maintain liquidity and to meet loan obligations through until 1965. The first nine months of 1962 had brought a net loss of £6.2 million. Qantas economics officer (research) Jim Somerville commented in January 1963: "KLM, like BOAC, is in big trouble. Heavy operating losses in each case have led to investigations of management policies by outside consultants . . . KLM is a firm believer in the philosophy of 'the freedom of the skies'; bilateral agreements are anathema to a country which has only one landing point in which to trade. However, for better or for worse, most countries of the world have turned their faces towards restrictionism and not free trade in air transport, and KLM is suffering in consequence."[2] KLM, in January 1963, had about nine per cent of the Australian passenger market, possibly inflated two per cent by the carriage of migrants. Qantas did not anticipate that the airline would be able to lift this percentage.

The general position for Qantas, as 1963 began, was that competition on the Kangaroo Route was aggressive and increasing. There was a possibility that Alitalia, TAI, KLM, and the German Lufthansa would combine in the Air Union pool to make a formidable opponent. Separately, Alitalia, TAI, and KLM were not, as could be expected, taking as much revenue from passengers departing Australia as from those they were bringing in. They had, however, eighteen per cent of the Australian passenger market, leaving the pool partners—BOAC, Air India, and Qantas—eighty-two per cent. Looking ahead with realism, and anticipating the entry of Lufthansa to Australia by 1965 on a weekly basis (with Alitalia going to twice weekly and TAI and KLM remaining weekly), Qantas expected the share of the pool partners to decline to seventy-two per cent by 1965. It was clear that without the tripartite pooling arrangements, Qantas would have been left with less than half the passenger traffic departing from Australia on the Kangaroo Route.

Eastward, across the Pacific, Pan American was the competitor. It was recognised by Qantas not only as the largest, but also as the strongest financially and most efficient international carrier. It provided, from its own resources, one-fifth of the total world international airline capacity, was twice as large as its nearest rival, BOAC, and six times bigger than Qantas. In 1962, on sales of $503 million, Pan American had made a net profit after tax of $15 million, equivalent to three per cent on turnover and ten per cent on shareholders' funds. (Pan American also operated a Guided Missile Range Division at Cape Canaveral and the wholly owned Intercontinental Hotels Corporation, but these contributed little to its overall result.) Its $1 shares had an asset backing of $22 and were, in 1963, quoted on the New York Stock Exchange at $35. Although its largest division was the Atlantic (forty-two per cent), the Pacific division (thirty per cent) was the most profitable, but the South Pacific route to Australia constituted only six per cent of the Pacific division as a whole. With passenger loads in and out of Sydney averaging only thirty-four (Qantas averaged forty-eight in a smaller aircraft), this was not, in Qantas's view, a profitable route for Pan American.

Qantas admired Pan American. Although faced with labour costs twice those of Qantas and European carriers, it was far more productive. In 1962, Pan American had produced 78,000 capacity ton miles per employee with a staff of 23,778. BOAC, with much the same staff size, had produced half this capacity. Qantas, though at an all-time high in their own efficiency, produced 43,500 capacity ton miles per employee. Economies of size, of course, influenced this disparity but it was, even so, staggering. (The Pan American fleet included fifty-six aircraft and about fifty piston-engined Douglas aircraft.) Qantas, in 1963, saw Pan American as their greatest rival and, at the same time, as an excellent mirror to hold up to themselves. Turner described Pan American as "our main enemy".[3]

Hudson Fysh, looking back on 1962, described it as "an amazingly good year for the Company. I can hardly think of a better one." He congratulated Turner for his leading part and remarked: "One notes better Board and Management work and relationships . . . better staff relationships and higher efficiency right through the Company".[4] Though most other airlines had suffered, Qantas had remained profitable. The government had approved the new hotel project. The fan conversion of the Boeing engines had proved itself. Difficulties had remained with the tripartite pool but the working relationship had been less acrimonious. While rate cutting by competitors had not ceased, Qantas had taken an increasing part in the IATA campaign to eradicate the practice. "In considering the whole of our work and interests, the one thing I am not happy about is the Australia-New Zealand and QEA-TEAL relationships in regard to trans-Tasman affairs and the future plans of TEAL – and how they fit in properly with our own interests", Fysh wrote. "The first step is to try and build up confidence with TEAL . . . convince them that we are not trying to wipe them out."[5]

Despite the fact that Qantas had been a partner in the jointly owned TEAL since 1939, relinquishing its shares following joint government agreement in 1961, confidence between the Australians and New Zealanders was markedly lacking. New Zealand feared the motives of the aggressive, expanding Qantas; Qantas was apprehensive about the financial consequences for pool arrangements if TEAL's plans for expansion into jet aircraft operation proved overambitious.

On the Tasman, both TEAL and Qantas were operating Electras in pool as 1963 began. BOAC was to commence services on the route from 1 April, but with Comet aircraft. There was adequate utilisation for TEAL's three Electras, in Qantas's eyes, but (even with plans to use Qantas Electras on the South African service from April) insufficient utilisation for the Qantas fleet of four Electras. Further ahead, a new international airport was being built at Auckland (to be available at the end of 1965). Qantas and other international operators planned to use their larger jet aircraft from that date on Auckland services. TEAL and the New Zealand government had no option but to consider buying jets if TEAL was to remain competitive after the new airport opened. (TEAL was looking closely at US jets but BOAC and the United Kingdom were making attractive offers on the VC10.) It worried Qantas that TEAL, originally reported as considering three jet aircraft, were now supposedly thinking of four. Too much capacity, in the Qantas view, would mean poor load factors.

Qantas was well informed about possible TEAL initiatives. TEAL's plans covered not only the trans-Tasman and New Zealand–Fiji areas, but also an extension of their Tahiti service to the United States and the establishment of a service through Sydney and Singapore to Hong Kong and Tokyo. The New Zealand authorities had been negotiating for traffic right that seemed to fit accurately with these perceived TEAL plans. The particular Qantas interest in TEAL's intentions flowed from the assurances of co-operation and assistance, and the inferences of continued pooling, contained in the intergovernmental agreement of 1961. Qantas was happy in principle to extend the policy of co-operation with TEAL but, before accepting any continuance of existing pooling arrangements as TEAL moved to large jet operations, wanted to examine fully what the cost might be to Qantas.

Turner, after examining capacity projections on possible TEAL routes, thought that a fleet of four jet aircraft "would be entirely unnecessary and ruinously uneconomical".[6] Qantas analysis showed that it would be impossible for a TEAL service to the Far East to achieve reasonable load factors and that any such TEAL operations would be a heavy drain on their pool partners – possibly as high as £1.7 million a year. The financial implications of TEAL expansion across the Pacific were difficult to assess as it was not possible to forecast what competitive services might be operated between Australasia and the United States through Tahiti. Turner did not think it reasonable to expect that a weekly TEAL service, even with trans-Tasman connections to Australia, could achieve load factors comparable with those of Qantas. If they proved appreciably less, there would be a further payment through the pool from Qantas to TEAL.

One important factor affecting the Qantas view of TEAL's proposed operations through Tahiti to the United States was the French attitude to traffic rights. The existing France-Australia arrangements were, of course, heavily weighted in favour of the French airline and were in the process of renegotiation. Recent negotiations between France and New Zealand provided TEAL with rights to operate through Tahiti, but were conditional on Australia agreeing to French demands to operate direct trans-Tasman services. A weekly TAI service Sydney-Auckland would, it was calculated, be worth up to £430,000 per annum in revenue. "It is certain", Turner told the Qantas board, "that New Zealand will apply strong pressure to grant trans-Tasman rights to the French and the Board should be fully aware of the grave dangers to Qantas interests that are involved."[7]

There was a further serious implication that the French

requests to Australia and New Zealand would, if conceded, permit not only the French airline but also TEAL (through Auckland) to drain Australia's trans-Pacific traffic through Tahiti. France, in fact, in talks early in 1963, refused to reach a solution with Australia that would have redressed the great imbalance in the existing arrangements. Turner feared that France would again raise a proposal that there be an exchange of round-the-world routings for the French and Australian airlines in which France would concede Tahiti and Paris to Australia in exchange for Sydney. Turner warned Don Anderson that this would be entirely unacceptable.[8] It was also conceivable that the outcome of Australia's difficulties with the United States (on rights through Tahiti) could result in Pan American being permitted to operate through Tahiti with Qantas being debarred from doing so. To greatly exacerbate the whole matter, from the Qantas point of view, Australia generated the most traffic of any country in the whole south-west Pacific area. Any trans-Pacific services depended on traffic to and from Australia. At the same time, Qantas could do little, if nothing, to affect what it saw as New Zealand's expansionist plans, even though Qantas considered them of vital concern and importance to itself.[9]

BOAC moved early in 1963 to bring Qantas into discussions on the proposed new supersonic airliner, asking Dick Shaw if he could attend a meeting in mid-February that would hear a statement on the present position and forecasts from British Aircraft Corporation.[10] BAC's managing director, George Edwards, wrote to BOAC's chairman: "A short while ago you suggested that it might be a good idea if you took the initiative in forming a committee of representatives of BOAC, Air France, Trans-Canada and Qantas to guide us in our deliberations on the supersonic transport . . . To bring everyone in would obviously be unwieldy and would be fraught with commercial security complications by the inclusion of US carriers, particularly now that the SST position in the United States is becoming more active." Edwards proposed an open symposium that would be "sufficiently broad not to reveal too many details and, on the other hand, would not result in any airlines feeling they had been left out . . .I think it would be very helpful if you could sound out TCA [Canada] and Qantas to see whether they would be willing to feed their ideas through your organisation."[11] Slattery agreed, commenting: "From our own point of view, we do want to have our two main Commonwealth partners, Qantas and TCA [on the committee] because we should each benefit by each other's opinions – and it should prevent you getting diametrically opposite views from these two potential customers on the many issues that will doubtless arise". [12] The Canadian airline, like Qantas, responded favourably to the BOAC invitation to hear BAC's exposition on the supersonic airliner project. Slattery commented to TCA's president, G. R. McGregor: "I seem to be very much in accord with your thinking. I do not find myself enthusiastic about the introduction of a supersonic transport but feel its advent is inevitable." [13]

Hudson Fysh turned to his diary again on 8 February to record his thoughts and to note an extraordinary stroke of fortune for his chief executive:

> A whole year since I made an entry. Never a diarist. My minister, Senator Paltridge, rang yesterday and told me he had seen Bob Menzies. It has been agreed that I be granted a renewal of my appointment as Chairman of QEA for another three years. It has to go to Cabinet . . . but no reason for it not being agreed to. I am 68 and a three year term from 30 June 1963 will bring me to 1966 when I will be 71. This means that if my health holds, I will be here at the great day – the opening of the new hotel. Thus after 40 years at the helm, I enter my last term. What will happen in these three years? As it appears now we were never set fairer, never in a more advantageous position from almost any point of view. However, if I know it, there will be some surprises as the international position is a mess and looks awful.

Fysh now noted the stroke of luck that had befallen Turner.

> Well, since a year ago, Cedric Turner has won the £100,000 Opera House Lottery. Tax free. And this has changed him, more for his good. He will come good now and this whole windfall [is] like a golden leaf fluttering down at his feet . . . Time passes and sees control change in all things. As 1963 opens I see Qantas at a peak of excellence, rarely attained by any organisation. 1. World high regard for excellence. 2. Making good profits. 3. Good staff relations. 4. Good relations with our own government, with our minister and with the DGCA. 5. Good board, excellent deputy chairman in Bob Law-Smith. 6. Excellent director-general of civil aviation in Don Anderson. Of all the DGCAs he is the best. Excellent minister in Senator Paltridge, now experienced in the business of civil aviation. With all this terrifying goodness one wonders when some thunderclap will occur. [14]

For the financial year that ended on 31 March 1963, Qantas was able to report the highest profit ever earned by the company. At £1,406,246 it was more than three times the profit for the

Her Majesty the Queen and the Duke of Edinburgh arrive by Qantas at Fairbairn RAAF base, Canberra on 18 February 1963. Waiting to the right of the stairs are the governor-general of Australia, Lord de l'Isle, the prime minister, Robert Gordon Menzies and Dame Pattie Menzies.

The royal compartment on Qantas 707-138B *City of Perth* which carried Her Majesty the Queen and the Duke of Edinburgh from Christchurch, New Zealand to Canberra in February 1963. The crew member is senior flight steward Brian Sewell. Note the Australian wildflower motif on the wall of the cabin; this motif was featured on the interiors of all Qantas 707s.

previous year. Revenue, for the first time, had exceeded £40 million while capacity operated had risen by more than one-fifth with no change in routes flown. The accelerated traffic growth that had followed buoyant world trade as the United States economy prospered posed, however, capacity problems for 1965 and it was clear that even more aircraft would be needed. The company's fleet stood at eleven Boeing 707-138B V-jets, four Electra L188C MkIIs, five Super Constellation L1049s, two Douglas DC4s, and one Douglas DC3. At the beginning of 1963, the airline introduced its first computer, an IBM 1401, for inventory control and stores accounting, with other functions such as labour analysis, costing, payroll and staff statistics, and aircraft component overhaul planned. It was the first modest step into equipment that would, over the years, become as important commercially to Qantas as their airliners.

Qantas was now among the top twenty Australian companies in size, measured in terms of shareholders funds. Though attempts were made to assess its position on the basis of sales, assets, net profits, and employees (as the US magazine *Fortune* did in its listing of the 500 top US companies), this was not possible. Australian organisations simply did not provide this data in their annual reports and balance sheets. The Sydney Stock Exchange agreed with Qantas that the only reliable yard-stick for comparison was that of shareholders funds. Leading the Australian list, and four times bigger than the next in size, was Broken Hill Proprietary with £238.1 million. Colonial Sugar (CSR) came second with £59.6 million. Qantas, at twentieth, had £21 million in shareholders funds. [15]

In late 1959 and early 1960, the government had approved the purchase of three additional Boeing 707s and agreed to Qantas's conversion of its existing fleet of seven Boeings to the fan engine configuration. Later, a further Boeing was approved under a lease-purchase arrangement, bringing the total Boeing fleet to eleven aircraft. (The leased aircraft was purchased in 1962.) This fleet acquisition programme was completed in January 1962 but now further capacity was needed. The fleet was flying at the rate of 3,200 hours per annum per aircraft, a high rate that left little spare capacity for insurance against accidents. Even in 1961–62, which had been a disappointing year for traffic growth, passenger miles for Qantas had increased ten per cent on the previous year. The 1962–63 year promised even stronger growth, with current trends then promising a rise of fifteen per cent, excluding Tasman operations. (The closing months of 1962 showed a phenomenal growth rate of thirty per cent.) Nevertheless, Qantas believed that anticipated growth to September 1964 could be accommodated by stretching further its aircraft utilisation to the very high rate of 10.8 hours per aircraft per day. Traffic growth beyond that date made an increase in fleet size unavoidable. Qantas asked its minister for approval to order a further two Boeing jets at an estimated cost of $11.1 million. (This was considerably less than the normal total price including spare engines. The excellent performance of the fan engines had given Qantas a surplus of spare engines from which they were able to supply the eight engines required for installation in the new aircraft.) Qantas advised Paltridge that it proposed financing the new purchase with a US dollar loan of $8.2 million, leaving a balance of $2.9 million to be met from the company's capital recoveries from obsolescence of the existing fleet. (Qantas now had £3 million in its self-insurance reserves, a figure expected to grow to £5.5 million by the time the new aircraft were delivered.)

As world air traffic grew strongly, there was also a marked swing from first to second class travel in the industry, a phenomenon that was clearly to influence Qantas strategies. The crossover from first to second class travel on international routes (in terms of total scheduled passenger miles) occurred for United States carriers in 1954 and in 1957 for Qantas. After World War II there had been only one class and it was not until 1952 that "coach" travel (introduced in 1949 in the United States) spread to the Atlantic. Qantas, like many other airlines, had initially opposed the idea of second class fares, fearing a substantial decline in revenue yields. It was not until 1954 that it introduced tourist fares and their fears were initially confirmed. There had been a forty-five per cent swing from first to second class in the first year. However, the effect had been cushioned because first class fares had been increased by IATA before the then twenty per cent tourist class differential was applied. At a subsequent IATA traffic conference a third class, economy, was introduced, which led to the decline and abandonment of the tourist fares. In 1963 fare differentials between first and second class were far from uniform and varied between twenty-seven per cent for Sydney-New York and forty-three per cent for the North Atlantic. First class travel, as a percentage of total passengers, had declined rapidly from twenty-four per cent in 1957 to nine per cent in 1962 on the North Atlantic, a route widely considered as not only the busiest but traditionally an experimental one that set world airline trends. For Qantas, traffic demands on the round-the-world route in 1963 made the most economic configuration twenty first class and eight-four economy class passengers, a standard that was also adopted on the Kangaroo and Far East services. (On the Pacific, to suit the traffic, there was a twenty-eight/sixty-six configuration.) Passenger revenue yields for Qantas and most large international carriers had declined steadily with the swing to lower class fares. The imponderable issue, in 1963, was the extent to which these lower fares had broadened the market and thus enabled airlines to expand and reduce unit costs. [16]

Boeing Aircraft Company's jet airliners had provided their users with high utilisation, economy of operation, and a safety record, despite some accidents, that compared well with other turbine-powered aircraft. There were, by the end of March 1963, 313 Boeing 707s in service with world airlines carrying, at any particular moment, about ten thousand passengers in the air. The Boeing 707 and Douglas DC8 jets ranked lowest in the table of aircraft accidents involving destruction of aircraft per 100,000 hours of flying. The Comet led this table at 1.34, the Electra was 0.73, and the Vickers Viscount 0.65. Both the 707 and DC8 were equal at 0.60. In terms of passenger fatalities per 100 million passenger miles flown, the average for 1961 was 1.10 (having fallen from 4.96 in 1945). The Boeing jet figure to March 1963 was 0.98. [17]

Sir Hudson Fysh and three Qantas directors (Law-Smith, Kirby, and Buttfield), with C. O. Turner, had an important meeting on 2 April with the minister and the director-general of civil aviation. Paltridge began the meeting by explaining what he believed to be his responsibility for Qantas affairs. A government instrumentality, he said, was usually covered by an act of Parliament, which laid down the powers and responsibilities of the board or commission and defined the duties of the minister. Qantas was not covered by act of Parliament, but was a public company registered in Queensland and operating under the terms of a financial directive. Qantas, said Paltridge, was the instrument of the government for the development and operation of international air services. He considered that as responsible minister he stood between the board and the government and had the responsibility to satisfy himself that the airline was properly managed and made an adequate profit to pay dividends on the government investment. When proposals to purchase new aircraft were put to him, he had to examine them very thoroughly to assure himself that the company was not making a mistake. He told the Qantas chairman and directors that in the light of Australia's international relations in many fields, the government often had to make decisions based on considerations other than purely commercial ones, which could affect the future of the airline. Paltridge cited the temporary arrangements made in Paris with the French. He knew they were unpopular with Qantas and worked unfairly against the company. He believed though that they could be validly defended as they related to Australia's relations with France. Australia, he said, had prevented TAA's order of the French Caravelle airliner, which had caused much illwill in trade circles at a time when the European Common Market negotiations were approaching and when Australia needed the goodwill of the French.

The government, said the Qantas minister, in dealing with overall problems facing Australia, might make concessions that could affect the profitability of Qantas from a commercial point of view. He wanted to emphasise, however, that the government took great care in choosing for Qantas directors with a wide commercial background to ensure that the affairs of the airline would be conducted in a way that would overcome any disability arising from international air agreements that had to be arranged on other than commercial grounds. It was a clear, unambiguous ministerial assertion that however hardly won were Qantas's achievements in competition with their international airline peers, they were considered by the government as fair fodder for barter in matters quite outside the influence and operating environment of the airline.

Behind the minister in these attitudes was, of course, his ambitious and able director-general with his department and his own prestige to forward and defend. Behind all Qantas submissions, though most went out under the signature of Hudson Fysh, was C. O. Turner. The potential for friction was ever present. Turner now had to listen while the minister, of necessity briefed by Anderson, questioned the Qantas argument for the purchase of two more Boeing jets. The factors affecting Qantas aircraft utilisation were, said Paltridge, changing day by day. Within a week of receipt of the Qantas proposal, he said, he had been advised by telephone from London of proposals by the United Kingdom that could vitally affect future utilisation of Qantas aircraft. The United Kingdom was prepared to concede additional rights to the United States to enable BOAC to operate on the South Pacific to Australia. There appeared little hope of the UK allowing Qantas to operate beyond Hong Kong until BOAC could operate on the South Pacific. Also, New

Zealand had only that morning (2 April) told him of their determination to buy three large jets for TEAL's expansion to Los Angeles through Tahiti. He wondered, he said, if the Qantas directors might like to reconsider the proposal to order two more aircraft.

Fysh answered these doubts while Turner listened; Paltridge then agreed to the purchase, while Anderson listened. The minister wanted assurances that Qantas would not be coming to the government with repeated requests for capital to tide them over financial difficulties because of sudden changes of circumstances.

When Paltridge turned to the paper that Qantas had prepared on TEAL's plans for expansion, Fysh emphasised the board's concern. The vital factor, said Fysh, was whether an acceptable agreement could be worked out between both the government and the two airlines.

Both Anderson and Turner made their contribution as the meeting came to an end. On the negotiations with the French, of such importance to Qantas, the director-general said that if the present Australian offer to France for a service Paris-Tahiti-Sydney in exchange for a Qantas service Sydney-Tahiti-London was not accepted by 1 May then all TAI services through Australia would cease as from 1 June. He had told the French, he said, that there was no hope of their being granted a service around the world via the Tasman. Turner intervened to point out that despite this advice to the French, they had gone to New Zealand and actually signed an agreement with the New Zealanders in which they agreed to give Tasman rights to the French airline. It was extraordinary, said Turner, that the New Zealanders would sign such an agreement unless they were confident of persuading Australia to give up the Tasman. The minister for external affairs had, the meeting was told, agreed that Australia should not negotiate on any basis on which the French used New Zealand to try and obtain additional rights from Australia. This was blackmail.[18]

Fysh thought the meeting had gone well. The request for two additional aircraft had been approved. The immediate problems that remained were related to TEAL's expansion, agreement with the French, a return to better relations with the United Kingdom, and clearance of Qantas rights through Tahiti with the United States. "Qantas", he told Law-Smith, "set the very greatest store on Tahiti . . . At the same time it is hardly practical politics for the French to be given notice to clear out of Sydney and the initialled agreement cancelled outright, as Turner goes all out for."[19]

Despite the atmosphere of accord between Qantas and their minister and director-general that Fysh had mentioned in his diary notes, Turner's constant pressures and well-argued submissions to government on the many complex problems that concerned them both were never less than forceful and made few concessions to the sensitivities of his political masters. The general atmosphere from the beginning of 1962 (as Fysh had noted) had been good and there had been no specific complaints but he now noticed an increase in sensitivity and warned Turner:

I am anxious that at all times extreme care is taken that letters signed by me to the Minister are right and proper as coming from the Head of a Government Instrumentality to his Minister as expressing the views of the Board, and are calculated to further the best interests of our undertaking. I think letters, at all times, should be expressive of our confidence and full co-operation with the Minister and his Administration, and calculated to keep them on side with us. I am anxious not to see an atmosphere grow up of putting the other fellow on the spot on paper . . . which must result in retaliation. As Chief Executive you and your assistants are the ones who draft the majority of letters to the Minister for Board consideration . . . The proof of the propriety of any letter is what one's reaction would be if receiving it oneself. I admit that this matter is giving me considerable concern . . .[20]

To his vice-chairman, Law-Smith, Fysh wrote that the maintenance of good relations between board and minister was vital for the company's wellbeing. "As a company, we have no politics. We are strictly the servants of the Government of the day, attempting to carry out their policy . . . It is, of course, unavoidable that a certain amount of antagonism arises at times in our dealings with the Minister and his Director-General and, as always, personalities enter into it. But it is up to us as Directors to keep these matters on the rails . . . matters are not over happy at the moment."[21]

On 29 April 1963, President John Kennedy approved a statement of a new US international air policy. It was, in essence, a nonprotectionist policy favouring equal opportunities for US carriers in route exchanges with foreign nations (together with reasonable fare rates) and opposing predetermined capacity restrictions on international routes. It also opposed the concept of one nominated airline as the United States "chosen instrument". The world air transport system, said the US paper, "must be as free from restrictions as possible, whether these be imposed by government or through inter-carrier arrangements. Any policy of arbitrarily restricting capacity, dividing markets by carrier agreements, encouraging high rates or curtailing service for which a demand exists, would be harmful to our national interests." It acknowledged that the US carriers' share of the market had declined and could decline still further but said: "US international air carriers should continue to grow at an impressive rate, one considerably greater than the growth rate of the economy as a whole. We are dealing with a US industry growing in size and maturity; not one which is sick and declining and can be expected to fade away to obscurity or death."

The new US policy supported the existing framework of bilateral air agreements. It was cautious on pooling arrangements and indicated that foreign carrier pools should be dealt with case-by-case. US carriers, however, would only be permitted to participate in pooling arrangements when the national interest required it. Despite the inherent free trade philosophy underlying the new policy, it gave general approval to the fare rate machinery of the International Air Transport Association, but with the blunt warning that it would press for reasonable rates by initiating government-to-government discussions. In one of the most significant sections of the policy, the statement affirmed the long-standing US position that its policy of having more than one international carrier was sound, and deserved to be reaffirmed: "We should continue to aim for a US carrier system in which one US flag carrier has access to world markets on a scale comparable to that of the flag carriers or combinations of carriers of other major civil aviation powers, and other US carriers continue to be authorised to serve one or more areas of the world in overall competition with this carrier".[22]

It was clear that the United States retained their strong reservations about pooling arrangements. Such arrangements did present considerable problems for the participants, which was evident in the conflict that now arose between Qantas and BOAC on the division of spoils within the tripartite pool. The basic principle of the tripartite pool was that India, the United Kingdom, and Australia were each entitled to 50 per cent of the traffic moving between their own country and the two other countries, 100 per cent of the traffic from their own country to any other country other than a partner's country, and one-third of all traffic both originating in and destined for ports outside the countries of the three partners. In practice, then, the entitlements of each carrier to third and fourth freedom traffic (traffic from or to their own country) were the main elements in arriving at the partners' shares.

It was BOAC's view that, having established pool shares on the basis of these traffic entitlements, it was unimportant which actual airline carried the traffic. BOAC emphasised the common selling by all three airlines of pool services as the underlying pool principle. No partner, said BOAC, should receive any advantage in revenue just because it carried more load responsibility. Otherwise, said BOAC, individual operators would be encouraged to channel traffic on to their own services, to the detriment of the pool as a whole.

This attitude, from the Qantas point of view, penalised any partner that carried excess traffic. To temper this situation it was agreed in 1961–62 and 1962–63 to limit the excess of traffic carried without compensation to one per cent (based on the main Group 1 of the pool), in order to ensure that each partner reasonably met its responsibilities for the carriage of traffic. (For example, this principle of limitation meant that on a total of £70 million from the pool, no partner could draw from the pool more than £700,000 in excess of its own carriage.) As a further complication, there was an overriding limitation formula specifically agreed between BOAC and Qantas designed to pro-vide a penalty (reduction in share of pool revenue) for one partner failing by more than five per cent to meet its respon-sibilities for load carriage.

In 1963, Sir Basil Smallpiece said that BOAC were no longer prepared to accept the idea of limitations and refused to renew them for a further year. C. O. Turner said that Qantas wanted limitations to continue. He believed, he said, that partners should meet their obligations to earn their share of pool revenue and, besides, it provided an incentive for the partners to sell to the maximum extent. Air India sided with BOAC, urging that limitation on settlements was directly contrary to the principle of a pool. Qantas regarded the position of its pool partners as "quite unacceptable".[23]

As pool payouts were based historically on traffic figures for the preceding year, the decline in airline traffic between November 1961 and March 1962 had provided an overstated figure on which the 1962–63 planning was established. Without a limitations formula, Qantas would have contributed £1,747,000 sterling to the other two partners, a very large sum and constituting 10.4 per cent of total Qantas pool carriage. The limitations formula reduced such a payout to £900,000. Further, during the first three years of the pool, Qantas and Air India had increased traffic but there had been a steady fall in the proportion of traffic carried by BOAC. It was little wonder that Turner was not prepared to accept sharing under the pool without some limitations formula.

Hudson Fysh had always regarded the tripartite pool agreement as an overcomplicated (if ingenious) creation of accountants, to which Turner had committed Qantas without board approval. To Law-Smith, Fysh commented: "The whole trouble goes back to a bad agreement by Turner in Bombay, and without reference to his Board. Some form of limitations should have gone in in the first place."[24] After the failure to agree on limitations at pool talks in mid-1963, Fysh commented: "Our argument with BOAC was that we are carrying traffic in excess of our agreed entitlements for which we are getting no credit; there is no financial regard for excellence; incentive is stifled; our financial results are affected. BOAC's only answer is that limitations are not in the original agreement and that . . . limitations will produce a most undesirable condition in which each partner will sell his own service, thus destroying the partnership idea." Fysh acknowledged that BOAC, in their existing unsatisfactory financial position, could hardly go to their government and recommend a heavy payout to Qantas, while Qantas could not tell the Australian government that they would forgo a large sum that they felt was well earned. "There is no doubt", Fysh wrote, "we should make every effort to stay in the pool. This is necessary strategically and politically if it can be reasonably effected . . . It looks as if the matter will have to go to our government for their advice." He also noted the future effect on Qantas and its attitude to the pool of the impending supersonic transports. "These aircraft could cost as much as £5 million each and . . . would be most expensive for an operator the size of QEA to introduce wholly on its own."[25]

Despite the tensions with BOAC on pool finances, it was Turner's strategy to involve Qantas in further pools where this helped contain competition. In September 1963, Japan Air Lines reopened the issue of a pooling arrangement between Japan and Australia that had first been discussed in August 1960. At that time the short-term Qantas aim was to try to contain the competition from KLM for traffic between Japan and Australia and protect the route for the two national carriers but Japan was not able to proceed. Now, Japan proposed talks aimed at developing what it called an interim joint service as a prelude to a pool. Turner told the board that it was still as important in 1963 as it had been in 1960 "to contain the operation of air services between Japan and Australia to the two national carriers". He believed, he said, that the long-range importance of Japan in the development of Qantas operations, not merely to the Orient but ultimately beyond, on trans-Pacific and trans-Polar routes, was of great significance. He wanted unrestricted Hong Kong–Tokyo rights for Qantas but advised that it would be necessary to insulate BOAC and Air India from the effects of any arrangement with Japan.[26]

By August, BOAC and Qantas had compromised on the pooling disagreements (with an ad hoc settlement of £200,000 to Qantas from BOAC).[27] Turner summarised for the board the outcome of a mid-year meeting of the chief executives of the three pool partners at which it was agreed that although the past, historical year would be used to determine the capacities allowed on the pool routes by each airline, the actual revenue sharing would be determined by current periods. "This change will not necessarily eliminate substantial settlements," Turner wrote, "but it should tend to reduce the magnitude of the settlements . . . In other words, in those years when the Australian economy is buoyant, our revenue will benefit but in periods when the Australian economy is depressed, our share of the revenue is likely to reduce . . ." The change, he said, had other benefits "by no means the least of which is the complete harmony that has now been reached between the three partners". Qantas had not had its original objective of limitations on settlements accepted as a permanent feature of the tripartite pool, but, Turner commented, "we have achieved an alternative which will produce somewhat the same result".[28] (One important part of the agreement was also that during the period of the tripartite agreement all the old pool principles between BOAC

May 1963. Many of the staff who had worked on the Super Constellations gathered at Mascot to farewell VH-EAG *Southern Constellation*. VH-EAG was the first L1049 to be delivered to Qantas on 15 April 1954 and the last to be sold. It flew out of Sydney on 3 May 1963. The sign was a play on the registration letters of *Southern Constellation*. It read:

> FAREWELL EAG
> Very good performer
> Held her reputation
> Enter service first
> Always reliable
> Going out last.

and Qantas relating exclusively to the Kangaroo Route would cease to apply. A further issue between BOAC and Qantas was settled. Agreement was reached that Qantas could extend beyond Hong Kong to London from 1 April 1964.)

Fysh was able to write to Rear Admiral Slattery: "How pleased we feel out here at the outcome of the difficult tripartite talks which have just concluded. Of course, nobody can get everything they want in a negotiation of this size and difficulty, but I feel what has been arrived at is a very good compromise." In that same letter Fysh referred to the issue of supersonic operations, "which seem to loom up ever increasingly as a difficult but intensely interesting problem ahead". The Qantas board, he said, had asked Turner to explore the possibility of protecting Qantas in the matter of deliveries of the Anglo-French supersonic Concorde airliner, if this could be accomplished in a reasonable manner. The United States attitude on supersonic transports was, said Fysh, even more obscure than that of the Anglo-French proposals. "What we would like, of course," said Fysh, "is a place on the Concorde line under something like the same conditions as BOAC, and in return we would undertake to protect you with American manufacturers to the best of our ability."[29] Air India's chairman, J. R. D. Tata, had come to a similar conclusion. He had told Slattery some weeks earlier, writing about Concorde: "We think the best and simplest solution would probably be for us to be included, through BOAC, in the tentative arrangements made with the Anglo-French manufacturers".[30] The pool partners were, on the issue of supersonic operations, starting off in step.

Though the general picture on supersonic airliners and their operation was indeed obscure in mid-1963, the United States had moved quickly in response to the Anglo-French initiatives. An official report by the US Federal Aviation Agency (FAA) acknowledged that, even if the existing design objectives for Concorde were modified as its programme developed, "it cannot be assumed that the net result will be to lessen the competitive impact of the aircraft. It would be unwise for the United States to assume that these [Concorde] objectives will not substantially be attained, since both the British and French Governments have fully mobilised their aeronautical resources and have earmarked approximately \$450 million for the development program."[31] The US Stanford Research Institute, in a comprehensive study, estimated that commercial air passenger-miles in the "free world" would grow from 81 billion in 1962 to 200 billion in 1973 and that forty-three per cent of this 200

billion, or 87 billion passenger-miles, would be available to
supersonic transports.[32] It assessed the market potential for a
US supersonic airliner capable of Mach 3 (three times the speed
of sound) and with trans-Atlantic range at 216 aircraft and, com-
plementing this, a Concorde market potential (Mach 2.2) of 128
aircraft. The FAA reported an estimated delivery price for the
Concorde of $7 million to $10 million each, excluding amortisation and development costs, which, it said, "would be absorbed
by the two Governments to keep the price within this range".
The agency reported that the cost for a US Mach 3, steel-
titanium supersonic airliner (based on estimates from four US
manufacturers) would be $22.6 million per aircraft, including
a normal twenty per cent profit and warranty, but excluding
amortisation of development costs. The total market, therefore,
of some 350 supersonic airliners was seen as massive. Like the
Anglo-French project, the FAA recommended that a United
States supersonic transport should have as a design objective
a New York to Paris capability, involving a range of 4,000 statute
miles. Less than fifteen per cent of the potential traffic available to it would, said the FAA, be beyond a nonstop range of
this order.

   The United States vision of its own supersonic airliner called
for a maximum gross weight of 350,000 pounds and a payload
of 35,000 pounds or more, based on 163 passengers in all-tourist
configuration and 2,000 pounds of cargo and mail. A design
speed greater than Mach 2.2 was called for, with the ability
to cruise without creating sonic boom overpressures greater than
1.5 pounds per square foot. The FAA recognised that "sonic
boom, which results from shock waves produced by an aircraft
in supersonic flights, will present a major problem. These
ground overpressures, like the sound of thunder, may be of
sufficient intensity to disturb the public along a flight path . . .
Booms will be noticeable at distances of approximately 25-30
miles to either side of the flight track. It is believed that there
will not be damage to ground structures." The FAA studies
promised a transport with "the potential for satisfactory
commercial characteristics and that there is a reasonable chance
that this aircraft will prove to be as good or perhaps better than
any transport operating today".[33] It called for an initial design
competition between all interested US airframe and engine
manufacturers, starting in August 1963. Its plan saw the United
States SST going into passenger service by June 1970, less than
two years after the prototype first flight. Qantas, recollecting
that the Boeing 707 did not enter commercial service until more

than four years after the prototype first flew, thought this FAA plan "quite unrealistic by at least three years". Government participation was required in the development programme, but not for the production programme.

Turner wrote to Basil Smallpiece in August that Qantas had received a proposal from British Aircraft Corporation that they reserve places on the Concorde delivery line (numbers 22–24) provided Qantas were willing to provide immediately £200,000 sterling deposit for three aircraft, a deposit that would be completely lost (plus an additional £200,000 damages) if Qantas were unwilling to enter into a definite contract later. Qantas, he said, would not accept these proposals. Turner asked that some joint arrangement might be made whereby BOAC could protect the interests of the partnership.

> I understood from you . . . that BOAC were not committed in any way to either accept the aircraft or to pay any money to assure a position on the line . . . As you know, we are closely investigating the supersonic airliner position and we have our Dr. Shaw on the Joint Committee of Commonwealth Airlines giving airline assistance to the manufacturers. On the other hand, we are keeping a close watch on the American position and our experts are in constant touch with the manufacturers in that country on all developments. In this latter connection I feel that we can be of considerable assistance to the Partnership with the technical information we obtain in these areas. Our Directors feel that by working together we could possibly protect each other for delivery places and in this way have the best of both worlds. [34]

BOAC's response to this Qantas request came from Slattery to Fysh in a "strictly personal and confidential" letter on 20 August.

> I made an application to the British Aircraft Corporation [he wrote] to increase our national reservations for the Concorde by a further six aircraft (making twelve in all) with the idea that I would hold two or three for Qantas—although, of course, I did not mention this to British Aircraft Corporation . . . I do not know whether BAC smelt a rat but they came back to me about a week later saying that it was quite difficult to fit further airlines into the list because they had to work jointly in this matter with Sud Aviation as the production lines are supposed to run parallel in the two countries. Unfortunately, they said, everyone is on holidays in France in August. The BAC representative then said that they would expect BOAC to pay something for this option for a further six aircraft to put them in line with other airlines. This I declined to do . . . Do you think Cedric Turner can have inadvertently let the cat out of the bag so that BAC knew we were trying to protect your position?" [35]

Securing a firm position on the delivery line for supersonic aircraft, if they eventuated, had become a matter of commercial importance in the closing months of 1963. The big world airlines were taking the possibility of supersonic passenger flight with sufficient seriousness to pay out substantial sums of money as deposits on what were still very much paper aeroplanes. Pan American had provisionally ordered fifteen of the US aircraft plus six Concordes, and had paid a deposit of $1.5 million on the US SSTs, though none on the Concordes. Trans World Airlines had ordered ten US SSTs and four Concordes (with a $1 million deposit for the US aircraft). American Airlines wanted six US aircraft and four Concordes (with a US deposit of $600,000). Japan Air Lines, Northwest, Alitalia, El Al, and Flying Tiger had all ordered the US aircraft, while BOAC, Air France, and Continental had all ordered Concordes. In total, by year's end, forty-seven US supersonic transports had been ordered and twenty-nine Concordes. On the provisional prices of both aircraft, these orders were worth approximately $1,352 million.[36]

The rate of growth in the Qantas expansion programme was accelerating as these new developments in airliner technology were promised. Its corporate confidence and its national role were reflected in the launching of a major exhibition, in August, illustrating the evolution of flight. Called "Da Vinci to Sputnik", it was shown progressively to the public around the world. Films on Australian art and artists were produced and won international awards. The company was experiencing the start of growth rates never before experienced. One main reason was a worldwide upsurge in passenger traffic augmented by a buoyant Australian economy. A second reason, coinciding with this upsurge, was the change in the agreed tripartite pool principles under which each partner was to provide services more closely related to its current levels of national entitlements, a change that particularly benefited Qantas and whose explosive result could not have been foreseen. Included in the expanded Qantas traffic as a substantial and growing part of the Qantas business was the carriage of government-sponsored migrants. Distinct from ordinary migrants who may have travelled with Qantas as full fare paying passengers (and of whom the airline had no records), the government-sponsored migrants fell into two main categories. First, there were those travelling to Australia under the aegis of the Intergovernmental Committee for European Migration (ICEM), and they were mostly carried in full-plane loads on charter flights. The second group were the United Kingdom migrants, most of whom were carried as fill-up loadings on Qantas and BOAC regular services. During the nine months from January 1963, there were thirty-seven ICEM Qantas flights, providing Qantas with a surplus of £103,000. In the eleven months from January, total uplift of United Kingdom migrants was 9,336. These migrants were carried at a government-directed fare of £130 sterling and the total revenue shared by BOAC and Qantas for the period was over £A1.5 million. This was almost all net gain from seats that would otherwise have remained unoccupied. Though the revenue gain to Qantas from migrant carriage was substantial, it was tiny compared with the amounts paid by government to the shipping companies to carry the majority of sponsored migrants.[37]

To crew the expanded services necessary for growth Qantas began, late in 1963, a drive to recruit large numbers of pilots, navigators, and flight engineers, projecting an increase in total pilot numbers of 280 in August 1963 to well over 400 by mid-1965.[38] In December, Qantas ordered more aircraft. This time, though, there was no question of ordering other than Boeing jets and a larger version of the Boeing 707 was chosen. Government approval was obtained for the purchase, in December, of three Boeing 707-338C aircraft, for delivery in February, April, and September of 1965. The 338C was longer and heavier than the 138B V-jets. It had the same first class and economy class passenger accommodation but could carry in special compartments almost twelve tons of cargo. Converted to an all-cargo configuration it could lift a payload of thirty tons over a range of 3,500 miles. The Qantas jet fleet, important commercially for Qantas, was now also an accepted and recognised element of Australia's defence infrastructure. In off-the-record talks with Turner, Australia's chief of defence forces, Sir Frederick Scherger, stated that it was necessary for Australia's defence that Qantas have long-range aircraft available to transport troops. RAAF planning, he told Turner, was all based on Qantas being the long-range troop carrier. Scherger went further, telling Turner that he thought the government might consider paying stand-by charges such as engineering maintenance and crew costs for aircraft purchased in excess of Qantas requirements, in order to ensure that a transport fleet was available. "On this basis," Qantas reported to the board in November 1963, "it is considered that we would have a strong case to present to the Government that additional 338Cs would be of overall advantage to Australia."[39]

Scherger's reflections on Qantas's role in providing long-range aircraft for troop transport were of more than theoretical import in 1963. The creation of the new and independent Commonwealth nation of Malaysia from the federation of the Malayan states, Singapore, North Borneo (Sabah), and Sarawak had provoked Indonesia to an outbreak of the most intense nationalism. President Sukarno regarded it with violent hostility as British neocolonialism and was committed to a policy of confrontation. Indonesian military units infiltrated Sarawak and Indonesian naval units operated provocatively in the Straits of Malacca. When the new nation was proclaimed on 16 September 1963, Australia had welcomed it publicly while Indonesia severed diplomatic relations with Kuala Lumpur and, in Djakarta, the British embassy was burned and sacked by unrestrained mobs. Australia was committed to assist Britain by providing Australian forces, not only in Malaya but in the new Malaysia.

Scherger's remarks also came at a timely moment for Qantas in its role as shareholder in Malayan Airways. Both Qantas and BOAC had been asked to facilitate the airline's equipment plans for modern jet aircraft over its network connecting Malaysia (including the Borneo Territories) with Hong Kong, Thailand, Indonesia, and possibly India. MAL at that time operated with Comets from the Kangaroo Route in 1965, forcing a simultaneous withdrawal of the aircraft from MAL, who could not fully maintain them at Singapore. Commercially, Qantas could not ignore the request from MAL for help. The value of third and fourth freedom traffic rights between Malaysia and Australia was estimated at £2 million per annum, with fifth freedom rights estimated at £650,000 per annum to Qantas by 1965. Both BOAC and Qantas had, however, agreed between them that they would not commit extra capital to MAL for their re-equipment with modern jets, though both agreed to investigate chartering aircraft. BOAC was able to provide VC10s and Qantas Boeing 138Bs. Turner noted that BOAC was likely to have surplus VC10 capacity in 1965 and they would be actively encouraged by the British government to supply this to Malaysia Airways, thereby increasing British influence in Malaysia and creating a possible market for additional VC10s. "This", wrote Turner, "would result in a decrease of Qantas and Australian influence in the area . . . It would be advantageous from the Qantas point of view and for Australia to have 707-138Bs available for MAL rather than the VC10 as this will bring considerable work to our engineering base and greatly assist the Australian image in Malaysia." He proposed that Qantas secure three more of the bigger Boeing 707-338Cs, making six in all, and conclude an agreement with MAL to use three 138Bs on the MAL-Thai network under a lease-purchase agreement. "One cannot over-emphasise the grave threat to our interests", Turner told the board, "if foreign airlines were able to replace the BOAC-Qantas interests in MAL." With a favourably disposed Malaysian government, he said, Pan American could become a major threat to the whole Kangaroo Route. If, on the other hand, KLM ousted the BOAC-Qantas interest it could, with its connections with Philippine Air Lines, have a stranglehold on air transport in South East Asia that would gravely threaten Qantas interests on both the Kangaroo and Far Eastern routes. "The political and defence support which the Australian Government has extended to Malaysia", he wrote, "should ensure a continuance of our present favourable position, provided we can offer an acceptable proposition for the re-equipment of MAL."[40]

There were few changes to the route network in 1963. In November, what presaged a major change was introduced when the Qantas service between Sydney and Tahiti began. The deadline for French acceptance of Australian counterproposals to their own proposals for round-the-world rights through Sydney, 1 May, had been extended several times. On 8 August the French finally accepted new arrangements in which they were to be given a weekly return service from France through the Middle East and South East Asia to Sydney and beyond to the United States (through Fiji and Tahiti), plus Sydney-Noumea and on to the United States. However, their traffic rights were to be limited to traffic between Sydney and places to the east. Australia, in return, was to have its weekly return service to Noumea and a weekly return service through Fiji and Tahiti and beyond to North America, Central America (or South America), and to London and beyond. (Qantas obtained rights through Mexico in late 1963 as part of Turner's overall strategy.) The French indicated that they wanted to limit the validity of these arrangements until the end of 1963, when they could be continued by agreement or denounced. This seeming breakthrough was greeted with heartfelt relief by Qantas. Turner told the board: "The French acceptance of this Australian proposal is the culmination of years of effort on our part to rectify the 1960 agreement with France which allowed the French airline to enjoy benefits out of all proportion to those obtained by the Australian airline".[41] But the ongoing battle between France and Australia over traffic rights made the new Sydney-Tahiti service short-lived. On 1 November, Anderson told Qantas that the French had given notice that their hard-won agreement would not be extended beyond 31 December. In the intervening period, Turner had pressed urgently for Qantas to begin the service through Tahiti, hoping that once in place, the French would be deterred from the major step of forcing its cancellation.

This tense situation was further complicated by pressures from the New Zealand prime minister Keith Holyoake, that Qantas should defer introduction of a Tahiti service "for fear that the commencement of the Qantas service would provoke the French to cancel TEAL's rights at Tahiti".[42] New Zealand also pressed for Qantas to relinquish completely its aspirations to operate through Tahiti and to allow TEAL alone to represent the Commonwealth on that route. To complicate matters even more, the United States Civil Aeronautics Board handed down a decision in mid-November awarding Pan American the right to fly from the West Coast through Tahiti and Auckland to Sydney. "This US decision", Turner wrote, "raises many complex problems for us."[43] Qantas firmly opposed the New Zealand request and Paltridge announced the introduction of the new Qantas service to Tahiti. It began on 22 November but was terminated after only five weeks. On 27 December, Paltridge was forced to announce: "France has cancelled the rights of Australia's overseas airline, Qantas, to operate jet services from Sydney to Tahiti from 31 December. It has also withdrawn French long-range jet services through Sydney from the same date . . . The French authorities had also said there was no immediate prospect of reconsidering reciprocal services between Sydney and Tahiti."[44]

In less dramatic changes to the network, Electras had replaced the Constellations on the South African service in April, and in September Queensland was included in the Pacific network when a weekly service began from Sydney through Brisbane to Honolulu connecting with Qantas services to North America and Europe. On the Tasman, new services started in October between Melbourne and Wellington and, in December, between Brisbane and Wellington. (The Sydney-Noumea Boeing service was interrupted when the French withdrew traffic rights at the end of December. To honour what Australia regarded as the intent of the agreement with the French government, specifying the use of propeller-driven aircraft, the Boeings were replaced by Electras on 2 January 1964, but the service ceased completely one week later. Arrangements were then made for a pool agreement with the French airline UTA and a weekly service resumed with Electras on 13 February 1964.)

In the closing months of 1963, Hudson Fysh was concerned with important personal matters that involved his pension rights, his chief executive, and the Department of Civil Aviation. On 25 September he wrote privately to Paltridge to explore the possibility of either a pension or a payment of some kind when his position as chairman of Qantas was terminated. "If I was not whole-time chairman, the question would not come up and, in this respect, I think I am unique", he wrote. "In reality I have been somewhat of an Executive Chairman . . . The retiring age in the Public Service is sixty-five and I was appointed to my present position at the age of sixty. I have never been avaricious for money but with my present responsibility it certainly does seem strange to see quite a number of QEA employees working under considerably better conditions than myself."[45] Fysh had, of course, received superannuation benefits on relinquishing his position as Qantas chief executive. His request now was for consideration of further benefits for his years as chairman. As a part-time chairman, he would have had no claim on the government. In the unusual position of "whole-time" chairman, the issue was clouded and, as he said, unique. The issue was sufficiently confusing to involve the prime minister, the chairman of the Public Service Board, F. H. Wheeler, and the secretary to the Treasury, Roland Wilson, and to occupy them until mid-1965.

Fysh clashed sharply with Turner on a matter that involved, in his judgment, his status as chairman and his chief executive's assumption of the chairman's prerogative in October. In obvious anger, he wrote to Turner:

> On my return from Rome last week I noticed a Press Release from our Press and Information Department in which you are quoted as commenting on our Annual Report. I was astonished to read this, as you are well aware it is the duty of the Chairman of the Board and no one else to make such a statement. If a statement was thought necessary I should have been approached. Actually, very good publicity was received when our Report was released in Canberra, on the Minister presenting it to Parliament.
>
> There is a directive in your possession regarding Company press statements which I would advise you to read and then thoroughly inform the Press and Information Department so that mistakes such as this cannot occur again. This is not the first time I have

had to complain about matters of this sort, but never before have I seen such a glaring mistake, and one which I feel requires an apology.[46]

On 30 December, Fysh was shocked to hear of a press report that his retirement as chairman was imminent, a report allegedly based on departmental information. He cabled Paltridge that a Sydney journalist had informed the Qantas Press and Information Department that "he had been told by a good source within the Civil Aviation Department that the minister would shortly be announcing that the chairman of Qantas would be retiring soon. As I have only recently commenced a three year term," said Fysh, "these rumours [are] most embarrassing and I suggest an investigation into the matter." Fysh sent his kind regards both to the minister and the head of the department concerned, D. G. Anderson.[47] It was an unsettling end to a year that had been a good one for both Qantas and its chairman.

Pilots versus Management; Turner versus Bland 1964

10   Senator Shane Paltridge dismissed Hudson Fysh's anxiety about the rumours of his impending retirement promptly. "The press statements contained in your telegram are quite without foundation", he told Fysh. "I am surprised that you have paid any serious attention to them."[1]

In England, in QEA's partner airline, BOAC, both the chairman, Sir Matthew Slattery, and the chief executive, Sir Basil Smallpiece, had been less fortunate. Both had been removed from their positions at year's end and replaced by a combined chairman and chief executive, Sir Giles Guthrie. There had been, according to the BOAC history, *Wings Across the World*, political manoeuvring behind the scenes and the British minister, Amery, had "devised the resignation of these two exemplary men". Guthrie's mandate was to produce, within twelve months, a sound plan for BOAC's future.[2]

Fysh pressed the matter of his pension rights as whole-time chairman. On 7 January 1964 he wrote to the prime minister directly, explaining that he had received a lump sum of £19,120.19.0 in lieu of pension when he had retired as chief executive of QEA on 30 June 1955. On being appointed whole-time chairman, he said, he had ceased being an employee of QEA. The difficulty Fysh saw for himself was that "under present conditions [he] would have to face a very sharp drop in remuneration, which would seriously affect the way of life of [himself] and [his] wife [on retirement as chairman]". He proposed that a sum be set aside towards an ultimate retiring allowance to cover his service from 1 July 1955 to the termination of his service as whole-time chairman. If, he said, such a payment were approximately £1,000 for each year of service as whole-time chairman, the sum total of such a benefit, when added to the lump sum received on retirement in 1955, would be roughly comparable to the benefit other top executives of the company were due to receive on retirement.

Prime Minister Menzies referred the matter to Paltridge, asking him to consult the chairman of the Public Service Board, F. H. Wheeler, and noting that Fysh had completed nearly nine years service since retiring as chief executive, and that he would have completed eleven years on 30 June 1966 when his present appointment expired. It was Wheeler's view, expressed to Paltridge, that there was no precedent for the type of payment sought by Fysh. Wheeler noted that the representations for the payment had come not from the Qantas board, but from Fysh.

There had been remarkable growth in all Qantas operations in the period from 1956 to 1964 under C. O. Turner as chief executive. Total revenue for the airline had more than doubled from £20 million to £45 million. The number of revenue passengers carried each year had grown from 156,000 to 293,000 and revenue passenger miles from 414 million to 1,159 million. The company's staff had not grown so rapidly (it was 5,695 in 1956 to 7,405 in 1964) but gross salaries and wages had risen from £5.7 million to £11.2 million. Shareholders funds had increased from £10.9 million to £20.5 million and fixed assets from £18.9 million to £41.6 million.

In these nine years the pace, for Qantas management and staff, had been hectic. Immediately prior to Paltridge's appointment as minister, orders had been placed in 1956 for Boeing 707s as replacements for Super Constellations. In 1957, traffic rights were obtained to extend the Pacific services from San Francisco to New York, the United Kingdom, and Europe and so make Qantas the first airline with round-the-world services via Australia and the United States. Qantas House, the new company headquarters, had been completed in the same year. In 1958, the round-the-world services were inaugurated and a year later the jet Boeing 707s and the propjet Electras were introduced. (The Boeings cut the elapsed time for the Sydney-London journey from sixty-one to thirty-seven hours.) In 1960, the government approved the company's technical judgment that the straight jet engines of the Boeings should be modified to the more efficient fan jets and, in a major commercial rearrangement of operations on the company's main Kangaroo Route, the tripartite pool with BOAC and Air India commenced. In that same year Qantas celebrated its fortieth anniversary. With the start of the new decade, Qantas began operations in 1960 in its own right across the Tasman in pool with the now wholly New Zealand-owned TEAL, bought four additional Boeing 707s, and received government approval to build a hotel next to Qantas House. The fleet was again to be extended massively in 1964, with orders for five additional Boeings. Now, as 1964 began, Qantas braced itself for yet another technical leap forward into a new airline age. Government approval was given for deposits to be paid to secure production line positions for supersonic aircraft – for four Concordes and six United States supersonic transports.

Fysh sent a generous cable of congratulations to Turner, who was in London, to applaud the payment of these deposits: "They mark another great step forward in Qantas progress under your chief executiveship". All had gone smoothly and expeditiously at home, he said, and the event was especially marked by co-operation between Qantas people and the Department of Civil Aviation.[3] Fysh also wrote an encouraging note to Capt. R. J. Ritchie, deputy chief executive, who had been closely involved, together with senior people of the Technical Development Department, in the studies of the two supersonic types. "There is no doubt", wrote Fysh, "that you have personally worked strenuously and well and never spared yourself in the heavy work which has resulted in the success we wished for. When eventually Qantas operates supersonically, with all its thrills and advancement, you will be able to look back with satisfaction to your own work and leadership in this matter. You have a big future in the coming sphere."[4]

In a special issue of the company newspaper, *Qantas News*, Fysh told Qantas employees that the decision of the federal government would enable Qantas to be fully competitive in the early stages of the supersonic era. It was, he said, too early for Qantas to select either the Concorde or the United States SST. Qantas were still negotiating with Concorde's manufacturers on the amount of the deposit to be paid and nothing would be paid until Qantas were satisfied that the Concorde's performance was satisfactory. "We intend to defer a final decision about the actual purchase of supersonic aircraft until sufficient detailed information is available for us to make our usual careful technical and economic analysis of the machines."[5]

BOAC noted and reacted to the Qantas move. In an urgent and confidential letter on 16 January, one day before the Qantas

public announcement, BOAC's new chairman and chief
executive, Sir Giles Guthrie, wrote to the permanent secretary
of Britain's Ministry of Aviation, Sir Richard Way. There was,
he said, a potentially serious competitive position developing
with the major airlines of the world committing themselves on
either or both the BAC-SUD Concorde or the American SST
delivery lines.

> BOAC's position on the Concorde delivery line is, of course,
> protected [he wrote]. We now feel it commercially necessary to
> obtain six suitable positions on the American supersonic transport
> delivery line. The cost of reserving six places would be $600,000,
> which amount would be refunded in full unless further commit-
> ments are entered into prior to 1 November 1965. The earliest
> position we can get, if we act extremely promptly, is No. 17. This
> situation is unlikely to remain for long; indeed, Qantas have now
> received authority from their Government to reserve delivery
> positions.

Guthrie summarised BOAC's attitude to the new airliners.

> The supersonic transport development, whether in Europe or
> America, is fraught with many difficulties and is advancing the
> general state of the art in civil air transport by a bigger margin
> than has ever been attempted before . . . It seems to us, from the
> information currently available, that the US supersonic airliner
> might fulfil a different role from that envisaged for the Anglo-
> French Concorde, yet a role which would suit admirably our
> planned network . . . Nothing in this letter should be taken as
> criticism of the Concorde.[6]

A public diplomatic row followed the cancellation by France
of QEA's Tahiti rights and Australia's quid pro quo in removing
France's right to operate jet services through Sydney. The
Australian manager of UTA-Air France was called before the
Australian director-general of civil aviation for breaching the
agreement between the two countries by continuing to operate
its jets. The department told the press that it was prepared to
overlook a flight on 1 January because it was so close to the
cancellation date. But flights on 7 and 8 January, it said, "were
clear breaches of the agreement". A strong note was sent to the
French ambassador. The atmosphere was tempered by rapid
negotiations and the authorities of both countries agreed to keep
open the Sydney-Noumea service with nonjet aircraft.[7]

Qantas took the occasion to have a close look at the operations
of the French airline. "UTA, the airline formed by the recent
marriage of TAI and UAT," said a management report, "is not
very large and is comparable in size with Air India, Iberia,

British United and El Al." Compared with Qantas it had six jet aircraft (DC8s) to Qantas's eleven Boeing 707s. It flew 153 million capacity ton miles to Qantas's 275. "It is ironical", said the report, "that the British airlines are constantly receiving bad publicity because of losses and high unit costs, while the French airlines, although consistently losing money and operating with high costs, manage to escape poor publicity . . . It is often overlooked that Air France receives a regular subsidy of about 7 per cent of total revenue from its owner, the French government." The independent airline TAI (since merged with UAT and operating as UTA) was one-tenth the size of Air France and had, it said, since 1960 also operated at a loss (£1 million in 1962). By contrast, the two British corporations, BOAC and BEA, had in the previous year lost a total of £A12 million and had accumulated losses at March 1963 of £A100 million. "Obviously," commented the report, "silence is golden. The French industry is not given to introspection or agonising reappraisals so that their inefficiency is comparatively unknown. The British air corporations, on the other hand, live in glass houses and are constantly under fire from press and public." UTA, born on 1 October 1963, was a private French airline, a little over half the size of Qantas. "While the present situation continues, it is clear that the French airline is suffering more than Qantas . . . The tripartite pool should therefore continue to enjoy the carriage of most of the former TAI traffic."[8]

There was support for Qantas in the Australian press. The *Sydney Morning Herald*, in an editorial on 14 January, commented:

> This is not the first time we have had trouble with French airlines, which are inclined to act in an arbitrary and high-handed manner . . . Qantas has a long and successful history as a world-wide carrier and has proved it can look after itself when it comes to negotiations with foreign airlines. Its principle is that it will accept competition for mutual benefits where a genuine flow of traffic exists. Unlike certain government-owned airlines, it is not a prestige symbol but a highly efficient money earner and in its negotiations it deserves the whole-hearted support of the Australian Government. We have few enough assets to match it.[9]

The *Bulletin*, on 11 January, commented that the Australia-France agreement had given the French

> a foothold on the highly competitive Australia-Europe run. Six airlines operate out of Sydney to Europe – QEA, BOAC, Alitalia, Air India, KLM and until this year TAI-UTA. Situated in elaborate premises on the ground floor of the Sydney Stock

Exchange building, only a good stone's throw from QEA head-quarters, with heavily accented switch girls and reception staff to provide the French colour, TAI and then UTA have managed to carve out a share of the Europe-bound traffic. More than a fair share, according to Qantas . . . It is no coincidence that Australia and America, in particular QEA and Pan American, tend to agree on the higher levels of airline diplomacy. Another bond of feeling is the Qantas firm drive under C. O. Turner, chief executive officer, towards being a self-supporting commercial under-taking . . . The Americans are openly critical of the "national prestige" airlines which . . . tend to lose money in over-expansion and reckless plane purchasing. In the razor edge financial world of international airlines finance, Qantas' profit record stands out against the losses of BOAC or the more spectacular accumulated losses of KLM. [10]

Despite the activities of other airlines, which included five more than those listed by the *Bulletin* (TEAL, Pan American, South African Airways, Canadian Pacific, and Trans-Australia Airlines, the latter operating under Qantas rights to the Solomon Islands and West Irian and to Portuguese Timor), Qantas had the lion's share of passenger, cargo, and mail traffic uplifted and discharged in Australia. (For the year ending 30 June 1963, Qantas had 51 per cent of passengers, 59 per cent of cargo, and 57 per cent of mail.) The tripartite pool partners (in the pool area comprising Sydney-London via the Middle East and Sydney-Hong Kong and Tokyo) together carried 90 per cent of passengers, 82 per cent of cargo, and 95 per cent of mail. Of the remaining traffic on these routes carried by competitors, KLM took 4.5 per cent of passengers, Alitalia 4.3 per cent, and TAI 1.1 per cent in that same year. (These three accounted for 18 per cent of cargo and 4.9 per cent of mail.) On the Pacific route, Qantas carried 72 per cent of passengers and 70 per cent of both cargo and mail. The Australian carrier's competitive performance was remarkably strong. [11]

C. O. Turner was the chief architect of these impressive achievements. Around him he had assembled a strong and loyal top management team. His deputy chief executive and deputy chief general manager was Capt. R. J. "Bert" Ritchie, erudite in aircraft and operational matters and a former pilot of long experience; C. W. Nielson was director of commercial services; P. W. Howson director of technical services; and F. C. Derham director of finance. Management strength continued well below these levels. Turner took a personal interest always in at least the top one hundred senior appointments. In an era of rapid change in airliner technology, Dr. R. R. Shaw, technical development manager, was a major strength. D. B. Hudson,

285

engineering manager, controlled an organisation whose efficiency and high standards were not bettered anywhere in the world. Capt. A. Wharton, who had distinguished himself as a World War II pilot, was manager, flight operations. T. E. Roff was commercial manager planning and H. M. Birch commercial manager marketing. G. G. Badgery, as cargo manager, was responsible for the successful Qantas performance in this field. Of great importance to Turner and unshakeable in his loyalty to him in his disputes with Hudson Fysh, the director-general of civil aviation, Don Anderson, or any airline, organisation or press outlet, was the chief press and information officer, John Ulm. Divisional managers, heading specific regions of Qantas operations, were Capt. L. R. Ambrose, manager western division; John Fysh (son of Sir Hudson Fysh), manager Tasman and Pacific Islands; A. A. Barlow, manager eastern division; and C. E. Oliver, manager Far East. As advisers, Qantas retained the services of Capt. G. U. "Scottie" Allan, Capt. Edgar Johnston (international adviser), and Capt. W. H. Crowther (as chairman, hotel project committee).

C. O. Turner, by international standards, was poorly paid for his responsibilities and achievements and was well aware of it. He had clipped from the June 1964 issue of the American magazine *Air Transport World* an article headed "How US Trunks Pay Top Executives" (and was to keep this cutting amongst his personal papers until his death). Presidents or chief executives of fourteen major US trunk airlines during 1963, the article said, were paid salaries ranging from $40,000 to $106,250 and averaged $75,000. Pan American's Juan Trippe and United's W. A. Patterson received $100,000. Delta's president and general manager C. E. Woolman headed the list at $106,250. By contrast, the board of Qantas was struggling, in November 1963, to have Turner's salary increased to £11,000 per annum (approximately $22,000). Turner's salary provided a margin of £500 per annum in excess of the salary of top government departmental heads of the Commonwealth Public Service as a token recognition by the government that higher salaries were paid in commercial organisations than by government. Under the government's financial directive to Qantas, Turner's salary level was not at the discretion of the Qantas board; its variation involved the careful deliberation of the country's most senior public servants. In February 1964 they responded to the board request for an increase in the salary of the Qantas chief executive. The Permanent Heads Committee recommended to the Higher Salaries Committee of Cabinet that the salary review

for the general manager and deputy general manager of Qantas
be held over until such time as there was a general review of
other top level statutory authority salaries.

Three members of the top management team – Ritchie, Howson,
and Wharton – supported by top executive staff, had spent the
closing months of 1963 and the beginning of 1964 working constantly on a widening disagreement with the airlines' pilots
involving aircrew rosters. It was now to erupt into open conflict with a strike by Qantas pilots.

There had been a significant change by Turner and his
management team in their attitude to negotiations with the
Australian Federation of Air Pilots in mid-1962. On 31 July
the Overseas Airline Pilots (Qantas) Agreement 1962 was
certified under the Arbitration Act and, in it, the parties were
not Qantas and the AFAP but Qantas and listed individual pilots
in Qantas employ. While this was an advance of a kind for the
pilots' federation, it had not prevented the holding of formal
proceedings before the Arbitration Commission or the formal
certification of agreements. The AFAP remained firmly
committed to its anti-arbitration views as it proceeded with yet
more negotiations. Qantas was just as firm in its determination
to seek legislation to contain possibilities for industrial action
by pilots. A year later, in July 1963, the AFAP team was
immensely strengthened when a former Qantas executive, Fred
Caterson, well versed in pilot-management relations, resigned
from Qantas to become manager of the AFAP's Sydney regional
office. By February 1964 negotiations on new rosters to vary
pilots' rest cycles broke down. On 12 February, the AFAP told
Qantas: "The Executive has authorised the Qantas pilots to
declare a stoppage if they should decide to do so. The matter
has been considered by the Overseas Branch and it has decided
to take this action. There will be a withdrawal of services
commencing midnight tomorrow, 2359 Thursday 13 February."

In a press release on 12 February, the AFAP manager, B. I.
Crofts, put the pilots' case to the public.

> Qantas pilots are withdrawing their services following failure to
> reach agreement on a new employment contract to replace the
> previous contract which expired on 30 June 1963. One of the main
> issues in dispute . . . is the limitation which the pilots seek placed
> upon duty hours, upon the number of days away from home base
> in each year, and the free time at home base following international
> flights . . . The operation of jet aircraft has dramatically affected
> the work cycle and working conditions of pilots. Recognition of

the fatigue inducing characteristics of jet flying is something which the Company is apparently not prepared to recognise. [12]

At that time the industrial agreement with the pilots provided for a minimum of sixteen free days for each pilot in each fifty-six day period. Typical duty periods for this fifty-six day cycle in January 1964 for Boeing pilots varied from thirty-nine duty days plus seventeen free days to twenty-six duty days and twenty-seven free days. Turner responded to the AFAP press release with a memorandum to all pilots. "On the matter of fatigue which earlier was not pursued by the Federation," he wrote, "[it] is now highlighted in the press. The Company has kept itself fully informed on worldwide discussion and investigation of this question. The most authoritative world medical opinion has so far found no discernible evidence of increased fatigue as a result of the operation of jet aircraft . . ."[13]

The pilots were in no mood to listen to Turner. In a four-page brochure they accused Qantas executives of an inability or a refusal to negotiate honestly and directly and emphasised "the pre-occupation, even obsession, of the Qantas management with the 'legal' approach as a solution to their industrial inadequacies". Pilots, said the federation, had "a feeling of personal insecurity due to the effects of cumulative fatigue". [14] (It was the view of Scottie Allan in his retirement that pilots suffered not from fatigue but from boredom.)[15]

Turner's tough attitude had now brought conflict not only with his pilots but also with his chairman, his minister (Paltridge), senior public servants, and other ministers. The prime minister himself was concerned that the national airline had stopped operating. On 15 February Menzies issued a statement strongly attacking the pilots. He made it plain that the government would not allow illegal stoppages against the airline when processes were in place that were available for them and all workers. The government, he warned, could enact special legislation to ensure that it and other parties would not be seriously disadvantaged by the action of the pilots, as had been done before in matters affecting the mining industry and the waterfront.

The strike itself ended at midnight on 16 February when the pilots returned to work. Qantas had lost £300,000 in revenue. The issues that had brought about the strike had not, however, been resolved. On 18 February, Fysh suggested to Paltridge and Anderson that an umpire be appointed to settle the dispute. "The Government", he wrote, "should prepare legislation aimed at avoiding future strikes by Qantas pilots and paralysing a great Australian essential service."[16]

Late on the evening of 19 February, Paltridge rang Fysh from Melbourne. He wanted Qantas to meet the pilots' federation under the chairmanship of the secretary of the Department of Labour and Industry, Henry Bland, in Melbourne on the afternoon of 20 February. Fysh rang Turner. His chief executive would not agree to go to Melbourne on the grounds that there was not proper time to get ready. Fysh was confronted by an impossible situation. "I . . . informed him of the Minister's request and instructed him to send our team to Melbourne and suggested Capt. Ritchie should go. Mr Turner refused", wrote Fysh. "I found Mr Turner quite unable to undertake a rational discussion and he appeared under great strain and stress." Fysh called a special board meeting for the morning of 20 February. Bland's minister, William McMahon, had by then also telephoned asking for the meeting with the federation, stating that it was the prime minister's wish. The board agreed to comply with the request, despite doubts that it could solve the company's long-term difficulties in dealing with the pilots.[17] "The Board requested that Mr Turner use Capt. Ritchie to the greatest possible extent in dealing with the pilots and industrial matters", Fysh wrote. "In my view, as far as possible the burden of critical industrial negotiations should be removed from Mr Turner's control."[18] In handwritten notes dated 20 February, Fysh wrote: "Turner sees no good in anything anyone suggests except himself. Never consulted me once for advice through the whole difficult time. I have great difficulty getting anything out of him. In fact, as usual . . . egotistical, bumptious, unyielding and dogmatic in negotiations. He allows personal egotism and dominance to enter in."[19] Fysh thought that Capt. Bert Ritchie, by contrast, had a realistic grip on matters. He wrote that the board decision was, "as for last time, a terrible defeat for Turner's personal pushing of extreme confrontation and no give. Turner [is] faced with the Board's action. Hated it like hell because it was somebody else's suggestion. A small man with the mind of an accountant."[20]

Despite the understandable bitterness of these comments, Fysh was still able to recognise Turner's strengths. He wrote to his vice-chairman, R. R. Law-Smith: "I have no confidence whatever in our Chief Executive in any top line negotiation when the position becomes necessary for him to compromise for a settlement and I am fearful that he will land the Company in trouble in the future as he has done in the past. Apart from this vital top angle the Chief Executive, of course, does a wonderful job in the interests of the Company and is highly efficient."[21] In Melbourne on 20 and 21 February, arrangements were finally agreed between Qantas and the AFAP, under Bland's chairmanship, for the settlement of disputes by mediation. If the two parties agreed that the mediator should settle any matter in dispute, then his decision would be accepted. "The parties have agreed to these unusual arrangements for the settlement of the conditions of pilots", the minutes of the meeting reported, "because of the particular relationships that necessarily exist between Qantas and its pilots." D. G. Apsey was nominated as mediator, and the first meeting with him set down for 25 February.

Fysh told Paltridge: "So far as mediation is concerned, the Board is not satisfied that this will resolve our problems with the pilots and believes that should mediation fail there must be final recourse to arbitration under the Commonwealth Conciliation and Arbitration Act if serious repercussions on all other sections of the industry are to be avoided".[22] Paltridge expressed his concern in such a way that clearly indicated he had listened closely to the message of the pilots. "Some apprehension is felt . . . that the Qantas management may not be entering into the mediation process determined to try to make it succeed. Lack of faith on the management side could do nothing but harm in the long run."[23]

As the pilots did not really want mediation, and as Qantas doubted its efficacy, it was little wonder that by 8 April the mediator, Apsey, reported: "Complete agreement could not be outlined on the issue in dispute . . . Discussion was confined to the question of hours of duty and free time at home base. It has proved impossible for me to bring the parties to a common ground . . . even on the basis of a trial period. I am bound to say that early in the proceedings I was concerned at what I term the poor state of industrial relations which appeared to exist between the Company and its pilots, a condition to which in my opinion both sides had contributed."[24] All that the mediator had managed to achieve was a basic recommendation that during an interim period the company should adopt a basis of two and a half days free of duty for pilots for each five days spent away from home. Qantas management and the AFAP accepted this as a basis for proceeding pending the outcome of an investigation into pilot fatigue. The matters in dispute were to occupy both parties throughout the year, beginning with this investigation. The pilots' strike had made their conflict with

Qantas management a public issue that was to occupy the airline and the media in the months ahead.

"Has anything been accomplished?" asked the AFAP rhetorically in their publication the *Australian Air Pilot*. It was their view that

> most definitely something has been accomplished, despite and in the face of the popular belief that no one, no party, can gain by any direct action. What has been achieved is the acceptance by Qantas management of *private mediation*, not compulsory formal arbitration. Additionally, it has been established that Qantas management has been totally and recklessly wrong in its complacently condescending conviction that Qantas pilots would not withdraw their services, no matter what the provocation.
>
> A stoppage of airline pilots in this country is generally regarded variously as sabotage, insurrection or treason and, as far as Qantas is concerned, almost sacrilege . . . This is one lesson we as a Federation must draw. We must be able on all such occasions to present our case with honesty, integrity and a conviction based on responsible and principled thought and deliberation.

The journal added ominously, with C. O. Turner in mind:

> It may well be that we should turn our attention to a review of the administration of Qantas as it currently exists. Commercial ability alone is insufficient in Management. Commonsense, understanding and an acceptance that staff are individuals . . . is also necessary. [25]

The AFAP now took the battle public and sent a pamphlet putting their case to all members of Parliament and many prominent members of the business community. Qantas was placed on the defensive and had no option but to respond. C. O. Turner distributed a closely argued criticism of the AFAP circular, saying that it "contains a collection of distortions, misstatements of fact and half truths which bear on the commercial reputation of a vital national instrument". The situation in which Qantas and its pilots now found themselves was extraordinary, and unparalleled in Australian airline industrial relations.

> While they [the pilots] complain of our "legal" approach [wrote Turner], it is noteworthy that in the last ten years they have been prepared to take Industrial Court and High Court actions to subvert the established systems of arbitration . . . During the negotiations leading to the current dispute, we made a number of major concessions in salaries and conditions. On 11 February we made further offers of concessions . . . On the major issue of hours of duty and free time at home base the Company made a compromise offer. All offers were flatly rejected by the Federation on the morning of 12 February. A deadlock had been reached and

conciliation had been exhausted. We proposed that the matters in dispute should be dealt with in accordance with the law of the land, i.e. by arbitration. The Federation flatly rejected this . . .

Turner went on to detail one of the most ingenious and disruptive elements of the pilots' strategy.

When the matter came before the Commonwealth Conciliation and Arbitration Commission on Thursday 13 February, the paid officers of the Federation indicated that they were not authorised to represent any pilot before the Commission and that the two hundred odd pilots party to the current agreement should be given the opportunity to appear in person. This is part of the pilots' policy of frustrating the working of the Conciliation and Arbitration Commission to prevent an independent arbitration.

The strategem of individual pilot representation before the Commission was engineered by the pilots in 1959 when they dissolved their association. (This was a "registered organisation" under the Commonwealth Conciliation and Arbitration Act and was thus vested with the rights and responsibilities flowing from the Act.) In its stead, the pilots formed the body known as the Australian Federation of Air Pilots. They deliberately did not register it under the Act. Notwithstanding this, all Australian airline operators agreed to recognise it as representing the pilots because of the promise given that it would make every effort to solve disputes by conciliation, and that no strike action would be taken without first taking a secret ballot of members. The employers also made it quite clear that they were bound by the Act and when conciliation failed, disputes would be referred to the Commission for settlement either by further conciliation or ultimately by arbitration.[26]

Turner was well aware that his unshakeable commitment to what he referred to as "the law of the land", coupled with his utter conviction that Qantas was headed for anarchy if management was denied the right to manage, had greatly disturbed the board. Hudson Fysh had, from the start, been critical of what he saw as Turner's egotistical inflexibility. Both chairman and vice-chairman could find him difficult to handle. (One example of this was seen in Turner's comments to reporters at Sydney airport. He described the overseas terminal as a disgrace and said that the main runway should be extended to 10,000 feet. Within twelve hours of Turner's remarks and without knowledge of them, Paltridge had released an official ministerial statement that the runway was to be extended to 9,000 feet. Turner's comments and the minister's announcement together made headlines and an angry Paltridge telephoned Law-Smith. "I went to Sydney immediately to reason with Cedric", Law-Smith wrote to Fysh, who was overseas. "I explained how thoughtless he

29 March 1964. Named after the Queensland town that was the first Qantas headquarters, 707-138B VH-EBI prepares to depart on the inaugural Sydney to London via Hong Kong service.

had been; that the only thing to do under the circumstances was for me to write a letter to the Minister stating that 'Mr Turner sincerely regrets any embarrassment he may have caused'. As you can imagine, it took some talking to get Cedric to agree to this letter." [27])

The pilots, having flexed their muscles with some success, had hinted darkly that they might now turn their attention to the Qantas management processes. There was an unusual note of anxiety, therefore, in a letter from Turner to Fysh on 9 March, when Turner learned that Qantas directors were to meet Paltridge without his being present. "I am greatly disturbed", he wrote, "at the proposed meeting of the Directors with the Minister in Canberra on Tuesday to which Management has not been invited. If the Company's Industrial Policy is to be discussed, it is essential that I should be present to put forward the views of our Management team on what are very vital issues to the Company. If other problems affecting myself are to be discussed, then I should at least be available to explain my position on them before the Minister." [28]

In fact, there was no need for his anxiety. The meeting between Paltridge and the directors was concerned primarily with the board view that the existing situation imposed by the AFAP, in its role as a deregistered union, was an impossible one and one that the government should address by legislation. The pilots' federation, convinced that its persuasive powers were working at the political level, claimed publicly that Qantas had the most to fear if there was no settlement to the unresolved

293

dispute. Captain Ritchie was now given management responsibility for dealing with the pilots and reported to the board: "Over the weekend of 2 and 3 May, a great deal of activity resulted from press statements by the pilots [and] there seemed no alternative to a [further] strike. Throughout the mediation and more critical strike threat situations . . . the Company's officers have been concerned that the Pilots' Federation has claimed to be assured of political support . . . Briefly, mediation has not been a success for either side."[29] The press, however, was critical of Qantas management, the pilots and the existing law. The *Sydney Morning Herald* commented on 6 May: "If the pilots had again stopped work, so soon after their three-day strike last February, further and more serious damage would have been done to Australia's reputation abroad . . . Relations between the airline and the pilots must be very bad if it has taken so long to arrive at what seems a simple compromise. It is not a very good advertisement for the vaunted flexibility of our arbitration system, nor does it say much for the attitude of the parties concerned."[30]

A new issue of contention now arose between the AFAP and Qantas management. Ritchie summarised it in a note to the board:

> The need to recruit experienced pilots capable of early appointment as captains has arisen. We have since learned that the Federation's executive will be pressing the Government to direct TAA pilots to be considered for captains' vacancies in Qantas and that TAA should step up their training to fill the gaps in their own ranks. It is also understood that they expect pilots from the Ansett Transport Industries group to contribute. From this it appears that the Pilots' Federation hope to achieve their long-standing objective of complete freedom of movement of pilots within the industry without loss of seniority. As the recruitment of captains could have a serious effect on our ability to crew aircraft next year . . . any attempt by the Federation to delay or frustrate the Company in this matter will have to be resisted strenuously.[31]

The AFAP carried its case on this new issue direct to the minister and wrote to Paltridge expressing its grave concern at the Qantas announcement that it proposed to recruit pilots on the understanding that they would receive immediate commands.[32] To Ritchie, Crofts wrote: "This constitutes a complete departure from the established practice . . . and would destroy the principle of seniority. This Federation cannot accept the employment of pilots on the basis proposed."[33]

Qantas's manager flight operations, Capt. A. Wharton, sent

a memorandum to all pilots in an attempt to defuse this new
source of conflict.

> Our present growth rate has produced the situation that we haven't
> sufficient pilots with the experience to fill all the command
> vacancies in 1965. Our withdrawal from New Guinea in 1960 con-
> tributed to this situation as this deprived us of a valuable command
> training system. I would make it quite clear that every present
> Qantas First Officer with the necessary ability and experience will
> begin command training at the same date as he would have done
> had the Company not found it necessary to employ experienced
> pilots. By filling our Captains numbers, this in turn creates more
> vacancies for our present Second Officers to become First
> Officers.[34]

A new possibility, beyond mediation, was now canvassed by
which a judge might act to settle disputes where mediation failed.
The AFAP indicated that it would be quite agreeable. "This
is our first step with the Government, to get this fixed", Fysh
wrote to Law-Smith. "However, it will be outside the actual
Arbitration Court, I feel . . . We have got to concentrate on
better Company-pilots liaison where we have fallen down in
the past. The pilots have done a magnificent job on our services.
At the right time we should publicly say so and let bygones
be bygones."[35]

Fysh left for a meeting of the IATA executive in Geneva and
commented on what he saw en route.

> The pilots appear bored and restless with their lot [he told Law-
> Smith]. [There is] too much concentration by Management on
> rapid advancement, new routes, new machines, and not enough
> on the things which make Qantas work. I found a deterioration
> in cabin service and all that goes with it. The thing has gone to
> seed and wants a complete facelift. We are no longer No 1 and
> live on our reputation.[36]

In a report, on his return, he wrote that he had spoken with
some twenty pilots and found all of them

> tremendously anxious to discuss the position and reach a lasting
> solution of an unfortunate position which they greatly regret and
> profoundly do not understand [sic]. All almost pray for a lasting
> amicable solution, and in no case was the Company or Manage-
> ment attacked. The type of information being fed them by their
> Association is the great difficulty . . . All pilots are agreed that they
> would accept an arbitrator but on no account will they accept an
> Arbitration Court judge, stating such is appointed by the
> Government, to which he must be biased, and that their case is
> entirely different from the usual Australian industrial disputes . . .
> During my tour I was much impressed with the attitude, standard

of behaviour, and operational ability of our air crews who are undoubtedly doing a very fine job. [37]

Despite these findings, Fysh told the board on 18 June: "Relations between the Company and the Pilots Federation are at a virtual dead end . . . The present position is hindering the Company from carrying out its work efficiently and if not checked must reach catastrophic proportions . . . The position is akin to a rudderless ship drifting in a gale." He urged that the federal government be called in in the interests of the company and that the pilots, which were indivisible, take urgent action to secure "rationalisation of the present dangerous position". An authority should, said Fysh, be set up either inside or outside the arbitration system to settle disputes which could not be settled by mediation. [38]

Law-Smith told Fysh: "I have spoken to Don Anderson and asked him to try and persuade the Minister not to get so involved directly with the pilots' dispute, as it has now reached the stage that the pilots are getting answers to their questions through the Minister. One thing I forgot to mention", he noted. "Cedric Turner received an invitation from Sir Giles Guthrie to attend a dinner in London to celebrate his thirty years with the industry. The Board agreed that he should go. I made no mention of us doing anything at this end . . ." [39]

Others, however, had initiated independently plans for a Turner dinner in Australia to celebrate his thirty years with Qantas. John Ulm and the widely known Sydney columnist and journalist, Jim McDougall, had been organising behind the scenes. On 28 April, McDougall told Ulm: "The Cedric Turner dinner is off the ground. Stan Utz [a prominent businessman] grabbed the idea with both hands and is terribly enthusiastic. He has an enormous affection for Cedric." McDougall saw timing problems for a June dinner (the anniversary month). "The Prime Minister will be overseas through June – Commonwealth Prime Ministers Conferences are always determined by the English Test series! However, Stan Utz is seeing the Prime Minister in Canberra and will sound him out . . . Secondly, Sir Daniel McVey is also overseas through June and early July. Stan Utz is anxious to team with Dan McVey on the dinner." Utz, said McDougall, wanted to limit the dinner to very personal friends. He himself thought it should be a tribute from a much wider representation. That Fysh-Turner politics had intruded was obvious not only from Law-Smith's enigmatic comment that he had not mentioned the possibility to Turner of any function to celebrate the occasion, but also from the attitude of the Turner supporters. "Stan Utz appeared anxious to vet and restrict the guest list", wrote McDougall. "At first conversation he wasn't anxious to have Sir Hudson Fysh. I told him I thought this would be a mistake . . ."[40]

On 22 June, the thirtieth anniversary of the day that Turner had joined Qantas, he was, ironically, on his way to London to attend the dinner to be given in his honour by BOAC. Ulm prepared press background notes on Turner's long career. He began with a quotation from a Fysh letter to the first Qantas chairman, Fergus McMaster, in 1934. "Turner, the new accountant has arrived, but it is too early to report on his capabilities." Turner, he wrote, had worked in the 1930s in London, Paris, and Rotterdam and was in Berlin when he was recruited by Imperial Airways to be chief accountant for the new airline formed by the original Q.A.N.T.A.S. and Imperial Airways to operate the Australia-Singapore leg of the new service between England and Australia by the jointly owned Qantas Empire Airways. Turner had left Berlin on the infamous "Night of the Long Knives" in 1934, at the age of twenty-seven. Qantas, at that date, had a staff of thirty. It had always been Turner's preoccupation, wrote Ulm, to run Qantas as a commercial organisation against commercial competition. His priorities were always clear: the right aircraft, the right routes, and, above all, the right politics, nationally and internationally.[41] While C. O. Turner was in the air en route for London through San Francisco on 22 June, Fysh cabled congratulations from himself and the board.[42] No moves were made to mark Turner's thirty years with Qantas in Australia. Even the dinner proposed by McDougall and Utz came to nothing; Turner himself did not think such a function appropriate.

Turner had succinctly expressed his philosophy as chief executive in a memorandum to directors in March.

> The concept of the Company continuing to act as a registered public company, as it has for the past seventeen years since Government ownership, is one which has preserved the Company's position distinct from other Commonwealth authorities or instrumentalities and has encouraged continuing respect from the public. It may be said that the vital Qantas image which has been built up over the years has resulted from the marriage of the vigour which flows from a strong commercial enterprise and the continuing stability associated with Government ownership . . . The image of Qantas as a commercial organisation is inextricably bound up with the fact that the Company has observed as far as possible the standards and practices of private enterprise rather than those of the Public Service . . . The roots therefore of our industrial

policies are firmly established in private industry and commerce.[43]

These attitudes, so firmly at the heart of Turner's management philosophy, were now being challenged by Henry Bland, secretary of the Department of Labour and National Service. It was Bland's view that the Qantas pilots' disputes should be the subject of continuous private mediation and that any agreement reached should not be registered in the arbitration court. Qantas management, wrote Turner, "believes this to be a wrong and dangerous course". The commissioners of the court, he said, agreed with the Qantas view; so did Qantas's legal advisers and their industrial consultant, W. C. Taylor. The employers' organisations were greatly concerned.

> The Department of Labour and National Service continually suggests that pilots represent a unique problem to be handled with other than normal machinery . . . Political interference in labour relations has led to disastrous consequences in airlines such as BOAC and KLM . . . In recent years, Qantas has been finding that dealings with the Pilots' Federation have tended to be more and more inhibited because of the increasing influence of Government Departments, particularly the Department of Labour and National Service. This influence has made itself apparent in the attitude adopted by the AFAP and the increasing assurance they have felt in the strength of their position as an unregistered association . . .[44]

In a letter to Bland, Turner summarised the ongoing confusion of the pilots' dispute as "the almost ludicrous situation which currently exists and the quite obvious shortcomings of the mediation process in February". The disorderly conduct of these industrial affairs, he wrote,

> as a result of the repetitious use of strike threats by the Pilots' Federation, makes anything other than a formal Conciliation and Arbitration System quite impracticable. I realise that arbitration itself brings many difficulties, but at least it is a system where controls are exercised on both parties, and both parties must submit to them. In the present situation this quite malicious suggestion which is from time to time mentioned even in Government circles of poor industrial relations in Qantas in its dealings with pilots is, in fact, the result of Government failure, so far, to regulate the Pilots' Federation and bring them under the Law.[45]

As government unease increased at what it increasingly saw as the political cost of the Turner approach to industrial relations, Qantas had to adjust to a new minister. Senator N. H. Denham Henty replaced Paltridge as minister for civil aviation on 10 June 1964. He made his presence felt within a matter

of days, confirming Turner's view of ever-increasing government intrusion into Qantas industrial matters. Referring to a
Qantas board decision to grant increases in incremental bonus
payments to workshop staff, Henty told Fysh on 16 June:

> This decision of the Qantas Board was the subject of a conference
> between representatives of Qantas, Department of Labour and
> National Service, Trans-Australia Airlines and my Department this
> morning. In the light of matters discussed at this meeting no action
> should be taken to implement or announce proposed wage increases
> to the Australian Council of Trade Unions without prior
> consultation and agreement with the major domestic operators on
> an industry approach, and further discussion with Labour and
> National Service on the broader question of wage increases to
> tradesmen in Government employment . . .[46]

The board met at once and responded that a stopwork meeting
had been held at Mascot the previous day and another was
threatened. There was only one way to avoid a strike, curtail-
ment of services, and heavy loss of revenue: "The Board is
unanimous that in terms of their Financial Directive to run the
Company as a commercial organisation immediate action must
be taken to implement the increased incremental bonus
payments as advised".[47]

There was an inherent paradox in the government attitude.
Qantas had moved with relative freedom in decisions on wage
payments above those laid down in court awards until November
1961 when they were directed by the minister to consult with
the Department of Labour and National Service on all such
matters. This direction had stemmed from a complaint by Ansett
in July 1961, when he had sought to offset an increase in payment of the basic wage, as set down by the court, against
overaward payments for certain of his staff. At various times
after acquisition of Qantas shares by the government in 1946,
they had been under union pressure to grant employees conditions of service equivalent to those in government employment. These had been resisted on the grounds that Qantas
operated commercially and was bound by the aircraft industry
award. Now, in 1964, the Department of Labour and National
Service was arguing that if Qantas increased its rates, this would
create untold pressure on the government in the field of government employment and that this pressure might be impossible
to resist. Qantas found it hard to accept that it could continue
to deny its employees Commonwealth conditions but, at the
same time, the government could not publicly allow that Qantas was different from other fields of government employment.

In mid-1964, Qantas employed 7,600 staff worldwide. It was party to twelve awards or agreements in Australia and seven with unions overseas. Only four of the agreements had been made as the result of arbitration; the rest were consent agreements or awards. In all, Qantas dealt directly with thirty different trade unions and was subject to industrial legislation in seven countries outside Australia. (By contrast, the world's largest airline, Pan American, had only six awards or agreements covering their 24,900 staff.) In general, Qantas had built up a stable and loyal staff, despite real difficulties in 1960, when efforts were made to introduce night shift work, and in 1961, when industrial unrest followed retrenchments. It was the government directive in 1961 to consult on all major industrial matters with TAA, Ansett, and the Department of Labour and National Service that had made it more difficult, and at times impossible, to deal promptly and effectively with problems raised by unions. The two domestic airlines often had their own conflicts on industrial policy. Even when they did not, compromise solutions with them were not always the best ones from the Qantas viewpoint. Further, the fact that Qantas was an international operator often dictated a different solution in industrial matters. Forced consultation with the department inevitably had led to delays in decisions in disputes. Qantas regarded the solutions offered by the department as often unrealistic. Despite all these pressures, Qantas was able in 1964 to produce indisputable figures showing its good record in working time lost as a result of industrial disputes and in its labour turnover. There was also no doubting that the high standing and integrity of the company's representatives with union officials was recognised. Qantas now had to convince its new minister of these arguments.

The introduction of jet aircraft had brought with it the pilot argument of jet fatigue, a strike, and intense ongoing pressures in industrial matters that disturbed Qantas relationships with government and brought bitter public debate, but the economic effect of this new method of aircraft propulsion had been a boon to airlines and their customers. "What a honeymoon we are having!" Qantas deputy chief executive Captain Ritchie told a meeting of the American Institute of Aeronautics and Astronautics in Seattle on 12 August 1964. "Break-even load factors of 45 per cent, unit costs down to an all-time low, reliability undreamed of a few short years ago! . . . International airline cost levels have fallen from a plateau of 36 cents per ton mile in the piston-dominated period of the late 1950s to 23 cents today, a decline of nearly 40 per cent. After many years of purely marginal operations we have at last turned the corner." Ritchie asked his audience to remember, however, Joseph's dream of the seven lean years and the seven good years. "From 1963 to 1970 we should be able to get some fat on our bones. But what of the future?" (His words were remarkably prophetic; from 1970 international airlines were to suffer substantial losses.) Ritchie was speaking to the Transport Aircraft Design and Operations meeting of the institute. He expressed his apprehension about the effect that supersonic transports would have on passenger fares. "It has been said by some cynic that instead of building a 1,500 miles per hour vehicle to carry 150 passengers, the industry should be endeavouring to produce a 150 miles per hour vehicle to carry 1,500 passengers." There was still great competition from shipping for the traveller, despite figures showing that sea travel had won only 22 per cent of Atlantic traffic and that Tasman Sea traffic, between Australia and New Zealand, was down to 15 per cent in 1963. The cheapest sea fare between Australia and Europe, said Ritchie, was still half the economy class air fare, even though labour represented only 30 per cent of airline costs compared to nearly 60 per cent for shipping. "We get only a small share of those many thousands of Australian tourists who flock overseas to the United Kingdom and Europe each year."

One of the great benefits of the jet engine, he said, had been the increase in reliability that it had brought. "It is not unusual for a Qantas 707 to operate up to twenty stages in a sequence of flights before returning to its home base and it is computed that the average Qantas aircraft is at any time 6,000 miles from its base. The Company operates to 35 stations, only five of which are in Australia . . . I mention these facts only to emphasise the importance of reliability of equipment." Ritchie compared engine reliability in 1958, a peak year of piston engine activity, with Boeing 707 jet reliability in 1963. Premature engine removals en route had dropped from 43 to 3; engines prematurely removed and completely overhauled had dropped from 53 to zero; in-flight engine shut-downs had dropped from 101 to 13. Overall safety had improved greatly. In terms of passenger fatalities per 100 million passenger miles it was, in 1963, the least it had ever been – four times better than in 1950 and twice as good as in 1960. "But," he said, "the accident rate is still much too high."[48]

Though the jet engine had helped airlines contain and reduce costs in an era of rising wages, Turner kept a close watch on other areas of cost and, when possible, of the Qantas performance relative to other international carriers. One area of mounting costs for the airline was communications. In 1964, Qantas spent approximately £900,000 worldwide on telephone and teletype communications. They were the second largest operator in Australia in the international telecommunications field, outstripped only by the government-owned Telecommunications Commission. Of its total communications costs, Qantas spent 72 per cent on passenger reservations. They evaluated their performance, therefore, by relating total communications costs to passenger revenue and found, comparing their figures with other airlines, a heartening result. Qantas spent 2.4 per cent of passenger revenue on communications, Pan American 4.0 per cent, and BOAC 3.8 per cent. The telecommunications network, a study concluded, was working efficiently and cheaply.[49] In a further study, the airline looked at the full annual cost of appointing one new clerical or works employee. It was the first time such an assessment had ever been attempted, and it was soon realised that there were doubtful areas in the allocation of overhead costs and how these moved in sympathy with staff strength. Supervision was one area, property costs another. The study concluded, however, that it cost the company £1,770 per annum for a new clerical employee and £1,576 for a new works employee, including supervision.[50] Looking ahead to 1966–67, and comparing themselves to BOAC in terms of overall efficiency, Qantas found, however, that under the new BOAC chairman's plans their pool partner intended to outstrip them in the rate of improvement. In 1963–64 BOAC was already, because of its great economies of scale, 5 per cent more efficient than Qantas in the production of capacity ton miles per employee (though BOAC was considerably less efficient than Pan American). BOAC planned, for the three years ahead, 40 per cent more business, 25 per cent more capacity, and 18 per cent fewer staff. Qantas planned capacity increases in the three years from 1964 of 33 per cent, 20 per cent, and 7 per cent, with necessary recruitment of staff, compared with the BOAC average increase per annum of 7 per cent. By 1966–67 Qantas expected still to be only half the size of BOAC. It was, however, more conservative in its forward estimates of load factor: BOAC planned for as much as 54 per cent in 1967–68, Qantas for only 45 per cent. This, as Qantas measured itself against its pool partner in their future projections, was easily the main reason

why BOAC could predict a disproportionately high revenue per
employee.[51]

The pilots' dispute continued, however, to overshadow every
other Qantas management preoccupation throughout 1964. In
mid-year, Qantas looked hard at special industrial legislation
in other industries, including coal and stevedoring. Still pressing
to bring the pilots under the Arbitration Act, Qantas proposed
the formation of a special tribunal under the act to deal with
all aircrew unions. It seemed, for a time, that this might be
acceptable. The Department of Labour and National Service,
the Department of Civil Aviation, TAA, Ansett, and Qantas
held a confidential meeting on 12 August at which it was agreed
that as all operators were facing direct action by the pilots, there
was an urgent need for special legislation. Bland undertook to
put the matter to his minister promptly.

The government, however, was not persuaded. In the light
of what it considered the success of mediation in holding off
strike action, it told Bland to draw up new procedures for
pilot-management conflicts.[52] As this cumbersome process
moved slowly onward, so too did the deep conflict of
personalities and philosophy between Bland, the powerful public
servant, and Turner, the brilliant airline executive. Their styles
and attitudes were starkly delineated in a biting exchange of
letters in September.

Bland referred to Turner's letter urging formal arbitration
procedures and commented:

> What really troubles me is the underlying tenor of your letter. It
> starts with a defensive attitude and this persists throughout. It seeks
> to convey the impression that the Pilots alone are the bad boys . . .
> It assumes that the worst is going to happen . . . It magnifies
> individual happenings that have occurred in your negotiations; yet
> other employers seem to be able to take like situations in their
> stride. Your last two paragraphs are perhaps the most revealing.
> You seem to forget altogether that your services have kept running
> during the mediation process regarding the pilots and, by contrast,
> that you have not been free of troubles in the ground staff area
> where the formal conciliation and arbitration system does operate.
> You complain of the pilots' use of strike threats, making "anything
> other than a formal Conciliation and Arbitration System imprac-
> ticable" and yet bend to strike threats by the unions controlling
> your ground staff, and are quite prepared to buy them off by
> negotiation without recourse to the formal arbitration machinery.
> In a nutshell, what these two paragraphs convey unmistakably is
> that you don't like negotiating with the pilots although you seem
> to be happy to do so with the militant industrial trade unions; that

303

you haven't yet come to recognise the prizes of better relationships with the pilots . . . but would prefer to hold the pilots off
at arms length in reliance on the formal arbitration system . . . If
I judge the situation correctly, it is because "Government circles"
have become increasingly aware of these attitudes that your
Company does not, I fear, enjoy in relation to its handling of its
industrial relations with the pilots, the respect and praise it does
as regards other aspects of its activities. [53]

These were by far the harshest words that Turner had ever
received in his dealings with government. He responded with
both careful argument and matching bile. His theme was Bland's
ignorance of the real airline world coupled with an evident
incapacity to understand the matters in question.

The most recent talks we had with you and representatives of the
Department of Civil Aviation and the airline industry encourage
me to believe that urgent action is about to be taken by the Government along the general lines which we have been advocating since
1961.

At long last, Turner was saying, the government had caught
up. He went on:

Your comments . . . while not unexpected do cause me
considerable concern, firstly because you seem to be at such pains
to defend your system of mediation and, secondly, because once
again there is evidence of failure to understand the depth of the
problems facing Qantas. Contrary to your statement that "other
employers seem to be able to take like situations in their stride",
the problems outlined in my letter centre around pilot demands
which have never been pursued to any like extent against the
Australian domestic operators.

They were problems, he said, that were causing concern to most
if not all international operators. Employers, if not governments,
were well aware that pilots' associations abroad were actively
pursuing radical policies laid down by the International Federation of Airline Pilots' Associations. "It would be difficult for
you to understand", wrote Turner, with the most careful choice
of words, "that some of the so-called 'success' of the internal
operators has been accomplished because they have been able
to avoid interference from your Department." The so-called
"private enterprise" Ansett-ANA, he said, was not subject to
Bland's direction and had usually led the way in giving
concessions to the AFAP. "The irony is that Ansett has
purchased peace with the pilots under pressure by repeated
costly concessions, to the embarrassment of everyone – but these
actions are apparently considered by you to be examples of good

industrial relations." Bland, he said, obviously did not appreciate that Qantas was five years ahead of TAA and Ansett-ANA in the operation of jet equipment, that this had precipitated Qantas, alone of the Australian operators, into the International Federation of Pilots' Associations disputes, that the pattern set by Qantas would set the pattern for the domestic operators. He told Bland that only the week before, in Washington DC, Qantas representatives had listened to twelve major US trunk carriers discuss the imbalance in bargaining with the pilots and the hopelessness of the mediation system. "Certainly, airline employers in the US are becoming alarmed about present developments which have led to the virtual elimination of final Arbitration. You should obviously inform yourself about what is happening . . . since you have always held up the US system of mediation as an example for us." It would not be placing the position too highly, wrote Turner, to say "that most employers in the industry regard themselves as the victims in this problem of negotiating with the pilot 'bad boys' and that 'the prizes of better relationships with the pilots' is a high-sounding cliche". It was a very serious charge indeed, he told Bland, to comment that Qantas did not enjoy government respect and praise in its handling of industrial relations with pilots. "I assume that in the context of your letter you regard yourself as 'the government', otherwise evidence should be produced that there are others that share your view, together with evidence (and not opinions) to support such loose charges. This is an unworthy comment to be coming from the head of a Commonwealth Department."[54]

The three chairmen of the major Australian airlines, Sir Hudson Fysh, Sir Giles Chippindall (TAA), and R. M. Ansett, were in direct contact as the AFAP maintained its pressure. At a farewell dinner for Paltridge in Melbourne, they had agreed on the need for an arbiter who could make decisions when mediation failed. Fysh followed this meeting with a proposal to Chippindall that the three chairmen should see the prime minister.[55] Chippindall responded that he agreed "that we cannot carry on much longer without having some 'umpire' with power to enforce his decisions". It was, though, Henty's view that it would be premature to seek an interview with the prime minister until all had clarified their views.[56] Fysh told Ansett some weeks later that he had managed a private word with Menzies at a farewell to Princess Marina when Menzies had "said he is looking forward to seeing the three of us". The interview, said Fysh, would be simply to try and see that the prime minister gave his full assistance in getting the urgent aircrew matters on a proper and effective basis, and he urged keeping the interview secret, "or it may be magnified and misconstrued".[57] Ansett strongly agreed with Fysh. "I realise our own Minister has the feeling that a meeting with the Prime Minister is not really necessary. However, I entirely agree with you that we should continue to press for such a meeting, as some legislation is imperative." He also agreed on secrecy. By 16 October, however, Henty was still not persuaded that a meeting with the prime minister was appropriate. Fysh commented to Ansett: "One can only take it that if we are not to receive agreement to see the prime minister, then the Government will most certainly attend to this very urgent matter in a manner satisfactory to us".[58]

There was an air of crisis. The pilots, in October, began a campaign for withdrawal of co-operation. On 12 October, the Brisbane *Courier Mail* carried a story quoting C. O. Turner as saying: "The pilots are a small, highly paid group. Many of them came to us from the RAAF. These pilots have not had real contact with the hard areas of life." B. I. Crofts, manager of the AFAP, brought this remark to the attention of the Air Force Association, describing it as an insult to the pilots. "Many of the Qantas pilots are highly decorated, having obtained their decorations in air combat", he wrote.[59] Capt. P. J. R. Shields, chairman of the operations group of the AFAP's overseas branch committee, told Fysh: "Any good that may have been done has, I feel, been dissipated by the content of the article . . . I again assure you that the Qantas pilot is a loyal and devoted employee, anxious to do the best job possible for the Company. Frivolous strikes have no part on his make-up. He is, however, most anxious to see an end to the bitterness that has characterised pilot-management relations in the past." He pressed for a meeting in an atmosphere of calm before irreparable damage was done to the good name of both the company and the pilots.[60] (Fysh wrote to Crofts that he shared his concern about the article that had quoted Turner.)

By the end of October 1964, while Qantas deputy staff manager B. J. Hinchcliffe was advising management that the company was still at loggerheads with the pilots on the provision of first class duty travel for pilots, Bland wrote to Turner: "I have not been idle since the talk we had in Melbourne on 12 August. Following my Minister's consideration of the conclusions then come to I have had discussions with the representatives of the Pilots' Federation. It seems to me that we are now

on the way to an outcome that might be acceptable to all concerned."[61]

On 5 November, Fysh made a handwritten note. "There is
no goodwill between pilots and management. The present
position . . . is a continuation of the tragedy of Turner versus
the pilots and the pilots versus Turner – triggered off by Turner's
criticism of pilots at his press conference and its subsequent
reporting . . . The press article undid all my work for better
relationships." The board, he wrote, was unable to control
Turner.[62]

On the following day, however, Bland's discussions with the
AFAP bore fruit and the immediate problems with the pilots
were ended with the signing of a three-year agreement. It was,
on balance, a win for the pilots. The agreement accepted the
AFAP proposals for a minimum of two and a half days of rest
after five days overseas, and it guaranteed pilots first class travel.
A remaining important issue on annual leave would, it was
agreed, go to mediation. The pilots had therefore, following
their strike action, incurred no penalties, avoided arbitration,
won independent mediation, and ended with appreciable gains.
Bland, the press reported, had also proposed to the AFAP that
an agreement between airlines, pilots, and the government
should be effected, a suggestion that Qantas opposed. The airline
still firmly believed that the arbitration system should not be
bypassed, that negotiations without a final arbitration would
make resistance to union demands almost impossible, that
moderate unions might be antagonised, and that to buy industrial
peace form the pilots would place immense pressures on
operating costs if such a principle spread through the industry.

With unconscious irony, the chairman of New Zealand's TEAL,
Air Marshal Sir Andrew McKee, wrote to Fysh only three days
later: "What a wonderful year you have had. Qantas must be
the envy of the world in its progress, management and worldwide operations." McKee referred to Ansett's ambitions for a
trans-Tasman service: "Rest assured, as far as the New Zealand
Government is concerned, they have promised that they will
never grant permission for Ansett to cross the Tasman under
any conditions".[63]

TEAL was itself within one year of a great expansion of its
South Pacific network to the Far East and the United States
with DC8 jet airliners. It had also, in its 1963–64 results,
substantially improved profitability. Qantas, however, was
doubtful of the optimism expressed in that report for the future.

It could not identify the source of the extra traffic that would be needed to fill the three-fold increase in capacity that the replacement of Electras with DC8s would bring. A Qantas report noted: "Few would disagree that conservatism and independence are words synonymous with New Zealand". It instanced "their five year late introduction of jet equipment despite obvious economic advantages". New Zealand had chosen the DC8, said the report, primarily for its range and payload advantages over the Boeing 707 on the Tahiti-US sector of its planned North American service. "It is rather ironic that TEAL's traffic rights at Tahiti were cancelled by the French earlier this year. Unless the French grant TEAL rights into and beyond Tahiti, both of their planned twice-weekly services to North America must be routed via Hawaii ... Naturally, TEAL will request admission to the Tripartite pool." Clearly, said the report, the next few years are the most important in TEAL's twenty-four years existence.[64]

Australia itself had finally reached agreement with the French. In October it was agreed that from 15 November 1964, Australia would operate via Nadi (Fiji) to Tahiti and beyond, either through Acapulco (Mexico), Mexico City, Nassau, and Bermuda or via San Francisco and New York to London and beyond via agreed ports back to Australia. France was to have a route via Athens and Cairo (or Teheran or Baghdad), Karachi (or Colombo, Bangkok or Rangoon and Singapore or Colombo or Djakarta to Darwin) and Sydney and beyond, to Noumea, Tahiti, and back to France. In addition it had been agreed that Australia and France would operate fortnightly services between Sydney and Noumea on alternate weeks.

Qantas was therefore able to inaugurate an alternative round-the-world service on 26 November 1964, which it called the Fiesta route, through Papeete, Acapulco, Nassau, and Bermuda on a weekly basis. It left Sydney under the command of Capt. R. Uren, flying the Boeing 707 *City of Launceston*. There had been great opposition from BOAC to the Qantas Nassau call but Turner, taking the view that it was essential to the commercial development of the service, had come to a financial agreement with BOAC involving the payment to BOAC of a percentage of the traffic revenue. In fact, Turner told Fysh, the negotiations with BOAC on the Mexico service had been difficult.[65]

Turner had also reached agreement with his two partners in the tripartite pool for the coming year. It provided for an increase in services that accorded with the Qantas five-year plan and with formula changes that promised an overall Qantas revenue share. If the pool, under this new agreement, held off opposition from other airlines then, Turner reported, Qantas was expected to exceed its forward revenue estimates until March 1966.

TEAL's chairman had been generous and accurate in his comment on the Qantas performance, even if his phrase "a wonderful year" had been less than appropriate in the light of management-pilot relationships. Despite the effect of the pilots' strike and the draining of management effort in the subsequent tensions, Qantas recorded the most successful year in its history in the financial year ending 31 March 1964 and continued this success into the new financial year to achieve new profit records. Recovery in world air traffic continued to strengthen. Revenue loads increased in the 1963–64 financial year by 14.3 per cent and load factor rose from 50.5 to 53.2 per cent (the best since 1959). Pilot strength, following an extensive recruiting campaign, rose 48 to a total of 335 on 31 March and, concurrently with the overseas recruitment campaign, a £7 million programme for the development of pilot training facilities was announced in July 1964 (including the purchase of two twin-jet HS 125 training aircraft and an additional simulator for the 707-338C). The active fleet strength was eleven of the Boeing 707-138B jets, with two more delivered during 1964, plus three bigger Boeing 707-338Cs ordered in September for delivery in 1965. There were four Electras, two DC4s, and two DC3s. In addition to the new Fiesta route in November through Mexico, new services to London via Hong Kong had been introduced at the end of March. Greater aircraft utilisation of 25 million ton miles of capacity had been achieved by improved methods of aircraft maintenance by the Qantas engineering team and there were 379 young men training under the company's apprenticeship scheme. In August, work had commenced on an additional line maintenance hangar costing £550,000, able to accommodate two Boeing aircraft side by side. Staff totalled 7,405, an increase for the financial year of 510. Productivity had increased by 3.8 per cent to 45,198 capacity ton miles per employee. Plans were completed for the installation of three IBM System 360 computers in Sydney in a data processing complex called Qantam, to provide message switching, reservations, and general commercial functions. World economic conditions, combined with an expanding Australian economy, promised continued growth in air traffic.

The long year of conflict with the pilots had at least ended in resolution, the even longer dispute with the French had at

The first Boeing 707-338C for Qantas, VH-EBN *City of Parramatta*, nearing completion, December 1964.

last been settled, and the arrangements for future tripartite pool operations had been negotiated to Turner's satisfaction. Qantas was now facing one of the biggest expansion phases in its history, limited only by a shortage of aircraft and the skilled people necessary to fly and maintain them.

Unparalleled Innovation
and Expansion
1965

At the beginning of 1965, the Qantas network of routes, with its pool partners and other associated companies, comprised the Kangaroo service to and from the United Kingdom; the Southern Cross route to and from the United Kingdom via Canada and the United States; the Fiesta route, to and from the United Kingdom via Tahiti, Mexico, Nassau and Bermuda; the Far East route to and from Hong Kong and Japan; the Wallaby route to and from South Africa; the Pacific Islands service to and from Norfolk Island and New Caledonia; the Australia–Malaysia–Far East–Europe–United Kingdom services; and the trans-Tasman services to and from New Zealand.

As Qantas continued its expansion, close attention was always paid to economic as well as operational performance by comparisons with other carriers, particularly the two tripartite pool partners, Air India and BOAC. They had markedly contrasting records. Qantas considered Air India an efficient airline, while BOAC had been continually beset with political interference since the end of World War II. It was not always easy to make valid judgments on comparative economic efficiencies. For example, the received wisdom of the day was that Air India's success was due to 'American income and Indian expenditure'. Air India operated with the remarkable break-even load factor of 39 per cent, which seemed to justify competitors' assessments that its low wage levels gave it an edge. Qantas's break-even load factor was 48 per cent and Pan American, which had just achieved the biggest airline profit in the history of aviation, had

11

a break-even load factor of 50 per cent. When Qantas looked more closely at their Indian partner they found, however, that there was another important factor involved. Air India earned more money from each seat sold, on average; in other words, they had a higher revenue yield than Qantas and Pan American. (Air India's passenger yield was 17 per cent more than that of Qantas and 15 per cent more than that of Pan American.) Costs for the three airlines were at about the same level per capacity ton mile (Air India 27.4 pence, Pan American 26.4, and Qantas 28.3.) Air India's break-even point therefore naturally reduced with higher revenue yield. This higher yield had a simple explanation. Air India carried a high proportion of its traffic on routes between India and the eastern Mediterranean, where fares were among the world's highest. If Air India's productivity per employee had matched that of Qantas and Pan American, its results would have been more spectacular. Average Air India salaries were half those of Qantas and one-quarter those of Pan American, but poor employee productivity kept costs up despite lower salaries.

BOAC's financial record was more complex. They had had the distinction in 1961–62 of achieving the largest loss in airline history (£50 million sterling). There were continual public investigations into their affairs. A further loss of £12 million in 1962–63 had led to the departure of Sir Matthew Slattery and Sir Basil Smallpiece with Sir Giles Guthrie replacing them (on their combined salary of £15,000 per annum). In the last half of 1964, BOAC had proposed cancellation of their Super VC10 order, shed uneconomic routes, and declared that 3,700 staff were redundant. The recently published annual report and accounts for the year to 31 March 1964 showed an accumulated deficit of £90 million sterling. A Select Committee on Nationalised Industries in 1964 reported that BOAC had equipped themselves with types of aircraft that had turned out to be uncompetitive and that, in addition, they had too many of them. The committee also criticised BOAC for not putting their commercial interest before that of the country as a whole. The criticisms were, of course, of interest to Qantas who were (as Paltridge had stated) at times expected to make decisions that put the national interest before commercial considerations and who were also, at times, subject to considerable pressures from parliamentarians with strong British loyalties to buy aircraft that Qantas felt were uneconomic. These strong Australian feelings for Britain as the head of the Commonwealth of Nations were, by 1965, not reciprocated by Britain. Indeed, as Alan Watt has pointed out in *The Evolution of Australian Foreign Policy*, an article in *The Times* of London on 2 April 1964 described the current Commonwealth as "a gigantic farce".[1] Britain's application to join the European Economic Community, which had so disturbed Menzies, was a clear demonstration of British sentiment in economic matters. In strategic and defence matters, the trend of disengagement was just as plain. As the *Times* article pointed out, Britain was a power, but a European power. She had ceased being a Far Eastern power years before and was no longer a Middle Eastern power; she should recast her defence policy on European lines. On 29 April, the Australian prime minister, Sir Robert Menzies, announced his government's decision to commit a battalion of troops to South Vietnam, to support the United States military effort there and to further Australia's policy of encouraging the American presence in what it saw as an unstable and possibly threatening region. Only three months before, Menzies had been a pall-bearer at the state funeral of Sir Winston Churchill on 30 January, an occasion that marked the passing of a man who had personified the sentiments of Empire and the sentiments of those who saw the Commonwealth as its cultural child. It also could have been a ceremony to honour the passing of those institutions as political realities. From the Crypt of St Paul's, in London, Menzies paid his tribute in a BBC telecast: "It was because he was a great Englishman that he was able to speak for the English people. It was because he was a great Commonwealth statesman that he was able to warm hearts and inspire courage right around the seven seas."[2] That deep, emotional link with Britain as head of the Commonwealth of Nations remained strong in many Australian hearts as it withered in the hearts of more realistic Britons. It was manifest in Australia in civil aviation by support for the British aircraft manufacturing industry through pressures on Qantas to buy aircraft such as the Comet, the VC10, and the Concorde.

BOAC had shown what the economic consequences were when politicians became the arbiters of airliner choice. Nevertheless, 1965 was a turning point for BOAC. Despite the controversy, humbug, and bitterness of the preceding two years, the airline was now making excellent financial progress. Unit costs were good, revenue was better, staff productivity and aircraft utilisation were above average. A Qantas report that analysed the latest (1963–64) results commented, however: "The presentation of the accounts is now so complex that understandably some will believe (as BOAC apparently desire) that there

313

was a profit of £8.7 million and others will be equally certain that there was a deficit of £10 million. Both are correct – it all depends which figures you choose."[3] What was incontestable was that a 5 per cent reduction in staff from 20,626 plus a 9.3 per cent increase in capacity had brought about a notable increase in staff productivity, allowing BOAC to jump ahead of Qantas for the first time. "As it is now widely accepted that staff productivity is related to the size of an airline, it is only right and proper that BOAC, more than three times as big as Qantas, should achieve greater output from their staff", said the report. BOAC, as at March 1964, owned fifty aircraft (twenty Boeing 707s, eighteen Comets, ten Britannia 312s, and two DC7F freighters); 1965 was to see a reduction in the Comet and Britannia fleets as VC10 aircraft were phased in. BOAC's break-even load factor was 46.2 per cent. However, with an accumulated loss of taxpayers' money of £90 million since World War II, BOAC was an inevitable subject for media controversy. Few remembered the government pressures on BOAC to buy British equipment, or the relentless replacement of its senior people when politicians saw a need for scapegoats. Since 1939, BOAC had had nine chairmen, twelve deputy chairmen, and seven chief executives. Qantas had had two chairmen (McMaster and Fysh) and two chief executives (Fysh and Turner), so that, in fact, only one individual (McMaster) had, because of age and health, disappeared from the leadership in all those years. Now, BOAC unit costs were at last down to those achieved by Qantas.

As 1965 began, it was clear to the pool partners that the next few years would see the continued operation of Boeing 707s, DC8s, and VC10s in varied forms. Beyond 1970, however – only a few years away – lay what seemed the inevitable beginning of the supersonic era. The first Anglo-French Concorde was scheduled for testing in 1968 and delivery to airlines in early 1972, seemingly well ahead of any American competitor. Russia was to unveil a model of its own supersonic airliner at the 1965 Paris Air Show, closely modelled on the Concorde. Qantas estimated that the delivery gap between the Concorde and the US supersonic transport could be as little as one and a half years or as much as three years. It was a gap of substantial significance. If small, Qantas could ignore Concorde; if large, they could be forced to order both types. The likely price of the Concorde, in 1965, was now £14 million. Hanging over both types was growing public controversy about the effects of the supersonic boom and whether supersonic airliners would be allowed to operate only over restricted areas.

314

As early as October 1963, Dick Shaw had done an economic
analysis of supersonic transport, with a further report in
November on delivery positions for the US aircraft. The Qantas
Technical Development Department watched the Concorde
closely. In January 1964, Ken Gould reported on Qantas's basic
interior layout requirements for the Concorde. The department
completed a Concorde route analysis in June 1964 and an
analysis of the Lockheed 2000 SST in December, together with
an analysis of supersonic transports in relation to available runway pavements. The effort applied to assessing the new
phenomenon of supersonic flight was considerable. C. O. Turner
told the British technical magazine the *Aeroplane* in November
1964: "While we do not yet know nearly all we need about the
technology of the SST, we know immensely more than we did
two or three years ago. We know enough to say with confidence
that it is possible to produce an SST which is as safe or safer
than our present subsonic jets, which will be compatible with
the aerodromes and other facilities which will be available in
the 1970s and which will be completely acceptable in flying
qualities to pilots of the same calibre as those we have today."
He thought that the commercial need for supersonic travel would
be justified by demand from business travellers. "I therefore
view arguments that claim that the money being spent on the
development of the SST would be better spent on developing
a very large, low fare, subsonic vehicle as rather confused. The
two developments are not in any sense opposed, they are both
important in their own right and could each have an impact
on about half our present market. They are separate and complementary decisions." If resources were short, said Turner, he
believed that the supersonic transport was the more important.
He felt the Concorde had sound market potential if the costs
of its development and production could be realistically planned
and strictly controlled and if the technical objectives were
achieved.[4] Fysh, in a report to the board, summarised the
impending arrival of both large subsonic jets and supersonic
transports and commented: "The one certain factor, given the
absence of world catastrophe, is that international air transport
is headed for a tremendous, if complicated, world expansion,
when undreamed of capital and operating commitments will
be entailed, establishing the business as one of the world's
premier endeavours with a most significant economic
impact".[5] Qantas in 1965 saw the immediate future, despite
the sustained record growth of recent years, as one of
unparalleled technical innovation and economic expansion.

Though it was possible always to order airliners in sufficient numbers to meet anticipated traffic, the provision of highly trained pilots to fly them was not as assured. In 1965, Qantas began its own cadet pilot training scheme to help solve this problem. In the past, the airline had recruited its pilot force from a number of sources both within and outside Australia. The Royal Australian Air Force and Royal Australian Navy and the two main domestic airlines had proved useful avenues of supply though, as expansion had continued, Qantas had usually also had to turn overseas. At the beginning of the decade, Qantas were approached by the Federation of Australian Aero Clubs to support a scheme in which young pilots could be trained through the clubs, with guaranteed employment at the end of their course. Qantas did undertake to accept a number of these trainees but the scheme itself failed because it lacked supporting formal teaching facilities. All but one of the Qantas graduates had not reached the required academic standard. Qantas also judged that this scheme had not inculcated in the trainees the high sense of discipline that they considered essential.

The 1964 Qantas pilot recruiting drive had produced fifty-one junior pilots from within Australia and eighty-six from overseas, mainly because the drive had coincided with large-scale reductions in pilot strength in the Royal Air Force and Royal Canadian Air Force. Qantas, however, was aware that they could not continue to rely on such sources for future pilot numbers. The airline estimated a need for approximately thirty-five new pilots each year. Of these, it seemed reasonable to budget for fifteen from traditional sources within Australia. The balance of twenty would have to be found overseas or trained through a company scheme. Aware that worldwide airline requirements for pilots fluctuated, Qantas told the Department of Civil Aviation in August 1964 that they believed a pilot training scheme should be started. They estimated the cost of such a scheme to Qantas at £90,000 per annum and asked the department to consider whether the airline scheme could be integrated with the Commonwealth's flying training scholarships scheme.[6] Qantas planned that the cadet pilots, on completing their course, would be seconded to general aviation organisations throughout Australia and New Guinea for a period of fifteen months to accumulate flying hours. The Department of Civil Aviation, however, hesitated at the request for support through the Commonwealth's scholarship scheme. It was felt that a substantial proportion of the annual Commonwealth subsidy of £50,000 would be absorbed by Qantas, and that this would cause political problems with the aero club movement and agricultural and other general aviation groups. The scholarships were not necessarily awarded on merit, but took into account an equitable geographical distribution to clubs and flying organisations throughout Australia. Qantas had to begin their scheme without financial support, except for cadets who had already qualified for Commonwealth scholarships. Despite the introduction of the Qantas cadet pilot training scheme in 1965, interim recruitment of other pilots was necessary before the cadet scheme began providing junior pilots to the airline in 1967.

Pilot numbers were far less of a problem in 1965 than pilot-management relationships. The plan that had been agreed at the top-level, confidential meeting between airlines and government departments in August 1964 to create, by legislation, a special tribunal to deal with all aircrew matters and impose on the AFAP the status of a declared organisation was not acceptable to the government. Henry Bland was instructed to prepare procedures to deal with management-pilot problems. The pilots, in the AFAP magazine the *Australian Air Pilot*, were blunt in describing what they saw as their strong position. "In industrial activities it [the pilots' federation] can operate as a law unto itself, for it is obliged to recognise no law", said an editorial article. "It remains immune from the penalties, normally a deterrent (if not a prohibiting force) against strike action. There have been, in the eyes of the Operators, past demonstrations of the use of the Federation's power, and they plead apprehension of the abuse of power, unrestrained in any other way than by the Federation itself in the future." The editorial recognised that any action taken by the Federation had unavoidable repercussions outside the industry itself "upon commerce and even upon the nation" so that there was an inevitable public concentration on the effect of any dispute, "the cause being frequently lost in the ensuing turmoil". It was against this background, said the article, that the Department of Labour and National Service as a government agency was moving.[7]

One issue at stake with Qantas was a pilot demand for extra payment to fly the bigger Boeing 707-338C. (The pilots were also pressing for five weeks annual leave and in dispute over the operation with two-pilot crews of the Australia-Noumea route.) Even Fysh was exasperated. "I feel that the £1,006 per annum claimed as extra compensation for a pilot to fly the 338C is quite ridiculous", he wrote. "It is the sort of claim that makes

The first Boeing 707-338C *City of Parramatta* prior to departure from Boeing Field at Renton. It arrived in Sydney on 15 February 1965.

negotiation well nigh impossible."[8] To his minister, Senator Henty, he wrote:

> I feel that the pilots' representatives are getting their case over, whereas we are not . . . It is upsetting to feel that the notion is still abroad that Qantas will have nothing of mediation and conciliation and that all we want to do is force the pilots into court. Indeed, mediation is an essential part of arbitration and we are tremendously in favour of it, but what we do say is that it can never stand alone as an end in itself, particularly in regard to a group who time and again have struck, and reserve the right to strike when mediation fails. I am personally not happy about the absence of a proper rational set up.[9]

At a meeting on 28 May 1965, Qantas and the domestic airlines discussed with Bland his new proposed procedures. Both TAA and Ansett, anxious to have the procedures in place to deal with an imminent AFAP log of claims on their Boeing 727 aircraft, wanted speedy acceptance. It was proposed that the procedural agreement and contracts made under it would not be registered and, in addition, that existing registered agreements would have no force under the new procedural agreement. The AFAP thought their membership would accept these proposals. If Qantas failed to do so, the AFAP indicated it would rethink its attitude to the domestic operators. Qantas was isolated. The board was apprehensive that such an experimental new system should be tried out on an industry of great national importance.

Though Trans-Australia Airlines had sided with Ansett on 28 May, it was Ansett that undoubtedly had the track record of pragmatism, putting immediate commercial considerations well ahead of what it considered unwinnable and costly battles to assert the abstract principle of management's right to manage.

318

Ansett's record of success and growth was such that few could critcise either the ability or the judgment of its chairman, R. M. Ansett. When Ansett Transport Industries was formed in 1946 (the original Ansett Airways Ltd was incorporated in 1937) its annual revenue was less than £1 million. By 1955 it had reached £5 million and with the acquisition of ANA in 1957, Queensland Air Lines and Butler Air Transport in 1958, Airlines of South Australia in 1959, Mandated Airlines in 1960, and MacRobertson Miller in Western Australia in 1963, it reported a 1964 annual revenue of £39.2 million. By February 1965, Ansett Transport Industries had seven separate airlines, operating in New Guinea and all states except Tasmania; it owned ten hotels, four motels, and the Hayman Island resort; it controlled ATV Channel 0 television in Melbourne and owned half of Channel 0 in Queensland and part of other television channels in New South Wales, South Australia, and Western Australia; it had seventeen manufacturing subsidiaries, 215 passenger coaches, and, in road freight, over one hundred prime movers and trailers. Ansett's group dominated Australian domestic aviation with fifty-four per cent of the capacity production. Though TAA and Ansett-ANA were much the same size, the inclusion of Ansett's subsidiaries made the group twenty-five per cent bigger. In terms of unduplicated route mileage, the Ansett group was double TAA's size. Nevertheless, with 152 million available capacity ton miles, it still remained much smaller than Qantas, with 383 million available capacity ton miles. The Ansett group had a mixed bag of 104 aircraft, compared with TAA's 63 and Qantas's 21. The largest were Boeing 727s (2), Electras (3), Viscounts (9), and DC6Bs (5) and the smaller were Fokker Friendships (10), DC3s (38), DC4s (6), helicopters (7), and 24 miscellaneous aircraft. The extraordinary Ansett success story had been marred only by its brief incursion into New Zealand but even there, Ansett had managed to withdraw by giving the airline (SPANZ), together with its debt to the New Zealand government, to the employees. The Ansett group, after earlier reliance on government loan guarantees, had repaid all moneys owing to lending institutions on which such guarantees were issued and had made arrangements to buy three Boeing 727s without recourse to further guarantees. Ansett moved strongly (though unsuccessfully) to take over East-West Airlines, an independent New South Wales intrastate operator, but was opposed not only by the airline but the state Labor government in what developed into a power struggle between the state and the Commonwealth on the right to license intrastate services.

319

Reg Ansett's record of past successes and his ongoing ambitions and vitality were of direct interest to Qantas. He had long wanted overseas routes, as evidenced by his fifteen per cent interest in Cathay Pacific. In 1965 he was pressing Qantas on three fronts. Ansett argued that Qantas should relinquish its local service to Norfolk Island in his favour, thereby giving him the possibility of a link with New Zealand; he was pressing for the right to fly from Port Moresby, in New Guinea, to Manila, in the Philippines, and so link there with Cathay Pacific; and he was campaigning to use his new Boeing 727 aircraft on the trans-Tasman route, claiming them to be cheaper to operate and able to fly into Wellington airport (something that neither Qantas nor TEAL could do with their jets). Underpinning Ansett's financial position was the federal government legislation that regulated Australia's unique two-airline system. He had acknowledged its value. "The value of this franchise cannot be calculated", said Ansett in 1962. "Nowhere else in the world is there such an arrangement which ensures civil aviation economic stability for such a period. Operating within this situation with efficient management controlling costs, reasonable profits are assured for fifteen years . . . No trunk aviation competitor will be permitted other than TAA and industry re-equipment with full jet aircraft will be gradual and over a period long enough to enable financial and economic digestion to take place without disruption of the industry."[10] The Ansett spirit and zest were extraordinary. Well aware that any change in the status quo on the Tasman required Cabinet approval in both countries, he was publicly unworried, even though his attempt to buy TEAL outright in 1960 had upset New Zealand. From 1958, Ansett had used his status as the saviour of privately owned civil aviation enterprise in Australia to press hard on a grateful federal government for support. He had easily won access to traffic on both the Darwin and Canberra routes by appealing to the arbitrator under the two airlines system (the director-general, Don Anderson). His opponents, as he bid for overseas routes, found it difficult to see why his 30,000 shareholders should receive federal government favours over and above those given the eleven million Australians who, through their government, owned TAA and Qantas. They thought it significant that a most senior policy adviser from the Department of Civil Aviation, Dr Harold Poulton, had left the department in 1964 to join Ansett and that there had since been continuous pressure for new routes both domestically and internationally.

Qantas was facing mounting pressure from their international competitors in 1965. Japan Air Lines had announced their intention to fly to Australia, Alitalia had expressed interest in a third weekly frequency, and Lufthansa began operations to Sydney in April. Lufthansa had a deservedly high reputation for their cabin service and an extraordinary record of growth. Ten years after the end of World War II, in 1955, the airline was formed with a capital of 50 million marks (£5.5 million), and by 1965 was the sixth largest international carrier. Qantas was twice the size of Lufthansa in 1956; by 1965 Lufthansa had become 38 per cent larger than Qantas (in capacity ton miles). Since 1958, Qantas had grown 300 per cent, Lufthansa 900 per cent. They did not, however, match Qantas's profit record. Losses from 1955 had totalled £37 million, recouped by government subsidy without which their rapid expansion would not have been possible. Qantas knew that should Lufthansa's new service to Australia prove uneconomic in the initial period, the airline would not be greatly concerned. It was the first time that Qantas was faced with formidable competition from a carrier with ready access to government sudsidy and there was little doubt that Lufthansa would make substantial inroads into the Qantas share of tripartite pool revenue. [11]

Concurrently with the new Lufthansa service, Qantas in April began a new twice weekly service through Vienna and in-augurated a Boeing 707 service between Sydney and Christchurch, New Zealand. Perhaps with Ansett in mind, Hudson Fysh was particularly generous in his phraseology when he reported to Henty: "It is an honour for us in Qantas to be entrusted by you to carry out the Australian part of these important trans-Tasman services". [12] Fysh was himself now approaching the end of his term as Qantas chairman. His request in 1963 for consideration of some form of additional pension payment for his service since his relinquishment of the managing director's position was still being considered by Australia's top public servants. Roland Wilson, as secretary of the Treasury, was of the opinion that if Fysh had not drawn his managing director's retirement payment in 1955, it would have accumulated in Qantas's hands to the same final sum as it did in Fysh's own hands, unless Fysh had had to pay tax on the annual income it generated. This, said Wilson, had been Fysh's own choice. However, he argued, a Qantas employee continuing in office whose retirement benefit was accumulated by the company suffered no reduction in salary. Fysh had suffered a reduction equivalent to £10,850 in take-home pay over the period concerned. He thought that the payment made to Fysh in 1955 should be treated as a loan, with interest due. To adjust matters, after taking income tax into account, Fysh should be credited with £10,850 plus certain contributions payable by Qantas under the pension scheme rules. This, said Wilson, would leave Fysh out of pocket by the amount of tax paid on the income from the amount paid him in 1955. It seemed to Wilson an appropriate penalty for Fysh to bear.

As the pilots and Bland waited for a decision by Qantas on the new Bland Procedures for governing management-pilot relationships, Fysh made a gesture of goodwill by sending to the AFAP's Capt. P. J. J. Shields a card from a satisfied Qantas passenger, commenting that Qantas aircrews had a wonderful name for efficiency and service and adding his congratulations on a job well done. Shields replied: "Your remarks . . . are particularly welcome at this time . . . As you know, the pilots are tremendously loyal and devoted to yourself and the Grand Old Company many of us have served for so long, and we have always been aware of your kindly and special interest in our welfare. You have frequently expressed appreciation of the pilots' contribution towards the outstanding success of the Company."[13]

On 22 June, Turner wrote to Bland (now Sir Henry Bland) advising that the Qantas board could not tie itself to the proposed procedures as presently drafted, particularly the suggested period of a five-year agreement. It would agree to observe the procedures for eighteen months without being tied to a specific agreement. One of the numerous other points detailed by Turner was: "The Board considers that the introduction of the new procedures should not lead to a changed position for pilots in the salary structure in Australia or a departure from the relationships with other industries that have long applied under the Conciliation and Arbitration Act".[14] Salary differentials between pilots and other groups was causing bitterness, as they were in airlines overseas. On 29 April, the British magazine the *Aeroplane* commented on the recently concluded strike by Pan American pilots that had grounded the airline for ten days: "Vast resentment has been fostered in the Pan American World Airways organisation between the pilots and the airline's ground staff and executive groups . . . Pan American pilots . . . receive an average of about $31,000 per year while the average non-pilot worker's salary is around $6,000."[15]

Fysh had always been critical of what he regarded as C. O. Turner's remoteness from the pilots and his inflexible attitude to the exercise of management prerogatives. He was equally concerned by the manner adopted by Turner in his dealings with BOAC. Keith Granville, BOAC's deputy chairman, had written a strong letter to Turner in April accusing him of an unpartner-like and insulting attitude.[16] On 27 May, Fysh left for a meeting of the IATA executive and spoke with BOAC's chairman, Guthrie, and with Granville. In his diary he wrote:

> Guthrie is worried about relations with Turner, who is arrogant and domineering—and when pushed, lies about the facts. They have more trouble dealing with Turner than in dealing with foreign concerns, yet we are partners. The tragedy in BOAC-QEA relations is that BOAC just can't stand Turner. Neither can TEAL or anyone else he has to negotiate with. Turner is good to his staff, those under him, when he dictates. Hopeless with staff he has got to bargain with, and when he is forced to see the other fellow's point of view. Hopeless with his Chairman, Minister, his Director-General and anyone he has got to agree with on an equal basis of discussion, and where a compromise is necessary. I said [to Guthrie and Granville] I thought Turner was much easier to deal with since he won his £100,000. They said "no", he was much more arrogant.[17]

Fysh commented on the drinking habits of his chief executive. "Sadly, I deduce Turner's . . . behaviour is common knowledge. It must also be common knowledge amongst a number of staff."[18] The Turner relationship with TEAL was even more abrasive than that with BOAC. "There was", said Maurice Davis (later chief executive of Air New Zealand), "a massive campaign by C. O. Turner to screw us. He did all he could to terrify New Zealand investors." There was, he said, a most bitter situation from 1964 to 1967. Davis also commented on Turner's habitual, heavy drinking. But his summing up was by no means bitter, or critical of Turner's abilities. "When his attention span was there, he was as acute as ever up to the time of his retirement. He had that faculty, in all his rudeness and abruptness, to think and analyse and make a commitment."[19]

The great Qantas expansion under the leadership of C. O. Turner, so evident in their round-the-world route network and increasing jet fleet, had made their headquarters building in Sydney increasingly inadequate. The Hunter Street site had been bought in 1949 but, because of inappropriate conditions in the building industry, the plan to build a new head office was deferred until 1953. By then head office personnel were distributed through eleven city buildings. Although the new head office had been designed to the maximum allowable size for the site and provided a substantial margin for staff expansion, events that could not have been foreseen when the site was purchased (including the BCPA takeover) meant it was almost fully occupied from the time of its completion in 1957. In 1965, the company faced a situation similar to that of 1953. Qantas House, with 76,000 square feet of office space available, was too small. In the adjoining Bligh House and in Swire House two blocks away, 32,000 square feet of space had been leased. It was estimated that by 1969 the company would need a further 23,000 square feet of space. Proposals were put to the minister, Senator Henty, for the erection of a large new building on the site of the old Wentworth Hotel and adjoining properties to accommodate head office staff for as far ahead as 1989. Qantas also suggested the acquisition of further properties close by for siting other office buildings that might be needed beyond this date. Henty took the Qantas proposal to Cabinet on 25 May 1965. Qantas, he said, forecast an average compound growth of 8.4 per cent in its operations over the next twenty to twenty-five years. The International Civil Aviation Organisation had forecast a 12 per cent per annum growth for the next five years. By 1969, said Henty, rentals paid by Qantas for leased premises were expected to reach £112,000 per annum and, on the forecast rate of staff growth, would become £650,000 by 1989. Projected costs had led the company to reject leasing as a long-term proposition.

With the completion of the new Qantas hotel in 1966, he said, the old Wentworth's value as a better class hotel would vanish, its age and size making it unsuitable for development, or for sale as a going concern. The Qantas board had suggested the acquisition of the whole city block bounded by Lang, Jamieson, Grosvenor, and George streets. It was clear that if these sites were not acquired now they would cease to be available. Henty's proposal was referred to a Cabinet committee. (It was not until 24 March 1966 that Qantas was finally authorised to go ahead.)

One rapidly growing area of traffic expansion for Qantas had been in the carriage of migrants, both from Britain and in meeting the requirements of the ICEM programme. By 1965 almost half of the intake of assisted passage migrants from the United Kingdom was by air. It was a far cry from the modest movements by air in the first years after Qantas, in 1958, had been directed to carry migrants as an insurance against the difficulties of obtaining sea berths. In the three years from 1958, migrant traffic from the United Kingdom averaged ten flights a month. In the depressed economic period of 1961, air movements were reduced to a minimum but in 1962 and 1963 they had risen to almost one hundred air passages each month. In terms of seats, by the end of 1963 they had risen to a thousand per month. In the first six months of 1964, Qantas carried 13,425 migrants. For the fiscal year 1964–65 the Department of Immigration advised that approximately 20,000 migrants would be carried, subsequently requesting the movement of an additional 5,000 by the end of 1964. Qantas contracted with the British independent airline, British Eagle, for fifty-one flights, which provided 5,865 seats in addition to those available through QEA and BOAC. For the first half of 1965 (again using some capacity from British Eagle), Qantas and BOAC planned for the movement of 22,916 migrants. For the Qantas financial year to March 1965, the carriage of British migrants provided a revenue return of £4,494,295. In this period 15,026 migrants were carried on scheduled flights and 12,618 on charter flights. From July 1964 to June 1965 Qantas dominated the carriage of ICEM-sponsored migrants with the arrangement of fifty-two charter flights. The net return to Qantas for the fiscal year to March 1965 for ICEM charter flights was £107,303. Fill-up ICEM migrants on scheduled flights provided an additional £34,000. (Qantas also carried Finnish and Italian migrants from London and Rome at special low fares.)[20]

The previous year, 1964, had been the most profitable in the history of civil aviation. Estimates by the International Civil Aviation Organisation showed operating profits for its member airlines of $US600 million, compared with $US326 million in 1963. As a percentage of revenue, the industry profit (excluding interest and taxes) was 7.3 per cent, a rise from 4.7 per cent in 1963 and 1.5 per cent in 1962. The highest return in the prejet airliner era had been 2.6 per cent in 1955. World airline traffic in 1964 continued to grow at a faster rate than the introduction of new equipment and, although revenue yields declined, so did cost levels. The result was that efficient airlines made money and the inefficient airlines lost less. Qantas followed the industry trend and revenue exceeded £1 million per week for the first time. Loads increased by 25 per cent and capacity by 22 per cent, giving a revenue load factor of 55 per cent, the highest since 1959. However, it was clear that many carriers were by now fully realising the economies of the long-haul jet airliners. Qantas could only anticipate slight reductions in cost per capacity ton mile over the next five years, with this decrease solely attributable to the lower unit cost levels of the Boeing 707-338Cs. With limited scope for further cost reduction and an inevitable decline in the revenue yield per ton mile, it was plain that to improve on the 1964 profit Qantas needed better load factors. The 1964 industry seat factor of 56 per cent, for example, was considerably below the best achieved in the piston-engined era, 63 per cent in 1956.

Qantas would have been in a poor financial state with such low load factors if their revenue yields had fallen to the level of some other international operators. Paradoxically, though fares had remained reasonably constant on Qantas's main routes in the past five years, passenger yield had fallen. There were three main factors influencing the level of revenue yields. The share of first class traffic had declined to eighteen per cent. First class fares were from thirty to eighty per cent higher than economy fares, depending on the sector travelled. Carriage of migrants on scheduled services, particularly heavy since April 1963, produced less revenue per seat. Return fare rebates on most routes, however, had been lowered from ten per cent to five per cent, effectively increasing fares. From 1960–61 to 1954–65, the yield per load ton mile average for the company had dropped from 68.7 pence to 63.2 pence. The lowest yield was on the fiercely competitive Atlantic sector, where it was 47 pence. If this yield had applied across all Qantas routes, their total revenue would have dropped by £9 million.

One Ansett argument for making the Tasman a domestic route was the higher fare level per passenger mile charged by Qantas. The company yield on the Tasman (62.8 pence) was just below the average yield but considered far too high by many who compared it with Australian domestic levels. There were, however, solid reasons for the difference. The Qantas Electras had ten fewer seats than normal because of the carriage of additional galley equipment and catering stores, life rafts, and requirement for crew rest areas. Two additional technical crew members (navigator and third pilot) were carried. Catering standards were higher, requiring two additional cabin crew. Passenger commissions to agents were higher than domestic levels. There were higher governmental charges for landing fees and customs overtime. The only favourable offset was a lower fuel tax, but it provided a bonus of only one-fifth of a penny per passenger mile. Compared with the domestic Sydney–Perth route, which produced a yield of 5.7 pence, Qantas's net effective yield on the Tasman (allowing for return fare and other rebates) was 6.42 pence, or thirteen per cent higher.

On the Qantas long haul routes the carriage of migrants at
lower fares depressed yield overall by about 3 pence per load
ton mile. However, a comparison of 1964 economy class
passenger mile yields excluding migrants showed Qantas, at 6
pence, in line with BOAC (6 pence), Alitalia (5.8), and KLM
(6.2) and below Air India (6.6), Lufthansa (7.2), and Air France
(6.5). Cargo and excess baggage produced a 1964–65 yield of
37.3 pence per load ton mile.

Mail carriage was interesting in its economics. The Universal
Postal Union, an agency of the United Nations, met every five
years to determine how much national post administrations
should charge one another for the carriage of international mail.
This archaic procedure, originally developed for the transport
of mail by ship where it was carried for a pittance, involved
postal experts from 104 countries gathering to discuss
appropriate conveyance rates. Airline assistance in these discussions was declined. The postal authorities had not passed
on to the public in the form of lower postal fees any reduction
in rates from the airlines. It was in Australia's interests to keep
mail carriage rates high because Qantas was a net earner of
foreign exchange as a result of carrying the mail of other
countries. On Qantas routes the rates had, since 1952, been four
gold francs per tonne kilometre (equivalent to 205 pence per
load ton mile) for first class mail and one gold franc for other
classes (51 pence per load ton mile). The mix of mail between
first and second class on Qantas had consistently been evenly
split. One of the best features of the Qantas revenue position
overall in the past thirty years had been their high mail volumes
in relation to other categories of load.

As in all forms of transport the innocuously phrased service
principle applied: what will the user pay rather than forgo? More
crudely, it meant: what will the market bear? Overall profitability depended on a judicious mix of loads. Qantas yields varied
from a high of 205 pence per load ton mile for first class mail
to 8 pence for foodstuffs, giving an average of 63 pence
(compared with a pence for rail and less than one penny for
sea). In the year to the end of March 1965, the Qantas source
of load ton miles was passengers and their free baggage 68 per
cent; cargo and excess baggage 23 per cent; mail 9 per cent.
Yields for all categories of load were tending downward, both
for Qantas and the industry generally. In terms of revenue yields
the Qantas position in relation to other carriers was much as
it was for costs; they fell between the low cost–low yield

American carriers and the high cost–high yield European carriers. [21]

Hudson Fysh returned from a meeting of the IATA executive committee in Beirut and a visit to the Paris Air Show and reported on some of the details that were part of the rich mix of airline operations. A blitz on charging fully for excess baggage carried by passengers was, he said, causing resentment by passengers. A lot of money was made by the international airlines from carriage of this excess, he noted, but better procedures were needed. Fysh noted that duty free liquor was delivered to passengers after they had weighed in with their baggage, which meant that "millions of bottles, mostly of Scotch, are being carried free by the airlines". He quoted figures for Bermuda, where all liquor stores in the town were able to sell special packs for duty free export. Some 1,875 bottles cleared the Bermuda airport each day, making 684,375 bottles a year weighing almost one million kilograms, equivalent to $814,000 in lost revenue. Fysh did not like the new Qantas hats for their air hostesses. He found them neither practical nor decorative and suggested they be withdrawn as soon as possible. He did, however, like the new uniform. Fysh also commented on an issue of more substance, which was to provoke much debate among international airlines in coming years. He had attended a demonstration of in-flight entertainment equipment at the Paris Air Show and found that "the majority of people were against in-flight movies as forcing them to see something they might not wish to see". It was felt, he said, that movies might well be acceptable for short flights across the United States but that for long flights, where many passengers wanted to sleep, they would not be nearly as acceptable. He agreed with Qantas management that more leg room between seats, particularly in the economy section, and increased baggage allowances "should take precedence over a very doubtful and expensive innovation such as in-flight movies". [22]

At the end of July, Fysh prepared a note for the board on the still unresolved dispute on pilot-management procedures. "We are in a weak position", he wrote. It was evident that the airline must go further in agreeing to the proposals put forward by Bland "or be out alone on a limb". TAA and Ansett-ANA had agreed to the proposals. The Department of Labour and National Service had largely taken over the problem of the Australian pilots. Qantas was a government instrumentality "and

much under the direction of our Minister". QEA management,
he wrote (referring to Turner) had failed to convince TAA,
Ansett-ANA, the department, and the pilots. "There has been
a movement away from the set Arbitration System as it applies
to our pilots . . . which I believe will not be reversed. I do not
feel we should stand out alone."[23] The Qantas board held a
special meeting on 10 September, under intense pressure from
Bland. Neither Roland Wilson nor Law-Smith was able to attend
because of the short notice. Fysh recommended that Qantas sign
the pilots' agreement but protest against the features in it that
were objectionable, subject to Henty's agreement. Fysh thought
that Bland would not be able to get agreement from the pilots
to alterations required by Qantas but the board was less pessimistic. Roland Wilson was angry at the pressure brought to
bear by Bland. "I take exception to Bland's attempt to deliver
an ultimatum to the Company with a 24-hour deadline", he said
in a message to the board from Canberra. "Similarly, I object
to the calling of a special meeting [of the board] at equally short
notice. I cannot attend and other directors may be in the same
boat." He criticised elements of the agreement put forward by
Bland and set out what he believed were the minimum Qantas
requirements, concluding: "I submit that we could not be worse
off without any agreement at all. The anxiety of the AFAP to
bludgeon us into early signing is clear enough evidence of this."

Emotions ran high within Qantas. Fysh noted that Turner
had headed off any agreement with the pilots, aided and abetted
by Taylor and with the agreement of the board. "Over the years
[we] drifted into a morass of mistrust and controversies", now,
he wrote, Wilson was supporting Turner against Bland. "An
agreement should have been signed by Qantas after the June
1965 Board . . . Turner said the Agreement would not be the
be all and end all of the trouble with the pilots as the Chairman seemed to think. I said it was a lie to say that. The trouble
with Turner is when defeated he blatantly lies."[24] Ritchie
reported to the board on 9 September that the effect of the proposed industrial relations procedures would be to "open the door
to many matters which are currently jealously regarded as
Management prerogatives . . . and subject [them] to mediation
and even inquiry procedures". On a current issue concerning
reduction in the size of the London basing of pilots, he said
that there was "a remote possibility of a mediator castigating
the Company . . . without the prior agreement of the
AFAP".[25]

Henty wrote to Fysh on 20 September that he was gratified to hear that the agreement was close to being signed.

> I am most apprehensive about the possibility of Federation members refusing to crew aircraft into areas where disturbed conditions exist . . . I well understand your concern about the possible intrusion upon what you regard as management responsibilities . . . All I can say is you are no worse off by signing the Agreement than you would be under the Conciliation and Arbitration Act. The truth is that under the Act . . . there are few, if any, decisions of management which cannot become industrial disputes . . . The great virtue as I see it of the proposed Agreement is that the Federation voluntarily agrees not to indulge in direct action while the procedures are in operation.[26]

(The AFAP had threatened not to crew aircraft flying within one hundred nautical miles of North and South Vietnam, or of the coastline of India and East or West Pakistan, as well as any other areas considered as "troubled" by the AFAP from time to time.)

On 27 September all parties signed what was to be known as the Bland Agreement, to be operative for a period of three years. It provided for negotiation between disputing parties, mediation, inquiry procedures, and a cooling-off period before industrial action could take place. There was also provision for participation by a government representative. Important to Qantas was a substantial restriction on the right to strike while negotiations were in process. There was no provision for penalties and the agreement was wholly outside the framework of the Conciliation and Arbitration Act. The pilots won freedom from compulsory arbitration (so fiercely fought for by Turner), though their freedom of action was limited to some extent, and Qantas gained a rational set of procedures for the settlement of disputes. Despite all the energies expended over months in its achievement it was not, however, to prevent the crippling disaster for which it was designed. A year later the most bitter confrontation between management and pilots in Australian civil aviation would shut down the airline for twenty-eight days.

Turner sent a critical memorandum to all Qantas departmental and outstation heads on 12 November, accusing them all of "playing it safe" in their attitudes to company budgeting. "How else can I view the matter", he asked, "when your estimates of manpower requirements have been consistently and almost universally overstated?" He listed the discrepancies between actual staff and budgeted staff from 1962 and found budget excesses for each year, with a high of 6.2 per cent in 1964. He also criticised the practice of budgeting for yearly staff increases as though all additional staff were required for the full year and from the same date. "Quite clearly your staff requirements do not occur suddenly at the beginning of the year." He was mindful, he said, that the employement situation in Australia had created many difficulties in obtaining suitable staff.

> The Board has in the past been rightly critical of the fact that Qantas labour costs are always well below budget, drawing the inference that, if the Company can still operate satisfactorily with about 3 per cent less staff than planned (worth £540,000 in the present year), then management is also "playing it safe" by deliberately padding staff requirements. As I am seriously concerned with such criticism I plan to take a particular interest in vetting your manpower requests for the budget year 1966-67 . . . If funds are earmarked for staff which are not really necessary, important capital projects (even the purchase of aircraft) may have to be deferred.[27]

Qantas had carried out a study of capital expenditure trends earlier in the year to find whether the company was, in fact, spending enough on capital requirements during the existing period of buoyant revenue. This study was in itself inconclusive but it raised the suspicion that certain functions at Mascot relied too heavily on labour and too little on mechanical aids. Further studies were made, beginning with a broad assessment of the total value of plant, machinery, and other ground equipment owned by Qantas worldwide in relation to total revenue. This showed that from 1961–62 to 1964–65, investment in such equipment had fallen from 21.9 pence per pound of revenue to 14.8 pence per pound, a fall of thirty-two per cent in just three years. Expressed in terms of assets per employee, investment in ground equipment showed a similar downward trend. The trend was more marked at Mascot. An unskilled cabin service employee cost the company each year (including direct and indirect overheads) just under £2,000. "At this rate," said the study, "we could buy £17,000 worth of equipment with every man saved without affecting profits by substituting depreciation (assuming a ten-year write-off), maintenance and interest instead of labour costs in the profit and loss account. This is, in fact, what appears to be happening in the USA where the airlines must be much more careful in employing staff because of extremely high labour costs." US airlines, the study commented, made it easier to obtain capital expenditure for the purchase of plant and equipment than to get staff; the opposite was true in Qantas. "Take a case in point. An additional 46 male cabin service staff have been requested because of 'peaking' of morning arrivals at Mascot, over and above that anticipated in the budget. Will this request receive the same consideration at Management and Board level as one for £750,000 worth of airport handling equipment? Yet the effect on profit is identical." This failure to recognise the relationship between unskilled labour and capital investment costs was, said the study, slowing down Qantas productivity growth in comparison with that of other airlines. [28]

These ongoing preoccupations with staff levels and levels of capital investment were not undertaken to pursue an abstract goal of ever-rising efficiency. Competition for Qantas traffic continued to rise. The newest competitor, in November 1965, was Philippine Air Lines, who joined the existing ten large international airlines serving Australia. Commonly referred to as PAL, it inaugurated a twice weekly service between Manila and Sydney using DC8 aircraft. PAL's jet operations were undertaken with important assistance from KLM, whose aid had been critical to PAL's economic expansion. This assistance, begun in 1962, came at a time when PAL was committed to buy two DC8s but was unable to finance and effectively operate them. PAL concluded an agreement with KLM under which KLM took over responsibility for the aircraft on order, leasing one back to PAL (which they later purchased outright). KLM also provided staff training and back-up aircraft during periods when the PAL aircraft underwent maintenance at Amsterdam. PAL and KLM were general sales agents for each other. Turner commented to Fysh on this new competitor. "The combination of KLM-PAL might well give us some trouble. In addition, although we have tried, we have been unable to prevent PAL introducing in-flight movies, which might have a novelty value for passengers." [29]

This growth in the activities of competitors was, of course, a reflection of the worldwide expansion in civil aviation that had made Qantas's own growth so spectacular. Net profit for the year ending 31 March 1965 had been a record £2,050,506. In September 1964, three new Boeing 707-338C combination passenger-cargo aircraft had been ordered for delivery from September 1965 to January 1966 and in October 1965 a further three were ordered for delivery in the first half of 1967. During 1965 the company was hard pressed to fill almost one thousand new jobs. There was a continuing shortage of pilots. Service frequencies were increased on most routes during the year and calls at Colombo and Kuala Lumpur were resumed in September. (The governments of India and Pakistan imposed severe restrictions on commercial aircraft in September, however, following the outbreak of hostilities between the two countries.) Boeing V-Jets replaced Electras on the New Zealand services to Christchurch (in April) and Auckland (in November) when new jet airfields became available (as they had done at Colombo and Kuala Lumpur). TEAL stretched its wings competitively when, with new jet airliners, it changed its name to Air New Zealand in December.

In the closing months of 1965 there was, Fysh wrote, "press speculation as to who would succeed me as Chairman of QEA". There was also speculation in government circles and within Qantas itself.

> Articles in the *Australian Financial Review* by John Gunn [wrote Fysh in the unedited manuscript of his third volume of reminiscences *Wings to the World*] starred five possible contenders in Sir Roland Wilson, Sir Frederick Scherger, D. G. Anderson, C. O. Turner and, as odds-on favourite, R. R. Law-Smith, the then deputy chairman. However, the articles pushed strongly for Turner and were embarrassing to the Federal Government and the QEA Board. They seemed inspired and well informed in some aspects. However, Turner and his Qantas publicity man, John Ulm, flatly denied all knowledge of the articles – Canberra strangely knowing about publication the day before they appeared.

There were two articles. The first, on 28 October, began:

> The annual general meeting of the International Air Transport Organisation which began in Vienna this week will be Sir Hudson Fysh's last. He is due to retire as chairman of Qantas on 30 June next and his valedictory in Vienna raises questions of succession and organisation in Australian aviation both within and beyond Qantas . . . No one inside the [Qantas] team, in government or amongst Australians conscious of their country's unique contribution to aviation would deny him . . . the gratitude due to him for his four and a half decades of service to Qantas and Australia.

It was the second article that Fysh had noted with more interest. In discussing the short list of contenders, it said:

> Sir Roland Wilson, so close to the heart of Government as Secretary of the Treasury, has been by far the most valuable and important member of the Qantas board . . . Sir Roland, indeed, would come very close to our picture of the ideal chairman [but] he happens to have a very interesting job where he is . . . Mr R. R. Law-Smith is vice-chairman of Qantas. He is a wealthy man with wide business and rural interests and is also a member of the

Australian National Airlines Commission (which controls
TAA) . . . Though he does not to me measure up to the specification in terms of international stature, expertise in international
aviation or toughness in dealing with governments, there is no
doubt at all that he is currently odds-on favourite for the job in
official circles . . . Mr D. G. Anderson, director-general of civil
aviation, would probably make a very good Qantas chairman if
one could first shoot the existing top Qantas management . . . It
is difficult to imagine Mr Anderson working happily within the
existing Qantas team . . . Sir Frederick Scherger, chairman of the
Chiefs-of-Staff Committee, retires in April. He is a man of immense
personality and has the international stature appropriate to the
job. Perhaps his one drawback is that he knows nothing about the
intensely technical and competitive field of international aviation.
With Sir Frederick as Qantas chairman, one might end up with
a board on which no one was expert in his subject [though] it is
unthinkable that the present chief executive of Qantas, Mr C. O.
Turner, would not move on to the board when Sir Hudson Fysh
retires. Mr Turner, as everyone in the airline world will tell you,
has been at the heart of the Qantas postwar achievement . . . Mr
Turner, indeed, has a top place on my personal short list. On the
debit side, his directness of manner has not made him loved in
government circles. One could whole-heartedly wish him the
succession for the sake of Qantas, while realising that it is much
more likely that he will be teamed as managing director with a
chairman who is not as dry, forthright and forbidding as
himself. [30]

There was, within Qantas management, considerable
agonising about the Fysh succession. Very close to C. O. Turner,
as the drama began to unfold, was Qantas press relations
manager, John Ulm. Ulm, son of the great Australian aviation
pioneer, Charles Ulm, had been an RAAF Spitfire pilot and
journalist before joining Qantas at Turner's invitation. He
prepared a remarkably frank, personal, and confidential paper
for Turner. What was at stake, and plainly recognised by Turner
and Ulm, was not merely the question of succession to the chairmanship. Fysh's departure was an opportunity for those who
wanted radical change in Qantas's leadership to force the
departure of Turner as well. Ulm addressed this issue. "The
continuity of the successful management is essential to the continuity of the company", he wrote to Turner. "The management is you. Your continuity is therefore vital. It does not really
matter to the company whether you continue as chief executive,
managing director, chairman or God or what. We must therefore
work against and set aside those factors which would make for
your departure. One of these", said Ulm bluntly, "is yourself."
There was, he judged, "no combination of forces outside the

company, or for that matter inside the company, which will
bring about your accession to the chairmanship at this stage.
Any move you make which is based on your personal requirement of becoming chairman in the near future is bound to
fail . . . You can cope with any chairman appointed." The team,
wrote Ulm, "is actively and variously cogitating on the future;
that is, your future". Ulm now spoke very plainly and intimately
to his chief executive. "I believe that fundamentally they [the
team] are all for you, or would be if they were not beginning
to lose heart in your cause. This is your own fault. You have
given them no lead as to the future and you are no longer a
rallying point . . . You must formulate a policy and commit all
your top people to it." Ulm urged that Turner publicly commit
himself to the principle that the new Qantas chairman, whoever
he might be, should represent the company in the decision-
making centre of the nation. He should live in Canberra. "We
have seen how our absence from Melbourne, while all the other
elements in civil aviation are at home there, has been a critical
and unsolved problem. The move of the Department of Civil
Aviation to Canberra in a very few years from now without a
balancing Qantas move would be disastrous to the company's
independence . . . The chairman's retirement can be used to
fix this glaring deficiency . . . As the company itself is rooted
in Sydney, it follows that the chief executive must be there,
developing top policy and leading the company overall."

Ulm now tackled Turner on his two most vulnerable points,
his perceived antagonism to the Qantas pilot body, and his
excessive drinking. They were issues, he said, on which he
thought Turner critically and possibly fatally vulnerable. On
the pilots, Ulm wrote:

> No matter how right you believe yourself and the company's
> industrial handling to be, there is no doubt whatever that any
> intelligent person examining this subject today could not but con-
> clude that the company has made no progress whatever in the eight
> years since the 1957 strike towards solving the problem . . . Those
> behind the pilots (not the pilots themselves) want to destroy
> you . . . You must take great personal initiatives in this yourself . . .
> by going directly to your pilots yourself and asking "What has gone
> wrong between us? Tell me where we have gone wrong?" . . . At
> one blow this would be calculated to have a genuine effect among
> the pilot body (away from their professional negotiators) and would
> publicly steal the initiative from the AFAP. Politically you would
> come through as trying to reach them. Unless you make some
> personal move of this kind . . . the company will continue to
> register to those outside who are concerned with its destiny that
> the management of Qantas is bankrupt of ideas, and therefore we

335

should try someone else ... The times require a dramatic innovation by you.

On Turner's drinking habits, Ulm was brutally frank. "This is the one item which is leading to despair within the team", he wrote. "What can we do with him?" Turner drank heavily when flying, drank excessively at public dinners and functions, and drank habitually in the company of his senior executives in his anteroom, No. 913. Ulm wrote: "You should make 913 by invitation only, and proclaim it so. You should have no 913 the evening before a jet base lunch. You should only do one jet base lunch in two. You should have no 913 on Monday night or Friday night. Everybody home early these nights, please. Outside the company," Ulm warned, "it is doubtful if you can survive on this issue."

Ulm concluded his note urging the idea of promulgating a policy for the new Qantas chairman to live in Canberra. "The beauty of all this is that it offers a dispassionate alternative to the moves which are already under way. It will enable all sorts of influential people to take an interest in the subject without having to take a position for or against given personalities. And from the muddying of the waters, who knows what we might come up with? We could well find a name which confounds them all. But it doesn't really matter. What matters is your continuity, in whatever form."[31]

There was much intelligence gathering as the issue of the Fysh succession gathered momentum. From Canberra came advice that it was unlikely Turner would go straight to the chairmanship; that it was usual for the vice-chairman to go into the chair. The minister, Henty, would have supported Anderson but had said that he could not spare him from the department. Sir Frederick Scherger was quoted as saying that he did not think he had the qualifications to become chairman of Qantas, but he did think he had them for the chairmanship of TAA. He could not, said the information, stand either Wilson or Law-Smith. He would be delighted to join the board of Qantas and work under Turner and take direction from him. "Believes Turner would be an excellent chairman but must curb his drinking", said one report.[32] Another short note reported that Hudson Fysh, on his return to Sydney from Vienna "vilified C. O. Turner to Capt. Shields in terms that Shields could not repeat". Shields, an official of the AFAP and a senior Qantas captain, was reported to have said that the pilots had discussed the succession and, though they had their differences with

Turner, were one hundred per cent behind him to succeed Fysh. "They all recognise that, although they make their contribution, the company's success is mainly due to Turner's organising genius."[33]

Hudson Fysh held a party in mid-November to launch the first volume of his autobiography, *Qantas Rising*. An article in the *Sydney Morning Herald* of 19 November led with the statement that Fysh did not invite Turner to the launch. Where was Turner at the time, asked the article?

> He was, in fact, working in his office on the ninth floor at Qantas . . . It is no secret that relations between the 71-year-old Sir Hudson Fysh and 58-year-old C. O. Turner have never been particularly warm and that some members of the present board would by no means relish the presence of the forceful and wealthy (Mr Turner won the £100,000 lottery three years ago) chief executive in the chairman's seat . . . When asked recently by an American television interviewer what he did at Qantas, Turner replied simply: "I set policy". This is true, but it is not the sort of truth that is palatable to the directors, all of whom are big men in their own fields.

It was not the kind of article likely to further the popularity of C. O. Turner. In fact, Turner's attitude to the Fysh volume was a strong one. "C.O.'s attitude", wrote Ulm, "is that if we get behind the book, then we are stuck with it. It is only Hudson Fysh's view of history. We might not agree with it. Bearing in mind that the chairman has stated he intends to spend the next two years writing the history of Qantas from 1934 up to the present, we will probably have strong views about the content, and obviously C.O. wants to reserve his position on this."[34]

From the Qantas office in Canberra came a report, based on conversations with Henty's secretary and his personal assistant: "We hope you are going to like your new chairman. It is Law-Smith. There is nobody else. C.O. will be better off under Law-Smith than he is now, as a part-time chairman in Melbourne. He should be able to run the company the way he wants." Sir Alister McMullin, president of the Senate, was quoted as saying that two businessmen had approached him to make sure that Turner succeeded as chairman. "McMullin said he liked C.O. and had never struck anyone who didn't like him. It would, he said, be a tragedy to lose him and a retrograde step. McMullin said he would have a quiet word with Henty." Henty himself, said a further Canberra report, was so positive that Law-Smith would be the next chairman that he had invited him to his office to congratulate him. "The minister sponsored Law-Smith. The treasurer sponsored Roland Wilson." The note concluded, however, that Law-Smith was rejected on account of his youth and his many other interests. "At the moment there is no thought of C. O. Turner moving on to the board . . . [This] will be looked at closer to his retirement date." This same note added: "Hudson Fysh has been writing right up to the last minute to try and get an extension [of his period as chairman] and in his last letter said something along these lines: 'It was a pity to have heard reports of C. O. Turner's behavior in Djakarta and Tokyo'. The minister is not concerned about reports of Turner's behavior."[35] A letter in the *Sydney Morning Herald* was published from the AFAP quoting a pilots' resolution that was strongly supportive of Turner. (The letter was from F. D. C. Caterson. Turner wrote to Caterson on 9 December expressing thanks for "informing me of the support for me by the overseas pilots. It gave me a great deal of pleasure to hear about it."[36])

From Tokyo, Turner, who had been unwell, wrote to Ulm:

Pills, rest and golf are working well and in another week I'll be fit to fight again. The AFAP letter caught me by surprise. Perhaps Bruce Hinchcliffe [QEA staff manager] could suggest to Caterson [AFAP] *verbally* that a copy of the resolution to the Minister might help. I don't know whether senior staff could do something on the theme "Who fights for Qantas? – i.e. anti-Commission [TAA], anti-Ansett, anti-Melbourne". Perhaps you could see Dan McV. [Sir Daniel McVey] personally . . . Suggest points to cover (1) Anderson [director general of civil aviation] appointed his wartime commanding officer [Law-Smith] to the Board of TAA and Qantas. Law-Smith was not known to Townley [the minister] at the time. (2) Anderson and Paltridge were working on a long-term plan for *one* Commission of Qantas and TAA. Whether this has been dropped in government circles might be smoked out. It would be disastrous to Qantas because under a two-airline policy it would let Ansett fly overseas. (3) Quote the disastrous loss of New Guinea services which resulted from promises made by Anderson to Ansett on the take-over of ANA. Law-Smith did not fight this in any way, although the consequences were made clear to him. (4) The department is based on Melbourne and [has been] close to Ansett and always looked with suspicion at Qantas in Sydney. Anderson's great claim to fame is his so-called two-airline policy which in his view saved the Liberal Party much embarrassment over their support for private enterprise against the government ownership of TAA. (5) Anderson and Paltridge were responsible in having Warren MacDonald removed as chairman of TAA once he started to fight

for TAA interests against favouritisation for Ansett. Chippindall,
a friend of Anderson, was appointed "because he knew Government policy". (6) Fysh is supporting Law-Smith mainly because
he finds no difficulty in handling him, whereas I disagree with
him. Fysh has been angling for a further three years appointment
but, failing this, wants an office, secretary and presumably a car
to continue ad infinitum (his writing). He probably realises this
would be an embarrassment to me as Chairman and probably not
so much to Law-Smith. (7) Tell David [David McNicoll, a senior
and respected journalist-editor-columnist who greatly admired
Turner] we will give him full details of the Mascot [airport]
mess . . . The theme of Tullamarine [Melbourne's new airport]
being already two to three years ahead of Sydney terminal [is]
evidence of Melbourne influence and must be pressed. (And now
they want to appoint a Qantas Chairman from the same stable!).
(8) Tell David confidentially that Fysh has done much harm to
me on personal issues. Much of it is slanderous but difficult to
nail down, and this is the way Fysh has worked all his life. In
some way we should get the issue before the Prime Minister . . .
I expect to be back on 5th December. [37]

Turner had referred to himself in the role of chairman. It
was clear that he wanted the position and would fight for it.
Within ten days, however, the issue was decided. The decision
was taken over the heads of Anderson and Henty by the prime
minister, Menzies, the treasurer, Harold Holt, and the secretary
to the Treasury, Sir Roland Wilson. Wilson himself was
appointed to succeed Hudson Fysh as chairman of Qantas from
30 June 1966. Unlike Fysh, however, his appointment was as
part-time chairman.

Although it was a personal blow to Turner, the appointment
of Qantas's most able director to the chair was by far the best
outcome for him short of his own promotion. It meant, it
seemed, achievement of the plan for a strong chairman in
Canberra and a strong chief executive in Sydney. (Turner wrote
to Sydney businessman W. J. Stack on 15 December: "As things
turned out it was the best I could have hoped for . . . I have
an immense admiration for Roland Wilson. He has without
doubt one of the top minds in Australia." [38])

Ulm recalled the sequence of events leading to the announcement of Wilson as successor to Fysh in a typewritten note for
one of his senior staff.

C.O. was in Tokyo having a break. Consistently I was getting back
from Melbourne and Canberra the unbending steer that Law-Smith
was to be the new chairman. The Minister's office was absolutely
certain and was, of course, reflecting the Minister's view and
intention. I caught a cold on Wednesday night, 1st December and
was in bed all day Thursday and Friday. At about 5 p.m. on Friday

> Max Newton [a senior journalist with the *Sydney Morning Herald*]
> rang . . . to say that it was about to be announced that Wilson was
> to be chairman. I phoned Bert Ritchie who responded: "How could
> they possibly have found out? I knew earlier in the week but was
> sworn to secrecy".

Ritchie, wrote Ulm, had been advised by E. John Bunting,
secretary of the Prime Minister's Department, and told the
decision was top secret. Ulm wrote that Ritchie said this "was
the big fix, way above Henty and Anderson — taken by
Wilson, Holt and Menzies". Ritchie realised that no one had
told Hudson Fysh of the decision, and Fysh was fishing in a
remote part of the Snowy Mountains. He was found, and
Henty phoned him on the Friday morning. "I asked Bert",
Ulm wrote, "if C.O. had been told. Bert said no, because he
was sworn to secrecy. I said I would now phone C.O. in
Tokyo as I had private information from Canberra and was
not bound to keep it to myself."

It was now just on 5.30 p.m. on Friday 3 December. The
telephone circuit to Tokyo was closed and Ulm could not reach
Turner. He dictated a cable as Fysh rang. "He sounded like
a dead man. He had just got back from the country . . . and
wanted to make a comment to the press. When would I like
it? By 8 p.m., I said. Then in came the press calls." In response
to these calls, Ulm quoted Turner as responding to the news
of Wilson's appointment with complete delight. "It is a superb
choice", were the words Ulm (who, of course, had not spoken
to his chief executive) attributed to Turner. They were perfectly
appropriate. When Turner arrived in Sydney from Tokyo on
the Sunday he was, wrote Ulm at the time, "quite delighted
because . . . he has a tremendous admiration for Roland as the
best brain in Australia". The atmosphere in the office, Ulm
noted, was wonderful. "All have picked up the point that this
was Plan A and we had achieved *exactly* what we want at this
stage. What stronger team could we have than Wilson in
Canberra and Turner in Sydney? Another way to assess the
victory is in terms of those who have been completely thrust
aside by the decision—Anderson, Henty, Law-Smith, Bland.
The victory is truly mighty but I warned C.O. that the moment
of great victory was the moment fraught with great danger,
because it is at this point that a man relaxes his guard." If Law-
Smith had been appointed, wrote Ulm, Turner would have
resigned. "This was the Melbourne plot. My assessment of the
office view up to the time of the decision was that C.O. had
had it. He would not survive . . . They virtually conceded defeat

before the battle was really joined . . . They're all for C.O. but
I wonder who really *did* anything about it? There comes a time
when one must nail one's colours to the mast. We have done
this—and we hold the heights."[39]

On 31 December, Hudson Fysh wrote a long, personal,
confidential letter to Roland Wilson. He was, he said, available
to continue as a director of Qantas "but am not anticipating
that I will be so appointed". He was available, also, to continue
not as chairman but as a director of the new Wentworth Hotel,
and he had spoken "to Denham Henty some time back about
this matter and he had no objection, saying it was entirely a
matter for the Qantas Board". He asked if the company "would
grant me the courtesy of use of an office with phone and facilities
to get typing done, and where I can settle in with my records
and make a start on the second volume of *Qantas Rising* . . .
In any event, after forty-five years with Qantas and QEA it will
be impossible to break off suddenly." Fysh made some critical
comments about Turner and Ulm. "Growing up with the
Company I had no difficulties [in regard to chairman's contact
with management and staff] till a crisis some years back when
for a period, till it was stopped, I found the General Manager
was not fully taking me into his confidence . . . You may wish
to consider a Private Secretary and, indeed, unless you are to
spend a great deal of time in the office, you might consider it
essential."

Fysh criticised the manner in which Turner involved the
company secretary, Fred Derham, and the assistant secretary
in additional heavy duties as executives.

> This involves some divided loyalties and as these officers come
> daily under the control of the Chief Executive they are "his men".
> However, I believe a Secretary's first duty is to his Board Chairman
> and Board and he should inform his Chairman on matters and
> happenings in the Company which are of interest to the Board . . .
> However, in our case, Mr Derham has well carried out dual duties
> of a difficult nature.

On John Ulm and the Qantas press relations organisation Fysh
was highly critical.

> I have never been in agreement with Mr Ulm being placed in
> charge as I felt him unsuitable [he wrote]. And the way the Chief
> Executive worked this section of our activities with him was not
> in the best interests of the Company. During my term I have been
> constantly engaged in a battle to keep Management from bad

341

On 10 December 1965, exactly forty-six years after he had welcomed Ross and Keith Smith on their arrival at Darwin, Sir Hudson Fysh attended a ceremony at Mascot. An Avro 504K formerly used by the RAAF in the 1920s had been lent to Qantas earlier in 1965 by the Australian War Memorial. The original rotary engine was replaced by a Sunbeam Dyak and the airframe repainted to duplicate the appearance of the first Q.A.N.T.A.S. Avro 504 in 1921. Sir Hudson donned flying helmet and goggles to taxi the old aircraft 330 yards (300 metres) along the tarmac and park alongside the 707 *Winton*.

publicity, bad public relations (a boasting attitude etc) and from infringing on the normal functions of the Chairman.

I purposefully refrained from press conferences, leaving this to the General Manager, as I felt I was receiving too much publicity elsewhere. However, this proved a mistake, and over the past two or three years a relationship dangerous to QEA relationships was built up with the press. I feel this whole section needs looking at.

He thought it vital that Wilson should attend executive committee meetings of IATA, though Law-Smith would be an acceptable alternative, but "with deep regret I must state my view that Mr Turner is psychologically unsuitable for this sort of appointment". On the general Qantas organisation he commented: "Generally I believe that the Qantas organisation is in splendid shape and that Mr Turner has done a splendid job of organisation, and in his selection and distribution of top staff. The pilots' troubles are, of course, always with us."[40]

A Splendid Life
1966

In January, Wilson responded to Fysh's letter: "I found your letter of 31st December particularly useful in giving me a bird's eye picture of what lies ahead of me as Chairman. I note your view that you do not anticipate that you will be re-appointed [to the board] and this squares with something the Minister said to me fairly recently. I share your hope that Bob Law-Smith will be continued as Vice-Chairman, in which position he will have my full support and confidence." Wilson said that he would have to reflect very deeply on the memorandum that outlined the responsibilities and duties of the chairman and the chief executive. He would, on the matter of the duties of the secretary, hasten slowly. Referring to Ulm and the public relations organisation, he wrote: "I share your views on this matter. But there is quite a question in working out some system that will be more suited to our needs. Again, it requires a good deal of thought." Wilson referred to the coming meeting of IATA in Mexico in October 1966 and said that the question of representation (of Qantas) had been raised with him by Turner. He had not yet given Turner a reply, he wrote, but "for your private information, and for no other ears at this stage, I fully expect to lead the Qantas delegation to the Mexico City meeting, and I will almost certainly wish to take over your position on the Executive Committee". [1]

Sir Roland Wilson had, ironically, first been approached about the possibility of succeeding Sir Hudson Fysh by the director-general of civil aviation, Don Anderson, but many months before the decision had been made to appoint him. Anderson was later,

12

said Wilson, to back away from this suggestion. He had more carefully considered the timetable of his own future and his own ambition to chair the Qantas board and this did not accord with a term as chairman by Wilson. "Anderson", said Wilson, "was overbearing and a bully, though his staff worshipped him. He ruled all his ministers except perhaps Paltridge." Anderson and Turner, he said, fought continuously.[2] The Wilson appointment was well received publicly, though there were powerful people who resented the rejection of Turner. Fysh noted in his diary that at a cocktail party at the Menzies Hotel, the autocratic chairman of Australian Consolidated Press, Frank Packer, "openly told my wife and self of his great admiration for Turner and his real determination to get Wilson out and Turner in. Packer", Fysh commented, "is a dangerous, vindictive, one-eyed buccaneer. This is a worry for Wilson in the future."[3]

As 1966 began, there were important changes in Australia's government. Australia's prime minister, Sir Robert Menzies, voluntarily retired from office and was succeeded on 26 January by the former treasurer, Harold Holt. On the same day, R. W. C. Swartz succeeded Denham Henty as minister for civil aviation. Menzies's concern, expressed in late 1964, at the possibility of war with Indonesia had been proved groundless. In Indonesia there had been a shift to anti-Chinese attitudes and a pro-Western stance in 1965, followed by a recognition of Singapore and an ending of confrontation in 1966. Menzies had, however, in November 1964, stressed his view of the dangers of the Vietnam situation and, in April 1965, an Australian infantry battalion had been despatched to Saigon. A communist takeover of South Vietnam, in Menzies's judgment, would be a direct military threat to Australia – a view that was increasingly contested within Australia. In March 1966, two months after Menzies's retirement, the government announced that Australian national servicemen would be sent to Vietnam. Qantas reported tersely in its annual report that "charter flights operated by Qantas included movements of Australian Defence Forces".[4]

In England, Qantas's partner airline BOAC had, under their new chairman, Guthrie, received massive support from the government. In November and December of 1965 the House of Commons had debated the United Kingdom Air Corporations Bill, which provided for the long-awaited financial reconstruction of BOAC. Under this legislation, £110 million of BOAC borrowings had been cancelled, the reduction being applied to eliminate the airline's huge accumulated deficit and increase its capital reserve by £27.5 million to £30.8 million. Total BOAC borrowings came down from £176 million to £66 million. The purpose of the bill, the minister had announced, was to free the corporation "from the incubus of the past".

BOAC, like Qantas a wholly government-owned body, now had the capital characteristics of a normal company so that, from 31 March 1966, Qantas were now able to review BOAC results on a comparable basis with other airlines. In the past this had not been possible because interest on government loans had been charged against profits and there was no equity capital on which the dividend was paid. The BOAC reconstruction brought considerable benefit by reducing interest charges. Qantas, with a capital of £16 million (sterling) and with a revenue of £44 million turned over its capital 2.7 times each year; BOAC's new capital total of £35 million and revenue of £114 million now gave it much the same ratio (after allowing for the contribution made by Cunard aircraft). Other comparisons showed a BOAC debt-equity ratio of 0.9 to 1 compared with Qantas 1 to 1, KLM 3.3 to 1, and Pan American 2.4 to 1. The British government white paper on BOAC attributed a great part of the corporation's deficit to "the disasters to the Comet 1, the delays over the Britannia and the resulting need to equip with a stop-gap fleet of different types of aircraft". In fact, BOAC, which had lost more money than any of its major competitors since World War II, was now in a stronger financial position than any of them.

Air India, the other partner in the tripartite pool, was also (since 1953) completely government-owned. Its capital structure was unusual as it had capital that was half equity and half interest-bearing, while being permitted to borrow extensively from outside organisations. On a capacity ton mile basis Air India was a little over half the size of Qantas and, with a total capital (including reserves and loans) of £41 million plus large cash balances of almost £14 million at March 1965, it was, compared with Qantas, comfortably overcapitalised. It had also enjoyed very satisfactory profit levels (£2.4 million in 1964–65).

Qantas's other pool partner, the newly renamed Air New Zealand, was not doing well on its expanded services with DC8 jets. Fysh wrote to Law-Smith and Wilson that "the pool with Air New Zealand is going even worse than expected". He was sympathetic.

> Even our own new operations take a considerable time to build up traffic-wise. This is natural. For an entirely new operation like

345

Air New Zealand (excluding the Tasman) this will, of course, take a lot longer. Even if we are carrying the majority of the New Zealand traffic, mainly because of our greater frequency, this traffic still belongs to New Zealand. We must do all possible to help Air New Zealand. However, the strictly correct method of pooling is that passengers carried should in the main be credited to the company carrying them . . . The same system should be applied to our Tripartite Pool arrangements and it has always been a very serious defect of the original Bombay agreement that this was not provided for – a position injurious to our interests which Management has been trying to get out of ever since, trying desperately. [This was, of course, a tilt at Turner.] The Bombay agreement made by Management, set a precedent and how can we deny anything less favourable to our close friend and neighbour, New Zealand?

As a final thrust at Turner, he suggested that the board should call for the actual figures clearly stated of the balances of payments between QEA, BOAC, and Air India over the full term of the tripartite partnership "which will show a huge total which QEA have paid out to the other airlines".[5]

Qantas was now, like the rest of Australia, to move from pounds, shillings, and pence in its accounts to dollars and cents. On 14 February 1966, Australia adopted decimal currency: one Australian pound was to equal two Australian dollars.

There was, twenty years after the end of World War II, a world airliner fleet in airline service of 4,826 aircraft. For the first time, pure jet aircraft exceeded in number turboprop aircraft (1,037 against 913). Although there was approximately the same number of four-engined piston aircraft as jets (1,028) and a similar number of twin-engined DC3s (1,052), the contribution to airline capacity was far from similar. Jets provided seventy-two per cent of total capacity in terms of ton miles, turboprops fifteen per cent, and piston-engined aircraft thirteen per cent. The jet engine had brought an improvement in accident rates, which had, for the fifth successive year, declined. There were now (at 31 December 1965) 445 Boeing 707s in airline service (19 with Qantas), flying almost five thousand hours each day with, at any one moment, an estimated 15,650 passengers flying in them. Since their introduction, 19 Boeing 707s had been destroyed in accidents, giving them an accident rate of 0.57 losses per 100,000 hours of flying, much the same as the Douglas DC8 (0.5), double that of the Boeing 727 (0.25) and well below that for the Caravelle (0.88), the Viscount (0.88), and the Fokker

F27 (0.77). Topping the accident rate was the Comet 4 at 2.34.[6]

Inseparable from aircraft accident statistics were levels of insurance premiums. The Comet disasters and other jet aircraft accidents had brought premiums by 1959 to more than five per cent of equipment value. Qantas had paid £495,225 in premiums for the year to 31 December 1959. The moneys had gone overseas, as the Australian internal insurance market could not, in Qantas's judgment, absorb the risks. The board, with government support, decided to self-insure, setting aside commercial levels of premiums in an insurance reserve and investing this in Commonwealth Bonds. Now, in 1965, as premiums dropped to more acceptable levels, Qantas went back to the market. On 31 March 1965 the insurance reserve stood at £12,496,582 (with the Qantas aircraft fleet valued at cost at £138,510,698 million).[7]

Insurance problems were not, of course, concerned only with aircraft. Liability for damages for passenger personal injury or death had always been a major airline concern, with governments coming together to agree limits on such liability. In Warsaw in 1929 an international convention was made and ratified by over one hundred countries, including Australia. In broad terms it provided damages for personal injury or death on an international flight without necessary proof of fault or negligence by the passenger to a limit of approximately £3,700. (However, the carrier was not liable if able to prove that all necessary measures to avoid damage had been taken.) This Warsaw Convention was amended by a protocol after a conference at The Hague in 1955, doubling the limit of the recoverable amount. Australia had applied these amended principles to its carriers so that the limit on the amount of damages recoverable for death or personal injury of a passenger was £7,500. The United States, at the Hague conference, had pressed for a much higher limit of $100,000, arguing that the agreed limit was unduly low for American passengers. It now not only proposed not to ratify the Hague protocol but also to denounce the Warsaw Convention. For international airlines, this would have left them with unlimited liability for passengers travelling to, from, or through the United States. On 15 November 1965 the United States gave notice that its denunciation of the Warsaw Convention would be effective from 15 May 1966. An ICAO conference was called to reach a compromise. On 4 May, the United States announced that it would withdraw its notice of denunciation if governments agreed to an upper damages limit of $75,000 per passenger for travel to or from the United States, including segments of journeys through that country (as well as renouncing rights to the defence under the Warsaw Convention of having taken all necessary measures to avoid damage incurred). On 10 May, Australia's minister for civil aviation wrote to the prime minister: "I feel that in view of the importance of keeping the United States Government within the Warsaw Convention system and thereby helping to preserve its wide application it would be wise for the Australian Government to notify the United States Government that it has no objection to the interim arrangement proposed . . .".[8] The Australian embassy in Washington notified Canberra on 13 May that the United States had withdrawn its notice of denunciation of the Warsaw Convention and had accepted the IATA interim arrangements.[9] The result, of course, was the creation of an anomaly in that a passenger travelling Sydney-London through the United States would have higher insurance cover than one travelling Sydney-London through India.

Fysh entered hospital on 25 February for prostate treatment and surgery. He was depressed and apprehensive. "Today I stood at midday in the brilliant sun; if not well, I was still a free man. Now, one month ahead in awful inhuman degeneration of functions – thirty days unable to leak at will. What will be the end? At best a terrible . . . change of life."[10] He had a comforting note from Australia's governor-general, Sir William Slim, thanking him for a copy of *Qantas Rising*. "What a splendid life you have had", wrote Slim. "How you have served Australia – and a lot of us, too."[11]

In the financial year 1965–66 Qantas had absorbed four additional Boeing 707-338C passenger-cargo aircraft into its fleet and sold one Electra (in April 1965) to Air New Zealand. At 31 March it owned and operated thirteen Boeing 707-138Bs and six 338Cs, as well as three Electras, two DC4s, and two DC3s. There were three more 707-338Cs on order and two small Hawker Siddeley HS125 twin jet training aircraft (delivered later in 1966). These HS125s, said vice-chairman R. R. Law-Smith had been part of the price paid by Qantas for British agreement to give Qantas London-Bermuda rights.[12] The introduction of the big 707-338Cs had caused capacity to expand faster than revenue traffic, with load factor dropping to 51.6 per cent from 54.8 per cent in the previous year. They had, however, enabled company productivity in terms of capacity

ton miles flown to rise by almost a quarter. Some normal services had been curtailed for short periods during the year to provide capacity for the movement of Australian defence forces to South East Asia. A shortage of pilots had necessitated the cancellation of some services and recruiting teams again visited the United Kingdom and other Commonwealth countries, bringing in fifty additional pilots and eleven technical aircrew. The first twenty-one cadet pilots introduced under the cadet pilot training scheme were due to graduate in September 1966 and a further twenty-six cadets had begun training in February. Qantas now employed 441 pilots, 97 navigators, 149 flight engineers, and three radio officers. Experienced tradesmen in almost every field of specialisation were, like pilots, also in short supply and there had been recruiting drives overseas as well as a doubling of the company's apprentice intake. An additional 241 apprentices began training early in 1966, bringing the total number in the company to 570. Total personnel employed had risen substantially during the year by 1,205 to 9,546. This year of expansion had made it necessary once again to obtain additional office space for staff in Sydney outside Qantas House, adding to the pressure for the construction of a new headquarters building.

The carriage of migrants from the United Kingdom (as assisted passage migrants) and from Europe, under the auspices of ICEM, remained an important part of business in 1965–66.

VH-ECE, the first of two Hawker Siddeley 125s in flight over England in May 1966. Both were in service as training aircraft by mid-July 1966.

349

For the year, the carriage of British migrants provided a revenue return of $A5,901,675 from scheduled flights and $A7,416,500 for charter flights. During the period, 18,159 adults and 397 infants were carried on the scheduled flights and 22,684 adults plus 518 infants on migrant charter flights – an increase over the previous year of more than 20 per cent on scheduled flights and almost 80 per cent on charter operations. (An arrangement was made with British Eagle International for the charter flights as Qantas could not, because of its other operational requirements, provide all the aircraft necessary.) For the ICEM migrants, regular weekly flights (with occasional extra flights) continued for 1965–66. Qantas was also not able, because of its commercial commitments, to provide its own aircraft for the ICEM flights after December 1965 and again turned to British Eagle International to provide capacity. Qantas was allocated forty-six ICEM flights for the year (83.6 per cent of the traffic). Direct charter revenue for all ICEM flights for the fiscal year totalled $A1,750,212.[13] Qantas also carried small numbers of ICEM-sponsored migrants from Europe on regular commercial services on a fill-up basis as well as Finnish and Italian migrants at special fares. (The total carriage of migrants by air to Australia for the year to 31 March 1966 was 47,761. It was made up of UK and ICEM migrants on Qantas and BOAC scheduled and charter flights, and British Eagle charter flights plus small numbers of Finnish and Italian migrants on Qantas scheduled flights.)

A Cabinet ad hoc committee met on 24 March 1966 with Qantas management to discuss the need for a new head office. Turner had written a personal letter to Wilson, in his role as secretary to the Treasury, on 25 February which ended: "I do hope we will soon get an answer to this vexatious problem of the Lang Park [headquarters] development, as the passing months do not help to solve our ever mounting shortage of Head Office accommodation".[14] Turner had briefed the board (including Wilson) on 7 February for its meeting with the Cabinet subcommittee. "The Lang Park block is ideally suited for this [head office] purpose, is basically undeveloped and can be purchased at relatively low cost. It is most improbable that a central city block will ever again become available under such favourable conditions." He recalled that Qantas had purchased the site for the existing head office in 1955 at a cost of £515,000 and that it was now valued at £1,300,000, an increase of 250 per cent.[15] In general notes for the board Turner said that the company was already leasing 54,000 square feet of office space in addition to Qantas House at an annual cost of £154,000. "Leasing of space is uneconomic," he wrote, "both in terms of direct rental costs and the liability that flows from split locations." In that heady period of uninterrupted expansion, the Lang Park development, planned in three stages, was seen as something more than a Qantas head office. The second stage, wrote Turner,

> must be so designed that it can cope with the Company's intention of creating an Air Centre for all airline operators and other allied interests, e.g. Trans-Australia Airlines and Overseas Telecommunications Commission. The Air Centre would provide for proper facilities for buses and other ground transport to and from Mascot, an extensive communications system including electronic computers, and appropriate offices for domestic and international operators . . . The total site has now been largely acquired by Qantas at reasonable cost and the balance outstanding can be secured gradually as opportunity arises. Qantas does not require any funding from the Commonwealth as finance can be provided within the Company's own ambit and institutional borrowings.

Qantas, he said, now required from Cabinet agreement in principle to develop the whole site, authority to exercise options expiring on 31 March, and authority to proceed with the first stage of the development.[16] These requirements were all substantially agreed to by the Cabinet subcommittee at its meeting on 24 March.[17] (In its other major property venture, the new Wentworth Hotel, there was a change of name of the company responsible for its construction on 28 March from Kenmaster Holdings Limited to Qantas Wentworth Holdings Limited. On the same day, the parent company of Wentworth Hotel Limited [the old Wentworth Hotel] changed its name to Lang Park Limited from Qantas Wentworth Holdings Limited. All three of these companies were wholly owned subsidiaries of Qantas. Wentworth Hotel Limited now operated through Lang Park Limited and Qantas Wentworth Holdings Limited. The old Wentworth Hotel facilities were well patronised during the year to 31 March 1966 and it carried on trading until the opening of the new hotel.)[18]

In March 1966, in the midst of all this fleet expansion, preparations for the opening of the big new Wentworth Hotel, and acquisition of a whole inner city block for the future Qantas headquarters, Boeing announced that it intended to build a new airliner that would dwarf even the existing 707s. The Boeing 747 announcement came in the middle of a Qantas study of their fleet projections. It was to be an aircraft of 750,000 pounds all-up weight carrying a planned 357 passengers at a cruising speed of 570 miles per hour, compared with the Boeing 707-338Cs in Qantas service with an all-up weight of 336,000 pounds, a passenger capacity of 140, and a cruising speed of 550 miles per hour. (The supersonic Concorde figures available to Qantas in 1966 showed an aircraft with an all-up weight of 389,000 pounds, a passenger capacity of 106, and a cruising speed of 1350 miles per hour.) The company's fleet projections in 1966 showed a requirement up to 1972 for approximately 33 aircraft of Boeing 707 size, made up of thirteen of the smaller 707-138B aircraft and twenty of the Boeing 707-338Cs.

The problems of crew availability for such a large fleet of Boeing 707s was to affect greatly the decisions on future fleet composition reached later in 1966.[19] Qantas was suffering heavily from their inability to provide crews for the existing fleet of nineteen Boeings. Daily utilisation of the airliners, in the forecast prepared to support their purchase, had been assumed to be 10 hours in the air each day. (This was not unreasonable; in 1963–64 Qantas had achieved a peak utilisation of 10.3 hours while in 1964, Pan American had averaged almost 12 hours, Lufthansa had achieved 11 hours, and Canadian Pacific an impressive 12.5 hours.) By 1965–66, the Qantas daily utilisation had dropped, because of aircrew shortage, to 9.4 hours and was budgeted to fall in 1966–67 to the dismal figure of 8.2 hours. The financial effect of this underutilisation was severe. Based on its existing fleet strength of nineteen Boeings, a drop in daily utilisation from the original, projected ten hours a day to the budgeted figure of 8.2 hours per day meant, with very simple arithmetic, that Qantas had three surplus aircraft. The financial penalty in the 1966–67 budget, in terms of obsolescence charges, insurance, maintenance labour, and interest charges totalled $2,655,000. In terms of projected profit diminution, this underutilisation promised even greater penalties.[20]

These pressures on profits from aircrew shortages were compounded by the decision in March 1966 to cancel two scheduled services per week on the Kangaroo service and one per week on the Pacific service in May and June to enable Qantas to meet Australian government requirements for the operation of twenty-five charter flights to South Vietnam (Saigon) in support of Australia's military commitment to United States involvement in that country. Qantas had no alternative, simply on the basis of lost crew days for the charters, to reducing commercial frequencies. However, a close look at aircrew utilisation in February showed that crews were not working to the limit of their capacity. The effective duty days for all categories of air-crew, expressed as duty days away from Sydney, had been steadily eroded in recent years. For line captains they had dropped from 159 to 144 days, with even greater falls for first officers and second officers. As days scheduled for duty at base, plus sick leave and annual leave, had not changed materially, the fall in duty days away from Sydney effectively meant a direct increase in off duty days. By April 1966 this increase in off duty days had reached a position where they were well in excess of the accepted level of three days off for every five days away. For the year ended February 1966 it was clear that line captains averaged four and a half days free of duty for every five days away, while first and second officers averaged five. However, senior Qantas operations personnel considered that any attempt by management to use these demonstrated extra duty free days, even during the ten weeks of the emergency charter operations to Saigon, would result in industrial suicide.[21]

Management-pilot problems involved much more than the question of duty free days. Turner told the board on 7 April: "The discipline problem with the pilots is now becoming more evident in a number of areas and is fast reaching a critical point . . . The reaction of Sir Henry Bland to these problems was favourable in that he appreciated that continuation of this indiscipline could not be tolerated." One substantial issue related to the refusal of captains to "give away landings to first officers" and so allow the first officers to maintain their proper level of experience and competence. Qantas' chief industrial officer, B. J. Hinchcliffe, raised the matter with B. I. Crofts, manager of the AFAP.

> Over the last two weeks [he wrote] there has been an unprecedented increase in the number of First Officers who have reached the Company's long standing and accepted thirty-five day "recent experience" limit in relation to landings. As a result, these pilots cannot be used on commercial flights without prejudicing the Company's safety standards . . . Whether or not a [federation] directive has been issued, the evidence of a concerted refusal to supervise First Officer landings in recent weeks confirms that a ban or limitation is being imposed. You are now informed that in respect of the seven "time expired" Boeing 338C First Officers and other First Officers who very shortly will reach the thirty-five day limit, no special training will be given to enable them to re-qualify to operate the Company's aircraft.

Direct confrontation was inevitable. Captain Ritchie and other members of management met for discussions with Sir Henry Bland on 13 April. Bland, Turner told the board, requested that special training should be provided for the Boeing first officers who were affected.

> Three pilots were called for this training on 14 April [wrote Turner], and were scheduled to fly to Darwin for it. Before departure from Sydney it was found that some . . . first class seats on the Air New Zealand service to Darwin had been oversold and as a result these pilots were unable to be accommodated in first class. (There were 48 vacant economy seats.) Two pilots then promptly refused to fly to Darwin for the training. We have informed Sir Henry Bland that our obligation in respect of these two pilots has been discharged and consideration is now being given to their immediate stand-down. Board members will appreciate that we are now facing a multiplicity of issues, any one of which could be the immediate cause of a strike—which is becoming more and more likely. [22]

Turner wrote to Fysh: "The pilot industrial position is changing daily". [23]

Over and above these detailed issues, the pilots had been pressing salary claims. On 18 March 1966, following an invitation from Bland, Professor Joseph Isaac of Monash University began an inquiry during which a completely new issue, which was to change the very basis on which pilots were paid, arose. A temporary suspension of the inquiry was granted to allow pilots and management to study the practice of an incentive bidding system used by pilots in the United States and Canada. Under this system, management-devised rosters for pilots were replaced by a procedure that gave pilots a minimum salary related to their agreed sixty-five hour minimum flying hours per month, plus the right to bid, in accordance with seniority rights, for extra flying hours, with a maximum of eighty-five hours per month for jet aircraft. In addition, pay was to be based on a formula that took into account the speed and weight of the aircraft flown. It meant, also, that with certain constraints pilots could decide their own roster and hours of duty. The Isaac inquiry finished on 27 May and he reported on 14 June that though some issues had been settled, that of salaries had not been. Isaac recommended a salary increase of fifteen per cent.

While these critical tensions continued as management and pilots considered the Isaac inquiry's recommendation, Qantas were considering the size and mix of their future fleet. It was abundantly clear that aircrew problems, particularly aircrew numbers, constrained fleet size. Replacement of the Boeing 707-138Bs with the bigger 338Cs would hold down aircraft numbers. Beyond the 338C was the promise of the recently announced Boeing 747 jumbo jet. On 3 May 1966 Qantas received a formal proposal from Boeing for the purchase of ten 338Cs, including a plan to help Qantas dispose of up to eleven of its 138Bs. Delivery of the new aircraft was scheduled at one per month beginning February 1968 and the basic price per aircraft was $US6,990,000. (Qantas revised this schedule to begin deliveries in October 1967; required Qantas changes to the aircraft added $US95,000, bringing the total price each to $US7,085,000.) A formula for agreeing the value of the older and smaller 138Bs was set out, Boeing proposing that they and Qantas would share equally in the profit or loss realised on the sale of any aircraft but limited to a maximum of $500,000 per aircraft. "Qantas", said the proposal, "shall have sole and exclusive control of the sale of the . . . aircraft and will use its best efforts to sell such aircraft at the highest price obtainable." Boeing also offered financial assistance if any of the 138Bs were not sold before delivery of the corresponding 338C.[24] The objective, Turner told the board, was to provide increased aircraft capacity to meet expanding commercial requirements, which had been limited by the current shortage of pilots. The timing of the sale of the smaller 138B aircraft was, in Turner's view, most important. They would be the first large American subsonic jets available on the second-hand market. "It is important", he wrote, "to appreciate that this is a replacement programme and we need more aircraft beyond February 1969. In our forward projections of fleet growth we forecast a maximum fleet of twenty-six 338 aircraft by March 1971, which is five additional to the ten we [now] propose."[25]

Only two and a half weeks later, Boeing made their first proposal that Qantas acquire three of the huge new Boeing 747s. The aircraft, said Boeing, was offered in three configurations — passenger, convertible, or freighter. The basic price of the passenger 747 was $US18,381,000. Boeing promised delivery in June, August, and September of 1970. For Qantas, as for the other major international carriers, this Boeing 747 initiative was to change radically the pattern of world airline operations. But this 20 May proposal for jumbo jets came too soon for Qantas. The airline was fully engaged in preparing for the sale of 138Bs and purchase of 338Cs. The project cost for the ten 338Cs alone was $US90 million and Turner considered it inappropriate to request a further sum in excess of $US100 million for 747 aircraft. This first Boeing proposal for acquisition of jumbo jets was allowed to lapse.[26] It had, Turner told the board, been given due consideration, together with the Concorde, for 1971–73 introduction, and the United States SST for 1975–76 introduction. "We believe we can introduce Boeing 747s in 1971–72 and Concordes in 1973–74 without creating a problem of over-capacity and without retiring our 707-338 aircraft prematurely", Turner said. Reviewing the company's future capital requirements, Turner thought it would be necessary to ask the government to provide approximately $20 million additional capital in each of the three years starting from 1968–69.

> This will not only improve our ratio of loan funds to equity capital but will ease the capital requirements in the 1970s, which are likely to be substantial . . . This is a relatively small contribution to such substantial capital outlay, particularly in view of the company's forecast Australian income tax payments of $15.3 million and estimated contributions to the nation's balance of payments of approximately $330 million during the five-year period. We also, of course, plan to continue to service capital with dividends involving an outlay of $14.9 million during the same period.

The company was, he said, projecting a turnover ranging from $123.3 million in 1966–67 to $214.4 million in 1970–71, and "even a small percentage drop in revenue could strain our resources".[27]

Hudson Fysh, recovering from his stay in hospital, received a letter from Law-Smith on 28 March responding to his requests on matters following his retirement.

> The Board is happy for you to have an office, telephone and typing facilities . . . Miss Isaacs may stay with you until 31 December 1966. You may have access to company records which would cover the period of the book you propose to write. This access would be done through Bert Ritchie . . . We had quite a lengthy discussion concerning the Hotel Board . . . The feeling of the Board is that if the hotel is not going to be floated as a public company, as was originally envisaged, the Qantas Board is responsible for its successful operation and therefore the whole Qantas Board should be the Hotel Board.[28]

Sir Roland Wilson, in a handwritten comment on this letter said: "Just prior to this I had asked Bob Law-Smith to take responsibility for dealing with matters arising out of Hudson Fysh's retirement, including his requests for continuing assistance after retirement. This arrangement continued indefinitely, with any important matters being submitted to the Board by Law-Smith."[29]

Fysh replied to Law-Smith: "I would like to say at this stage that though I retired from the Chairmanship of QEA by 'mutual consent' I am disappointed at my apparently not being asked to continue as a Director". (In his book *Wings to the World*, Fysh commented: "For some political subtlety, unfathomed by me, I was pressed to resign, but declined to do so. It was agreed that my resignation should be by mutual consent and honour was resolved by this compromise, which did not mean anything anyhow."[30] Continuation as a Qantas director, Fysh told Law-Smith, would have opened the way for him to continue on the hotel board.

> I confidently expected so to continue and had cleared the matter with the late Minister if the Board so wished to appoint me . . . The unfortunate fact is that owing to the decline in the value of money I will be left with quite an inadequate income to live reasonably on, even after really severely cutting all expenses. After selling all but five acres of my Dural property and receiving the Commonwealth Pension of £14,450 in July, I will be able to muster £56,000, which I estimate on a reasonable average will bring me in £3,360 per annum. Now rent, household allowances and wife's dress allowance (cut to half), taxation, running a car, two Clubs only and expenses, plus annual holidays is estimated to absorb exactly that amount which, of course, is only a portion of what one's expenses will be . . . Obviously I should be working in with Qantas or a Qantas association if this is possible. That I have to go out after all these years of pioneering and carrying on Qantas in financial circumstances so completely out of line with the rewards [that would have resulted] from similar service in private industry – and when one sees the sumptuous wealth displayed on every hand by successful people not in Government positions – does indeed seem unfortunate.[31]

To the new minister, Reginald Swartz, Fysh wrote on 13 May: "I must confess a feeling of disappointment exists in regard to the way things are turning out". He suggested that he be retained in an advisory capacity to the board for an annual fee equivalent to that of a director.

> I find I will definitely need to augment my income in order for my wife and I to live in reasonable comfort, after heavily curtailing expenses . . . I retire after forty-five years creative service having foregone the fortune, expensive homes and cars etc which the great majority of my friends and associates have as a result of their private enterprise. I can't help being conscious of being the main lasting factor in building what is today a great Commonwealth enterprise.[32]

Hudson Fysh found time, amidst these personal worries, to write a note to the steward of the Epsom summer race meeting in England, the Duke of Norfolk, at Arundel Castle, Bognor Regis, chiding him for one aspect of the conduct of the meeting. He complained that he had had a bet of £1 on a horse called Caterina at odds of seven to four. His horse won.

> Repeated presentation of the ticket for payment failed to produce payment or acknowledgement of the bet [Fysh wrote]. The bookmaker was a big, swarthy, dark, greying haired man who said nothing. There was also a gullible little fat man who did the smooth talk and, finally, the penciller who was, I think, one-legged, very abusive and a bad type. I realise that these conditions could either be regarded as warranting a good laugh or, alternatively, as disastrous to the honour of England, when viewed by a visitor from Australia where racing is properly regulated and bookmakers must themselves record the bet on the back of the card. English racing, of which you are a Steward, owes me £1 . . .[33]

Though Hudson Fysh was appointed for a brief time as "consultant" to the board and was given an office and secretarial assistance, his long service with Qantas now ended. It had been Fysh's wartime pilot, Paul McGinness, who had been the prime mover in winning the support of Queensland grazier Fergus McMaster for the formation of the original Queensland and Northern Territory Aerial Services Limited in 1920, but it had been Fysh whose application, industry, and tenacity had, at first under McMaster's chairmanship, led the tiny but growing enterprise over the decades. His own words most accurately described his role. He had been "the main lasting factor". He was given a farewell lunch in Canberra by the minister, a dinner by the Qantas board, and a staff send-off. Other functions in Australia and overseas honoured his going and his long service to Qantas and international aviation. At a final function in Launceston, Tasmania, where Fysh had been born on 7 January 1895, he was granted the freedom of the city. The prime minister, Harold Holt, wrote to him on 27 June: "I feel I should write to you in formal terms how much I have in mind that this is your last week in the position you have filled so admirably. It is in fact the culmination of the great public service which you have rendered to this country for what truly constitutes a great many years in the life of any man."[34] The last living link with the company's beginnings was now severed.

Qantas, in mid-1966, faced an operating situation in which crew shortages meant effective overcapacity in aircraft numbers as pressure was building from the United States to add to the competition across the Pacific. Continental Air Lines were, in May, seeking authorisation from the US government to operate scheduled international air services across the North Pacific to Japan and Singapore, and across the South Pacific through Hawaii, Tahiti, and other points to New Zealand, Sydney, Melbourne, and Perth – and beyond to Singapore. Continental was basically a US domestic carrier, ranking tenth largest among US domestic airlines. Their headquarters were in Los Angeles and they employed approximately 3,500 people, serving twenty-one cities in the western half of the US. They had a fleet of eight Boeing 707s and four Boeing 720B jets and they had, demonstrating their ambition, reserved delivery positions for three Concorde supersonic airliners. Continental were, however, only one of twenty-two American carriers seeking authorisation from the Civil Aeronautics Board to operate in the Pacific area. Most had applied for the Northern Pacific routes but there were seven seeking to enter the South Pacific to Australia (American Airlines, Braniff Airways, Eastern Air Lines, Trans International Airlines, United Air Lines, World Airways, Continental). The hearing of their applications before the CAB was a protracted matter, and the outcome depended ultimately on the approval of the US president.

This upsurge of interest in the South Pacific route was a concern to Qantas. Under the Australia-United States Air Agreement of December 1946, there were rights for either country to designate more than one airline to operate its agreed services under the bilateral. Pan American were currently the only airline so designated but it was open to the US authorities to authorise others. Australia was still in dispute with the US on Tahiti, maintaining that Tahiti was an authorised point for both countries' airlines to call at. The United States maintained that rights at Tahiti were conferred only on their carrier. Pending settlement of that issue, neither Qantas nor Pan American was currently able to include Tahiti on their routes. In mid-1966, Pan American operated four services weekly to Sydney and Qantas nine services weekly from Sydney to San Francisco (three of which extended beyond to New York and London). Other direct services connecting Australia with North America were operated by Qantas (twice a week to Mexico City), Canadian Pacific Air Lines (fortnightly to Vancouver), and the French airline UTA (weekly to Los Angeles). The total market for which they competed into and out of Australia on all trans-Pacific services in 1965 had totalled 87,000 passengers (out of a grand total for passenger traffic on all routes into and out of Australia of 511,000). What was of interest to the competing US contenders for the South Pacific was the traffic growth rate. Traffic had grown by fifty-six per cent from 55,000 in 1963.

These pressures, and the unresolved conflict with the pilots, faced Sir Roland Wilson in his new role as part-time chairman of Qantas. He was no stranger to either pressure or high office. Wilson remained (for a time) in his position as secretary to the Treasury, was a member of the board of the Reserve Bank of Australia, a director of the Commonwealth Banking Corporation, and a member of the council of the Australian National University. He had been a member of the Qantas board since July 1954. Like Hudson Fysh, he was a Tasmanian by birth. Son of a carpenter-cabinet-maker, he was born at Ulverstone in the timbered country one hundred miles from Launceston on Tasmania's north-western coast. A product of the state school system, his education was set back for a time by rheumatic fever but, when he came to study at the University of Tasmania under Australia's eminent economist, Sir Douglas Copeland, he was regarded as Copeland's brightest pupil. His degree and a Rhodes scholarship took him to Oriel College, Oxford, where he earned his doctorate with a thesis on the import of capital. Wilson went for a time to the University of Chicago for further research, lectured in economics at the University of Tasmania from 1930 to 1932, then joined the statisticians branch of the Commonwealth Treasury. In 1936, at the age of thirty-two, he was appointed Commonwealth statistician and economic adviser to the Treasury. In World War II he established and directed the Department of Labour and National Service but returned to his post as Commonwealth statistician from 1946 to 1951 (spending three years in the United States as member and chairman of the Economic and Employment Commission of the United Nations). His appointment as secretary to the Treasury in 1951 was followed by his knighthood in 1955. Wilson retained his father's love of craftmanship; his hobby throughout his life was cabinet-making.

Wilson had carefully pondered the letter that Fysh had written to him in January raising the relationship of chairman to chief executive and the functions of Qantas's Press and Information Department. On 23 June 1966, one week before he formally took up his appointment, a board memorandum under Law-Smith's signature was given to C. O. Turner. It was, said the preamble, "a guide to assist the Board, the Chairman, the Vice-Chairman and the General Manager and Chief Executive in carrying out their respective functions". It was explicit in its language: "The main function of the Board is to direct and control the policy and management of the Company". The board, it said, "from time to time delegates certain of its functions to the Chairman and others to the General Manager, who is the Chief Executive officer of the Company". The general manager was "responsible for the operations and day-to-day management of the Company". It was a document intended for Turner and a clear statement from Wilson that it was the board, under his chairmanship, that set policy—not Turner.

On publicity, the memorandum stated: "Board decisions or Company forecasts on policy matters, or on matters affecting relations with governments or other operators, will be publicly announced solely by the Chairman". It listed such policy matters carefully: routes, aircraft orders or acquisitions, new or modified pooling arrangements, important personnel policies, financial results, or important innovations or changes in Company practices or operations. The general manager could make public statements in amplification, or with reference to day-to-day operations. The Press and Information Department would, said the memorandum, assist the chairman as well as the general manager in publicity activities. No publicity release relating in any way to the board or its members, or to board decisions or discussions was to be made without the prior consent of the chairman.[35] Although this memorandum made plain the new chairman's views on the limits of the authority of the chief executive, Turner was not prepared to change his ways. It was, said Law-Smith, impossible to discipline him.[36] (Turner did not think the government had made the best decision when Wilson was appointed chairman. At a meeting with myself in Turner's house soon after the announcement, with Ulm present, I asked Turner who would have been the best choice for chairman. "I would", he replied bluntly.)

There had been other changes to the Qantas board. One year before, on 30 June 1965, M. C. Buttfield had retired and been replaced by J. M. Fotheringham. On 30 June 1966, the formal date for Fysh's retirement, Sir Norman Nock had retired as a director. From 1 July 1966 there were two new appointments to the board, T. J. N. Foley and K. C. Wilkinson. John Ulm suggested to Turner on 5 July that the new board, particularly its new chairman, be introduced to Qantas staff through the company's staff newspaper. Turner turned down the suggestion. In a handwritten note he told Ulm: "Hold for a few months until Roland gets out of the Treasury".[37]

Wilson wrote directly to the prime minister on the question of his salary as part-time chairman of Qantas, pointing out that

The Qantas Board, August 1966. From left: F. C. Derham, secretary; C. O. Turner, chief executive and general manager; J. M. Fotheringham, director; R. R. Law-Smith, vice-chairman; Sir Roland Wilson, chairman; Sir James Kirby, director; K. C. Wilkinson, director; T. J. N. Foley, director; Capt. R. J. Ritchie, deputy chief executive and deputy general manager.

his current public service salary and allowance had for some time past been at least equal to the salaries of both the chief executive and general manager of Qantas and the managing director of the Commonwealth Banking Corporation (each of whom earned $18,500 per annum). The remuneration of the chairman of the Banking Corporation was, he said, thirty-five per cent of the managing director's salary. He suggested the same figure for himself at Qantas ($6,500). This salary level was approved.

Sir Roland Wilson assumed the chairmanship of what was, using the yardstick of total assets, the twentieth largest enterprise in Australia (excluding such dissimilar organisations as banks and insurance companies). Other yardsticks of comparison were hard to find because many large Australian companies, including the biggest, Broken Hill Proprietary, still refused to disclose the most meaningful of comparative figures: sales. Of the nineteen companies larger than Qantas in terms of assets, however, seven were owned and controlled by overseas interests — Shell, General Motors Holden, ICIANZ, Mobil, BP, Conzinc Rio Tinto, and Mt Isa Mines. On this basis, Qantas was therefore the thirteenth largest Australian enterprise, rather than the twentieth largest enterprise in Australia.

Qantas was proud of its status as one of the few representatives of Australian economic life in 1966 that was not dominated by foreign capital. Australia did not, for example, have its own shipping line. It controlled only three per cent of its pharmaceutical industry, five per cent of oil refining and distribution, six per cent of its motor vehicle industry, and fifteen per cent of Australian oil exploration. A recent survey by the Department of Trade and Industry had shown that 748 companies engaged in manufacturing were controlled by overseas interests; of these, 506 firms were one hundred per cent overseas controlled and owned assets worth $3,355 million. Between twenty-five and thirty per cent of Australian secondary industry was, in 1966, controlled by foreign capital.

By contrast, Qantas (owned, of course, completely by the Australian government) not only earned foreign exchange for Australia but repaid their owner, in 1965, by way of dividend and taxation $7.4 million on an investment of just under $40 million. Qantas, with foreign currency income of $74 million, were seventh on the list of Australia's export industries. Since World War II they had doubled in size every five years and expected to continue their rapid growth. By 1970, Qantas projected that export earnings would place them fifth in the national economy, after wool, wheat, meat and ores, and well ahead of sugar and fruit.

Qantas were by far the biggest aviation organisation in Australia when Wilson became chairman. With a revenue of $2.3 million each week, they were larger than TAA and Ansett-ANA combined. Internationally, in terms of capacity ton miles flown, passenger miles flown, and seat miles available they ranked nineteenth among the world's airlines and ninth among those operating international routes. The driving force and genius behind the growth of the airline had been its general manager and chief executive, C. O. Turner.

Dominating the thinking of Turner (and most other major world airlines) in mid-1966 was the reality that the industry was in transition from Boeing 707-size jets to very much bigger aircraft. The first upward movement from the 140-passenger 707s, taking the industry into 1968, was represented by the 250-passenger Douglas DC8-60 series. US carriers had placed orders for it. Beyond, the Boeing 747 promised a passenger capacity approaching 400. Pan American, under its visionary leader Juan Trippe, had announced their order for twenty-five 747s plus an option for a further ten. Boeing already had a full-scale wooden mock-up of the airliner. It was due to enter airline

363

service in 1969, only three years ahead. Qantas were unwilling to move to the stretched DC8 because of the attendant crewing and engineering problems with a mixed aircraft fleet. Boeing, for technical reasons, could not stretch their 707 design further. Their only option had been to produce a completely new type. Boeing had been unsuccessful in the competition to provide the United States government with its huge new C5A military troop and cargo carrier but found an outlet for the expertise acquired in its studies in the concept for a big new civil airliner. An airliner of such size depended, of course, on the availability of a suitable engine. There had, as a result of the design competition for the giant troop carrier, been a breakthrough in the field of engine design. General Electric had developed a new engine for the C5A producing 41,000 pounds of thrust. Their competitor, Pratt & Whitney, had developed an engine of similar power. As the General Electric engine was to power the military carrier, Boeing saw the opportunity to use the Pratt & Whitney turbofan in their design for the huge new 747. (Douglas also had their own jumbo jet civil design, the DC10. In 1966 it was at a less advanced stage than the Boeing 747 project as Douglas saw no requirement for such a large airliner before 1975.)

The only supersonic airliner with a definite delivery date was the Anglo-French Concorde. Qantas had reserved delivery positions for four of them. "At this stage," wrote Capt. Bert Ritchie in 1966, "the Concorde project is reminiscent of the Comet. It promises to be a pretty comfortable, smallish aeroplane for which Qantas has a use – but that's as far as it goes. In the matter of speed and size, the designers elected to aim only as high as they could encompass with existing technology – existing metallurgy and an existing powerplant. On the other side of the Atlantic, the Americans are thinking bigger and faster; aiming higher." The Americans, for their SST project, had organised a government-sponsored competition in which over eighty experts were to evaluate the entries. Boeing and Lockheed were the competitors, and the result of the competition was to be announced early in 1967. Even in its initial concept, the United States supersonic transport was much bigger than Concorde. Some 270 feet long, it promised to have twice the passenger capacity and be forty per cent faster, with the same range. "But it will cost something like $35 million", wrote Ritchie. "Two to three times the price of Concorde. Much profound thought will precede any decision to commit ourselves to this sort of outlay."[38] Qantas, nevertheless, had reserved their place for six US SSTs on the production line.

Turner, in mid-1966, saw these new jumbo jets, as they had already been christened, as complementary to the coming supersonic airliners. The one would provide high speed without reduction in fare levels, the other promised a drop in passenger mile costs, in his view, of about fifteen per cent. "The other big problem", he wrote, "is aircrew – firstly to train the scores of new crews we need and, meanwhile, to obtain the highest possible productivity from the crews we have already. Undeniably, productivity is down, to the extent that we find it difficult to maintain our present pattern of services, let alone expand. Unless crew productivity can be lifted, utilisation of our aircraft which is essential to our economics is going to fall."[39]

Aircraft magazine, in the editorial of its July 1966 issue, referred to a possible Qantas investment programme for supersonic and subsonic aircraft and equipment "of staggering proportions – $600 million or more". It commented, however: "In its approach to these and other normal problems of a big airline, Qantas is completely realistic and unafraid. It is much more concerned with those problems arising from the current shortage of pilots . . ."

Qantas were even more concerned with the worsening conflict with their existing pilots. They had already paid to the pilots the fifteen per cent salary increase recommended in the Isaac report (though they had not been a party to the Isaac inquiry). It was a move undertaken at the urging of Sir Henry Bland with the aim of getting overseas pilots to remove various sanctions against Qantas operations. By doing this Qantas had, in Turner's view, lost any effective bargaining power to settle other outstanding differences. He told the minister for labour and national service (now L. H. E. Bury) that there still remained twenty unresolved matters. "We would", he wrote, "be very seriously compromised if the Domestic Airlines accepted the present demands of the AFAP." Applied to Qantas, the AFAP demands would, said Turner, give a Qantas senior training captain a salary of $16,800 and the airline's chief pilot, training and development, a salary of $17,472. By comparison, Qantas's deputy general manager's salary was $15,000 and that of the chief executive $18,500. "It will be seen", Turner commented, "that proposed pilots' salaries if agreed to would exceed those of every company executive with the exception of the Chief Executive".[40] Only four days later, Turner wrote to Wilson:

"In view of the cave-in by Ansett, followed meekly by TAA, the next assault by the AFAP will be on Qantas and we can expect heavy pressures almost immediately". The latest claim by the AFAP would, said Turner, give Qantas pilots at the top of the salary scale $20,500 per year. "However, the famous Harry Bland procedures must be observed": a mediator would be necessary. Turner hoped that it could be a qualified person "a Presidential Member of the Arbitration Commission and not some odd Socialist professor".[41]

On 8 August, the Australian Federation of Air Pilots proposed that Qantas introduce the North American bidding system for its pilots. The new Qantas chairman acted speedily. On 18 August the Qantas board met both the minister of civil aviation and the minister of labour and national service. The object of the meeting, he told the ministers, was to inform them of the likely cost of the carry-over into Qantas of the domestic airlines' settlement, the latest AFAP claims, and other related issues in dispute, some involving costs, others disciplinary and operational problems and the repercussions in other wage and salary areas "of any settlement conceivably satisfactory to the pilots". It was the view of the directors, Wilson told the two ministers, "that it is becoming increasingly difficult to maintain operational integrity under current conditions". The loyalty of senior staff and their preparedness to carry on was, he said, fast being exhausted. Wilson also, he said, wished to express the directors' intense dissatisfaction with the present organisation of industrial relations with Qantas aircrews. He wanted guidance from ministers on its future conduct.

Wilson pointed out the possible extraordinary flow-on effects from salary levels sought by pilots. First, the top company pilots, who had been promoted to management appointments because of their outstanding operational performance, could not reasonably be expected to continue functioning in these positions unless they, too, received similar salary adjustments, and "several have already indicated that they are not willing to do so". An extension of such salary increases to the top executive staff of the company, said Wilson, could not then be avoided. "Thus, in respect to the two top Management appointments, we get into the area of the Higher Salaries Committee of Cabinet, and this has implications which can lead to a general flow into the salaries of higher Public Servants, Judges, Arbitration Commissioners and others. A flow-over into the workshop area is probable . . ." Directors were, he said, concerned about the company's ability to operate services efficiently and effectively and at the same time maintain proper safety standards and discipline. "The industrial procedures under which we are now operating appear to have accentuated the problem of indiscipline which has now reached a critical stage. I have been shown a most disturbing letter today from the Company's Manager of Flight Operations [Capt. A. Wharton], himself an ex-pilot and appointed to that position because he was one of the best pilots in the Company." Wilson quoted from the letter:

> It is my considered opinion that the next few months will prove disastrous to Qantas . . . Over the last month it has become absolutely clear that the AFAP's intention is to ensure that during their employment with the Company, pilots – in conjunction with the AFAP – will have the sole rights over their disposition during their working life . . . A joint QEA-AFAP committee which has been operating to assess pilot capabilities is proving that the AFAP representatives are not objective in their consideration of operational capabilities of pilots. Almost every decision made in the Operations Department is challenged by the AFAP . . . The AFAP dictates on all matters affecting pilots' careers is gravely undermining the supervisory pilots' role in ensuring safety of operation and proper administrative control. Indeed, if no halt is made to the demands and dictatorial attitude of the AFAP . . . it is doubtful that the supervisory element amongst the pilots will remain in their jobs – and this must inevitably result in a disintegration of the Company's flying operations.

Wilson commented: "Ministers should appreciate that these people have quite simply reached the stage where they feel they cannot and will not carry on any longer under circumstances where they are subjected to personal abuse and to refusals by pilots to accept Company decisions". Morale generally amongst senior Qantas staff had been affected. The pilots had been given attention because of their militancy whereas senior administrative and executive staff, particularly in regard to salary questions, had received less effective consideration. "These people are the backbone of the Company's administration and management. They are the people with whom I personally, some three or four months ago, had to plead with to carry on in what I had to admit were quite untenable circumstances." Wilson stressed that it was necessary to introduce a new system for the management of industrial relations and disputes. [42]

The shortage of pilots and the lower than optimum aircrew productivity had limited Qantas growth in 1966 to below half that of the world average of 15 to 20 per cent. Since 1961, however, when growth had also slowed, Qantas had shared in the consistent world traffic growth. One result of the 1966–67 restraint on growth had been a minimal increase in employee productivity (in terms of capacity ton miles per employee) of only 1 per cent. (In 1962–63, by contrast, productivity had grown by 18.5 per cent.) For the first time in Qantas's postwar history, staff numbers were now increasing at a faster rate than work performed. Past records of the industry had shown that for large international carriers, staff should grow at less than half the rate of airline capacity. In Qantas, staff numbers had been allowed to rise by approximately five hundred in the last part of the previous financial year in the belief that the company needed strengthening in certain areas and as a result of various long-term development projects (Qantam data processing centre, supersonic studies, cadet pilot training etc). "The only consolation which we can gain from the present deplorable situation in regard to staff productivity", said a report in September 1966, "is that our existing staff would, with some exceptions, be capable of handling the additional workload if we were able to mount the services which we have either cancelled or not dared to schedule because of aircrew shortage . . . The present aircraft fleet and staff could probably cope with at least twenty per cent more work." Labour, said the report, constituted about one-third of total costs and was the only part of total expenditure where management had room to manoeuvre.[43] (In actual airliner operation, however, fuel was the largest single item of recurrent cost and constituted the biggest load put aboard passenger aircraft. Of approximately $1 million dollars per year in typical total expenditure for fuel and engineering replacement parts for a standard 707-DC8 type jet airliner, fuel took $650,000.)[14] Low aircraft utilisation, combined with increased salaries and reduced load factors resulting from increased competition, foreshadowed reduced profits for Qantas in the year ahead. "Our current cost levels are . . . being adversely affected by reduced utilisation of aircraft, which is progressively diminishing as we attempt to gain maximum flying from our depleted crew resources by operating route patterns which conserve crew requirements", Turner wrote to Swartz on 28 September.

Qantas had, at the beginning of September rejected the AFAP proposals to introduce a North American bidding system for pilots and had insisted that the earlier pilots' salary claims should be dealt with under the agreed procedures for mediation. Mediation began under D. C. Apsey on 24 October but it was soon evident that the attitudes of Qantas management and pilots were irreconcilable. On 7 November the AFAP asked Apsey to terminate mediation and informed him that they would submit a new claim on salaries. On 17 November Apsey reported, as he was required to do under the agreed procedures, to Sir Henry Bland. On the same day the AFAP announced that a strike ballot would be held. Three days later, on Sunday 20 November, almost ninety per cent of Qantas pilots voted in favour of a strike. The AFAP met Bland in Melbourne the next day and talks with Qantas were organised by Bland for 23 and 24 November. The federation met Qantas delegates, led by Captain Ritchie, in Qantas House.

The AFAP opened by asking: "Are you empowered to negotiate?" The Qantas answer was: "Yes". The AFAP asked: "Are you prepared to negotiate through to a settlement?" Again, the answer was: "Yes".

The AFAP then tabled a schedule of ten industrial claims. Then, for the first time in the whole series of industrial discussions, two operational questions were raised. One was the Qantas plan for resumption of night landings into Djakarta, once weekly, on London-Sydney flights. The other was the proposed introduction by Qantas of two-pilot crews (plus flight engineer and navigator) on the routes to New Zealand and Noumea from 1 February 1967. The AFAP asked for an undertaking that the company would make no further attempt to force pilots to accept two-pilot operations or night operations into Djakarta and make no alterations to operational practices unless such resulted from "normal approach to and evaluation of such practices by the Company and the Federation". The AFAP undertook to process normally and help solve any operational problem raised by the company and, when better relationships existed, examine without prejudice the two-pilot concept.

Qantas replied with a new offer on salary and conditions that increased salaries for supervisory and senior line captains by just under twenty-two per cent and for junior line captains by as much as thirty-six per cent. First officers, second officers, flight engineers, and navigators were all offered rises of approximately twenty-three per cent. The cost to the airline of the increases alone per annum totalled $1,573,899. Ritchie, however, insisted for the company that the federation no longer frustrate the company's plans, approved by the Department of Civil Aviation, for resumption of night operations into Djakarta or the introduction of two-pilot crewing on the short-range New Zealand and Noumea flights. At this point the meeting ended. The AFAP walked out, delivered an ultimatum, and declared that Qantas pilots would go on strike from midnight, Thursday

24 November. At fifteen minutes past midnight on Friday, Qantas pilots due for departure from Hong Kong, refused to fly. Qantas passengers and aircraft at various points around the world were abandoned by their crews. It was the beginning of a crippling strike that was to ground Qantas and last for twenty-eight days.

While the AFAP talks with Ritchie were in progres, C. O. Turner issued a message to all Qantas staff. "If the pilots proceed with the strike and the stage is reached where we have to stand down staff, the Company will try to minimise as far as possible any hardship for all members of staff by such measures, for instance, as allowing you to take arrears of leave". The company, he said, had made application to the Conciliation and Arbitration Commission for stand-down provisions to be inserted where necessary in awards covering staff.[45] One day after the airline's operations ceased, Turner, in a special issue of *Qantas News*, summarised the salary offer made to pilots. At the top of the scale, a Boeing captain was offered $15,250 per annum, an increase of $2,808. "They are", wrote Turner, "demanding a top pay of $17,160 and, in addition, they want the Company to introduce a formula pay system which could raise the earnings of some individual senior pilots (who would be in a position to demand that they operate the most favourable routes) to a figure in excess of $20,000 per annum." The operational principles in dispute, he said, were of serious concern. "In simple terms, the pilots' attitude amounts to a denial of authority by this small but highly paid group of key employees – not only Company authority but Government authority as well." The pilots, said Turner, were attempting to deny management authority to control operational practices. It was a situation that the company would not accept.[46]

With the national airline grounded, the conflict between the pilots and Qantas management was now debated vigorously before the public. The AFAP argued, in a press release:

> The major matter of principle in dispute is the Company's requirement that Aircraft Captains accept direction by the Company in matters of operational judgement, provided of course, such are not prohibited by the Department of Civil Aviation. The pilots point out that this blanket proposal would strip the aircraft commander of his final authority in the exercise of his operational assessment but still leave him with final responsibility in the event of a mishap. This was dangerous and intolerable and contrary to law under Air Navigation Regulations.

The release said that the navigational and landing aids at

Djakarta were so substandard that safe operations could not be conducted at night. "The Qantas pilots state that, while they have certain obligations as employees to Qantas, the employer, this relationship is subordinate to their obligations to their passengers . . . They cannot and will not reverse these priorities." The AFAP said that pilots were willing to examine the proposal for two-pilot crews on some routes

> given time and the details of the training programme . . . but cannot accept directions to operate in this way until satisfied that the elimination of the third pilot does not detract from the safety level available with a co-ordinated three-pilot operation . . . The Federation is most critical that its agreement to waive this principle of individual or collective responsibility in the areas of safety should have been sought by Qantas as part of a settlement of some outstanding industrial issues . . . No doubt the Company will attribute this stoppage to these and decry operational matters. The truth is, these industrial issues appeared possible of solution. It was these that had led to the threat of a strike, and if the Federation's assessment of the possibility of their settlement was correct, there would have existed no cause for the stoppage, except for the Company's insistence that the operational matters referred to and the principle involved be considered in conjunction with them and conceded as part of the package deal. [47]

Qantas prepared a background paper rejecting this argument. "it is impossible to accept the suggestion underlying the Federation's stand – that its conclusions about basic standards should over-ride the decisions of the Department of Civil Aviation and the Company . . . The Federation's views on these matters come from a majority vote of a part-time committee whose members serve on a year-by-year basis. The unique safety record of Qantas reflects the soundness of the DCA-Qantas judgements." The AFAP's demand was impossible, said Qantas. It wanted the right to make decisions on the safety of flight operations, the most important part of the technical activities of the airline. It wanted these relinquished by the department and the company to the federation. On the two operational issues, Qantas quoted from a Department of Civil Aviation statement: "The proposals have been checked out and approved by us as safe operating procedures. They are completely in line with standard operating practices in the world's leading airlines." Other major international airlines, said the department, were operating at night through Djakarta. Qantas prepared similar briefs on particular industrial issues including AFAP proposals that pilot seniority should govern pilot promotion, pilot insistence on first class travel whether first class seats were or were not available (and the guarantee of first class seats for pilots' wives and families), AFAP demands for the reintroduction of long-term crew postings to London, and meal allowances.[48]

The government backed the Qantas management stand. William McMahon, as acting minister for labour and national service, had warned the pilots on 28 November that they should return to work or face the consequences. After consultation with Swartz, he issued a press statement:

> The issue in the current strike by the pilots of Qantas is simple. Is Australia's international airline to be run by Qantas, subject to the rulings of the Department of Civil Aviation, or by the dictation of the Pilots' Federation? The responsibility of a Captain of a particular aircraft faced with a particular situation that goes to the safety of that aircraft and its passengers is not in question: that is laid down in the Air Navigation Regulation. The Pilots' Federation goes far beyond this. It is engaged in a deliberate challenge to the authority of the Management of Qantas and the Director General of Civil Aviation . . . The present dispute has to be seen against a pattern of activity over a number of years. The current strike is the latest attempt to force acceptance of this on Qantas and the Director General . . . On the purely industrial side, the Federation's behaviour has been equally arrogant . . . The Government will not allow pilots, any more than any other group in the community, to act with such contemptuous disregard of the interests of Australia's international airline . . . The present anarchy cannot be tolerated.[49]

The AFAP responded on 30 November by asking the International Federation of Airline Pilots' Associations to consider taking action if the Australian government should take strong action against striking Qantas pilots, calling McMahon's statement "post electoral arrogance". The federation warned that the strike could spread to the domestic airlines.

From midnight on Thursday 1 December, 4,530 Qantas staff were stood down and the company warned that more would be put off as sections of the company's operations were closed down. In Canberra, McMahon said: "This is our hour of decision. We are not stopping now." He had, he said, had amendments to legislation drafted ready to introduce to bring the pilots within the arbitration system before the end of the previous Parliament. "I did not go ahead because I believed they would honour their undertaking to exhaust all processes of negotiation before resorting to strike action. They have failed to do so and we shall certainly go ahead now."[50]

Goodbye to "Empire" 1967

Although flights on some Qantas routes were operated on limited frequencies within forty-eight hours from the end of the pilots' strike, the progressive build-up to normal operations was not completed for almost four weeks. The effects of the grounding of the airline were felt for much longer as passenger and cargo traffic was diverted to other airlines. The company estimated that the strike caused a direct loss in revenue of $12 million. C. O. Turner, in a letter to Dr Walter Berchtold, president of Swissair, commented on 12 January:

> Our pilots' strike was a completely stupid affair (as all these types of strikes are). It seems to me in retrospect that nothing we would have done could have avoided it because the pilots built themselves up into a psychological state of mind where they had to have a strike to show how powerful they were. Also, perhaps, to line themselves alongside their brother pilots in many other international airlines who have gone on strike or threatened strike over the last year or so. In a time of very severe shortage of pilots worldwide, this "ganging up" on an international basis is a most serious affair. I am not sure what we, as Presidents of airlines, can do in order to combat it, but I certainly feel it is worth an exchange of ideas between us.[1]

Although Sir Roland Wilson, backed by the Australian government, had given Turner full support when the pilots had finally decided to use their powerful strike weapon, the strike was a blow to Qantas that some saw as a manifestation of Turner's rigidity in management-pilot relations and his failure, over a period of eight years, to effect a workable modus operandi. As Ulm had pointed out in his blunt note to Turner, the failure

373

of management to resolve the long and intensifying conflict with the pilots was one of two issues on which Turner was vulnerable. The other, which Ulm had identified simply and clearly, was Turner himself and his drinking habits. "Outside the company," Ulm had written with some prescience at the time of the Fysh succession, "it is doubtful if you can survive on this issue."

Turner was not to survive. Although Wilson's appointment as chairman had been seen by those close to Turner as the best possible one, short of Turner's own appointment, it soon became clear to both men that they would clash. Wilson had, after careful deliberation, set down specific guidelines for the definition of the role of the chief executive. They were faultless in their perception of proper chairman-chief executive relationships. But they took little account of Turner's style of management over many years or of his personality. It was Turner's style to lead. He had built a team around him who, in every facet of the airline's operations, were immensely competent and utterly loyal. The policies and strategies that had been developed under his leadership in the demanding postwar years had won for Qantas the respect of the airline industry worldwide. The Qantas board and the Australian government had, almost without exception, recognised the rightness of his views and accepted them. In that sense he had led the board and the government as well as the management, though the contributions of both to Qantas's growth and success had been vital elements. In essence, however, Turner had asserted his own vision and his own will with little restraint from others. When he met opposition from his peers or his betters and he had before him the alternatives of compromise or conflict, he preferred to fight. He fought endlessly with the director-general, Don Anderson; he drove successive BOAC leaders almost to despair by his single-mindedness; in New Zealand he was seen over many years as a threat to the emergence of an independent national airline; with the pilots' federation he was not prepared to concede even in the slightest way management's right to manage. He lacked completely any reverence for his institutional betters. As Law-Smith observed, it was impossible to discipline him.

He now had a chairman whose contribution to Qantas in financial matters, particularly in their implementation through the highest levels of the bureaucracy and the ministerial maze of Canberra, had been invaluable. He respected Wilson. But he was not able to defer or to submit to constraints, however proper or subtle. Sir Roland Wilson, in his service as secretary to the Treasury, chairman of the Commonwealth Banking

374

Corporation, and chairman of Qantas was, by any standards, a man of vast achievement and a great Australian. In early 1967 he was still at his post as secretary to the Treasury and was part-time, nonexecutive chairman of Qantas. He had, however, indicated to the prime minister, Harold Holt, that he wished to leave the Treasury. It was also his intention, though only part-time chairman of Qantas, to devote a considerable proportion of his time to the airline. Wilson had been head of the most influential of all government departments in the national capital for many years. If Turner knew how to lead, Wilson knew how to rule. Turner, under his new chairman, continued to manage in his accustomed way and made no attempt to moderate his drinking. He soon found himself, however, excluded from some sessions of board meetings. Those close to him, like his able and long-serving personal assistant, Colin Porter, tried to warn him that there was a battle in progress and that his future was at stake. Within a few months of Wilson's appointment, it began to dawn on Turner that his advisers were right, and that he had lost the battle.[2] He was told that he would be retired at the age of sixty, with effect from 30 June 1967.

Turner resisted the move. In a letter to Wilson he set out an unemotional but reasoned case why he should, in the interests of Qantas, continue on in his position beyond the age of sixty. There was a meeting in Wilson's office of the two most senior board members, the new part-time chairman, and Robert Law-Smith, vice-chairman. Wilson showed Law-Smith Turner's letter and asked for his comments. "He mustn't stay", was Law-Smith's reply. Wilson agreed with him. The two men pondered what was a potentially explosive situation.

"I wonder how we should handle it", mused Wilson. There was only a short pause, then Law-Smith replied: "I think we should get him a knighthood".[3]

Wilson took the matter of a knighthood directly to the prime minister and was delighted, if surprised, at Holt's ready acquiescence. Anderson and Swartz were, said Wilson, furious that all this was done without reference to them. In Wilson's words, C. O. Turner's knighthood was arranged "to sweeten the pill of his retirement".[4]

On 15 April 1967 a press release was issued:

> The Chairman of Qantas Empire Airways Limited, Sir Roland Wilson, said today that Mr C. O. Turner CBE would be retiring from his position of Chief Executive and General Manager of the Company on 30 June next. Capt. R. J. Ritchie, who has been Mr

Turner's deputy since the retirement of Capt. G. U. (Scottie) Allan in 1961, will succeed Mr Turner as General Manager and will be the chief executive officer of the Company . . . Mr Turner has been invited to devote part of his time in the future to special advisory work for Qantas in fields where his special knowledge and experience would be of great assistance to the airline.[5]

The letters to Turner, following this announcement, poured in from all over the world. To Courtlandt S. Gross, Lockheed's retiring chairman, he replied: "When I wrote to you on 21 February about your retirement the final details of my own retirement had not been worked out. Our retiring age is officially the 30 June after reaching sixty years and since I was sixty on 13 February 'the time has come', so to speak."[6]

To Lockheed's Australian representative, E. L. Heymanson, he wrote:

It is something to have reached sixty. Many of my good friends have passed away before this and I know what a great loss Bill Taylor was to us at the early age of fifty-seven. I am lucky to be able to retire when I am fit and well . . . I am not anxious to be over-burdened with Committees or Boards. Particularly, I want to avoid any commitment to Government service in the future! . . . Tremendous developments will come in aviation. Jets have literally changed the world in the last ten years. The job of my successors will be to try and convince the Government in big enough terms in order that Qantas can pace it with the big boys such as Pan Am, TWA, the Germans and the French.[7]

Dick Shaw, technical director of the International Air Transport Association and former Qantas technical development manager, wrote to him: "I sense that this announcement has come as the result of some crisis and no doubt will be associated in your own mind with some disappointment . . . I, and I am sure every one of your colleagues in the Company high and low, have the most tremendous admiration for what you have done as Chief Executive to bring Qantas from a very small and remote airline into one of the greatest carriers in the world."[8] Turner responded: "To some extent I have had my fill of politics and civil servants and pilots' problems and on reflection over the last few weeks I believe it is best for me to have a rest and rearrange my thinking . . . As you well know and have so ably expressed it, the technical developments of civil aviation are really far ahead of the ground developments. The immense capital outlays required over the next twenty years are likely to frighten governments—and this particularly applies to Australia in my mind."[9] Turner wrote to M. Herries, of

Jardine Matheson, in Hong Kong: "As you are aware, we have a new Chairman and almost completely a new Board and to a significant degree it has altered the relationships within the Company itself, and after very careful consideration the Board has decreed, and I am going to agree, that I will retire as Chief Executive on 30 June . . . In all the circumstances it is probably best that we reorganise now with a new Management team, not only to initiate the expansion [ahead] but also to carry it on in the next ten to fifteen years."[10] Air Chief Marshal Sir Frederick Scherger, chairman of Trans-Australia Airlines, wrote: "To me, Qantas is a great airline which has achieved its enviable position because of your imagination, drive and judgement".[11] Turner confided to Sir Basil Smallpiece, who had written warmly to him: "Perhaps it was inevitable that once I missed out on the Chairmanship myself, that I should end up retiring at our normal retiring age of sixty".[12] From F. D. C. Caterson, who had fought him so hard as an official of the Australian Air Pilots Association, came a personal tribute: "I did want to say how sorry I am personally to see you go at such a critical stage of Qantas' history . . . I have often been privileged to say . . . that the best boss I ever had was C. O. Turner."[13] There were many more such letters. In an interview with the *Australian Financial Review*, Turner summed up some of his feelings. The two most difficult challenges, he said, had come after World War II when Qantas was under enormous political pressure to buy British aircraft. "Politically and emotionally we were committed to buying the British Tudors", he recalled. "It was a tremendous problem to persuade the Government to let us buy the Constellation. The man who backed Qantas and let us do it was Ben Chifley." The next big crisis, he said, came with the Comet. "We had everyone, from royalty down – tremendous pressure – on the side of the Comet. We believed in our own judgement and didn't order, and events proved us right."

The *Financial Review* article commented on Turner's imminent departure: "The appointment of Australia's top civil servant to the position of chairman, and the incorporation of his particular vision of Qantas' future, can hardly have been without effect". One of the major Qantas achievements during Turner's career, it said, came after four years of preparation and the most careful timing. "He decided that the airline would offer the United States all rights in, through and from Australia in return for the Qantas right to fly across the United States. That particular right, won in 1957, coupled with the Qantas

377

absorption of British Commonwealth Pacific Airways, made Qantas a big airline." The article concluded: "To the outsider, Mr C. O. Turner's most vehement antagonists in public have been the Qantas pilots. Perhaps it is worth recalling their tribute to him a little over a year ago in a letter from the pilots' Federation to the *Financial Review*: 'We [the pilots] have played an important part, we hope. But the whole thing has revolved around Turner and we recognise this'. Most other Australians, Mr Turner, will also recognise it."[14] Lester Brain, who as chief pilot of Qantas had been largely responsible for the inculcation of its high operational standards before World War II and who was to become first general manager of Trans-Australia Airlines, intimately knew of Turner's contribution to Qantas. He wrote:

> It was with real pleasure that I read in Monday's *Financial Review* the comments and credits accorded to you for your performance and achievements as Chief Executive of Qantas. You carried the major role in planning and decision making right from your appointment years before as Assistant General Manager. I would hesitate to conjecture what Qantas would be today were it not for you and the collaboration you had from time to time from vice chairman Taylor . . . The Chief Executive cannot refer a vital decision down or up. Even when it must be referred to the Board for authority, the Chief Executive must make his firm recommendation. And what Board would veto the considered judgement and recommendation of its Chief Executive in such matters? If he is right, then they in due course enjoy the credit. If he is wrong, then they can blame him or replace him . . . Because of my past associations and experience I am much more familiar than most Australians with the history of Qantas events and the extraordinary political and personal problems with which you have had to contend over the last twenty years and I heartily concur in the comments by John Gunn in the *Financial Review*.[15]

Pressure on Qantas increased sharply at the beginning of 1967 to commit the airline to an order for Boeing 747s. The response to Boeing's daring decision to build the airliner, on the then basis of orders from only a few airlines, had been dramatic. Sixteen airlines had announced orders for ninety-nine 747s and Boeing had made a further decision to increase the peak delivery rate to eight and a half aircraft per month by late 1970, one year after the first aircraft were due to enter airline service. On 10 February 1967, Boeing advised Qantas: "Due to the very recent increased activity by customers for the 747 we find we are unable to protect any longer the . . . quotes we have made to Qantas . . . the first customer to commit will receive the deliveries".[16]

The minister for civil aviation, R. W. Swartz, referred to Qantas needs for Boeing 747s in February when he told the government, after referring to its approval to replace the airline's existing eleven Boeing 138Bs with ten 338Cs in the previous October, that "the company has not yet crystallised its forward planning because many significant technical and financial details of the so-called jumbo jets and SSTs are still uncertain. However, it is clearly necessary for Qantas to plan on introducing these advanced types. It is likely the jumbos will be available for delivery in 1971–72 . . . and the United Kingdom-French Concorde around 1972–73, with larger US versions some three to four years later." Qantas, said Swartz, had tentatively estimated a need for four Concordes and six US SSTs costing overall at least $320 million, plus an initial five jumbos costing $120 million. Deposits, he said, would have to be placed at an early date. In addition, normal traffic growth would necessitate the acquisition of additional Boeing 338Cs from 1969 onwards. (In the United States the government-organised SST competition had been won by Boeing. Turner wrote to Lockheed's retiring Courtlandt Gross: "It must have been a great disappointment for you to lose the SST Competition. It is no secret now that Lockheed had our vote, but I am convinced that the weight of Pan American's opinion swayed the decision. I will not be active at the time the 'monster' is flying, but I hope I will be alive to see it.")[17]

Boeing, in mid-March, offered Qantas tentative delivery dates for three 747s in August, October, and November 1971 but the dates were "subject to prior sale" and, in order to obtain firm delivery, Qantas was required to make an initial down payment of $100,000 per aircraft and to sign a letter of agreement. Boeing further expected that this letter of agreement would be followed by the signing of a definitive contract three months later with a further payment of 2.5 per cent of the value of the aircraft, less the amount of the deposits paid – amounting in total to approximately $500,000 per aircraft. In mid-March, Qantas concluded that the earliest possible date on which it could make the required deposit of $100,000 per aircraft was the end of July but on 30 March the director of technical services, R. J. Yates (later to become chief executive of Qantas), recommended payment of the deposit as soon as possible to avoid losing the delivery positions offered by Boeing. "I feel the payment of the initial $100,000 is to allow Boeing Sales to demonstrate to

Boeing Management that Qantas is sincere in its requirements to obtain early delivery of the 747 aircraft", he wrote.[18]

These impending commitments, on a scale never previously experienced by Qantas, came as the airline faced a difficult 1967–68 fiscal year, partly because of rising labour costs and partly because of the continuing low utilisation of aircraft and staff. A full year in which salary increases granted in 1966 would apply coincided with stagnation in staff productivity. (Productivity in capacity ton miles per staff member had risen only marginally from 49,476 in 1965–66 to a projected 51,700 for 1967–68.) It was apparent that the airline was over-staffed.[19] These unwelcome facts were evident as R. M. Ansett increased his representations to the government to restrict the carriage by Qantas of international traffic in Australia unless it was part of a continuous journey without break to or from a place overseas. (In other words, Ansett wished to prevent a traveller from overseas who broke his journey at Perth, for example, from proceeding later to Sydney either by the same or a different international operator.) Turner responded with his usual vigour in a letter to the director-general of civil aviation, Don Anderson, a man Turner had long regarded as a firm Ansett supporter. The adoption of the Ansett policy, wrote Turner, quite clearly would be contrary to the interests of overseas travellers and would discourage tourism.

> Quite apart from the unsoundness of the suggested restrictions, there are legal and political obstacles . . . The imposition of the restrictions would . . . in a number of cases be a breach of Australia's international obligations under its current Air Services Agreements and could be effected only by negotiating new agreements. Apart from the political problems of denouncement and the costs involved in re-negotiating numbers of international agreements, it is quite likely that in the re-negotiations, the privileges allowed abroad to the Australian carrier would be reduced in retaliation.[20]

Wilson responded, on 28 March, to Swartz's letter of 5 January proposing that the Qantas board consider a change of name for the company. "This was considered at our meeting last week," he wrote, "when the directors decided to recommend to you that the name be changed by the deletion of 'Empire'—i.e. to Qantas Airways Limited . . . It is estimated that the cost of the change of name will be to the order of $20,000 to cover the printing of new tickets, other documentation and registration in Australian States and some twenty-two overseas countries. We estimate that four clear months will be required . . ."[21]

On 1 May 1967 there was an informal gathering in the board room at Qantas House to mark the final dissolution of British Commonwealth Pacific Airlines as a company. Qantas had taken over the Pacific operations of BCPA in 1954 in the single biggest postwar expansion of their routes. Liquidation of BCPA commenced in that year but was delayed by extensive litigation in the United States following the serious accident of a BCPA aircraft at San Francisco. (BCPA board and management was completely vindicated by the United States Supreme Court.) The gathering to mark the end of the long, drawnout liquidation process was proposed by the liquidator himself, A. C. Joyce, and attended by Wilson, Law-Smith, Ritchie, other former Qantas directors, BCPA's former general manager, Alex Barlow (now Qantas manager Far East and Tasman), Edgar Johnston, Arthur Coles, and former BCPA chairman, Norman Watt. As a result of the completion of the BCPA liquidation process, Qantas's issued capital rose by $4 million to $39.4 million when four million shares of $1 each were issued to the Commonwealth government in settlement of cash and residual assets acquired by Qantas from BCPA.[22]

In 1967 Qantas saw the spread of a new form of international airline competition from a proliferation of charter companies. The movement had started in America two years before and spread rapidly. To counter it, a number of European airlines (Lufthansa, KLM, SAS, Air France, Sabena, and Alitalia amongst them) had created separate charter companies of their own to operate outside the restrictive orbit of the International Air Transport Association's fare structures. Qantas had, a year before, made approaches to the government to be allowed to develop an internal charter organisation to fit in with the company's pilot training scheme but, because of the restrictions of the domestic two-airline policy, were prevented from going ahead. Turner now proposed to his successor, Captain Ritchie, that before disposing of the remaining eleven Boeing 138B aircraft, they should have a close look at the development of a separate company to operate international charters.

> I think we should work up a scheme to show the possibility of retaining, say, four or five aircraft basing the initial economics on the carriage of migrants and the operation of defense charters, later to be expanded to operate group charters, particularly on the Pacific. I think we ought to form a separate company and my thought is that if we can get some outside capital into it, it might make the approach easier from the point of view of the Govern-

381

ment. The company certainly should operate outside IATA if we cannot meet competition by being within it . . . It will be recalled that we did suggest to the Government that the RAAF should buy three of our 138s for Transport Command but they turned the scheme down . . . Whereas the Government on the score of their two-airline policy could object to our previous proposal for an internal charter organisation, it seems to me that they would find it difficult to object to an overseas charter operation and at the same time allow other charter companies, such as World Airways, to operate to Australia.[23]

A market survey and a broad operational study were undertaken. It was apparent that, in Ritchie's words, the European subsidiaries of the major airlines were "shoe-string operations". He considered

that in the case of our charter company no catering or engineering staff would be employed as all work would be subcontracted or purchased from outside organisations . . . A small commercial department would be necessary to handle marketing and arrange contracts . . . The Director of Commercial Services [Ritchie advised Turner] believes that the formation of a charter company is feasible and envisages a limited amount of charter work in the early stages. A substantial reduction in rates for Inclusive Tours could tap a large market but the trick is to encourage this business without taking away passengers from Qantas and its pool partners.[24]

By 4 May, the director of technical services, Capt. P. W. Howson, advised that Qantas had good prospects of consummating the sale of six more 138B aircraft, leaving five for disposal between August and December 1968, with every indication that these, too, could be disposed of; so "allowing a period of crew training, the earliest practicable date for commencement of a charter subsidiary would therefore be 1 January 1969". By taking up Australia's share of migrant traffic, which a shortage of pilots had previously prevented, said Howson, the charter company would remove the constant threat posed by British Eagle and would, by satisfying the Australian military requirement, prevent further disruption of Qantas scheduled services (such as occurred in 1966). Further, should United States supplemental carriers already licenced by the CAB to operate charters on the Pacific come to Australia, Qantas would be able to compete on equal terms. "The possibility of seeking equity capital on the open market has been considered and discarded. The prime purpose of the subsidiary is not to make large profits (for in doing so it would damage Qantas) but to complement Qantas by performing work which the parent company cannot contemplate because of pilot shortage due to standards which must be maintained, plus IATA restrictions." He recommended acquiring aircraft for the subsidiary on lease-purchase arrangements, but warned that without migrant traffic its operations would not be viable. "It appears that migrant requirements are declining . . . and the future is obscure." Even on the most optimistic basis, broad estimates of revenue and expenditure showed that a Qantas charter company would be only marginally profitable in the early stages. Howson recommended "[making] haste slowly".[25]

The forward assessment of requirements for the main Qantas fleet had meanwhile been studied closely in the light of Boeing's offer on 747 deliveries. Ritchie was able to tell Boeing on 14 April: "We have been working over our figures to see how we could stretch our fleet of twenty-one 707s into the 747 period without taking in more 707s and we believe we can do it – certainly we will not need the fleet of twenty-six 707s that we contemplated in our earlier studies, provided we can obtain four 747s on the dates discussed – August, October, November and December 1971, with an option for a further two in November and December 1972. As far as Qantas management is concerned we have decided we must have 747s . . ."[26]

This Qantas decision to commit to the new generation of huge passenger airliners two and a half times greater than their existing 707-338Cs in passenger capacity had more than the usual financial implications for consideration by the government. Before the board could consider a proposition to approve the purchase of 747s, it needed, Wilson told the minister, "some indication of the Government's policy regarding the availability of suitable aerodromes and terminals for this type of aircraft in Australia". Qantas considered, he wrote, that the 747 would be less demanding on runways and taxiways than the Concorde or Boeing SST and that any improvements contemplated for the introduction of these aircraft would be satisfactory for the 747. "The Concorde could be operating on Qantas routes late in 1972 and the Boeing 747 in late 1971. Therefore if the Boeing 747 is to be operated by Qantas at Australian airports, the runway and taxiway improvements necessary for the Concorde will be required to be completed one year earlier . . . Some additions to the capacity of the terminal buildings at Australian airports will be required."[27] Qantas had, in fact, advised the department that a runway length of approximately 11,000 feet would be required for the 747 and a length of 12,000 feet would be needed for the Concorde and Boeing SST. The department had, as a result, planned a runway length of 12,000 feet for Sydney, Tullamarine (Melbourne), Brisbane, and Nadi (Fiji). The existing runway length of 10,500 feet at Perth was considered satisfactory for both Concorde and 747 operations between Perth and Singapore. Sydney and Nadi were the two airports where most time was needed for improvements to be completed. At Sydney the major work required extension of the existing runway into Botany Bay, with reclamation and rock wall protection to be carried out and the newly made ground consolidated before a start could be made on the runway pavement itself. (In purely technical terms, the 747 was considered by Qantas, despite its size, as employing similar technology in its structure, systems, and power plant to the 707, with few technical innovations.)[28] To permit the introduction of the 747 in 1971, Qantas had concluded that it would be necessary to eliminate all or some of its planned additional 338C aircraft, previously considered necessary to cover expansion needs in the 1969–71 period. Studies showed that the 707 fleet could be held at twenty-one aircraft provided higher seat load factors were accepted, some marginally economic services were sacrificed, cargo growth was restricted, daily aircraft utilisation was increased, and no provision was made for the development of new routes before 1971.

The board considered a memorandum from Ritchie on the 747 procurement programme on 18 May. The total cost of the project to purchase four 747s, he said, including aircraft, spare engines, ground support equipment, simulator, training aids, and buildings and hangars was estimated at $109 million (later revised to $134.5 million). The Department of Civil Aviation had estimated that $60 million would have to be spent on airport work and buildings for both Concorde and the 747, of which approximately $10 million would be attributable to the peculiar needs of the 747. Management, said Ritchie, would make a full submission in June covering the period 1968–69 through to 1974–75 showing the programme of services and aircraft utilisation, estimates of revenue and expenditure, and forecast cash position. Pending that full review he asked board approval to commit $US400,000 to hold delivery positions.[29]

On 1 June, Boeing offered Qantas firm delivery dates for four 747s in August, October, November, and December 1971. On 18 June, Qantas accepted these proposals, subject to government approval, and committed the airline to the coming new world environment for international airline operation in which the mass transit of travellers from a huge and previously untapped market would replace the more sedate and personal approach of the movement of individual travellers. This was the period of change that lay ahead for the chief executive-designate, Capt. R. J. Ritchie. On 30 June 1967, Sir Cedric Turner CBE retired from Qantas.

Capt. "Bert" Ritchie differed in almost every way from C. O. Turner. In temperament he was a courteous, friendly, and like-able man. He had had extensive operational experience as a pilot and was a man of great technical erudition. Born in Sydney in 1915, he had joined Amalgamated Wireless Australasia Limited in 1929 as a cadet telegraphist, convinced even at the age of fourteen that radio and flying were somehow inexorably mixed and would complement each other. He started learning to fly at Kingsford-Smith Aerial Services Limited, Mascot, in DH60 aircraft in 1933. By 1937, he had a commercial pilot's licence, then the top flying licence attainable, plus a first class wireless telegraphy certificate and a second class navigator's licence. (First class certificates dealing mainly with astro-navigation were not available in Australia at that time; Ritchie won one of the first when the examinations were held here.) His routine was to finish work at AWA in the city at six in the morning, then ride his bicycle to Mascot to do some flying.

Bert Ritchie did some part-time flying for Kingsford-Smith Aerial Services until, one Sunday morning, a voice called to him over the fence at Mascot to offer him a job. (Lester Brain, chief pilot for Qantas, had previously offered him a post with the Flying Doctor Service at Cloncurry but Ritchie had declined.) The voice at the fence was that of W. R. Carpenter's first pilot in New Guinea. Ritchie went to New Guinea for two years with Carpenters, then was transferred to Sydney to fly the mail route between Sydney and Rabaul. When the Japanese advanced southward in World War II, he took part in the evacuation of New Britain, New Guinea, and Papua in 1941–42 and in the supply flights into forward areas. In 1943 he saw Lester Brain again and was invited to join the new Qantas service in Perth flying Catalinas across the Indian Ocean. He joined Qantas in October 1943 as a first officer and was promoted to captain in January 1944, flying Catalinas and, later, Liberators and Lancastrians. In all, he made eighty-one nonstop crossings of the Indian Ocean.

After service as flight captain from 1946 on the Sydney-Karachi Lancastrian service, he went to the United States in June 1947 to supervise the flying training programme for the

Constellation 749s and was appointed flight captain, Constellations, from the introduction of these aircraft in December 1947. In June 1948, he was appointed flight superintendent Kangaroo Service. A year later he was appointed assistant operations manager and he ceased regular flying for Qantas in 1951. He became technical manager in 1955 and director of technical services in 1959. Two years later, in 1961, he became deputy chief executive and deputy general manager under C. O. Turner.

Ritchie's reaction to his appointment as chief executive was clear from a letter he wrote to Edgar Johnston on 24 April 1967: "I'm sure you realise that I would have preferred to see things otherwise for some time to come, but our masters thought differently. A great pity and I am indeed sorry for C.O.'s sake."[30]

The new Qantas chief executive, greatly experienced in all operational and technical matters, had closely followed Boeing's introduction and development of the 747. The concept of the 747 was, he said, an accident rather than an objective Boeing initiative. Its birth sprang primarily from two factors: Pratt & Whitney did not win the engine contest for the C5A Galaxy aircraft and Boeing's competitors in civil aircraft, Douglas, were trying to retrieve a competitive position by lengthening their DC8 jet airliner by over thirty feet, to make it the 60 Series DC8. Boeing, very successful in their 707 sales, had optimised the design of their airliner in the initial stages with a short undercarriage. Any attempt to lengthen the 707 to match the bigger DC8 was impossible, simply because the short undercarriage, on take-off rotation, would have produced tail drag along the pavement. The Douglas DC8 stretch promised fifty extra seats per aircraft; Boeing could only stretch by some twenty seats. Boeing saw customers begin to move away.

It was in these circumstances that Pratt & Whitney offered their big new engine (42,000 to 44,000 pounds thrust) to Boeing who polled the world's airlines on the acceptability of a big, new airliner. There was a supporting consensus, but a requirement, since the airlines then believed much future traffic would fly in supersonic airliners, that any big subsonic civil aircraft should have good capability for conversion to a freighter. Freight pallets and container sizes had been internationally agreed at eight feet wide by eight feet high and the aviation industry adopted this standard. Boeing decided that two such containers should fit in their new 747 design side by side, with working clearances at either side and between them. The new airliner, therefore, was given an eighteen feet internal diameter and the pilot's cockpit was placed on top of the main fuselage. In the initial specification, there was no upper lounge, only a cockpit with a vertical ladder leading to it. "Boeing were boxed in to the size of the aeroplane by the size of the engine", said Ritchie. Qantas favoured the general design but were not interested in the first 747 because of its lack of range. Also, in the beginning, it was to prove, both on the drawing board and in airline operation, too big. When Pan American introduced it into airline service, they found it grossly oversized and, so that they would not be perceived as flying large quantities of empty seats around the world, began to give away seats on the most generous terms to employees of almost any airline. (Qantas employees found that they could get much cheaper fares and better discounts flying Pan American than they could with their own company; even employees' parents were offered discounts to fill the new airliner.)

Qantas pressed Boeing for more range in the 747 and Pratt & Whitney for greater engine thrust to preserve take-off performance and rate of climb and initial cruise. More range meant additional tankage and a stronger structure to withstand this higher gross weight. With these modifications adding 33,000 pounds in gross weight, the initial 747 became the 747B. Qantas was the first airline in the world to order (and operate) the 747B. Qantas, said Ritchie, pressed hard for improvements to the 747, in particular mentioning the rough ride experienced by passengers in the very back of the aircraft. The aircraft was so long that in turbulence the autopilot would sometimes be positioning the rudder so that it was sympathetic to a turn it should have been opposing. The fuselage moved within itself and there was pronounced tailwag. Qantas did much exploratory work on the problem and it was overcome by an additional sensing device that took account of the wracking of the fuselage. There were other numerous modifications proposed by Qantas. The most obvious, in terms of cost and physical change to the 747, was the positioning of the aircraft's galley on the lower freight deck in the Qantas aircraft.[31]

Ritchie assumed the leadership of Qantas after a bad financial year in which, to 31 March 1967, the company had suffered a loss of $1.5 million. Widespread increases in wages and salaries, price rises throughout the year, and heavy expenses absorbed while the fleet had been grounded had seriously affected costs. The pilots' strike had been a heavy blow. Operationally, the financial year had seen the withdrawal of Electra aircraft on 28 March from the Wallaby route to South Africa and their replacement by Boeing 707s. On the Kangaroo Route to London regular calls at Amsterdam began and calls were resumed at Bahrein after a lapse of several years. In April, Malaysia-Singapore Airlines began the charter of Qantas 707 aircraft to operate a weekly Singapore-Sydney service through Djakarta and Perth and several charter flights were undertaken for the Australian defence forces. The outbreak of hostilities between the Arab countries and Israel in June 1967 caused a temporary omission of Cairo from the Kangaroo Route and, in April, Karachi was dropped from the route as a port of call. With the introduction of BOAC services on the South Pacific and four Qantas services to the US West Coast per week, the pool partners were able to provide a daily flight from Sydney to London through New York. In Sydney, the Qantam message switching and reservations project began its first stage of operations in May with the transfer of telecommunication message handling and switching to the Qantam Computer Centre in Qantas House. (Reservations control became fully integrated at the end of 1967.) The Qantas fleet, at financial year's end, comprised twelve Boeing 707-138Bs and three Electras (all to be sold) and eight Boeing 707-338Cs (with a further thirteen 338Cs on order).

In a memorandum to Qantas outstations in June 1967, Ritchie summarised the airline's situation.

> To put the matter in a nutshell Qantas, like most other carriers, is experiencing a sharp increase in cost levels (mainly due to wages, which now constitute thirty-five per cent of our total expenditure), revenue yields are falling and this year we have made way on the Pacific and Singapore-Australia for our pool partners BOAC and MSA respectively. As from 1 April, the Company entered into new pooling arrangements across the Pacific with BOAC and Air New Zealand, coinciding with the introduction of BOAC's London-Sydney via San Francisco operations. In addition, with the inauguration of Sinagpore-Australia services by MSA, a new Australia-Asia pool embracing Qantas, BOAC, Air New Zealand, Air India and MSA commenced on 1 April 1967. These new operations have influenced our revenue results quite significantly.

(Qantas revenue in the Pacific had been severely reduced in successive years by the introduction of Air New Zealand and BOAC operations and was, in 1967, subjected to a determined onslaught by Pan American, who not only had the advantage of serving all important US traffic ports but also exercised cabotage rights denied to the pool partners.)[32] On an industry basis, wrote Ritchie, the most significant trend was that the reducing unit costs experienced in previous years had halted. Generally speaking, the airline industry had achieved all of the cost benefits possible with existing subsonic aircraft. This trend in unit costs had come when revenue yields were declining and it seemed unlikely that the profitability of the industry generally could be maintained without an appreciable increase in load factors.[33]

On 11 July, a new company organisation was announced. It had been twelve years since the last major reorganisation, a period in which staff had grown from 5,400 to 10,150, passengers carried from 135,000 to 480,000, and revenue earned from $32 million to $132 million. The new organisation gave the company two deputy general managers: Capt. P. W. Howson became deputy general manager (technical) and C. W. Nielson became deputy general manager (commercial). New departments and new positions were created and various departmental responsibilities realigned. The changes were extensive. The aim,

The Qantas management group July 1967. From left: F. C. Derham, secretary and director of finance; C. W. Nielson, deputy general manager (commercial); Capt. R. J. Ritchie, general manager; Capt. P. W. Howson, deputy general manager (technical); C. E. Oliver, director of policy development; and B. J. Hinchcliffe, director of administration and personnel.

Ritchie told staff, was to concentrate on important areas of the company's expanding business at a time of sharply increased competition.

On 25 July 1967 Sir Roland Wilson submitted to the government a formal proposal that Qantas should buy four Boeing 747s for delivery from August 1971, plus take out options for a further two. "The introduction of the 707-338C aircraft is progressively reducing our 707 operating costs and this trend should continue as we move towards an all-338C fleet. Seat-mile costs will then be as low as can be achieved with 707 aircraft and would be expected to rise gradually thereafter. To offset this rise, a more economic aircraft is required and our recent studies show that the seat-mile costs of the larger 747 will be ten to fifteen per cent lower than those of the 707", he wrote. The 747 would also, Qantas believed, have much greater passenger appeal. "This view is supported by the eighteen major airlines, including our pool partners and major competitors, which have already placed firm orders for 109 Boeing 747s and by others which are stated to have placed deposits on a further forty to fifty aircraft." Qantas had, said Wilson, examined the alternative of buying eleven or twelve additional Boeing 707-338Cs. Such a project would cost about eleven per cent less than the Boeing 747 purchase but would mean, he wrote, purchasing obsolescent aircraft with higher seat-mile costs and poorer passenger appeal. "We have therefore paid the Boeing Company a holding deposit to secure delivery positions . . . this will be refunded if Government approval is not obtained." Qantas had also, he said, obtained options for two additional 747s. "These options would provide some cover for the possibility that we decide not to proceed with the Concorde purchase. We have definite doubts as to its passenger appeal and economics and are awaiting further information before making a decision late in 1968. Three 747 aircraft would be required to provide the same productivity as the four Concordes which we have reserved. The Boeing 2707 supersonic transport, which should be available to Qantas by the end of 1975, is expected to be a more economic aircraft than the Concorde."

Wilson summarised the capital requirements for the Boeing 747 project. Four fully equipped aircraft would cost $A74 million; spare engines, initial aircraft spares, ground support and workshop equipment, tools, simulator, and training aids would cost $A49 million; additional hangars and buildings would cost $A11.5 million. The total project cost was estimated

at $A134.5 million." (The two aircraft on option involved an additional $A48 million.)

The 747 purchase was not, of course, the only aircraft project facing Qantas. There were outstanding orders for a further thirteen Boeing 338Cs ($82 million), $30 million by March 1983 on Concorde progress payments, and $A8 million in progress payments for the Boeing SST project.

Wilson wrote that "in planning a development programme as large as this, it seems essential to seek additional capital from the Government to avoid a progressively increasing imbalance in the Company's capital structure . . . The last capital subscription from the Commonwealth was in July 1962." He proposed an additional $50 million in capital that "would approximately restore the 1973 asset-capital and loan-capital ratios to their 1967 values".[34]

While Qantas were now firmly committed (subject to government approval) to the introduction of the new jumbo jets, future involvement in supersonic operations was less certain. Three and a half years previously, in January 1964, Qantas had reached agreement with the US Federal Aviation Agency to reserve delivery positions for six US supersonic airliners and had paid initial deposits of $US100,000 per aircraft. The agreement called for a further $US100,000 per aircraft six months

July 1967. Signing the purchase agreement for the first four Boeing 747s. From left: Phil Howson, Qantas; John Anderson, Boeing; Bob Heleniak, Boeing; Rudy Hillinger, Boeing; Bob Walker, Qantas; Graham Kench, Qantas; Tim Applegate, Boeing; George Marshall, Boeing; Capt. R. J. Ritchie, Qantas (seated).

after the start of construction of the prototype. In January 1967 it was announced that Boeing had won the US supersonic airliner design competition with their Model 2707 variable geometry wing proposal and on 1 May the US government contracted with Boeing for the development and flight testing of two prototype SSTs. Qantas was advised that its second payment was now due on 31 October 1967.

Qantas did not expect to make any firm commitment to a definitive purchase of the big American supersonic airliner before mid-1969. No exact specification of the aircraft had been given to the airlines but Boeing and their SST customers had set up a number of technical committees to evaluate and advise Boeing on all aspects of the SST design and operating characteristics. (Twenty-six airlines had reserved delivery positions for 129 aircraft; Qantas held delivery positions 28, 34, 48, 60, and 68 with an initial delivery date expected in 1975.) A board memorandum of 16 August 1967 described the Boeing design as promising, with potential for future development. "From initial studies its operating costs, although not as low as the B747's, are expected to be better than the Concorde. We expect the Boeing SST will be our main supersonic vehicle in the 1975–85 time period, irrespective of whether or not we proceed with the purchase of the Concorde." Management recommended that the six delivery positions be retained by making the second required payment to the US Treasury. [35]

The large sums of money needed for additional 707-338Cs, the new 747Bs, and the supersonic airliners, together with expenditure on airport runways and terminal facilities, had to be justified carefully to government. Swartz, in putting forward the Qantas requirements, referred to the steady increase in international air traffic since 1960–61, and the anticipated growth rate for the current year of approximately eighteen per cent. Cargo traffic was increasing at an even faster rate. Qantas (except for the year of the pilots' strike) had regularly exceeded the average industry growth rate. Qantas, said Swartz, believed current trends would continue and that passenger traffic into and out of Australia would double from the 1966 level by 1970 and triple by 1973. Again, cargo would grow even more rapidly. The company, he said, envisaged healthy growth beyond 1973 and their estimates agreed with those of the International Civil Aviation Organisation. Particularly rigorous competition was expected from the highly capitalised and well-equipped US airlines. Qantas, he said, thought the Boeing 747 was the next logical step, particularly if the company decided against the Concorde. They would introduce the aircraft at a maximum operating weight of 710,000 pounds, requiring a runway length of approximately 12,000 feet at Sydney, Melbourne, and Brisbane (though possible escalation of weight to about 750,000 pounds as engine thrust increased might push the required runway length to 12,500 feet).

The Swartz submission was given general support and the government, on 24 October, reaffirmed its commitment to the continued development of Qantas as a major operator of international air services. Authority was given to place firm orders for Boeing 747Bs, conditional on financing arrangements satisfactory to the treasurer. (Qantas was not, itself, to borrow overseas as this was considered a matter for the Commonwealth government.) No approval was given at this stage, however, for the programme of necessary airport and airways works.

The background to the Qantas plans for continuing and substantial fleet expansion was the sustained growth in demand for international air travel into and out of Australia. International air passengers in and out of the country had exceeded 560,000 in 1966, with an average annual passenger growth rate of over eighteen per cent for the previous three years, a rate in excess of the world growth average. The capacity provided by the scheduled international airlines serving Australia had not only matched the traffic offering but had enabled the encouragement of additional traffic. Australian government policy had been to avoid excess capacity in total but to stimulate traffic growth of end-to-end traffic. To accomplish this, it had insisted on the inclusion in the various bilateral air agreements of principles that ensured traffic expansion while guaranteeing the strength of Qantas together with opportunities for the efficient foreign airlines.

The government had addressed itself particularly to the problem of the necessarily high cost of travel between a remote Australia and other world centres. Despite the growing complexity of international airline operations and the larger units of capital involved in equipment and facilities, the international airlines had been remarkably successful in achieving stable international air fares against a backdrop of rising prices in other goods and a general decline in the purchasing power of money. The airlines had continued to introduce systematic reductions in fares for tourists with inclusive tour basing fares and group fares. The cost per mile for international air fares on world air routes was consistent with costs for journeys to and from Australia. In November 1967 the cost per mile in Australian cents for typical one-way economy class journeys between Australia and points abroad and for similar journeys between other countries was: Sydney-San Francisco 6.28 (cents per mile); Sydney-New York 5.73; Sydney-London via USA 5.10; London-Tokyo 6.63; London-Rome 9.19; New York-Karachi 6.89; Vancouver-Tokyo 6.84; Sydney-Tokyo 6.66. There was firm evidence of the stability in international air fares for the period 1960–67. The economy fare between Sydney and London had remained unchanged at $A620; between Sydney and San Francisco the fare had dropped slightly from $A500 to $A473; between Sydney and New York it had dropped from $A596.10 to $A580; the Sydney-Tokyo fare had risen slightly from $A405 to $A425.

The government had recently revised its policy on group charter flights, giving increased incentive to their promotion by creating a fare differential between the minimum rate for the charter flight passenger and the group fare on regular services. From 1 November 1967 the minimum rate for charter flight passengers had been reduced from seventy per cent of the normal IATA economy fare to sixty per cent. Despite the stability of the air fare structure, Qantas profits had risen steadily from $775,848 in the year ending 31 March 1961 to $4,030, 183 in 1966. (The 1967 year had, of course, ended with a loss because of the pilots' strike.) At 30 June 1967, Qantas operated seventeen return services a week Australia-New Zealand; fifteen return services a week Sydney-London (via Asia, USA, and Mexico); five return services a week Sydney-San Francisco (one extending to Vancouver each fortnight); four return services a week Sydney-Hong Kong (three extending to Tokyo); one return service a week Sydney-Mexico City, Sydney-Johannesburg, and Sydney-Noumea.

On 1 August 1967, reflecting the long attenuation of Empire links and sentiments between Britain and Australia and the immense changes in Britain's circumstances since the end of World War II, the change of company name from Qantas Empire Airways Limited to Qantas Airways Limited became effective.

Throughout 1967, as the airline made its careful commitment to the future composition of the fleet and as the top leadership and management changed, under the new chairman, Sir Roland Wilson, Qantas and the government had addressed the problem of the unique and massive industrial power of the pilots. The process was a slow one, but the government recognised that the pilots' strike had demonstrated the failure of the Bland Procedures for mediation. The minister for labour and national service, Leslie Bury, told his colleagues in April that, apart from the Crimes Act, the only real sanctions available against the pilots were public opinion and the ultimate one of sweating out a strike. The latter had prevailed in the twenty-eight day strike and the pilots had been shown, in Bury's view, to be as subject to economic pressures as ordinary mortals. In the Australian airline industry as a whole, Bury recognised that Ansett-ANA could not stand the financial consequences of even a short strike and that, as a consequence, Ansett would always be prepared to concede terms of settlement in a dispute that would offer more than anything awarded by an arbitrator. Bury proposed that the Bland Procedures should be replaced by setting up a special tribunal to deal with aircrew disputes, and that responsibility for this area of industrial relations should not be vested in the Conciliation and Arbitration Commission.

At Qantas, negotiations with the pilots on their demand for a North American bidding system type of contract proceeded steadily and an agreement was finalised in September 1967. On 14 September, Captain Holt announced the new agreement to the AFAP convention. "This Federation has an industrial strength that is unique", he told his colleagues. "We can do anything we like—we can do anything lawful that we like."[36]

The pilots had seemingly demonstrated, with great skill and perseverance, that it was possible as a union to operate outside the constraints of the accepted federal system for the settlement of industrial disputes. They had, in the Bland Procedures, been recognised by the government as a unique group. They had both immense power and no great restrictions on its use.

Sir Hudson Fysh, who had now been away from the battle for over a year, commented on the outcome of the pilots' negotiations in a handwritten note on 4 October. He was critical of the Qantas board and of management and summarised his own perspective on the development of the pilots' conflict over the years:

> Now the pilots' trouble is over for the time being and they have been accorded virtually all they asked for, even to the North American type contract. They were fought by Turner over many years. The key point is that practically all that the pilots have been given should have been conceded years ago—and $14 million in one year alone would have been saved, and much goodwill. All right! Why were the concessions not given? That is the question.

395

It goes back to my bitter row, week in week out, with Turner. Also with Taylor. Both hated the pilots and accused me of being on the pilots' side.

QEA management naturally backed Turner. The Board backed Turner. They refused to allow me as Chairman to come into the top action. During this early bad time I had McVey against me too. Jealousy. Law-Smith was with me, but too weak to support me in the Board . . . These were difficult years when I held many views contrary to the Board and when a question came up on an essential pilot matter I found myself the one divergent figure. I made it a rule as Chairman not to isolate myself as one against all when the questions on Turner and the pilots came up. I agreed with them, bowing to their one hundred per cent affinities. My resources? . . . Resignation. I went to Paltridge, the minister, with this possibility. Turner's studied insolence against Paltridge, Williams, Anderson, Smallpiece and against me in the Board-room . . . [is] surely borne out in my private papers, in my correspondence and diary. Yes, but I [too] later berated the pilots for their direct action, strikes and refusal to arbitrate. But this extreme attitude grew up over the years from their long failure to obtain redress.[37]

Despite this sympathetic and conciliatory attitude by Fysh during his years as chairman, Qantas had formally pressed hard for special legislation by the government, from the time of the formation of the pilots' federation, to order and contain the industrial might of the unregistered AFAP. Turner had never wavered in his view that a process of compulsory arbitration was a necessary last step for the settlement of disputes with pilots as it was for other Australian unions. His view was now to prevail. The pilots, by the exercise of the unconstrained industrial power available to them in shutting down the national airline for twenty-eight days, had demonstrated to the government much more forcefully than Turner's sustained arguments, that special legislation was a necessity. A month after Holt's exultant comments to the AFAP Convention, the federal government, on 19 October 1967, introduced into Parliament an amendment to the Conciliation and Arbitration Act creating a special Flight Crew Officers Industrial Tribunal designed specifically to deal with industrial disputes with pilots, navigators, and flight engineers. The new legislation provided for compulsory arbitration. Though the creation of the tribunal was a clear recognition that the government considered flight crew officers to be a unique body, it brought the AFAP firmly back into the accepted and traditional Australian industrial system.

Swartz announced in Parliament on 2 November the government's approval for the order of four Boeing 747s by Qantas
for delivery in 1971 and for options on a further two aircraft.
Approval was also announced to pay the second round of
deposits on the Boeing SST aircraft. In November 1967 Qantas
formally placed its order, the largest single aircraft order in the
history of the company, for four Boeing 747 airliners. They
would, said Qantas, "keep Australia in the forefront of international civil aviation and contribute substantially to the national
balance of payments, to which Qantas has long been a significant
contributor".[38] In December, the minister for civil aviation
recommended to government that the first tower of a revised
twin-tower design for Qantas's future headquarters in Sydney
be erected. The airline was preparing for a new era in international air travel.

Cost Pressures;
Revenue Threats
1968–1969

14 In December 1967, a week before Christmas, the prime minister, Harold Holt, had died in tragic circumstances. A keen and experienced skin diver, the prime minister had entered the surf in challenging conditions, close to the entrance to Melbourne's Port Phillip Bay, from the ocean beach near his house. He was never seen again. The deputy prime minister and leader of the Country Party, John McEwen, formed an interim ministry until, on 10 January 1968, John Gorton succeeded him as prime minister. Civil aviation affairs remained under the control of R. W. C. Swartz. Wilson wrote to Fysh: "It was indeed a sad occasion when Harold Holt passed from us as he had been a long and intimate personal friend and very good friend to Qantas. He will be greatly missed but I hope his successor will be no less useful to us, even if somewhat of a newcomer to the airline industry."[1]

Early in 1968, a dramatic change of attitude by Boeing to their design concept for a supersonic transport altered completely the Qantas time perspective for the possible introduction of its preferred supersonic aircraft. Boeing had, with its swing-wing, variable geometry design, beaten Lockheed's proposed delta wing concept in the US government's SST design competition. Boeing now found that their 2707-200 model SST would have a payload-range performance that was quite unacceptable. Prototype studies showed that there would be only a 1,600-nautical mile range capability, compared with the requirement for an ultimate production aircraft of 3,200 nautical miles. In February, therefore, Boeing was forced to ask for a government directive to cease work on its prototype programme, recommending a complete review aimed at producing a new design by 15 January 1969.

The major changes now proposed by Boeing affected the size of the aircraft and meant the abandonment of the revolutionary swing-wing design. The 2707-200 aeroplane was a 750,000-pounds, 300-passenger aircraft in which the wing could pivot as speed increased, swinging back and integrating with the tailplane for supersonic flight. Boeing now envisaged a fixed wing and a considerably smaller aircraft of less take-off weight carrying about two hundred passengers. For Qantas, this radical change in approach meant that Boeing could not begin commercial deliveries of its supersonic airliner before 1977 at the earliest.

As the new Boeing design developed over the months, it was to become less attractive. "Earlier indications that the Boeing SST, now being redesigned, would have a relatively better payload and significantly lower seat mile costs than the Concorde are not borne out by the latest Boeing figures", Captain Ritchie was to advise the board. "The design looks very much like a Concorde doubled in size and available five years later. Its airport noise levels are likely to be even higher."[2]

The earlier Qantas view that the Boeing SST was favoured to become the airline's main supersonic airliner in the mid-1970s now had to be abandoned. The delay in the American programme provided a much needed boost for the Anglo-French Concorde. There was, said Ritchie, even more justification for protecting Qantas's position on the Concorde delivery line than existed when deposits were paid in January 1964. "The interval between the possible advent of the Concorde and the United States SST into commercial service has gone from two to about five years and the original five airlines that had placed orders in 1964 has expanded to eleven. Thus we would face severe competition if the aircraft was successful."

That the Concorde would be commercially successful on Qantas routes was doubtful. As the months passed, the Qantas view firmed that the Concorde was likely to be technically sound but limited in range, with only a marginal ability on the important Sydney-Singapore route. It was definitely more costly to operate per seat mile than existing Boeing 707s and it was also limited in operation to routes that were mainly over water because of the sonic boom it created. "Airport noise is recognised as being one of the biggest problems, with no solution in sight.

399

Certainly if criteria defined recently by the US Federal Aviation Administration is applied, it could not operate from United States airports", wrote Ritchie. With these operational problems came significant price increases for the Concorde during the year. Development costs had risen sharply as its gross weight increased from 260,000 pounds in 1964 to 385,000 pounds in late 1968. The anticipated selling price of the Concorde now quoted by British Aircraft Corporation and Sud Aviation increased to $US19.4 million, compared with the contract formula price including escalations of about $US13 million.[3] The Concorde prototype was, however, due to fly in late 1968. Qantas, despite their misgivings, could not afford to ignore it. (In fact, the prototype did not fly until 2 March 1969.) Ritchie recommended to the board on 17 February 1969 that the letter of agreement reserving delivery positions for the Concorde be extended for a further fifteen months to 30 June 1970.[4]

Important as it was for Qantas to watch closely the emergence of supersonic airliners, it was the subsonic Boeing 747 programme that dominated forward planning in 1968. Within the approved 747 budget of $123 million, cash outflow requirements for 1968–70 were relatively low, with the major payments coming between 1970 and 1972. In 1968 considerable specialist effort was necessary for the ordering of the new ground support and essential workshop equipment.

Qantas was not impressed with the initial 747 performance. "The Qantas philosophy in assessing aircraft is to look first to adequate range", said Ritchie. "The first 747 lacked range." Qantas pressed Pratt & Whitney for more thrust from the engines and pressed Boeing for more range. These were soon to become available. Already, since board approval had been given to buy four 747s, Boeing had offered two major product improvement modifications that would increase the total project cost by over $3 million but also improve its operating efficiency and economics. In March 1968, Boeing advised that the take-off thrust of the Pratt & Whitney JT9D-3 engine would be increased from 43,500 to 45,000 pounds by the use of water injection. With some additional structural modifications this increase in take-off thrust would enable the 747 gross weight to rise from 710,000 to 733,000 pounds, giving it improved payload-range capability. On Qantas long-range sectors this promised a valuable payload increase of approximately 11,000 pounds and an increase of 6,000 pounds out of airports with restricted runway lengths. (The cost of this gross weight modification was $434,475 per aircraft.) A second modification

400

was the underfloor galley arrangement. It was the Qantas view (not shared by all other airlines) that the galley occupied prime space on the passenger deck, space that could more profitably be used to carry up to fourteen additional passengers. United Airlines and American Airlines had already committed to this underfloor galley. Ritchie advised the board in June:

> Although the potential revenue to be derived from the additional passenger capacity would more than offset the increased capital outlay [$359,000 per aircraft], there are a number of other benefits to be gained. Firstly, they are loaded through the normal baggage hold doors and not through the passenger doors . . . This means that galley loading will not interfere with passenger loading and will not disturb passengers who remain onboard during transit stops. Secondly, there is a potential saving in specialised ground handling equipment, since the equipment used to load the under-floor cargo containers may also be used for loading the galley.

On the debit side, he said, there was a loss of about one-third of the aircraft's deadload capacity.[5] Ritchie also pressed Boeing to extend the length of the upper deck lounge and to increase the number of windows in it. Qantas managed to have the rear bulkhead of the lounge moved aft, increasing its length by a third. Ritchie was not impressed, however, by the current euphoria about the beautiful lounge. "That was piffle", he said. "It was the most expensive piece of real estate in the world. We did have to use it as a lounge for a time because that was the going thing. But we aimed at its ultimate exploitation for

A change in the 707s markings was introduced in March 1968. QANTAS – Australia's Overseas Airline was gradually replaced by QANTAS AUSTRALIA as shown here on VH-EAC *City of Sydney*.

passenger seats which we knew would come with improvements in power and economic pressures."[6]

The effects of the 1966 Qantas pilots' strike on traffic and revenue had been prolonged and had depressed results throughout the following year. They were compounded by work stoppages by local employees in the United States and Fiji during the period from October 1967 to February 1968 as well as a strike by Qantas flight stewards in January that stopped services for twenty-four hours. Despite these setbacks, 1967–68

A light-hearted advertisement placed in the US technical press in 1968 seeking buyers for the smaller 707-138B aircraft that were being replaced in service by the last batch of ten 707-338Cs.

Flown only on Sundays by a little old pilot from Pasadena.

Negotiations for the purchase of several Qantas Boeing 707–138B jets are now open to interested parties. These fan jets, noted for their original high standard specification, unmatched operational economy, and general efficiency, compare favourably with new aircraft of their type. Each can be expected to operate efficiently for at least eight years, and may be purchased for not more than half the price of similar new flying machines. They will be fully overhauled and will meet FAA certification requirements prior to delivery. Delivery positions currently available are one each month for April, May, June, October, November, December 1968, and January 1969. Complete information may be obtained from Mr. J. K. McSweyn, Qantas Airways Limited, 183 Utah Avenue, South San Francisco, California. Phone (415) 583-9508. The aircraft may be inspected at San Francisco and Sydney, Australia. Stop by and kick the tires.

was a year of continuing growth for the company and Wilson
was able to report an after-tax profit to 31 March 1969 of
$2,867,289 compared to the $1,510,000 loss for the previous
year. Turner's shrewd timing in disposing of the Boeing 138Bs
brought an additional capital surplus from the sale of the first
five aircraft of almost $4 million. (Qantas was to be less success-
ful with the disposal of the remaining 707-138Bs. The market
for these aircraft slumped and Qantas found they had, for a time,
six of them lying idle. Attempts were made to sell them to Ansett
and TAA for domestic use but, despite the backing of Prime
Minister Gorton, who saw such a sale as a means of conserving
US dollars, they were unsuccessful. By 31 March 1969, seven
had been sold and the remaining six were sold by year's end.
In total the disposal of the eleven 707-138Bs returned a net
capital surplus of $5.2 million over their depreciated book
values.) Revenue for the 1968–69 financial year reached a new
peak of almost $144 million, an increase of 16.6 per cent. On
8 April the new bid-system for pilots came into full operation
and the AFAP, reconciled to the legislation of 7 December 1967,
accepted the reality of compulsory arbitration under the newly
appointed academic economist, Professor Joseph E. Isaac, as
the neutral tribunal.

In February 1968, the board had decided that Sir Hudson Fysh's
furnished office and secretary be discontinued at year's end. In
June, the board reviewed Fysh's appointment as consultant to
the company at a yearly fee of $2,000 and agreed to a final
extension of the appointment to 30 June 1969. Fysh wrote to
Law-Smith:

> I will, of course, miss the fee very much . . . You have all been
> most generous . . . You were also generous to Arthur Baird and
> George Harman. They both needed it, but in their cases the
> arrangement, I think, ended in their deaths. For some peculiar
> reason fate ruled that I should live on. I will now be forced to
> sell my property at Dural . . . My only complaint – having nothing
> to do with the Board – is that despite my record, which deserved
> more, I have never been able to get into a financial position
> approaching most of my associates and contemporaries, having had
> a fortune snatched from under my nose while new millionaires
> arise almost daily in our land – made from speculation, making
> ladies' hats, bricks, patent medicines and so forth. I have never
> been one to make money a god, but I would have liked to help
> more than I can some needy members of my family . . . However,
> this is not a Board matter and I do thank you and Roland Wilson
> and the other members of the Board for your consideration since
> I retired.[7]

(Fysh was to write more critically of his treatment by the board at a later date though, in fact, the board was eventually to agree to a continued and increased payment as a "consultant".[8])

The board was reminded by Ritchie on 19 June that Capt. G. U. (Scottie) Allan's appointment as consultant would expire on 30 June. "Capt. Allan, who is now sixty-eight years of age, represents Qantas as Chairman of Fiji Airways Limited and as a Director of Malaysia-Singapore Airlines until 30 June 1968 when this latter appointment will be terminated and the vacancy filled by the appointment of Capt. R. J. Ritchie", Ritchie wrote.[9]

Ritchie was to join the board of Malaysia-Singapore Airlines at a time when it was of growing importance to Qantas. A board paper in March had drawn attention to the withdrawal of Great Britain from the region and the consequent decrease in stature of British airlines. There was, said the paper, a potential increase in the importance of Qantas in the area. (The Malaysian and Singapore governments had increased their shareholding in Malaysia-Singapore Airlines Limited during the 1967–68 financial year and together held 78.8 per cent of the issued capital. The balance was held by Brunei, 6.8 per cent; BOAC and Qantas, each 6 per cent; and the general public, 2.4 per cent.) Qantas had always followed closely the involvement and strategies of their partner, BOAC, in South East Asia and Hong Kong. When BOAC and Qantas had first become joint major shareholders of Malayan Airways, BOAC were pursuing an active British aviation policy in South East Asia based on the premise that with declining British influence in Singapore and the Federation of Malaya, the linchpin of their continued dominance must be active support of Hong Kong-based commercial aviation (resulting in the deliberate restriction of MAL's regional expansion).

In 1956 there were two airline companies based on Hong Kong – Cathay Pacific and Hong Kong Airways. Hong Kong Airways was jointly owned by BOAC and Jardine Matheson and, by an agreement with the government of the colony endorsed by Whitehall, Cathay Pacific were to operate routes generally to the south of Hong Kong and Hong Kong Airways routes generally to the north. At this time, the Singapore–Hong Kong route was a British cabotage route and a BOAC monopoly.

Jardine Matheson and BOAC were wrong in their assessment of future opportunities for Hong Kong–China expansion and in the rate of growth of Hong Kong–Japan traffic. In the meantime, Jardine Matheson's principal competitor in Hong

Kong shipping and merchant circles, Butterfield and Swire, acquired a significant financial interest in Cathay Pacific. Despite BOAC faith in the future of Hong Kong Airways, Jardine Matheson withdrew their financial support and the airline was wound up. BOAC now took a financial interest in Cathay and continued their efforts to promote Hong Kong interests to the detriment of Malayan Airways Limited (MAL). In the late 1950s the policy of the United Kingdom was thus to develop Cathay Pacific as a strong British regional carrier in the Far East. This policy was opposed by Qantas, with the result that the renamed MAL, Malaysia-Singapore Airways (MSA) gradually developed into a regional carrier. (Qantas had acquired their interest in Malayan Airways Limited on 19 March 1958.)

After the seccession of Singapore from Malaysia in 1965, the two governments, on 14 May 1966, entered into an agreement in which Malayan Airways Limited acquired the status of a joint national airline and its name was later changed to Malaysia-Singapore Airlines Limited. The British position deteriorated further as Cathay's traffic rights into Singapore and Malaysia were heavily restricted at the end of 1966. BOAC's own rights beyond Singapore and Malaysia to Australia and New Zealand were allowed but subject to frequency restrictions that were subsequently reviewed when MSA participated in a pool with BOAC, Qantas, Air India, and Air New Zealand.

It was the Qantas view by 1968 that, with diminished British interests in South East Asia, and with the uncertainty surrounding Hong Kong's future, British ability to influence aviation politics in South East Asia would be negligible by the early 1970s and that a partial vacuum would be created. Cathay Pacific, Qantas judged, would not be able even partly to fill this vacuum because its traffic rights were restricted and because it was in no position to fund the acquisition of new equipment. At the same time, there had been an injection of further capital by the governments of Malaysia and Singapore in MSA in April 1967, a course that had little Cabinet support but was favoured by Singapore's deputy prime minister. One consequence of these internal Singaporean politics was that the deputy prime minister, anxious to ensure the success of MSA, took an excessive interest in the day-to-day affairs of the company. The result was to antagonise government officers in Malaysia and to lower morale in the company itself as Singapore government officials took it on themselves to question airline personnel responsible to the airline's general manager. That general manager was seconded Qantas officer, Keith Hamilton. The relationship between the governments of Malaysia and Singapore in their joint airline worsened and, on 27 August 1968, came close to being terminated when a letter from the Singapore government criticising Hamilton was tabled at a board meeting. Singapore's prime minister, Lee Kuan Yew, told the Australian high commissioner that Hamilton must go. There had, he said, been a long history of commercial mismanagement. Hamilton was accused of badly prepared board papers, an incomplete brief on the recent purchase of aircraft, and for running uneconomic routes to East Malaysia. He was also accused of turning on special flights just to send Malaysia's head of state his newspapers when he was in East Malaysia. Singaporeans believed that the airline was not profitable and that the main reason for this was that the Malaysians had too great an influence over Hamilton. Lee put it plainly: "He no longer enjoys our confidence and without that we cannot agree to his further employment". Lee did not, however, want a break-up of the airline and, in his conversation with the high commissioner, was at pains to make the point that as Hamilton had come from Qantas (and had been supported by Qantas representative Sir Cedric Turner when he was criticised), he hoped that Qantas would not encourage the Malaysians to fight in support of Hamilton.

On the day following this meeting, Australia's high commissioner in Kuala Lumpur was told in the strictest confidence that Malaysia's Tun Razak had decided that Malaysia would withdraw from MSA. Hamilton, he said, had been offered the position of general manager of Malayan Airways and had accepted. (Hamilton had, following the board criticism by Singapore, submitted his resignation from MSA. It was Malaysia's view that Singaore's antagonism to Hamilton was largely because he had expressed dissatisfaction with Singapore's rigid application of regulations denying work permits to Malaysian employees of MSA.)

The conflict had by now concerned the Australian government, which saw that a dissolution of the airline partnership between Singapore and Malaysia could have implications for Australia if a public breach occurred in an atmosphere of recrimination. The high commissioners in Singapore and Kuala Lumpur were informed by telegram from the Department of External Affairs in Canberra that they were not to become involved in any questions relating to the management of the airline. "Our dominant interest at this stage is with the political effects of an open breach", said the cable. Intensive negotiations

between Singapore's prime minister, Lee Kuan Yew, and the
permanent head of the Malaysian Ministry of Foreign Affairs
averted a breach but continuing divergent pressures were to
develop. Qantas remained keenly interested in these developments as they worked to retain close links with both countries
to ensure safe operation of civil aviation in the area and to
preserve favourable traffic rights.[10] (It was not until 25
January 1971 that the two governments announced in a joint
statement that they had agreed to review the May 1966 agreement with a view to the reconstruction of MSA to establish
two national airlines.)

Of much more immediate commercial significance to Qantas
than the fate of MSA in 1968 was the strong pressure from the
United States for a significant increase in the frequencies
operated across the South Pacific by Pan American. There was,
in the view of the Australian government, a real threat that the
capacity situation would get out of hand and exacerbate the
effects of the already low load factors being experienced on the
route. For more than a decade, the United States government
had sought to increase competitive United States flag services
on the Pacific air routes, beginning with initiatives by President
Eisenhower in 1959. Under the terms of the Australia-United
States Air Agreement in 1946, America was empowered to
designate a second US operator for the South Pacific, though
any such designation raised the problem of frequencies and
capacity. Both President Kennedy and President Johnson
renewed American pressures and in 1967 what became known
as the Trans-Pacific Route Investigation took place to determine the future pattern of air services by US flag carriers. The
advisory arm of the Civil Aeronautics Board expressed the view
that the South Pacific was the least competitive, most highly
priced, and most profitable market in the world, strongly
inferring that Qantas and Pan American were responsible.
Qantas rejected these views, pointing out that per mile costs
of travel on the route compared favourably with other world
routes, including the competitive North Atlantic, while
passenger load factors fell far short of what IATA considered
to be a viable minimum. By 1969, Pan American frequencies
on the route matched those of Qantas at nine flights per week.
Within the United States, however, there was an intense battle
by competing carriers to become the second US airline on the
route. Australia's concern was not the choice of the US carrier
but the result of increased US competition. The growth rate

in traffic in 1968 was low (about five per cent to March 1969). There were already six major carriers operating twenty-six frequencies weekly on the South Pacific trunk route between Australia and the United States. All had plans for expansion. In 1970–71, the introduction of Boeing 747s promised a further large increase in capacity. All six carriers on the route were currently experiencing uneconomic load factors. Qantas was concerned that the introduction of a second US carrier would mean serious losses for them.

In the previous August, the government had rejected Pan American's attempt to increase its frequencies and had allowed only two services a week instead of a proposed five. Pan American pressed for a third frequency. The minister for civil aviation, Swartz, commented in a letter to Wilson in September: "Our judgement was that it would not assist our objective of persuading the United States authorities to assist us in maintaining a sensible and orderly relationship between traffic and appropriate capacity with a fair and equal opportunity for each of the national airlines if we refused now to approve the third frequency. If we have to have a major confrontation with the United States authorities on this question of capacity and frequencies, it will be essential to select a suitable occasion and pretext." Swartz emphasised that the government had not yet succeeded in solving any of the major problems affecting the application of the bilateral agreement with the United States. "There is no doubt that the United States authorities will resist strongly any action which they regard as an attempt on our part to introduce pre-determination of frequencies and capacity into our air services arrangements. The maintaining of the Bermuda-type approach, as they see it and interpret it, is vital to their arrangements with many countries on world routes." Australia's concern, he said, was the possible creation of overcapacity. The issue was very serious. Whether such a situation should, wrote Swartz, "be met by negotiation and possible compromise or by a resort to more drastic measures which could even involve the threat of a possible breakdown of air services would have to be determined in the light of the circumstances". There was no government disposition "to permit the swamping of Qantas services by those of Pan American or any other United States operator".[11]

In October 1968, Boeing advised that they had replaced the modified 747 aircraft, known as the 747A, with a new model to be known as the Boeing 747B. This new version met Qantas

Everett, Washington,
30 September 1968. Qantas
promotions officer Pat Tudor
sits on the edge of the intake to
the prototype Boeing 747's
number 3 engine. Pat is
holding a bottle of champagne
that she will use to christen the
747 when it is towed out of the
assembly building.

Cabin crew members,
representing the twenty-six
airlines that had placed orders
for the Boeing 747, pose for
photographs with the 747
prototype inside the vast
assembly building at Everett,
north of Seattle, on
30 September 1968. Pat Tudor
representing Qantas is fifteenth
from the left.

requirements for range. Externally it was identical to the earlier aircraft in terms of wing span, body length, and aerodynamic shape. It gross weight, however, had now risen to 775,000 pounds. It was offered at that date with either the JT9D-3 wet engine of 45,000 pounds thrust (restricting gross weight to 740,000 pounds) or the JT9D-7 wet engine with 47,000 pounds thrust. The new 747B was also able to carry an additional 2,000 gallons of fuel. The more powerful engine was not available until February 1972, restricting Qantas initially to the JT9D-3 engine. Even so, the increase in gross weight available provided additional range of 700 nautical miles and enabled a full pay-load to be carried on the Sydney-Singapore sector, as well as improving take-off performance. The additional cost of the Boeing 747B was $US918,000 per aircraft or, for the four Qantas aircraft, a total capital increase of $A3.4 million. Boeing also announced price increases for all 747s delivered from 1972 onwards of $A2,351,300 per aircraft, increases affecting the two 747s Qantas had on option. Ritchie was concerned, however, at increases in the base price for the four Qantas aircraft, announced by Boeing, of $A230,000 per aircraft.

On 9 February 1969, the first flight of the Boeing 747 proto-type took place. On the grounds of cost Qantas, in March 1969, decided to reject the Boeing 747B offer. However, within only two months there were more significant changes evident in the relative performances and economics of the 747A and 747B models. In May, therefore, Ritchie recommended purchase of the 747B fitted with JTD9D-7 dry engines. Traffic demands

The first flight of the Boeing 747 occurred on 9 February 1969. The badges of the airlines that had ordered the giant aircraft are painted from the nose back; the Qantas symbol is directly below the B of Boeing.

during its early operating life would not, he reported, require Qantas to operate it at its maximum gross weight of 775,000 pounds. Boeing had agreed that initially the aircraft could be certified to a restricted gross weight of 725,000 pounds. (There was an incidental saving for Qantas of $160,000 a year from lower airport landing fees from the reduced weight.) It was also clear, by May 1969, that the future development of the 747 would be based on the 747B version.

A significant item of noncapital costs flowing from the 747B purchase was for the training of technical aircrew. Fleet composition in Qantas had changed so much in the four years from 1965 that it was no longer meaningful to compare training hours per pilot and the airline's productivity statistics from year to year but only on a general trend basis. In fact, in the previous four years, two-thirds of training costs were incurred for the benefit of post-1969 operations. The fleet changes, and consequent training demands, had been considerable. At the end of the 1965–66 financial year (31 March 1966), Qantas operated six of the bigger Boeing 707-338Cs, thirteen 138Bs, three Electras, two DC4s, and two DC3s. By 31 March 1968 this mix had changed to fifteen 338Cs, seven 138Bs, one Electra, and two each of the DC4s, DC3s, and the twin-jet training aircraft, the HS125. One year later, at 31 March 1969, there were twenty-one 338Cs (and six remaining 138Bs that were not in service) with the same DC4s, DC3s, and HS125s. In the period

March 1969. In the left and right background of this photograph taken from the roof of the International Terminal at Mascot are Qantas Boeing 707-138Bs withdrawn from service and awaiting sale.

from 1965–66 to 1968–69, capacity ton miles operated had increased by forty-six per cent and revenue hours flown by nineteen per cent. This change in fleet composition, combined with the growth in revenue flight hours, had created different demands each year for crew training. The introduction of the HS125 jet trainers and the expanding use of simulators had helped to hold down the costs of promotional training and endorsement hours but costs were rising.

In 1959, when Qantas 707s were put into service, there were no industrial restraints on the company. Qantas were able to choose the pilots they assessed as being the best for the task. In the following decade, as the pilots' federation applied more and more industrial pressure, there was a marked lessening of this discretionary authority. By 1965, following the series of conferences under the chairmanship of Sir Henry Bland, the company was forced to concede the principle of seniority for promotion or accept industrial anarchy. Heavy cost penalties resulted. In 1965–66, under these burdensome new rules, Qantas were compelled to give a second chance to a number of pilots who had been passed over for promotion. Predictably, many did not qualify and the high failure rate meant costly, wasted effort. In 1967, when the new pilots' contract was negotiated, the rights of the company were further whittled away with the introduction of the American type contract, which operated on a strict seniority system and under which the company could no longer be selective in pilot choice and training for promotion. Overall, from 1965–66 to 1968–69, total training costs had grown from $4.25 million to $5.95 million, an increase of almost forty per cent. The trend had been greatly influenced by the 1966 pilots' strike (which had severely disrupted endorsement training) but continuing fixed training costs had also grown with the acquisition of the HS125 jets and additional Boeing 707-338C simulators. The company also still felt the effects in training costs of its exclusion from New Guinea operations, which had provided a fine environment for pilot training. (The loss of the internal New Guinea routes had led directly to the purchase of the HS125s and DC3s for pilot training.) In mid-1969 budgeted training costs for 1969–70 were $6.25 million. Beyond that date, future training costs would inevitably include not only the higher operating cost per hour of the jumbo jets, but also the need to build up a pool of pilots to permit continuation of 707 services while 747 conversion training was in progress. (Projected salary increases for aircrews were also substantial.)[12]

While pressures on costs mounted in 1969, other external influences threatened Qantas revenue. Within Australia, the minister for trade and industry and deputy prime minister, John McEwen, and the minister in charge of tourist activities, Peter Howson, supported the strong public argument from the Australian Tourist Commission that lower international air fares to Australia were essential to help develop the tourist industry. International tourism, McEwen argued, was big business. World receipts in 1968 had totalled $13 billion, exclusive of international air transportation payments, which themselves had totalled $4.5 billion. Australia's competitive position in this huge market was, said the Australian Tourist Commission, worsening and the main reason was the high absolute and relative cost of international air transport charges both to and within Australia. The tourist industry was highly critical of the fare structures of the scheduled international carriers and pressed hard for a substantial increase in services by cut price charter companies and for the establishment of an Australian supplemental carrier, with Qantas participation. Qantas responded to these pressures and arguments within government through its minister, Swartz. Commenting on the publication of a Tourist Development Programme by the Australian Tourist Commission, Swartz said that it did not deal with the basic, long-standing civil aviation policy considerations that had governed the establishment and evolution of international scheduled airline operations into and out of Australia over the previous twenty-five years. "A fundamental element in this situation has been the setting up and the progressive expansion of our own international airline, Qantas, which has become not merely a national symbol and a major foreign exchange earner, but also an asset in many fields of Government activity. Government capital investment in Qantas, moreover, has reached $40 million while Qantas assets are valued at $200 million and will exceed $300 million by 1971." Current declining revenue yields and load factors, experienced at a time when Qantas was about to face very heavy capital re-equipment programmes, were causing concern, said Swartz. There had, nevertheless, been a considerable growth in charter travel over the preceding eighteen months as a result of the efforts of the scheduled carriers, especially Qantas. He did not see that the establishment of a supplemental carrier, with Qantas participation, would be a step forward. Despite this support, Qantas was to experience ever-increasing competition from nonscheduled charter operators, particularly on

413

routes west of Hong Kong and Singapore, with severe effects on revenue from the Kangaroo Route operations.

Another important, if nonglamorous, element of Qantas revenue was under pressure in 1969. The Universal Postal Union, of which Australia was a member, was to hold its quinquennial congress in Tokyo in October and was to discuss rates of payment for the carriage of international airmails. All international airlines carried the mails of their own countries and those of any other country that chose to use them. They were paid by their national postal administrations, which, in turn, met these costs from the postages collected and claimed on foreign postal administrations as necessary. In 1969, UPU agreed maximum rates for letter class carriage were three gold francs per tonne kilometre in Europe and four gold francs per tonne kilometre elsewhere. There was strong pressure for a substantial reduction in the latter rate, which would adversely affect Qantas revenue and Australia's balance of payments. (It was estimated that by 1970–71 Qantas revenue from all overseas letter class mail would be of the order of $12 million at the four gold francs rate.) Qantas, however, recognised that though a proposed reduction of the rate to three gold francs would mean a revenue loss of $3 million annually, it was unlikely that Australia could gain support for continuance of the higher rate. Qantas therefore took the view that it would be in their best long-term interests to agree to a three gold francs rate, but

Sir Roland Wilson, Prime Minister John Gorton, and Capt. R. J. Ritchie at Mascot, March 1969.

nothing lower. It was supported in this attitude by the Australian government.

Qantas was now settling down under its new chairman. Wilson had announced his resignation from the Treasury from Mexico (where he was attending the IATA meeting) late in 1968 and was no longer a public servant. Formally, he was part-time chairman of Qantas, not executive chairman. Ritchie regarded him highly as a good general (but not necessarily as the ideal) Qantas chairman. He had, said Ritchie, been a working government servant all his life. His mental approach was that of a permanent head and he had come to Qantas with the reputation of being a very strong and powerful man in his Treasury position for many years. One significant, though not necessarily over-ruling, consideration in his thinking was, thought Ritchie, what would please government and Canberra. This perception of his new chairman in no way diminished his respect for him. "I consider . . . that when Australian history is written in relation to his period of service both as secretary to the Treasury and chairman of the Commonwealth Banking Corporation, as well as chairman of Qantas, he must show up as a very great Australian."[13]

Wilson was something of an enigma to those under him. John Ulm proposed to Ritchie that this should be changed. "The Company does not know its chairman — and it should", he wrote in January 1969. "We all know that RW is having difficulty communicating with the staff. His style is inhibiting and his humour, after the first taste, is having a negative effect on people. This is pretty common talk around the shop. What I propose is a profile of him in Staff News at considerable length."[14]

His predecessor, Hudson Fysh, now wrote more frankly about his treatment by Wilson and the board, which he did not regard as kind. Wilson had taken care, in his proper way, to distance himself from Fysh by arranging that requests to the board for assistance or for consideration of his affairs should come through Robert Law-Smith. On 7 February, Fysh wrote sadly to Law-Smith:

> I have had a month of it at home here in the flat and, of course, have missed the old facilities in the ANZ Bank building very sorely. At my age, when I needed a bit of sympathetic consideration, I am afraid it has put an end to any further serious work. No one can understand why I had to leave the city office, in view of my long and creative service in Qantas . . . The Australian government, when it took over Qantas, proceeded to cash in on the

pioneering work of a few private individuals . . . who have never
been suitably recompensed. Perhaps they could not have been.
It is rather amusing to think of the great fortunes being made today
in Australia. My shares in the old Qantas and then in QEA—which
I was a very active leader in—should have been worth two million
dollars today. Pioneers, of course, traditionally do not make money.
Classic cases are Columbus, Kingsford Smith, Charles Ulm and
company . . . You will remember the great struggle I had to stay
on as long as I did in the face of an arbitrary notice to quit. [He
asked Law-Smith to mention] how I felt very deeply the loss of
some sort of city office accommodation, and receipt of a notice
that I am no longer wanted as a consultant after 30 June 1969,
when my stipend will cease, and all connection with my old
Company . . . Bert Ritchie has been more than kind and so
different to any Director. He came down personally to see if I was
OK, and to arrange for storage of some of my papers. He was
apprised of the large amount of my correspondence and records
handed back to the Company, and which I pray and trust will not
fall into the hands of Ulm and Gibson, who I have no confidence
in. [15]

His letter reflected his long conflict with C. O. Turner, which
was well documented, and hinted at what he saw as injustice
from Wilson. In fact, Fysh during his chairmanship had given
Wilson some cause to feel bitter towards him personally. Deeply
ingrained in Fysh's personality—and a source of both his
strengths and weaknesses—was a set of values and responses
that, in their Victorian rectitude, determined his attitude to
people and behaviour. They had been evident over the years
in his reaction to Turner's heavy drinking. They had been at
work, too, in his relationship with Wilson. Fysh had disapproved
strongly of certain conduct by Wilson in private matters that
had caused widespread gossip, and that, because of Wilson's
position as a Qantas director, Fysh felt reflected on the company.
That the supposed harm came from the gossip and the gossipers
rather than from Wilson's conduct did not occur to him. Fysh's
disquiet originated during a visit to the Qantas New York office
in the mid-1950s where he saw a new appointee on the staff,
Joyce Chivers. He asked who had appointed this attractive and
vivacious woman and was told by the office manager that it had
been arranged by Roland Wilson. Such an appointment would,
of course, have been impossible without the specific approval
of C. O. Turner. Fysh was disturbed that it had taken place
without his knowledge and suspected some arrangement by his
chief executive with Wilson that undermined his own authority
and position. On a later visit to New York, Fysh heard rumours,
though he could not remember who told him of them. He

unwisely asked Qantas's head of security, Gordon Fraser, to check on the rumours and the existence of gossip. When he learned that, indeed, the gossip existed (but nothing else), he was convinced that Wilson was being indiscreet in his position as a director of Qantas. Fysh decided to raise the matter with other Qantas directors, Taylor, McVey, and Watt. He told Turner that it might be best if Chivers were to leave the company. Turner took no action but, in January 1959, Wilson confronted Fysh. He had witnesses, he said, who were prepared to state that Fysh had mentioned matters to them in a way that defamed him. His association with Chivers, said Wilson, was only that of an old friend of the family whom he had known from his youth in Tasmania. He was, he said, considering legal action.

Instead, Wilson raised the matter at a board meeting on 19 February 1959, accusing Fysh of telling others that he and Joyce Chivers had misconducted themselves, and that Fysh had had Fraser investigate the matter. He asked for an apology. Wilson asked other board members if they had heard from Fysh on the subject. All said "Yes". McVey added that he had never believed such rumours.

Fysh apologised. Fysh also wrote a letter of apology to Joyce Chivers, in New York. In a postscript to this storm, written by Fysh in 1969, he referred to Wilson's attitude to him, and to his treatment after he retired: "I still think my attitude was correct but I got nowhere on it and have suffered for it, of course". He also noted that his treatment had not gone unnoticed. At a Qantas function, he said, the New South Wales premier, Robin Askin; the president of the Liberal Party, John Atwill; and the director-general of civil aviation, Don Anderson, all "shuffled past me at the function and said: 'I don't like the way they're treating Huddy' ".

On 1 August 1969 officials of the Overseas Branch of the Australian Federation of Air Pilots delivered to Qantas a copy of their proposed agreement on salaries and conditions to replace the existing award. Twelve days later, the domestic airlines were each served with a proposed agreement. The pilots sought significant changes in salaries, workload, and other matters.

The salary changes sought included increases in the maximum pay of Boeing 707 line pilots ranging from sixty to seventy-seven per cent, bringing the existing salary of $19,018 per annum for a captain to $30,544. These were basic increases only, with changes in various credits from bidding and scheduling procedures adding up to an additional ten per cent. No specific salary claims were included for Boeing 747 aircraft but an extension of the speed-weight formula put forward by the AFAP would, Qantas calculated, bring the salary of a 747 captain in 1971 to a minimum of $38,004 and a maximum of $47,505. It was estimated by Qantas's operations branch that the more restrictive work rules proposed would mean fifty per cent increase in captains' strength and thirty-nine per cent increase in other pilot categories on Boeing 707 aircraft to handle the existing workload of revenue flying. A massive increase of one hundred and fifty pilots would be needed.

These were not the only pilot proposals. Compulsory union membership was now sought with union dues deducted by the company through the payroll. The company was asked to terminate pilots who did not become and remain AFAP members. The federation also asked that it negotiate salary levels for all supervisory pilots, including chief pilots. The estimated annual cost of the new claim for Qantas was $8.36 million.

Qantas responded, on 29 August, in concert with the domestic airlines by serving a counterlog of claims on the pilots. ("We were somewhat disappointed at the lack of enthusiastic support from the domestic operators who, in our view, gave little more than token support to a common industry approach", Ritchie advised the board.)[16] The Flight Crew Officers Industrial Tribunal (Isaac) was notified of a dispute on 8 September and ordered the parties to negotiate. The two domestic airlines were brought into line by the federation by a twenty-four hour stoppage on 12 December and reached an immediate settlement. Qantas was subjected to a non-cooperation campaign and a one-day stoppage on 17 October and demanded arbitration. Uncertainty and antagonism persisted and it was not until 18 February 1970 that the tribunal brought down a new award. (The Airline Pilots Qantas Award 1970 gave senior Boeing 707 captains a salary increase of 23.9 per cent. The award was to operate for two years.)[17]

As this dispute intensified, two other grave issues faced Qantas in the closing months of 1969. In the United States, American Airlines had been designated second US carrier for the South Pacific route and had filed for the introduction of a daily service, to add seven more flights per week to the existing nine weekly services by Pan American. The second was that Qantas, like other international carriers, was facing an unprecedented

June 1969. One of four
707-138Bs sold by Qantas to
Braniff International. This
aircraft was formerly VH-EBI
Winton.

increase in the hijacking of and unlawful interference with
civilian aircraft.

Wilson wrote to Senator Robert Cotton, who had succeeded
Swartz as minister for civil aviation in 1969, that while Qantas
had accepted Swartz's judgment that the issue of Pan American's
flight frequencies at the end of 1968 was not an appropriate
one for a confrontation with the United States authorities, it
was basically the same issue as the American Airlines proposal.
It was one, said Wilson, that the minister might like to raise
with the US if a major confrontation now developed out of the
American Airlines thrust.

> My board desires me to acquaint you with the view that the present
> case of the American Airlines filing — involving as it does the
> introduction of a second US operator as well as the extraordinary
> increase in capacity proposed — seems a most favourable
> opportunity to have this whole capacity problem clarified . . . If
> we fail to do so or if we should accept any compromise arrange-
> ment it leaves the major question of the proper application of
> capacity provisions still unsettled . . . We are certain in the future
> to be faced with a continuing series of demands. [18]

(At the same time as this US problem faced Qantas, Australia
received a diplomatic note from the Soviet Union suggesting
a direct air link between the two countries. Qantas advised the
government that possible future traffic between the two countries
did not warrant Qantas and Aeroflot operating a once weekly
service, the minimum possible.)[19]

There had been more than eighty cases of hijacking or
unlawful interference in 1969. It was a phenomenon that began
with the diversion of US and Latin American domestic civil
airline flights to Cuba and an international conference (attended

by sixty-one nations, including Australia) was called in Tokyo in 1963 to try to address the problem. The resulting Tokyo Convention had no practical effect. Four years were to pass before a subcommittee on unlawful seizure was established, following the sixteenth session of the ICAO Assembly. (Australia was a member.) However, this committee's terms of reference provided that it would "deal only with the aircraft aspects of the cases of unlawful interference and shall refrain from considering any cases which may involve the committee in matters of a political nature or in a controversy between two or more states". These terms greatly limited the subcommittee's capacity to take effective action. On 29 August 1969 a spate of incidents in the Middle East culminated in the hijack of an American aircraft en route to Syria and there was action in the United Nations. After lengthy private negotiations, a draft resolution was tabled on 10 November under the sponsorship of twenty-eight countries, including Australia. It was a compromise but it urged full support for measures making the unlawful seizure of aircraft a punishable offence and called on all states to ensure that persons perpetrating such unlawful acts be prosecuted. Wilson, at the request of the director-general of IATA, Knut Hammarskjold, had earlier in 1969 passed on IATA's concern to Swartz. [20] Events were to show that these earnest procedural activities would in no way lessen the increasing attraction of airliner hijacking as a means of gaining worldwide media attention for the varied causes of determined political activists. Australia's Department of External Affairs told Australian embassies in Cairo, Beirut, Tel Aviv, and London in December 1969:

The interest in this 1969 photograph lies in the hangar behind the Qantas 707. Hangar 96 was built to accommodate the 707-138 aircraft which was 128 feet 10 inches (39.3 metres) in length. The 707-338 was over 16 feet (4.8 metres) longer and Hangar 96 had to have an extension built on at the front.

Qantas has intensified its precautions and its crews in the area are
operating in a high state of alert . . . In the last resort, the
effectiveness of Qantas precautions depends largely on warnings
being given to civil aircraft by the authorities concerned of
impending danger. In cases such as the surprise low level pene-
trations by Israeli jets of Egyptian defences . . . the possibility of
civil aircraft receiving any warning is remote. There is . . . the
added hazard of defensive measures by the air defence systems
which, in all probability, would go into action without warning
to civil aircraft in the area . . . There seem to be no precautions
that would be completely effective.[21]

Qantas faced the new decade of the seventies and its fiftieth
year of existence with many challenges and problems.

New Imperatives
for a Jumbo World
1970

15 Qantas began its second fifty years on the crest of economic success. The 1968–69 year had seen a record net profit of $7.1 million. The 1969–70 year increased this net profit to $8.166 million and brought substantial gains in traffic and a total revenue of $198.9 million, sixteen per cent more than the previous year. In the preceding decade, the seat miles available provided by the fleet and the passenger miles actually flown had increased by almost five hundred per cent while the cost of providing each capacity ton mile had fallen by a third. In terms of investment, the nation and the government had done well. Though the government had injected $21 million in capital into Qantas between 1956 and 1962 to bring its shareholding to $39,400,000, there had been no further provision of capital. Since 1962, however, the assets of Qantas had grown from $114.76 million to $250 million, to provide an asset backing of over $6 per $1 share. There was no doubt that further expansion lay ahead. What was questionable was the prospect of continuing prosperity.

The environment for the operation of international airlines was changing rapidly in 1970. Pan American, the giant of the industry, had posted a $25 million dollar loss for the previous year. Growth was not the problem; measured in ton miles, the annual growth rate of the international airlines had been almost fifteen per cent since 1948. But costs were rising faster than revenue and revenue yields were declining sharply year by year. Qantas had seen its revenue yield per load ton mile decline by eleven per cent in five years as it was forced to match the

422

proliferation of promotional fares offered. More passengers were travelling but at reduced fares and the return per passenger mile had reached an all-time low. Load factors fell dramatically on the Kangaroo Route as passengers flocked to the cheap British charter operators.

At the beginning of the seventies, as revenue yields fell, for the first time in the history of civil aviation improved technology and labour efficiency were unable to counter rising cost levels. During Qantas's first fifty years the greatest challenges came mainly from technical and operational changes. Sir Roland Wilson now saw the three main factors dominating the airline's corporate life as finance, marketing, and industrial relations. Of these, finance and marketing were, he said, "the most important factors in any airline that wants to survive and remain profitable".[1]

On 2 February 1970 the new and mounting competitive pressures were evident in discussions that began in Melbourne between United States and Australian authorities on the request by the newly designated US Pacific route carrier, American Airlines, to operate seven frequencies per week. Australia's director-general of civil aviation, D. G. Anderson, was blunt in his opening statement. There were already five carriers on the South Pacific route operating a total of twenty-six frequencies with an average load factor of only forty-five per cent. American Airlines wanted to provide an additional 980 seats each week and lift US capacity by seventy-eight per cent, yet Pan American's existing load factor was only forty-three per cent.

HS-125 VH-ECF, winner of the jet section of the BP England to Australia air race in January 1970, returns to the Qantas jet base. The Qantas crew flew from London in an elapsed time of 27 hours 30 minutes 29 seconds, crossing the finishing line at Adelaide almost 1 hour 56 minutes ahead of a Canadian Armed Forces fan-jet Falcon. Note the fiftieth anniversary symbol near the entry door.

Further, Pan American planned to introduce the large Boeing 747 on three of its existing frequencies and to increase these frequencies from seven to ten per week. Altogether, Pan American planned to provide an additional 2,060 seats per week.

Though the immediate issue was a commercial one (a battle for market share and a disregard for profitability), the implications went far beyond this, promising a major confrontation between the Australian and United States governments. The minister for civil aviation, Robert Cotton, was quick to advise Prime Minister Gorton of the high stakes.

> In spite of the very clear indications we had given them over the past two years at diplomatic level concerning the serious problems that would arise if the United States Government should designate a second major carrier on the South Pacific route to Australia, the initial proposition of the United States officials at the recent consultations involved a tremendous increase in the US flag carrier seat capacity . . . Qantas could not hope to remain competitive should the United States carriers proposals be approved. The best Qantas could do within the limits of aircraft availability would be to step up its frequency from eight to twelve per week. Even with this maximum competitive response, Qantas' market share would drop significantly and the result would be a loss to the order of $15 million in the first twelve months. In short, the acceptance of the initial United States position would be ruinous for Qantas' financial position . . . Simply stated, the United States is asking us to agree to an over-capacity situation in which there would be 600,000 seats available on airlines operating on this route catering for 200,000 passengers during the next twelve months.

Australia, wrote Cotton, had made an offer, after consultation with Qantas, equivalent to a total of thirteen Boeing 707 frequencies per week, which it regarded as an absolute limit. "Qantas estimated that this offer would cost them a total of $8 million which is almost the amount of the airline's profit before tax . . . The offer was not accepted. These developments appear to me to justify a firm stand on our part." The financial impact on Qantas was, he wrote, a crucial issue both immediately and over the longer term.

> From its gross profits Qantas would normally pay taxation and dividends to the Commonwealth while retaining a proportion to assist in financing the purchase of new aircraft etc. Any substantial decline in its profitability such as would be involved in accepting the United States proposal would undoubtedly reduce or eliminate contributions to Commonwealth revenues and, as a further consequence, the Government could be called upon to provide more than $150 million in capital for which the Company has already foreshadowed a need over the next two or three years . . . I con-

424

sidered it necessary to inform you fully of the major considerations affecting the attitude we have taken . . .[2]

The South Pacific battle was only one of many new pressures on an expanding Qantas. "Senior executives in all significant areas of Qantas management emphasise their consciousness that past efforts have only been a prelude to the battle of the seventies", wrote *Aircraft* magazine.[3] Preparations, across the whole gamut of the airline's activities, were on an unprecedented scale. In fleet planning, despite the decision to buy jumbo jets, the re-equipment programme required intense study of three alternative fleet structures involving expenditure that drew from *Aircraft* the comment that their common element of cost "has its initial shocks for those who think that defence equipment (such as, for instance, the F-111 programme) touches the zenith in modern top aircraft provisioning".[4]

The three possible future fleet programmes each retained ten of the existing twenty-one Boeing 707-338C aircraft. In the first, nineteen Boeing 747s would be added, which, with $50 million in additional support investment, made a total capital cost of $544 million. In the second, only five more 747s would be bought plus eighteen of the new wide-bodied trijets (the McDonnell Douglas DC10s or the Lockheed L-10011s). With support investment of $60 million the total cost was $586 million. The third alternative under consideration involved purchase of fifteen more 747s and eight Concorde supersonic airliners for a total cost of $658 million.

These were initial capital costs only. Over a ten-year operating period, and exclusive of loan servicing and insurance costs, *Aircraft* estimated the total programme cost for the first two alternatives at $4.5 billion, rising to $4.75 billion for the Concorde mix. (Qantas had made it clear, however, that trijets would not be considered unless the Concorde was rejected.)

The engineering planning and property management programmes were on a commensurate scale. R. J. Yates, director of technical services, wrote: "With a unit cost of $20 million and a revenue earning potential of $5,500 per hour per [747] aircraft, considerable planning is an economic necessity to ensure that each aircraft goes into service without delay and at the highest utilisation. In the engineering field alone, over 100,000 manhours of planning will have been spent by the time our first 747 arrives in Sydney." Facilities needed included a new hangar (big enough for a stretched 747), a new workshop annex to the hangar for airframe component repair, an extension to the engine overhaul workshop to handle the huge JT9D engine, extensions to component overhaul workshops, a new jet test cell, expansion of the central store, a new training building, a new flight kitchen, and the installation of an advanced 747 flight simulator. In total, almost a million square feet of additional floor area, costing approximately $23 million, was needed. (One big problem was shortage of land within the airport boundaries; Qantas acquired eighteen acres of land on the airport's northern boundary at a cost of $1.7 million.)

In Sydney, the first stage of the new Qantas International Centre was under construction. Five underground floors, excavated from rock, were in preparation to house Australia's largest computer centre (due for completion in August 1971). In 1970 it was expected confidently that the 600-feet tower block would be finished by the end of 1973 and that, by 1978, it would be completely filled by Qantas staff. In North America, Qantas were building a new headquarters in San Francisco and in Perth, Nadi (Fiji), Honolulu, and London various other work was under way. There was enthusiasm, and even the beginning of initial negotiations, for a completely new Qantas round-the-world route through South America and South Africa.

There was, too, a further important element necessary for the commercial success of Qantas that was not concerned directly with the operation of an airline fleet. Airlines had to be confident that they could provide suitable hotel accommodation for their passengers. The new Wentworth Hotel in Sydney had proved its worth. Qantas had also, during the year, acquired minority shareholdings in the companies operating the Mocambo Hotel and the Fijian Hotel, in Fiji. In Australia, however, there remained a critical shortage of accommodation in all capital cities and tourist resorts. The Qantas response in 1970 was to arrange a consortium of hotel organisations in which the airline did not plan any heavy financial involvement for itself. Qantas submitted to Cotton a proposal in May 1970 that it participate on an equal basis with these organisations in the formation of a company that would sponsor the construction of a limited number of hotels. Putting this submission forward, Cotton provided an insight into the government's assessment of its chosen instrument as Australia's international airline. He wrote:

> Three factors have contributed to Qantas being in a sound financial position at the present time. First, the Government has been able to secure satisfactory exchanges of traffic rights in negotiations with other governments; second, the airline has reliable and appropriate modern aircraft available to it at all times, financing

them largely through loans raised by the Commonwealth; thirdly, it has been an efficiently administered organisation which has established a solid reputation as a skilful and safe operator in a highly competitive industry.

The international airline industry is now experiencing an intensification of competitive pressures accompanied by steadily rising costs of operation, very great pressure for lower fares and consequent lower yields. All these factors are affecting Qantas and, despite an increasing volume of traffic on all its routes, the airline's ability to make a profit is being severely tested.

A special factor affecting the Qantas position is the extent to which other international airlines are wanting to provide an increasing number of services into and out of Australia. There are now fourteen major international airlines operating to and from this country and, without exception, they are either extending or aiming to extend the frequency of their operations. Additionally, numerous other airlines are seeking to enter the Australian market, including at least five significant European operators (e.g. Swissair and Scandinavian Airlines).

The Qantas share of the total traffic carried annually into and out of Australia has fallen from 51 per cent in 1962 to below 46 per cent in 1969. This is a trend which could well continue if constructive counter measures are not employed.

Cotton stressed the importance of the new pressures on the South Pacific from the United States and concluded:

At least twelve other major airlines, the majority of whom compete with Qantas on routes to and from Australia, are . . . participating in the hotel industry. The Qantas competitive position demands that the airline be able to provide adequate accommodation in Australia as well as have access to accommodation of the right type at the major destination points.

Qantas had a brief respite from problems that turned thoughts from the future to their origins. On 30 March 1970, Qantas flew the Queen and the Duke of Edinburgh from Auckland to Sydney to begin a tour of Australia. In Queensland, they visited the town of Longreach, where Qantas had begun its pioneering operations, and saw an exhibition mounted in the original Qantas hangar that traced the company's fifty-year history. In that same month, Sir Roland Wilson drew his minister's attention to the board's efforts to define the airline's goals for the future.

It seemed to us desirable to set down as clearly as we could . . . appropriate corporate objectives for Qantas . . . However, in view of the fact that Qantas Airways Limited is wholly owned by the Commonwealth Government, it was agreed that it would be proper for me to let you see our own formulation of desirable objectives for the Company and seek any comments you may wish to make before they are promulgated.

427

Wilson listed them:

> (i) To build and foster Australia's international airline in such a way that it will contribute significantly to Australia's progress and development and be identified strongly with the traditions and character of the Australian people.
>
> (ii) To operate the airline on a sound financial basis by seeking to earn an adequate return on funds invested.
>
> (iii) To advance the Company's place in international civil aviation by seeking out and exploiting opportunities for sound economic growth in its airline and related activities.
>
> (iv) To earn and to exploit the highest reputation for efficient, reliable and friendly service.
>
> (v) To encourage and promote the growth of tourism, especially to Australia and associated territories.
>
> (vi) To conduct the affairs of the Company on the highest plane of business ethics.
>
> (vii) To maintain and develop an effective corporate organisation, with highly trained and qualified personnel who will take a responsible and enthusiastic attitude towards the fulfilment of their defined tasks and objectives.[5]

Cotton responded favourably, adding his extra twopence of ministerial wisdom. The first objective was modified to include the words "in the light of Australian Government policy". The fourth had the word "safe" inserted before "efficient, reliable and friendly service", but not before Wilson had made it plain that "airlines have a traditional reluctance to talk too much about safety—mainly, I understand, because they feel it could be embarrassing in the event of some untoward event [*sic*].[6]

On 25 June, Cotton announced that Sir Roland Wilson had been reappointed as Qantas chairman for a further three years, with Robert Law-Smith continuing as vice-chairman. Captain Ritchie, general manager of Qantas, was appointed to the board to replace Sir James Kirby. Hudson Fysh wrote him a note of congratulations. "It was very kind of you", Wilson responded, "to take the trouble to write to me on my reappointment to the Qantas Board. As you know, I find it both interesting and challenging. We were all pleased to see Bert Ritchie appointed to the Board . . . but he is not Managing Director. He is still General Manager and has been appointed as a Board member for three years, the same as the rest of us. I will be looking forward to seeing you at the opening of Melbourne Airport."[7]

It was increasingly likely by mid-1970 that any "untoward event" in the operation of civil airliners, as Wilson had put it in his letter to Cotton, would be an airliner hijack of some kind. On 11 June the *Australian Financial Review* wrote: "From the airlines' point of view, hijacking is becoming distressingly fashionable. There were eighty-nine last year but in the first month of this year alone an estimated one hundred and ninety took place. Australia's most recent was at Sydney last month, where a young man tried to take over a DC-9 with a toy pistol." In fact, the problem had become so threatening and widespread that the International Civil Aviation Organisation convened an "extraordinary and emergency meeting" in Montreal on 11 June solely to consider "the protection of civil airliners". Australia was represented by senior officials of the Department of Civil Aviation, Qantas executives, and representatives of the Australian Federation of Air Pilots. The Montreal assembly had before it papers for consideration on the prevention of hijacking by the use of devices and procedures on the ground, over-powering hijackers in the air, and for an international agreement that hijacking be regarded as a crime and procedures be implemented under which hijackers would be extradited to their home countries to face court action and strong penalties. "Together," wrote the *Financial Review*, "they won't eradicate the insane and dangerous practice but they might have the effect of making it harder and far less certain of success."[8] (Subsequent years were to show that even this modest hope was unfounded.) The conclusions of the ICAO Montreal meeting were sent to the prime minister. Cotton commented in a letter to Gorton on 17 September: "The letter deals with a subject of considerable gravity and importance. So far we have escaped in Australia serious hijacking incident but the possibility of a more organised attempt being made to hijack an aircraft within Australia cannot be ignored. There is, of course, the equally important consideration that our own international airline, Qantas, could even more easily be involved in such an incident whilst operating its services through various sensitive areas on its world routes." He advised the prime minister, in replying to the ICAO letter, to point out that "Australian law and practice have been reviewed to ensure that measures of the kind recommended by the Assembly can be applied in this country. Our domestic legislation has for some time prescribed severe penalties for acts of violence against aircraft."[9]

Though governments and airlines heeded ICAO's words, the world's hijackers did not. Captain Ritchie told the board in October:

> Last month the Board was informed about the piracy of four aircraft, one of which — a Pan American 747 — had been destroyed at Cairo. The remaining three were subsequently destroyed at

Zarka on 13 September by Jordanian guerillas after all passengers had been moved to Amman. At this time 234 passengers remained prisoners of the rebel forces, the balance having been released and evacuated by the International Red Cross . . . By 14 September all but 54 had been set free. These people were kept prisoners of the guerilla forces in various parts of Amman, the last group being freed on 29 September following a cease fire agreement between the Jordanian Government and guerilla forces.

On Tuesday 15 September, three men and a woman of Hungarian nationality hijacked a BAC.111 of Romanian airlines and forced the pilot at gun point to divert to Munich . . . On 15 September, an attempt was made by a man to hijack a TWA 707 aircraft on the ground at San Francisco and have the crew fly him to North Korea . . . The hijacker was shot by a security guard . . . Security checks at Kennedy Airport uncovered revolvers on the persons of two Americans on 27 September.

These acts of violence against civil airliners had all taken place in areas through which Qantas operated.

Ritchie summarised the increased precautions taken by Qantas to avert hijacking but concluded:

> There is no positive way to prevent a determined person hijacking an aircraft. We have implemented security precautions which are in line with other international airlines and at the moment the threat seems to have diminished . . .[10]

The risk to Qantas aircraft from hijackers or terrorists had financial implications for the airline's insurance costs that coincided with the introduction to airline fleets of the much larger and costlier jumbo jets. Nevertheless, Cotton brought pressure on Qantas to make use of the self-insurance reserve it had built up in the years when the airline had declined to pay the high cost of insurance premiums in the market. Cotton's motive was to avoid or minimise future government contributions of capital to Qantas as it moved rapidly into the jumbo jet era. On 13 July 1970 he wrote to Wilson that in the light of total Commonwealth budget considerations,

> no provision is being made in 1970–71 estimates for any capital subscription to Qantas. This proposed course of action raises the question of what should be done about the self-insurance reserve, now that Qantas is largely insuring against its risks on the commercial market. In effect, the major part of the reserve (which stood at just under $18 million in 1970) could be recognised as accumulated profits . . . It could be appropriate for Qantas to make a bonus share issue based on transferring the reserve, or part of it, to shareholder's funds.[11]

Wilson responded firmly that higher insurance premiums were

imposing heavier financial burdens on international airlines. Although this was associated to some extent with the increasing exposure to risks, the larger and more expensive Boeing 747 aircraft were the primary cause, according to Wilson. "Premiums are rising and it would not appear prudent to weaken our bargaining position with underwriters just at the time we are about to seek quotations for Boeing 747 aircraft", Wilson said. The board, he added,

> was greatly disturbed on the more important issue of capital subscription . . . [it] has been mindful of the very heavy demands that will be imposed on the Government over the next few years and has endeavoured to spread the load. Since 1967 the Company has kept the Government informed of the unusual financial burdens which will need to be met in the early 1970s. Our need for $50 million was acknowledged by the Treasurer in 1967 and confirmed on a number of occasions since then . . . Every effort has been made by the Board to alleviate this demand on the Commonwealth. The Company has spread its tax burdens arising from the sale of its Boeing 138B fleet over the life of the Boeing 707-138C aircraft. Operating profits have been maintained at satisfactory levels, computers have been acquired by lease finance, and there has been considerable deferment of essential building projects. Despite these efforts the need for additional capital can only be deferred for a limited period and the Board is most concerned that the very heavy demands now arising will create significant embarrassment to the Commonwealth unless progressive injection of capital is achieved . . . . [12]

There was more than a little irony in the fact that Qantas, in their fiftieth and most successful ever year of operations, were now under financial siege on all fronts. Their one shareholder was reluctant to provide essential additional capital, their costs were rising sharply, the yield from each revenue seat mile flown was declining, and direct airline competitive pressures were mounting. All these things were happening as they faced increases in capital spending for aircraft and supporting services on a scale never before encountered, as well as the certain prospect that the arrival of wide-bodied aircraft in the world's airline fleets would mean substantial overcapacity. Rapid change had been the only constant in the Qantas environment since their beginnings as a pioneer airline in Queensland. The industry was poised for massive change in 1970 in its equipment and its market.

On 2 July the most immediate threat to Qantas's future profitability became reality. Cotton informed the prime minister that the United States had accepted the Australian offer of a total of thirteen equivalent Boeing 707 frequencies for US flag carriers serving Australia on the Pacific route. The agreement "allowed" Qantas to increase its own weekly frequencies on the route to thirteen to match the American total. American Airlines was to operate on the route with three frequencies weekly and Pan American were to have one extra frequency. "This . . . amounts to an increase in US flag carrier capacity of 45 per cent over the present level", wrote Cotton. It also marked the start of unprofitable operations on the route for all three airlines.

On 7 August 1970, Qantas announced plans to meet head-on the combined competition of Pan American and American Airlines. Qantas, said Wilson, would increase its frequencies to the maximum permitted. "It foresees a real slogging match with our efforts to maintain Australia's share of this very valuable foreign exchange market . . . This will probably mean a loss operation on the Pacific for most operators for some time."[13]

Captain Ritchie, visiting the United States in August, told *Aviation Daily* that the Qantas decision on whether to order additional Boeing 747s or buy the McDonnell Douglas DC10 trijet would be made within a month. Considerations, he said, were price (the Boeing 747 was $22 million and the DC10 $16.5 million), the cost of introducing different types, and operating costs. Air New Zealand's recent decision to buy the DC10 "has no impact" on the Qantas deliberations, he said. They would begin Boeing 747 services on the Sydney-California route in September 1971, extending to New York and London in 1972. Qantas, said Ritchie, favoured continuation of the American supersonic airliner project. "The Boeing SST appears much better from a size standpoint than the Concorde."[14]

Size was, in the Qantas view, the only competitive virtue of the Boeing SST. Ritchie reported to the board that since its redesign in 1968, the availability gap between the Boeing 2707-300 and the Concorde had widened to five or six years, making delivery of the American aircraft unlikely before 1980. "The new design has fixed wings rather than variable sweep but is still to be built of titanium to provide Mach 2.7 capability." Despite its higher speed in comparison with the Concorde Ritchie commented: "Its advantage on block speed is surprisingly small. It is an aircraft of about twice Concorde's weight, carrying twice the number of passengers and costing twice as much. Despite Boeing's forecasts it is difficult to see any major gain in seat-mile costs over the Concorde . . . The noise levels beside the runway at lift-off are certainly a problem. Politically, the cry of 'pollution' is a potent weapon." The Concorde, Ritchie reported, had in the eighteen months since its first flight made 121 flights with two prototypes, including thirty-one hours of supersonic flight. The highest speed reached had been Mach 1.5 (1,000 miles per hour) and the highest altitude 47,000 feet. Mechanically, the aircraft had operated without a single unscheduled engine shut-down and airline pilots had reported favourably on its handling qualities. "For some time most airlines have deferred detailed analysis of the Concorde and concentrated their efforts on wide-bodied subsonic aircraft, believing that the Concorde might never eventuate. This attitude has been fostered by frequent postponements of the certification date which is now estimated at late 1973. However, the time of decision now seems imminent . . . For a 1974 delivery, Qantas would be committed to a decision by mid-1971, by which time the Pan American position should be known."[15]

These, then, were the preoccupations of Qantas as it prepared to celebrate the fiftieth birthday of the company at a jubilee dinner in Sydney on 16 November 1970. The two overriding problems—the urgent need for more capital and the importance of the right aircraft choice—had not changed in kind since the company's very first years. Now, however, the operating environment was not the blacksoil plains of Western Queensland but routes that circled the whole world. They were routes that had to be won by hard negotiations between Australia and a host of foreign governments and that had to be operated in competition with the biggest and most efficient of the world's airlines. If Qantas were somewhat bigger in 1970 than they had been in 1920, and if their Boeing 747s could carry four hundred people while their first little Avro 504K could take only one passenger, the challenges that faced the men who led the airline in 1970 were hardly less daunting than those that faced Hudson Fysh, Paul McGinness, Arthur Baird, and Fergus McMaster in the 1920s.

Qantas growth in the years since World War II had been dramatic. In 1945, with a staff of 1,500, the airline had flown 11 million capacity ton miles and earned revenue of $4 million. Ten years later, with a staff of 5,400, they had flown 84 million capacity ton miles and earned $32 million. By 1969, with staff at 11,200, revenue was $200 million and capacity ton miles flown 804 million.

Compared with other international airlines Qantas was efficient. Their productivity per employee in capacity ton miles was 72,000; Lufthansa's was 70,000, KLM's was 76,000, UTA's

433

72,000, and Swissair's 57,000. None matched the large American carriers whose route density and size enabled productivity almost double that of Qantas. Comparisons in aircraft utilisation were also good. Qantas had lifted its daily utilisation of Boeing 707 aircraft to almost 12 hours per day compared with Lufthansa's 12.3, Swissair's 13, Pan American's 11.4, KLM's 11.2, and BOAC's 10.5. In size among the 104 members of IATA (using 1968 figures), Qantas ranked seventh in route mileage, twentieth in capacity ton miles flown, twenty-first in passengers carried, and twenty-second in number of employees. Qantas had earned $108 million in foreign exchange for Australia in 1969, making it the country's ninth largest earner.

Sir Roland Wilson, in his speech to the many distinguished guests that attended the jubilee Qantas birthday party at Sydney's Wentworth Hotel said: "We like to think that responsibility and enthusiasm – with, hopefully, the odd touch of genius – have in the past and will in the future continue to characterise the people of Qantas". [16]

The first Qantas Boeing 747B *City of Canberra* at Boeing's Everett airport in early July 1971. This aircraft made its first flight on 8 July 1971 and arrived in Sydney on 16 August.

Some few months later, in mid-1971, the *Australian Financial Review* wrote: "At midnight on 9 June, Qantas poked its nose into the jumbo world when the first of its four 747Bs rolled out of the 23-acre Boeing factory building at Everett, north of Seattle". [17]

Appendix

Qantas Fleet: Aircraft Owned and Operated, 1954–1970

Aircraft Type	Registration	Constructor's Number	Aircraft Name	Registration	Disposal	Remarks
Douglas DC-4	VH-EDA	42917	*Pacific Trader*	23.09.59 (ex VH-EBK, 15.02.49)	19.08.77	Sold to Air Express Ltd
Douglas DC-4	VH-EDB	7458	*Norfolk Trader*	11.04.60 (ex VH-EBN, 18.07.49)	19.08.77	Sold to Air Express Ltd
De Havilland DHC-3 Otter	VH-EAW	241	*Kikori*	27.05.58	01.09.60	Sold to TAA as VH-SBQ
De Havilland DHC-3 Otter	VH-EAX	247	*Kokopo*	27.05.58	01.09.60	Sold to TAA as VH-SBR
De Havilland DHC-3 Otter	VH-EAY	253	*Kieta*	04.07.58	0.09.60	Sold to TAA as VH-SBS
De Havilland DHC-3 Otter	VH-EAZ	258	*Kerowagi*	21.08.58	01.09.60	Sold to TAA as VH-SBT
Lockheed L188C Electra	VH-ECA	2002	*Pacific Electra*	04.11.59	06.06.67	Sold to Air California as N359AC
Lockheed L188C Electra	VH-ECB	2004	*Pacific Explorer*	04.11.59	21.08.67	Sold to Air California as N385AC
Lockheed L188C Electra	VH-ECC	2007	*Pacific Endeavour*	23.11.59	18.04.65	Sold to Air New Zealand as ZK-CLX
Lockheed L188C Electra	VH-ECD	2008	*Pacific Enterprise*	03.12.59	30.04.70	Sold to Air New Zealand as ZK-TED

Aircraft Type	Registration	Constructor's Number	Aircraft Name	Registration	Disposal	Remarks
Hawker Siddeley H.S. 125 Series 3B	VH-ECE	25062		15.06.66	08.10.81	Sold to G.D. Onus/ withdrawn from use
Hawker Siddeley H.S. 125 Series 3B	VH-ECF	25069		08.07.66	29.11.72	Sold to McAlpine Aviation Ltd as G-BAXL
Boeing 707-138	VH-EBA	17696	City of Canberra (roll-out) City of Melbourne (from July 1959)	07.06.59	03.11.67	Modified to B. 707-138B standard Sold to Pacific Western as CF-PWV
Boeing 707-138	VH-EBB	17697	City of Canberra (delivery flight) City of Sydney (from July 1959)	26.06.59	04.05.67	Modified to B. 707-138B standard Sold to Standard Airways as N790SA
Boeing 707-138	VH-EBC	17698	City of Melbourne (delivery) City of Canberra (from July 1959)	09.07.59	04.05.67	Modified to B. 707-138B standard Sold to Standard Airways as N791SA
Boeing 707-138	VH-EBD	17699	City of Brisbane	12.08.59	01.02.68	Modified to B.707-138B standard Sold to British Eagle as G-AVZZ
Boeing 707-138	VH-EBE	17700	City of Perth	24.08.59	15.05.68	Modified to B.707-138B standard Sold to Standard Airways as N793SA
Boeing 707-138	VH-EBF	17701	City of Adelaide	10.09.59	26.03.68	Modified to B.707-138B standard Sold to Standard Airways as N792SA
Boeing 707-138	VH-EBG	17702	City of Hobart	24.09.59	13.03.68	Modified to B.707-138B standard Sold to British Eagle as G-AWDG
Boeing 707-138B	VH-EBH	18067	City of Darwin	06.08.61	21.09.69	Sold to British West Indies Airways as 9Y-TDC
Boeing 707-138B	VH-EBI	18068	Winton	19.08.61	28.06.69	Sold to Braniff Airways as N105BN

Type	Registration	C/N	Name	Date	Date	Disposal
Boeing 707-138B	VH-EBJ	18069	*Longreach*	26.08.61	04.07.69	Sold to Braniff Airways as N106BN
Boeing 707-138B	VH-EBK	18334	*City of Newcastle*	31.08.61	08.12.68	Sold to British West Indies Airways as 9Y-TDB
Boeing 707-138B	VH-EBL	18739	*City of Geelong Winton* (10.12.65 only) *City of Geelong* (from 11.12.65)	21.08.64	19.06.69	Sold to Braniff Airways as N107BN
Boeing 707-138B	VH-EBM	18740	*City of Launceston*	12.09.64	24.06.69	Sold to Braniff Airways as N108BN
Boeing 707-338C	VH-EBN	18808	*City of Parramatta*	15.02.65	02.09.74	Sold to Singapore Airlines as 9V-BFW
Boeing 707-338C	VH-EBO	18809	*City of Townsville*	08.03.65	17.11.72	Sold to Singapore Airlines as 9V-BFN
Boeing 707-338C	VH-EBP	18810	*Alice Springs*	16.08.65	17.11.72	Sold to Trans World Airlines as N14791
Boeing 707-338C	VH-EBQ	18953	*City of Ballarat*	18.09.65	22.02.74	Sold to Malaysian Airlines
Boeing 707-338C	VH-EBR	18954	*City of Wollongong*	05.02.66	28.06.74	Sold to Malaysian Airlines System as 9M-ATR
Boeing 707-338C	VH-EBS	18955	*Kalgoorlie*	09.03.66	11.10.73	Sold to Malaysian Airlines System as 9M-ASO
Boeing 707-338C	VH-EBT	19293	*City of Bendigo*	28.02.67	17.04.78	Sold to British Midlands Airways as G-BFLE
Boeing 707-338C	VH-EBU	19294	*City of Broken Hill City of Parramatta* (from July 1975)	30.03.67	03.11.76	Sold to Air Niugini as P2-ANH
Boeing 707-338C	VH-EBV	19295	*City of Tamworth*	06.09.67	05.04.77	Sold to Zambia Airways as 9J-AEL
Boeing 707-338C	VH-EBW	19296	*City of Armidale*	10.10.67	12.05.75	Sold to British Caledonian Airways as G-BDEA
Boeing 707-338C	VH-EBX	19297	*Port Moresby City of Port Moresby* (from April 1972) *City of Parramatta* (from Oct. 1974)	24.10.67	28.04.75	Sold to British Caledonian Airways as G-BCAL

Aircraft Type	Registration	Constructor's Number	Aircraft Name	Registration	Disposal	Remarks
Boeing 707-338C	VH-EAA	19621	City of Toowoomba	12.12.67	27.04.77	Sold to Irel Equipment Management Co as 00-YCK
Boeing 707-338C	VH-EAB	19622	City of Canberra Winton (from June 1971)	12.01.68	27.12.77	Sold to Irel Equipment Management Co as 00-YCL
Boeing 707-338C	VH-EAC	19623	City of Sydney Longreach (from Oct. 1971)	07.02.68	30.10.78	Leased to British Caledonian Airways 08.10.75 to 09.01.76 as G-BDKE. Sold to Irel Corporation as C-GRYN
Boeing 707-338C	VH-EAD	19624	City of Melbourne City of Newcastle (from June 1971) City of Ballarat (from April 1974)	29.03.68	30.03.79	Sold to RAAF as A20-624
Boeing 707-338C	VH-EAE	19625	City of Brisbane Swan Hill (from Aug. 1972)	06.04.68	23.02.78	Sold to Irel Corporation as G-BFLD
Boeing 707-338C	VH-EAF	19626	City of Adelaide City of Townsville (from June 1973) City of Armidale (from May 1976)	07.05.68	03.04.78	Sold to Korean Airlines as HL7432
Boeing 707-338C	VH-EAG	19627	City of Hobart Alice Springs (from Feb. 1974)	18.05.68	30.03.79	Sold to RAAF as A20-627
Boeing 707-338C	VH-EAH	19628	City of Perth City of Launceston (from Oct. 1971)	14.06.68	11.06.78	Sold to Korean Airlines as HL7433
Boeing 707-338C	VH-EAI	19629	City of Darwin City of Kalgoorlie (from Apr. 1974)	24.08.68	07.11.75	Sold to British Caledonian Airways as G-BDLM
Boeing 707-338C	VH-EAJ	19630	City of Geelong City of Broken Hill (from Apr. 1975)	03.10.68	24.03.76	Sold to British Caledonian Airways as G-BDSJ

Type	Registration	Construction no.	Name	Date	Date	Remarks
Boeing 707-349C	VH-EBZ (ex EI-ASO)	19354	City of Swan Hill	17.09.70	29.09.71	Leased from Aer Lingus, returned as EI-ASO
Boeing 707-327C	N7099	19108		05.01.71	16.10.71	Leased from Braniff International Airways (freighter aircraft)
Douglas DC-3	VH-EDC	12874		12.07.61	15.11.71	Sold to Queensland Pacific Airways Pty Ltd
Douglas DC-3	VH-EDD	13922/25367		22.01.64	15.12.71	Sold to Queensland Pacific Airways Pty Ltd
Boeing 747-238B	VH-EBA	20009	City of Canberra	30.07.71	08.06.84	Sold to Guinness Peat Aviation as 4R-ULF.
Boeing 747-238B	VH-EBA	20009		01.09.86		Leased from British Caledonian Airways
Boeing 747-238B	VH-EBB	20010	City of Melbourne	14.08.71	06.07.84	Sold to Guinness Peat Aviation
Boeing 747-238B	VH-EBB	20010	City of Melbourne	07.07.84	22.10.85	Leased from Guinness Peat Aviation (thence to Air Lanka as 4R-ULG)
Boeing 747-238B	VH-EBB	20010	Island of Viti Leeu	16.07.87		Leased from Aerospace Finance, to operate in Air Pacific livery under commercial arrangement with Air Pacific
Boeing 747-238B	VH-EBC	20011	City of Sydney	21.10.71	04.12.84	Sold to Boeing Equipment Holding Co as N747BM (thence to People Express as N607PE)
Boeing 747-238B	VH-EBD	20012	City of Perth	08.12.71	21.03.85	Sold to Boeing Equipment Holding Co as N747BN (thence to People Express as N608PE)
Boeing 747-238B	VH-EBE	20534	City of Brisbane	23.08.84	08.01.86	Leased from Boeing Equipment Holding Co (thence to People Express as N609PE)
Boeing 747-238B	VH-EBF	20535	City of Adelaide	01.08.73	22.08.84	Sold to Boeing Equipment Holding Co

Aircraft Type	Registration	Constructor's Number	Aircraft Name	Registration	Disposal	Remarks
Boeing 747-238B	VH-EBF	20535	City of Adelaide	23.08.84	28.02.86	Leased from Boeing Equipment Holding Co (thence to People Express as N610PE)
Boeing 747-238B	VH-EBG	20841	City of Hobart City of Fremantle (from Aug. 1985)	19.03.74		
Boeing 747-238B	VH-EBH	20842	City of Newcastle City of Parramatta (from Aug. 1985)	24.05.74		
Boeing 747-238B	VH-EBI	20921	City of Darwin City of Dubbo (from Aug. 1985)	10.10.74		
Boeing 747-238B	VH-EBJ	21054	City of Geelong City of Newcastle (from Aug. 1985)	30.05.75		
Boeing 747-238B	VH-EBK	21140	City of Melbourne Island of Viti Levu (from Mar. 1985) City of Sale (from Sept. 1987)	07.11.75		Operated in Air Pacific livery under commercial arrangement with Air Pacific, 23.03.85 to mid-November 1987.
Boeing 747-238B	VH-EBL	21237	City of Townsville City of Perth (from July 1985) City of Ballarat (from Nov. 1986)	29.06.76		
Boeing 747-238B	VH-EBM	21352	City of Parramatta City of Darwin (from Aug. 1985) City of Gosford (from Apr. 1987)	15.08.77		
Boeing 747-238B	VH-EBN	21353	City of Albury	20.12.77		
Boeing 747-238B	VH-EBP	21658	City of Fremantle City of Adelaide (from Aug. 1985)	16.10.78		

Type	Registration	C/n	Name	Date	Date	Notes
Boeing 747-238B	VH-EBQ	22145	City of Bunbury	10.12.79		
Boeing 747-238B	VH-EBS	22616	Longreach	30.11.81		
Boeing 747-238B Combi	VH-ECA	21354	City of Sale	27.10.77	17.07.87	Sold to City Corp. Canada (Air Canada) as C-GAGC
Boeing 747-238B Combi	VH-ECB	21977	City of Swan Hill	14.11.79		
Boeing 747-238B Combi	VH-ECC	22615	City of Shepparton	15.10.80		
Boeing 747SP-38	VH-EAA	22495	City of Gold Coast/Tweed	19.01.81		
Boeing 747SP-38	VH-EAB	22672	Winton	31.08.81		
Boeing 747-338	VH-EBT	23222	City of Canberra	13.11.84		
Boeing 747-338	VH-EBU	23223	City of Sydney	24.01.85		
Boeing 747-338	VH-EBV	23224	City of Melbourne	15.04.85		
Boeing 747-338	VH-EBW	23408	City of Brisbane	31.03.86		
Boeing 747-338	VH-EBX	23688	City of Perth	12.11.86		
Boeing 747-338	VH-EBY	23823	City of Darwin	01.05.87		
Boeing 767-238ER	VH-EAJ	23304	City of Wollongong	03.07.85		
Boeing 767-238ER	VH-EAK	23305	City of Townsville	11.07.85		
Boeing 767-238ER	VH-EAL	23306	City of Geelong	27.09.85		
Boeing 767-238ER	VH-EAM	23309	City of Lake Macquarie	12.12.85		
Boeing 767-238ER	VH-EAN	23402	Alice Springs	05.02.86		
Boeing 767-238ER	VH-EAQ	23403	City of Cairns	19.03.86		
Boeing 767-238ER	VH-EAQ	23896	City of Launceston	27.08.87		

Notes

In citing sources in the notes, abbreviations have generally been used. Sources frequently cited have been identified by the following:

AA   Australian Archives

BA   British Airways archives, RAF Museum, Hendon, London

CTP   Cedric Oban Turner Papers (in the possession of the author, supplied by C. O. Turner's son, Ross Turner)

EJP   Edgar Johnston Papers (in the possession of Edgar Johnston)

HFP   Hudson Fysh Papers (Mitchell Library, Sydney)

JUP   John Ulm Papers (in the possession of the author, supplied by John Ulm)

RWP   Sir Roland Wilson Papers (in the possession of the author, supplied by Sir Roland Wilson)

Chapter 1

1. Fysh diary, 20 February 1950. There are seventy-one Fysh diaries in the Hudson Fysh papers, Mitchell Library, Sydney. They cover the period from January 1918, when Fysh qualified as a pilot at the end of World War I, to December 1973. Most are in notebooks. The entries are often scrappy and difficult to read, though there are some extended comments.
2. Ibid.
3. Fysh manuscript of *Wings to the World*, p. 334, HFP. This manuscript, much edited and abridged and without Fysh's comments on many sensitive issues, was published as *Wings to the World*. (Differentiated from the published book hereafter by the HFP location.)

4. Ibid., p. 338.
5. Ibid., p. 442.
6. Ibid., p. 339.
7. Ibid., p. 338.
8. Minutes of BOAC-Qantas meeting in London, 6 April 1954, BA.
9. Minutes of QEA-BOAC meeting London, 12 April 1954, BA.
10. Fysh to McVey, 22 July 1954, HFP.
11. Board memo by C. O. Turner, 26 May 1954, file SP1844, AA.
12. Information bulletin from C. O. Turner, 1 June 1954, file SP1844, AA.
13. Memo by A. Barlow, manager Pacific Division, 26 May 1954, file SP1844, AA.
14. Fysh to Anthony, 11 June 1954, file SP1844, AA.
15. Report on Aircraft Developments, September 1954, by Captain Allan, file SP1844, AA.
16. Private and confidential memorandum to BOAC board members from Sir Miles Thomas, 21 September 1954, BA.
17. Fysh, *Wings to the World*, p. 137.
18. Fysh to Townley, 30 August 1954, file SP1844, AA.
19. Townley to Fysh, 2 September 1954, file SP1844, AA.
20. Fysh to Wilson, 22 November 1954, HFP.
21. Fysh to Townley, 6 December 1954, file SP1844, AA.
22. Sir Daniel McVey to Viscount Swinton, 17 December 1954, BA.
23. Viscount Swinton to Sir Daniel McVey, 8 February 1955, BA.
24. Sir Miles Thomas to Phillip Hood, 8 March 1955, BA.
25. QEA Twenty-first Annual Report to 31 December 1954.
26. Fysh, *Wings to the World*, pp. 137-38.
27. Minister for air and civil aviation, Athol Townley, to Fysh 1 January 1955, file SP1844 (1943–63), AA.
28. External Affairs cable to Australian embassy, Washington, 25 January 1955, file SP1842 (1946–67), AA.
29. Note to US government from Australian ambassador, file SP1842 (1946–67), AA.
30. Australian embassy, Washington to Department of External Affairs, 2 March 1955, file SP1842 (1946–67), AA.
31. Australian embassy, Washington to Department of External Affairs, 7 March 1955, file SP1842 (1946–67), AA.
32. Acting minister for civil aviation to Fysh, 8 February 1955, file SP1844 (1943–63), AA.
33. Qantas board memo, 27 January 1955, file SP1844 (1945–52), AA.
34. Qantas press release, 17 February 1955, file SP1844 (1945–52), AA.
35. Phillip Hood to BOAC deputy chief executive, 20 January 1955, BA.
36. Whitney Straight to Sir Miles Thomas, 1 February 1955, BA.
37. Townley to Fysh, 2 May 1955, file SP1844 (1943–63), AA.
38. Smallpiece to Hood, 9 March 1955, BA.
39. Hood to Smallpiece, 14 March 1955, BA.
40. *New Zealand Herald*, 3 March 1955.
41. Hood to Smallpiece, 25 March 1955, BA.
42. External Affairs to Washington, 4 March 1955, file SP1844, AA.
43. Smallpiece to Turner, 17 March 1955, BA.
44. Turner to Smallpiece, 30 March 1955, BA.
45. Hood to sales planning manager, Brentford, 6 April 1955, BA.
46. Hood to Sir Miles Thomas, 29 April 1955, BA.
47. Spender to Townley, 3 May 1955, file SP1842 (1946–67), AA.
48. McVey to Fysh, 19 May 1955, HFP.
49. Board paper, 27 May 1955, file SP1844 (1945–52), AA.
50. McVey to Fysh, 6 June 1955, HFP.
51. Fysh to Townley, 9 June 1955, file SP1844 (1943–63), AA.
52. Hood to BOAC deputy chief executive, 24 June 1955, BA.
53. Board memo from Turner, 23 June 1955, HFP.
54. Bristol Aeroplane Company to Qantas, 10 June 1955, file SP1844 (1945–52), AA.
55. Minutes of board meeting, 24 June 1955, file SP1844 (1945–52), AA.
56. Qantas press release, 24 June 1955, HFP.
57. Fysh to Turner, 28 June 1955, HFP.
58. Qantas press release, 28 June 1955, HFP.
59. Turner board memo, 24 August 1955, file SP1844 (1945–52), AA.

60. Smallpiece report on discussions with Turner, 7 September 1955, BA.
61. Turner board memorandum, 27 July 1955, file SP1844 (1945–52), AA.
62. Memo from financial accounting division, June 1955, file SP1782 (1949–66), AA.
63. Turner memo to board, 28 July 1955, file SP1844 (1945–52), AA.
64. Turner memo to the board, 25 August 1955, file SP1844 (1945–52), AA.
65. Captain Allan report to Turner, 12 September 1955, file SP1844 (1945–52), AA.
66. Turner memo to board, 27 October 1955, file SP1844 (1945–52), AA.
67. Fysh memo to Turner, 15 November 1955, HFP.
68. Draft of joint paper for presentation to their respective governments by BOAC and QEA, 25 November 1955, file SP1844 (1945–52), AA.
69. Second Christopher Hinton lecture, "The British Aerospace Industry: A National Asset", by Sir George Edwards, 29 November 1982.
70. Turner board memo, 23 November 1955, file SP1844 (1945–52), AA.
71. Board memo, 23 November 1955, file SP1844 (1945–52), AA.
72. Turner board memo, 23 November 1955, file SP1844 (1945–52), AA.
73. QEA press release, 20 December 1955, HFP.

Chapter 2

1. Draft joint paper with amendments by Edgar Johnston, 6 January 1956, file SP1842 (1946–67), AA.
2. Hood to BOAC deputy chief executive, 4 January 1956, BA.
3. Smallpiece to Hood, 23 January 1956, BA.
4. Transcript of telephone conversation between Turner and Allen, 2 Februry 1956, Boeing company archives.
5. Allen to Turner, 8 February 1956, Boeing company archives.
6. Turner cable to Allen, 14 March 1956, Boeing company archives.
7. Author's interview with Peter Mingrone, Los Angeles, 1983.
8. Ibid.
9. Cable from Vernon Crudge to Wellwood Beall, Boeing, 27 April 1956, Boeing company archives.
10. Author's interview with Peter Mingrone, Los Angeles, 1983.
11. Transcript of telephone conversation between Schwartz, Lockheed and Beall and Skeen, Boeing, 2.55 p.m. 30 April 1956, Boeing company archives.
12. Transcript of telephone conversation between Schwartz, Lockheed, and Skeen, Boeing, at 4.15 p.m., 1 May 1956, Boeing company archives.
13. Crudge to Beall, 2 May 1956, Boeing company archives.
14. Ibid.
15. Turner to Anderson, 6 March 1956, file SP1842 (1946–67), AA.
16. Turner to Johnston, 23 April 1956, file SP1842 (1946–67), AA.
17. Townley to Fysh, 24 May 1956, file SP1844 (1952-56), AA.
18. Fysh, Wings to the World, p. 195.
19. Ibid., p. 443, HFP.
20. Author's interviews with Johnston and Allan, 1982.
21. Author's interview with Capt. Scottie Allan, 1982.
22. Edward C. Wells to William Allen, 17 May 1956, Boeing company archives.
23. Gordon Seven, Boeing, to Wellwood Beall, 17 May 1956, Boeing company archives.
24. Crudge to Beall, 24 May 1956, Boeing company archives.
25. J. O. Yeasting, Boeing vice-president controller, to Beall, 24 May 1956, Boeing company archives.
26. Ken Holtby to Beall, 29 May 1956, Boeing company archives.
27. Fysh memo to Turner, 18 May 1956, HFP.
28. Allan to Fysh, 12 June 1956, HFP.
29. Fysh diary, 16 July 1956, HFP.
30. Board report on international affairs, 16 August 1956, file SP1842 (1946–67), AA.
31. Fysh to Townley, 6 July 1956, file SP1844 (1952-56), AA.
32. Director-general's memorandum to secretary, Prime Minister's Department, 17 August 1956, file A463 Item 56/542, AA.
33. Capt. Ritchie interview with the author, 5 July 1982.
34. Author's interviews with Capt. Ritchie and Bob Walker, 1982.

35. Press release by the minister for civil aviation, Townley, 6 September 1956, file A463 Item 56/1326, AA.
36. Chief executive's *Outstation Bulletin*, September 1956, HFP.
37. "Planning the Qantas Jet Base, Mascot", paper by W. Hudson Shaw.
38. Fysh to Senator Paltridge, 20 November 1956, HFP.
39. Address by Hudson Fysh, IATA annual general meeting, Edinburgh, September 1956, HFP.
40. Hood to BOAC managing director, 27 July 1956, BA.
41. Turner to Keith Granville, 16 November 1956, BA.
42. Watt, *Evolution of Australian Foreign Policy, 1938–1965*, pp. 303, 307.
43. Paltridge to Fysh, November 1956, file SP1844 (1943-63), AA.
44. Commonwealth Relations Office memorandum, 22 November 1956, file A1209 item 57/4347, AA.
45. Fysh to Paltridge, 27 November 1956, HFP.

Chapter 3

1. Fysh to Turner, 3 January 1957, HFP.
2. Fysh to R. Law-Smith, 17 January 1957, HFP.
3. Granville to Hood, 18 January 1957, BA.
4. BOAC-prepared aide-memoire for Sir Miles Thomas, 13 February 1957, BA.
5. Statement by QEA, 20 February 1957, HFP.
6. Turner board memo, 25 February 1957, HFP.
7. Turner to Fysh, 26 February 1957, HFP.
8. Turner memo to directors, 28 February 1957, HFP.
9. Blain, *Industrial Relations in the Air*, p. 25.
10. Information contained in a letter from P. Howson, operations manager QEA, to Turner, 28 March 1957, HFP.
11. Turner letter to all pilots, 9 April 1957, HFP.
12. *Qantas News*, 10 April 1957.
13. Statement by Sir Arthur Fadden, 11 April 1957, HFP.
14. *Australian Air Pilot*, April-May 1957, HFP.
15. B. I. Crofts to Fysh, 16 May 1957, HFP.
16. Fysh, *Wings to the World*, p. 356, HFP.
17. Statement from senior staff meeting, 19 April 1957, HFP.
18. Finding by Commissioner Portus, 18 September 1957; Blain, *Industrial Relations in the Air*, p. 26.
19. Handwritten notes by Fysh, mid-1957, HFP.
20. Fysh paper, "To Strike or Not to Strike", 25 June 1957, HFP.
21. Fysh diary entry, 24 April 1957, HFP.
22. Anderson to Turner, 4 April 1957, file SP1844 (1943–63), AA.
23. Statement by Sir Percy Spender at the opening of the Australia-US air agreement discussions, 15 May 1957, Qantas files.
24. Letter and notes from Anderson to Fysh, 1968, HFP.
25. Brogden, *Australia's Two-Airline Policy*, p. 60.
26. Ibid., p. 135.
27. R. G. Menzies to Capt. Ivan Holyman, 28 March 1952, file A463 Item 57/2576, AA.
28. Fysh handwritten notes, 3 July 1957, HFP.
29. Transcript of telephone conversation between Turner and Smallpiece, 28 June 1957, BA.
30. Smallpiece to Turner, BA.
31. Turner to Smallpiece, 26 July 1957, BA.
32. Smallpiece to Turner, 8 August 1957, BA.
33. D. G. Anderson to Fysh, 15 July 1957, file SP1844 (1943–63), AA.
34. Board memorandum, 22 July 1957, file SP1782 (1949–66), AA.
35. Turner to Smallpiece, 9 August 1957, BA.
36. Fysh to Paltridge, 12 August 1957, file SP1844 (1943–63), AA.
37. Hansard, 3 September 1957, pp. 190-94.
38. Menzies speech, 28 October 1958, *Wings to the World*, p. 151.
39. Memorandum, Hood to Smallpiece, 30 September 1957, BA.

40. Smallpiece to Hood, 7 October 1957, BA.
41. Turner to Smallpiece, 10 October 1957, BA.

Chapter 4

1. Turner to Smallpiece, 6 January 1958, BA.
2. Fysh to Turner, 6 January 1958, HFP.
3. Brogden, *Australia's Two-Airline Policy*, pp. 136-47.
4. Department of External Affairs cablegram to Australian embassy, Paris, 14 January 1958, file CRS A463 Item 58/1163, AA.
5. Turner management proposal, 29 July 1958, HFP.
6. Fysh private notes, 19 August 1958, HFP.
7. Letter from Fysh to Norman Watt, 16 September 1958, with attached notes, HFP.
8. Statement to New Zealand House of Representatives by J. Mathison, minister-in-charge of civil aviation, distributed as a TEALAGRAM supplement by TEAL, September 1958, file SP1846 (1946–67), AA.
9. Extract from Report on International Affairs, December 1958, AA.
10. Fysh to Paltridge, 7 August 1957, file SP1844 (1943–63), AA.
11. Attachment to letter from Turner to Fysh, 28 November 1958, file SP1844 (1943–63), AA.

Chapter 5

1. Paltridge to Fysh, file SP1844 (1943–63), AA.
2. Paltridge to Fysh, 30 December 1958, file SP1844 (1943–63), AA.
3. Fysh notes, 7 January 1959, file SP1844 (1943–63), AA.
4. Fysh to Turner, 5 January 1959, file SP1844 (1943–63), AA.
5. Fysh to Paltridge, 6 February 1959, HFP.
6. Fysh to Turner, 10 February 1959, HFP.
7. Fysh, *Qantas Rising*, Foreword, pp. v-vi.
8. Author's interviews with Colin Porter, recorded and transcribed.
9. Author's interview with Captain Allan, recorded and transcribed.
10. Author's interview with Captain Ritchie, recorded and transcribed.
11. Author's interview with Captain Johnston, recorded and transcribed.
12. Author's interview with Colin Porter.
13. This incident was described to me by both John Fysh and Qantas press relations manager, John Ulm.
14. Author's interview with John Fysh.
15. Memorandum from J. Somerville, economics officer (general) to secretary and finance manager, 6 February 1959, Qantas files.
16. Review of Canadian Pacific service to Australia sent at Turner's request to W. C. Taylor and other Qantas directors on 27 February 1959, HFP.
17. Fysh to Turner, 18 March 1959, HFP.
18. Hood to general manager Eastern Routes BOAC, 28 April 1959, BA.
19. Minutes of QEA-BOAC partnership discussions, San Francisco, 20 and 21 April 1959, HFP.
20. Ibid.
21. Cable from Department of External Affairs to Australian embassy, Paris, 10 April 1959, file A463 Item 58/1163, AA.
22. Report of the Qantas, DCA Boeing 707 Survey Group, June 1959, AA.
23. Letter from Scottie Allan to Fysh, 22 July 1968, HFP.
24. Interview with the author.
25. Cable from Fysh to Beall, 30 July 1959, AA.
26. Paltridge to Fysh, 28 July 1959, file SP1844 (1943–63), AA.
27. Parliamentary Debates, 22 April 1959, file SP1844 (1943–63), AA.
28. Paltridge to Fysh, 28 July 1959, file SP1844 (1943–63), AA.
29. Minutes of BOAC-QEA meeting in Sydney, 29 October 1959, BA.
30. Fysh, *Wings to the World*, pp. 168-69.

31. Fysh, *Wings to the World*, p. 437, HFP.
32. Fysh to G. P. N. Watt, 7 December 1959, HFP.
33. Paltridge to Menzies, 21 December 1959, file A1209 Item 67/7264, AA.
34. Paltridge to Fysh, 8 December 1959, HFP.
35. QEA submission to Paltridge, 16 December 1959, HFP.
36. Ibid.
37. Fysh to Paltridge, 1 December 1959, HFP.
38. Paltridge to Fysh, December 1959, file SP1844 (1943–63), AA.
39. Fysh to Turner, 31 December 1959, HFP.

Chapter 6

1. Fysh, *Wings to the World*, pp. 444-45, HFP.
2. Letter from Oliver to Turner with copy of letter to the minister attached, 28 January 1960, HFP.
3. Minutes of board meeting, 17 March 1960, HFP.
4. Fysh to Turner, 11 February 1960, HFP.
5. *Australian Financial Review*, 3 March 1960.
6. Press release by Department of Civil Aviation, 4 March 1960, file SP1844 (1943–63), AA.
7. Fysh to Paltridge, 24 March 1960, HFP.
8. Fysh, *Wings to the World*, p. 99.
9. Handwritten comment by Turner on small card. Some of these cards were given to the author by Turner's son with the few papers that he left on his death.
10. Fysh to Taylor, 1 April 1960, HFP.
11. Holt to Fysh, 1 April 1960, HFP.
12. Fysh to Holt, 1 April 1960, HFP.
13. Turner to Fysh, 1 April 1960, HFP.
14. *Sydney Morning Herald* editorial, 1 April 1960.
15. Board memo from Turner, 4 April 1960, HFP.
16. Transcript of telephone conversation, Fysh to Barwick, 5 April 1960, HFP.
17. Cable from Australian High Commission London to Department of External Affairs 15 September 1959, file A1209 Item 61/80, AA.
18. Record of Menzies' answer in Prime Minister's Department records, 19 September 1959, file A1209 Item 61/80, AA.
19. Statement by Paltridge, 7 September 1959, file A1209 Item 61/80, AA.
20. Turner to Fysh, 9 May 1960, HFP.
21. Turner to Smallpiece, 25 June 1959, BA.
22. *Qantas News*, June 1960, p. 6.
23. Second Sir Ross and Sir Keith Smith Memorial Lecture delivered by D. G. Anderson CBE, director-general of civil aviation, to the Adelaide branch, Australian division, Royal Aeronautical Society, 22 April 1960, *Journal of the Royal Aeronautical Society*, September 1960.
24. Fysh to Wilson, 22 June 1960, HFP.
25. Fysh, *Wings to the World*, p. 446, HFP.
26. Fysh diary note, 1960, undated, HFP.
27. Fysh, *Wings to the World*, p. 451, HFP.
28. Ibid., pp. 456-57.
29. Fysh board notes for a meeting with Paltridge, 13 July 1960, HFP.
30. D. E. Fairbairn to Paltridge, 14 July 1960, file SP1844 (1943–63), AA.
31. Paltridge to Fysh, 28 July 1960, file SP1844 (1943–63), AA.
32. Qantas evidence to the Government Members Civil Aviation Committee, 24 August 1960, file SP1844 (1943–63), AA.
33. Paltridge to Menzies, 28 July 1960, file A1209 Item 68/9520, AA.
34. Nash to Menzies, 5 August 1960, file A1209 Item 68/9520, AA.
35. Internal memo, Prime Minister's Department, 11 August 1960, file A1209 Item 68/9520, AA.
36. Menzies to Nash, 31 August 1960, file A1209 Item 68/9520, AA.
37. Smallpiece to Turner, 15 July 1960, BA.
38. Turner to Smallpiece, 4 August 1960, BA.
39. Fysh, *Wings to the World*, p. 434, HFP.

40. Hood to Smallpiece, 26 September 1960, BA.
41. Turner to Smallpiece, 15 September 1960, BA.
42. Smallpiece to Turner, 30 September 1960, BA.
43. Ministry of Aviation to Smallpiece, 25 October 1960, BA.
44. Turner to Smallpiece, 21 October 1960, BA.
45. Smallpiece to Turner, 30 November 1960, BA.
46. Slattery to Fysh, 8 December 1960, BA.
47. McVey to Fysh, 7 December 1960, HFP.
48. Fysh to Law-Smith, 13 December 1960, HFP.
49. Hood to Smallpiece, 18 December 1960, BA.
50. Fysh to Slattery, 28 December 1960, BA.
51. Fysh, *Wings to the World*, p. 452, HFP.

Chapter 7

1. Paltridge to Menzies, 17 January 1961, file A463 Item 65/1034, AA.
2. Paltridge to Menzies, 14 February 1961, file A463 Item 65/1034, AA.
3. Blain, *Industrial Relations in the Air*, p. 40.
4. Joint statement by Paltridge and McAlpine, 7 March 1961, file A1209 Item 68/9520, AA.
5. *Sydney Morning Herald*, 21 March 1961, file A463 Item 61/4584, AA.
6. *Daily Telegraph*, 22 March 1961, file A463 Item 61/4584, AA.
7. Paltridge to Menzies, 8 March 1961, file A463 Item 61/4584, AA.
8. Fysh, *Wings to the World*, p. 166.
9. Cable from Department of External Affairs to Australian High Commission, London, 29 March 1961, file A1209 Item 61/80, AA.
10. Davis, *History of the World's Airlines*, p. 511.
11. Fysh to Wilson, 4 July 1961, HFP.
12. Turner to Fysh, 15 July 1961, HFP.
13. QEA Annual Report for the fifteen months to 31 March 1961.
14. Slattery to Thorneycroft, 14 April 1961, BA.
15. Technical development controller to engineering manager, 4 May 1961, file SP1844 (1943–63), AA.
16. Watt, *Evolution of Australian Foreign Policy*, pp. 309-10.
17. Fysh notes, 14 June 1961, HFP.
18. AFAP circular to all members, 1 June 1961, HFP.
19. Fysh memo to Turner, 13 June 1961, HFP.
20. President Qantas Senior Staff Association, E. H. Aldis, to Paltridge, 21 June 1961, HFP.
21. Company memo, unsigned, headed Pilots' Organisation, June 1961, HFP.
22. Management memorandum, 15 June 1961, HFP.
23. Fysh note to directors and management, 19 June 1961, HFP.
24. Fysh to Paltridge, 19 June 1961, HFP.
25. Handwritten Fysh note, 21 June 1961, HFP.
26. Staff notice, 22 June 1961, HFP.
27. Commonwealth Public Service General Orders, Sub-section (B), Termination of Employment 13/B/1, Order of Discharge 1961.
28. Fysh to Law-Smith and Sir Roland Wilson, 23 June 1961, HFP.
29. Fysh handwritten note, 27 June 1961, HFP.
30. Blain, *Industrial Relations in the Air*, pp. 38-39.
31. Turner memo to pilots, 31 August 1961, HFP.
32. Fysh, *Wings to the World*, p. 455, HFP.
33. Fysh to Turner, 2 August 1961, HFP.
34. Fysh, *Wings to the World*, p. 453, HFP.
35. Fysh to Watt, 2 August 1961, HFP.
36. Watt to Fysh, 2 August 1961, HFP.
37. Fysh to Watt, 4 August 1961, HFP.
38. Paltridge to Fysh, 11 August 1961, HFP.
39. Fysh to Menzies, 8 August 1961, HFP.
40. Fysh, *Wings to the World*, pp. 172-79.
41. Ibid., p. 177.
42. Fysh to Paltridge, 1 September 1961 file SP1844 (1943–63), AA.

Chapter 8

1. Fysh diary entry, 9 January 1962, HFP.
2. Fysh to Turner, 5 January 1962, HFP.
3. Paltridge to Fysh, 8 January 1962, file SP1844 (1943–63), AA.
4. Fysh to Paltridge, 21 December 1961, file SP1844 (1943–63), AA.
5. Townley to Paltridge, 16 May 1962, file A1209 Item 62/582, AA.
6. Secretary Defence Department to secretary Defence Committee, 14 June 1962 file A1209 Item 62/582, AA.
7. Smallpiece to Slattery, 26 January 1962, BA.
8. Slattery to Smallpiece, 29 January 1962, BA.
9. Slattery to Fysh, 22 January 1963, HFP.
10. Economics officer memo to chief executive, 16 February 1962, file SP1844 (1943–63), AA.
11. Economics officer memo to international advisor, 28 March 1962, file SP1844 (1943–63), AA.
12. Turner to Fysh, 25 May 1962, HFP.
13. Board memorandum from chief executive, 25 May 1962, HFP.
14. Smallpiece to Patel, 18 June 1962, file SP1842 (1946–67), AA.
15. Isitt to Fysh, 18 April 1962, HFP.
16. Turner to Anderson, 8 June 1962, file SP1842 (1946–67), AA.
17. Qantas international affairs report, June 1962, file SP1842 (1946–67), AA.
18. Paltridge to Menzies, 14 June 1962, file A1209/T2 Item 69/7262, AA.
19. Cable from Paltridge to Menzies, 14 June 1962, file A1209/T2 Item 69/7262, AA.
20. Menzies to Kennedy, 29 June 1962, file A1209/T2 Item 69/7762, AA.
21. Kennedy to Menzies, 15 July 1962, file A1209/T2 Item 69/7262, AA.
22. Paltridge to Menzies, 19 July 1962, file A1209/T2 Item 69/7262, AA.
23. Fysh notes on trip abroad, 26 June 1962, HFP.
24. QEA Annual Report, 1962–63.
25. Report by economics officer (research), Qantas, 25 July 1962, HFP.
26. Report by economics officer, Qantas, 16 August 1962, file SP1844 (1943–63), AA.
27. Fysh to Hildred, 18 June 1962, HFP.
28. Board memorandum, 12 December 1962, file SP1842 (1946–67), AA.

Chapter 9

1. Economics officer (research) report, 21 January 1963, HFP.
2. Report by economics officer (research), 21 January 1963, HFP.
3. Turner to Fysh, 19 July 1963, file SP1844 (1943–63), AA.
4. Fysh to Turner, 3 January 1963, HFP.
5. Ibid.
6. Board memorandum, 15 March 1963, HFP.
7. Ibid.
8. Turner to Anderson, 23 February 1963, HFP.
9. Ibid.
10. C. H. Jackson, BOAC assistant chief engineer, to Shaw, 15 January 1963, BA.
11. Edwards to Slattery, 24 January 1963, BA.
12. Slattery to Edwards, 28 January 1963, BA.
13. Slattery to McGregor, 28 February 1963, BA.
14. Fysh diary, 8 February 1963, HFP.
15. Economics officer report, 28 March 1963, file SP1844 (1943–63), AA.
16. Economics officer report, 23 April 1963, file SP1844 (1943–63), AA.
17. Technical development manager report, 2 April 1963, file SP1844 (1943–63), AA.
18. Notes of discussions between minister and QEA board, 2 April 1963, file SP1844 (1943–63), AA.
19. Fysh to Law-Smith, 3 April 1963, HFP.
20. Fysh to Turner, 24 April 1963, HFP.
21. Fysh to Law-Smith, 24 April 1963, HFP.
22. Report by chief press and information officer John Ulm, 29 April 1963, file SP1844 (1943–63), AA.

23. Turner board memo, 20 May 1963, HFP.
24. Fysh to Law-Smith, 20 May 1963, HFP.
25. Fysh memo, 14 June 1963, HFP.
26. Turner board memo, 12 November 1963, HFP.
27. Fysh, *Wings to the World*, p. 435, HFP.
28. Turner board memo, 24 July 1963, EJP.
29. Fysh to Slattery, 1 August 1963, BA.
30. Tata to Slattery, 9 July 1963, BA.
31. Qantas Technical Development Department summary of FAA report, 16 July 1963, file SP1833, (1943–63), AA.
32. Ibid.
33. Ibid.
34. Turner to Smallpiece, 19 August 1963, file SP1842 (1946–67), AA.
35. Slattery to Fysh, 20 August 1963, BA.
36. Technical Development Department memo, December 1963, file SP1844 (1943–63), AA.
37. Turner board memo, December 1963, EJP.
38. Memo to all pilots by Capt. A. Wharton, manager flight operations, 25 June 1964, HFP.
39. Turner board memo, 13 November 1963, EJP.
40. Ibid.
41. Turner board memo, 20 August 1963, EJP.
42. Turner board memo, 5 November 1963, EJP.
43. Turner board memo, 5 December 1963, EJP.
44. Ministerial press release, 27 December 1963, file SP1842 (1946–67), AA.
45. Fysh to Paltridge, 25 September 1963, HFP.
46. Fysh to Turner, 22 October 1963, HFP.
47. Telegram Fysh to Paltridge, 30 December 1963, file SP1844 (1943–63), AA.

Chapter 10

1. Telegram Paltridge to Fysh, 31 December 1963, file SP1844 (1943–63), AA.
2. Fysh, *Wings Across the World*, pp. 226-27.
3. Fysh to Turner, 17 January 1964, HFP.
4. Fysh to Ritchie, 17 January 1964, HFP.
5. *Qantas News*, 17 January 1964.
6. Guthrie to Way, 16 January 1964, BA.
7. *Sun*, Sydney, 8 January 1964.
8. Report by economics officer, 29 January 1964, file SP1842 (1946–67), AA.
9. *Sydney Morning Herald*, 14 January 1964.
10. *The Bulletin* 11 January 1964.
11. Economics officer memo, 14 February 1964, CTP.
12. AFAP press release, 12 February 1964, HFP.
13. Turner memo to pilots, 14 February 1964, HFP.
14. AFAP brochure, February 1964, HFP.
15. Interview with the author.
16. Fysh statement to Paltridge and Anderson, 18 February 1964, HFP.
17. Typed statement by Fysh, 20 February 1964, HFP.
18. Fysh notes, 26 February 1964, HFP.
19. Handwritten Fysh notes, 20 February 1964, HFP.
20. Ibid.
21. Fysh to Law-Smith, 28 February 1964, HFP.
22. Fysh to Paltridge, 21 February 1964, HFP.
23. Paltridge to Fysh, 12 March 1964, HFP.
24. Apsey report, 8 April 1964, HFP.
25. *Australian Air Pilot*, Vol 1, No. 3, February-March 1964.
26. Turner paper commenting on AFAP circular, 3 March 1964, HFP.
27. Law-Smith to Fysh, 21 May 1964, HFP.
28. Turner to Fysh, 9 March 1964, HFP.
29. Ritchie board memorandum, 18 May 1964, HFP.
30. *Sydney Morning Herald*, 6 May 1964.

31. Ritchie board memo, 18 May 1964, HFP.
32. AFAP to Paltridge, 12 May 1964, HFP.
33. Crofts to Ritchie, 12 May 1964, HFP.
34. Wharton memo to pilots, 25 June 1964, HFP.
35. Fysh to Law-Smith, 17 May 1964, HFP.
36. Fysh to Law-Smith, 25 May 1964, HFP.
37. Fysh trip report, 16 June 1964, HFP.
38. Fysh statement to board, 18 June 1964, HFP.
39. Law-Smith to Fysh, 3 June 1964, HFP.
40. McDougall to Ulm, 28 April 1964, JUP.
41. Ulm press material, JUP.
42. Fysh to Turner, 22 June 1964, HFP.
43. Turner board memo, 9 March 1964, JUP.
44. Ibid.
45. Turner to Bland, 24 July 1964, CTP.
46. Henty to Fysh, 16 June 1964, HFP.
47. Fysh to Henty, 19 June 1964, HFP.
48. Ritchie address to American Institute of Aeronautics and Astronautics, Seattle, US, 12 August 1964, supplied by Captain Ritchie.
49. Paper by economics officer, 21 August 1964, CTP.
50. Economics officer study, 25 August 1964, CTP.
51. Economics officer memo, 12 October 1964, CTP.
52. Blain, *Industrial Relations in the Air*, p. 44.
53. Bland to Turner, 4 September 1964, CTP.
54. Turner to Bland, 4 September 1964, CTP.
55. Fysh to Chippindall, 24 August 1964, HFP.
56. Chippindall to Fysh, 28 August 1964, HFP.
57. Fysh to Ansett, 8 October 1964, HFP.
58. Fysh to Ansett, 16 October 1964, HFP.
59. Crofts to Sdn. Ldr. C. H. Vautin, NSW Division, Air Force Association, 3 November 1964, HFP.
60. Shields to Fysh, 29 October 1964, HFP.
61. Bland to Turner, 30 October 1964, HFP.
62. Fysh handwritten note, 5 November 1964, HFP.
63. McKee to Fysh, 9 November 1964, HFP.
64. Economics officer, J. Somerville, report, 29 October 1964, supplied by J. Somerville.
65. Turner to Fysh, 22 October 1964, HFP.

Chapter 11

1. Watt, *Evolution of Australian Foreign Policy 1938-1965*, p. 317.
2. Pamphlet issued by Australian High Commission, London, 1965, CTP.
3. J. Somerville economics officer (research) report, 23 November 1964, CTP.
4. *Aeroplane*, 26 November 1964.
5. Fysh board report, 29 June 1965, HFP.
6. Capt P. W. Howson, director of technical services Qantas, to R. D. Phillips, DCA, 28 August 1964, CTP.
7. *Australian Air Pilot*, February-March 1965.
8. Fysh note, 15 February 1965, HFP.
9. Fysh to Henty, 2 March 1965, HFP.
10. Ansett Transport Industries Ltd Annual Report, 1962.
11. Economics research report, 10 March 1965, CTP.
12. Fysh to Henty, 14 April 1965, file SP1844 (1943–63), AA.
13. Shields to Fysh, 4 May 1965, HFP.
14. Turner to Bland, 22 June 1965, HFP.
15. *Aeroplane*, 29 April 1965.
16. Referred to in Turner letter to Granville, 21 April 1965, CTP.
17. Fysh diary, May 1965, HFP.
18. Fysh diary, 1965, undated.
19. Interview with the author, Los Angeles, 1984.

20. Management report, 28 June 1965, file SP1844 (1943–63), AA.
21. Economics officer research report, 30 June 1965, CTP.
22. Fysh report, 2 July 1965, HFP.
23. Fysh board note, 29 July 1965, HFP.
24. Handwritten Fysh note, September 1965, HFP.
25. Ritchie board memo, 9 September 1965, HFP.
26. Henty to Fysh, 20 September 1965, HFP.
27. Turner memo, 12 November 1965, J. Somerville papers.
28. Economics officer (research), J. Somerville, study, 23 November 1965, CTP.
29. Turner to Fysh, 6 October 1965, file SP1844 (1943–63), AA.
30. *Australian Financial Review* articles by John Gunn, 28 and 29 October 1965.
31. Ulm typewritten note, JUP.
32. Typed note headed 'Intelligence from Canberra', 12 November 1965, JUP.
33. Typed note, 17 November 1965, JUP.
34. Typed note, 21 September 1965, JUP.
35. Typed notes, 26 November and 8 December 1965, JUP.
36. Turner to Caterson, 9 December 1965, CTP.
37. Turner to Ulm, 25 November 1965, handwritten, JUP.
38. Turner to Stack, 15 December 1965, CTP.
39. Typed notes by Ulm, December 1965, JUP.
40. Fysh to Wilson, 31 December 1965, RWP.

Chapter 12

1. Wilson to Fysh, 13 January 1966, RWP.
2. Interview with the author, November 1984.
3. Fysh diary, February 1966, HFP.
4. QEA Annual Report, 1966-67.
5. Fysh to Law-Smith and Wilson, 23 March 1966, HFP.
6. Report by Qantas safety research, January 1966, CTP.
7. Fysh, *Wings to the World*, pp. 170, 171.
8. Henty to prime minister, 17 January 1966 and 10 May 1966, file A1209 Item 66/7254, AA.
9. Cable from Australian embassy to Department of Civil Aviation, 13 May 1966, file A1209 Item 66/7254, AA.
10. Fysh diary, 23 February 1966, HFP.
11. Slim to Fysh, 26 February 1966, HFP.
12. Interview with the author, 3 February 1983.
13. Memo from E. C. Johnston to C. O. Turner, 22 June 1966, CTP.
14. Turner to Wilson, 25 February 1966, RWP.
15. Turner board memo, 7 February 1966, RWP.
16. General notes for the board from Turner, 23 March 1966, RWP.
17. Ad hoc committee minutes, Decision No. 106 (HOC), 24 March 1966, RWP.
18. QEA 1965-66 Annual Report, p. 22.
19. *Aircraft*, September 1940, article by Capt. R. J. Ritchie.
20. Memo to Turner from economics officer (research), 1 April 1966, CTP.
21. Memo to Turner from economics officer (research), 1 April 1966, CTP.
22. Turner board memo, 15 April 1966, HFP.
23. Turner to Fysh, 15 April 1966, HFP.
24. Boeing to Qantas, 3 May 1966. Papers supplied by R. Walker, Qantas Technical Development Department.
25. Turner board memo, 13 September 1966, RWP.
26. P. W. Howson to Anderson, 27 July 1967, Qantas files.
27. Turner board memo, 13 September 1966, RWP.
28. Law-Smith to Fysh, 28 March 1966, RWP.
29. Handwritten note on Law-Smith letter, RWP.
30. Fysh, *Wings to the World*, p. 186.
31. Fysh to Law-Smith, 19 April 1966, RWP.
32. Fysh to Swartz, 13 May 1966, RWP.
33. Fysh to the Duke of Norfolk, 26 May 1966, HFP.
34. Holt to Fysh, 27 June 1966, HFP.

35. Board memorandum, 23 June 1966, CTP.
36. Interview with the author, 3 February 1983.
37. Ulm to Turner; Turner to Ulm, 5 July 1966, JUP.
38. Ritchie article, *Aircraft*, July 1966, p. 25.
39. *Aircraft*, July 1966, p. 23.
40. Turner to Bury, 7 July 1966, CTP.
41. Turner to Wilson, 11 July 1966, CTP.
42. Minutes of chairman's opening statement, board meeting with ministers, 18 August 1966, RWP.
43. Economics officer (research) report, 13 September 1966, CTP.
44. Technical Development Department report, September 1966, CTP.
45. Turner staff message, 23 November 1966, JUP.
46. *Qantas News*, 25 November 1966.
47. AFAP press release, November 1966.
48. Qantas background brief, 28 November 1966, JUP.
49. McMahon press release, 28 November 1966, JUP.
50. McMahon press statement, 1 December 1966, JUP.

Chapter 13

1. Turner to Berchtold, 12 January 1967, CTP.
2. Interview with Colin Porter by the author.
3. Conversation recounted to the author by Law-Smith, February 1983.
4. Wilson interview with the author, Canberra, November 1984.
5. Qantas press release, 15 April 1967, JUP.
6. Turner to Gross, 27 April 1967, CTP.
7. Turner to Heymanson, 2 May 1967, CTP.
8. Shaw to Turner, 25 April 1967, CTP.
9. Turner to Shaw, 9 May 1967, CTP.
10. Turner to Herries, 3 April 1967, CTP.
11. Scherger to Turner, 17 April 1967, CTP.
12. Turner to Smallpiece, 12 May 1967, CTP.
13. Caterson to Turner, 19 April 1967, CTP.
14. *Australian Financial Review* article by John Gunn, 17 April 1967.
15. Brain to Turner, 20 April 1967, CTP.
16. Boeing to Ritchie, 10 February 1967, RWP.
17. Turner to Gross, 21 February 1967, CTP.
18. Technical development manager memo, 30 March 1967, Qantas files.
19. Economics officer (research) memo to Turner, 31 March 1967, CTP.
20. Turner to Anderson, 21 March 1967, file SP1842 (1946–67), AA.
21. Wilson to Swartz, 29 March 1967, file A463 Item 67/1939, AA.
22. Handwritten notes by Norman Watt given by him to the author.
23. Turner to Ritchie, 6 April 1967, CTP.
24. Ritchie to Turner, 21 April 1967, CTP.
25. Howson to Turner, 4 May 1967, CTP.
26. Ritchie to Boeing Aircraft Company, 14 April 1967, RWP.
27. Wilson to Swartz, 8 May 1967, RWP.
28. Engineering and planning division Boeing 747 project budget, May 1967, RWP.
29. Ritchie board memorandum, 18 May 1967, RWP.
30. Ritchie to Johnston, 24 April 1967, EJP.
31. Author's interview with Ritchie, June 1982.
32. Board memorandum, 20 October 1967, CTP.
33. Ritchie memorandum to outstations, June 1967, JUP.
34. Wilson to Swartz, 25 July 1967, RWP.
35. Ritchie board memorandum, 16 August 1967, RWP.
36. Blain, *Industrial Relations in the Air*, p. 52, quoting the *Australian*.
37. Handwritten Fysh note, 4 October 1967, HFP.
38. Qantas Annual Report 1967-68, p. 3.

Chapter 14

1. Wilson to Fysh, 11 January 1968, RWP.
2. Board memo, 17 February 1969.
3. Ibid.
4. Board memo, 17 February 1969, Qantas files.
5. Board memo, 19 June 1968.
6. Interview with the author.
7. Fysh to Law-Smith, 18 July 1968 (Qantas board papers 1968), HFP.
8. Fysh refers to this increase in a letter to Wilson in June 1973, RWP.
9. Board memo, 19 June 1968.
10. Board memo, 21 March 1968, file A1209 Item 68/8820, AA.
11. Swartz to Wilson, September 1968 (Qantas board paper files).
12. Board memo, 20 June 1969, Qantas files.
13. Interview with the author, June 1982.
14. Typed paper by Ulm given to the author, JUP.
15. Fysh to Law-Smith, 7 February 1969, HFP.
16. Board memo, 19 September 1969, Qantas files.
17. Blain, *Industrial Relations in the Air*, pp. 63-64.
18. Wilson to Cotton, November 1969, Qantas files.
19. Board memo, 13 November 1969, Qantas files.
20. Wilson to Swartz, 16 January 1969, Qantas files.
21. Department of External Affairs cable, 17 December 1969, file A1209 Item 69/7272 pt. 2, AA.

Chapter 15

1. *Aircraft*, September 1970, p. 22.
2. Cotton to Gorton, 19 March 1970, file 1209/T2 Item 69/7262, AA.
3. *Aircraft*, September 1970, p. 58.
4. Ibid., p. 62.
5. Wilson to Cotton, 9 March 1970, RWP.
6. Wilson to Cotton, 5 May 1970, Qantas files.
7. Wilson to Fysh, 29 June 1970, Qantas files.
8. *Australian Financial Review*, 11 June 1970.
9. Cotton to Gorton, 17 September 1970, file A1209 Item 69/7272 pt 2, AA.
10. Board memo, 8 October 1970, Qantas files.
11. Cotton to Wilson, 13 July 1970, Qantas files.
12. Wilson to Cotton, August 1970, Qantas files.
13. Qantas press release, 7 August 1970, Qantas files.
14. *Aviation Daily*, 6 August 1970.
15. Board memo, August 1970, Qantas files.
16. Wilson speech, Wentworth Hotel, 16 November 1970, Qantas files.
17. *Australian Financial Review*, 16 June 1971.

General Bibliography

Alexander, F. *Australia Since Federation.* 3rd ed. London: Nelson, 1976.

Allen, R. *Pictorial History of K.L.M. Royal Dutch Airlines.* London: Ian Allan, 1978.

Baitsell, J. M. *Airline Industrial Relations: Pilots and Flight Engineers.* Boston: Harvard University, 1966.

Behr, J. *Royal Flying Doctor Service in Australia 1928–1979.* Manuscript in the possession of Federal Council of the Royal Flying Doctor Service of Australia.

Bennett-Bremner, E. *Front-Line Airline: The War Story of Qantas Empire Airways Limited.* Sydney: Angus and Robertson, 1944.

Blain, N. *Industrial Relations in the Air.* St Lucia: University of Queensland Press, 1984.

Brackley, F. H., comp. *Brackles: Memoirs of a Pioneer of Civil Aviation.* Chatham: W. & J. Mackay, 1952.

Bray, W. *The History of BOAC: 1939–1974.* Surrey: The Wessex Press, n.d. (This book was printed and bound but, by the decree of the British Airways board, it was never published. The board considered it "divisive".)

Brogden, S. *Australia's Two-Airline Policy.* Carlton, Vic.: Melbourne University Press, 1968.

Butler, C. A. *Flying Start: The History of the First Five Decades of Civil Aviation in Australia.* Sydney: Edwards & Shaw, 1971.

Carter, I. R. *Southern Cloud.* Melbourne: Landsdown Press, 1963.

Clark, C. M. H. *A Short History of Australia.* New York: New American Library, 1963.

Corbett, D. *Politics and the Airlines.* London: George Allan & Unwin, 1965.

Crome, E. A. *Qantas Aeriana.* Edited by N. C. Baldwin. Sutton Coldfild: Francis J. Field, 1955.

Davis, R. E. G. *A History of the World's Airlines.* London: Oxford University Press, 1964.

Donne, M. *Leader of the Skies: Rolls-Royce: The First Seventy-Five Years*. London: Frederick Muller, 1981.

Friedman, J. A. *A New Air Transport Policy for the North Atlantic: Saving an Endangered System*. New York: Atheneum, 1967.

Fysh, H. *Qantas at War*. Unedited manuscript. Mitchell Library, Sydney.

Fysh, H. *Qantas Rising*. Sydney: Angus and Robertson, 1965.

Fysh, H. *Taming the North*. Rev. and enl. ed. Sydney: Angus and Robertson, 1950.

Fysh, H. *Wings to the World: The Story of Qantas 1945–1966*. Sydney: Angus and Robertson, 1970.

Gibson, R. J. *Australia and Australians in Civil Aviation: An Index to Events from 1832 to 1920*. Vol. 1. Sydney: Qantas Airways Ltd., 1971.

Harvey-Bailey, A. *Rolls-Royce – the Formative Years 1906–1939*. Historical Series No. 1. Derby: Rolls-Royce Heritage Trust, 1982.

Higham, R. *Britain's Imperial Air Routes 1918 to 1939: The Story of Britain's Overseas Airlines*. London: G. T. Foutlis & Co. Ltd., 1960.

Hocking, D. M. and Haddon-Cave, C. P. *Air Transport in Australia*. Sydney: Angus and Robertson, 1951.

Jackson, A. J. *Avro Aircraft Since 1908*. London: Putnam, 1965.

Mackenzie, R. D. *Solo: The Bert Hinkler Story*. Sydney: Jacaranda Press, 1962.

Mansfield, H. *Vision: The Story of Boeing*. New York: Popular Library, 1966.

Miller, H. C. *Early Birds*. Adelaide: Rigby, 1968.

Mollison, J. *Playboy of the Air*. London: Michael Joseph, 1937.

Moody, J. D. *Qantas and the Kangaroo Route*. Ph.D. thesis, Australian National University, Canberra, 1981.

Munson, K. *Pictorial History of BOAC and Imperial Airways*. London: Ian Allan, 1970.

Pattison, B. and Goodall, G. *Qantas Empire Airways Indian Ocean Service 1943–1946*. Footscray, Vic.: Aviation Historical Society of Australia, 1979.

Penrose, H. *Wings across the World: An Illustrated History of British Airways*. London: Cassell, 1980.

Scott, C. W. A. *Scott's Book: The Life and Mildenhall–Melbourne Flight of C. W. A. Scott*. London: Hodder and Stoughton, 1934.

Shaw, A. G. L. *The Story of Australia*. London: Faber & Faber, 1955.

Smith, C. B. *Amy Johnson*. London: Collins, 1967.

Stroud, J. *Annals of British and Commonwealth Air Transport 1919–1960*. London: Putnam, 1962.

Thomas, M. *Out on a Wing: An Autobiography*. London: Michael Joseph, 1964.

Turner, P. St. J. *Pictorial History of Pan American World Airways*. London: Ian Allan, 1973.

Ward, R. *A Nation for a Continent*. London: Heinemann, 1979.

Watt, A. *The Evolution of Australian Foreign Policy 1938–1965*. London: Cambridge University Press, 1967.

Younger, R. M. *Australia and the Australians: A New Concise History*. Adelaide: Rigby, 1970.

Index

466